THE FUTURE
DOES NOT COMPUTE

Transcending the Machines
in Our Midst

THE FUTURE DOES NOT COMPUTE

Transcending the Machines in Our Midst

Stephen L. Talbott

O'Reilly & Associates, Inc.
103 Morris Street, Suite A · Sebastopol, CA · 95472

The Future Does Not Compute:
Transcending the Machines in Our Midst
by Stephen L. Talbott

Copyright © 1995 O'Reilly & Associates, Inc.
Printed in the United States of America

Editor: Tim O'Reilly
Book Design: Nancy Priest
Printing History: May 1995: First Edition.

This book is printed on acid-free paper with 85% recycled content, 15% post-consumer waste. O'Reilly & Associates is committed to using paper with the highest recycled content available consistent with high quality.

ISBN: 1-56592-085-6   [7/95]

For Phyllis
and for the future
of Gene, James and Jonathan
and for my parents

TABLE OF CONTENTS

1. Can Human Ideals Survive the Internet?

*The Internet has become the most highly perfected means yet for
the scattering of the self beyond recall. Unless we can recollect
ourselves in the presence of our intelligent artifacts, we have no
future.*

PART 1

MAN, COMPUTERS, AND COMMUNITY

2. The Machine in the Ghost

*The one sure thing about the computer's future is that we will
behold our own reflection in it. What I really fear is the hidden
and increasingly powerful machine within us, of which the
machines we create are an outward expression. Machines
become a threat when they embody our limitations without our
being fully aware of those limitations.*

PART 3

THE ELECTRONIC WORD

PART 4

OWEN BARFIELD, COMPUTERS, AND THE EVOLUTION OF CONSCIOUSNESS

Appendix C

(An introduction to Waldorf education.) The true human capacities pass through dramatic transformations. What we sow in the child must sink down into his being in seedlike child-forms before it can emerge again, mature, and flower into an adult capacity.

FOREWORD

In the fall of 1992, O'Reilly & Associates published a book that became an instant bestseller: *The Whole Internet User's Guide and Catalog*, by Ed Krol. The book spawned a host of imitators; together, they have sold millions of copies. Within months, the Internet was a household word and on the front page of newspapers everywhere. The Internet craze was on.

When we published *The Whole Internet User's Guide and Catalog*, we had no idea that the Internet, then a tool of academic researchers, computer scientists, and students, was about to become a social phenomenon that would transform American social policy, educational practice, and the dreams of a new generation of entrepreneurs.

But we were happy to ride the wave. We published more books about how to use the Internet. We created an information service called the *Global Network Navigator* (*GNN*), the first commercial presence on the World Wide Web. We worked with a software company to create *Internet In A Box*, a product designed to make the Internet accessible to anyone with a PC and a modem.

Then one of our editors, Steve Talbott, began to raise some questions in a series of articles written for *GNN*. Hasn't the hype about the Internet gotten a bit out of hand? he asked. Does the ability to communicate with others through the faceless, anonymous medium of computers lead to the formation of "virtual communities" or does it isolate us further from contact with the very people who used to form our community? Will the "information highway" really bring us closer together, or will it perform the same function as our asphalt highways, encouraging us to seek the promise of better things in the distance? Will the euphoria that now greets the Internet be replaced in 20 or 30 years with the dismay that now surrounds the once-bright promise of television?

Beneath these pointed questions lay one far deeper: is there something in the nature of the computer itself that takes us away from the characteristics that make us uniquely human? Does the increasing computerization of our society pose dangers that we are only on the brink of recognizing?

It soon became clear that Steve had more to say than would fit into a series of columns. He needed to write a book.

We realized that this was a very different kind of book than the practical "how to" computer books O'Reilly & Associates is known for. We thought of looking for another publisher, but then we realized that we were the right one after all. When a leading publisher of computer and Internet books also publishes a book questioning the role of computers in our society, it just might make people think.

And that is what this book is designed to do—make you think. You probably won't agree with everything Steve has to say. He may make you angry. But if you step back and look with fresh eyes at things you've taken for granted, if you look more carefully at claims that technology can only make our lives better, this book will have done its job.

Computer technology is with us whether we like it or not. And whether you are in love with the possibilities (as I am) or concerned about them (like Steve), you will be a more thoughtful user of that technology after reading this book.

—Tim O'Reilly

ACKNOWLEDGMENTS

The most difficult thing to acknowledge is all the authors I ought to have read but have not. In my extraordinarily slow and plodding program of study, I have yet to catch up with many works forming the "standard background" for the discussion I have attempted here. A good example of this bibliographic gap is Theodore Roszak's classic, *The Cult of Information* (re-issued with a lengthy new introduction in 1994). I have indeed read this book—but only during the last checking of page proofs before going to press. Where I would surely have adverted to Roszak many times in these pages, I have in fact only managed a last-minute footnote. Other worthy scholars must remain altogether unnoted.

Of those who read various versions of the manuscript, in whole or in part, and gave me valuable comments (not always heeded), I mention especially David Flanagan, Rob Kling, Lowell Monke, Andy Oram, Gerald Phillips, Christian Sweningsen, Tom Talbott, Stuart Weeks, Frank Willison, and Jeff Wright.

David Sewell reviewed the entire manuscript, offering numerous helpful stylistic suggestions. His careful eye taught me how much I have still to learn about editing.

Among my extraordinary colleagues at O'Reilly & Associates, Edie Freedman designed the cover; Nancy Priest handled the interior design; Lenny Muellner, constrained by a shortened schedule, implemented the design in software; Seth Maislin offered great, last-minute advice on the principles of indexing; and Clairemarie Fisher O'Leary and Kismet McDonough-Chan, with their ever discerning eyes, assisted in the final production of the book. Sheryl Avruch managed the whole process, and the entire crew put out the kind of dedicated effort and long hours that cannot be *required* of anyone.

Special thanks are owing to Tim O'Reilly, president of O'Reilly & Associates, who is not only my publisher and editor, but also my employer. Tim read through the manuscript several times, offering incisive commentary and helping me find my way—often hollering and clawing at the keyboard—toward a proper balance. Despite the fact that my views are not his views, he devoted far more of his resources toward enabling me to write this book than he has any reasonable hope of recovering. He believed the book is important. That stance of conviction symbolizes a good part of the reason why I work for O'Reilly & Associates.

I am indebted above all to a man whom I have met only through his published writings: Owen Barfield. It was no small part of my hope in producing this book that it might introduce a few people to Barfield's work who might otherwise never encounter it. The risk is that such a brief exposure as I can give here not only may fail to lay bare the heart of Barfield's accomplishment (I take this for granted), but for that reason may encourage readers to pigeonhole Barfield along with one or another more familiar thinker.

Certainly Barfield does say some things that many others have been saying. But the pigeonholing quickly misleads. The core insights underlying all his work remain among the most original scholarly achievements of this century. So original, in fact, that these insights are still largely "impossible" to accept—even impossible to *think*. One has to escape the most deeply ingrained, least conscious habits of modern thought in order to entertain the full import of what Barfield is saying. This is not easy to do, so that the tendency is to take him as merely repeating a more conventional wisdom. No one, however, who has once wrestled through to a close understanding of *Saving the Appearances* or *Worlds Apart* will ever again be able to stand within the intellectual traditions of our culture in quite the same way as before.

T. S. Eliot said of *Worlds Apart* that it is "an excursion into seas of thought which are very far from ordinary routes of intellectual shipping." I have spent some seventeen years trying to follow Barfield on that excursion—with only partial, if nevertheless satisfying, success. During most of those seventeen years I was working with computers, and it slowly became clear to me that the central issues bedeviling all of us who try to understand the relation between the human being and the computer are issues upon which Barfield began throwing light some seven decades ago. *The Future Does Not Compute* is my attempt to reflect a little of that light toward the reader.

CAN HUMAN IDEALS SURVIVE THE INTERNET?

SOCIAL HEALING, IT SEEMS, approaches us from the Internet. If the hopes clustered about this miraculous, Hydra-headed gift of the information age are fulfilled, it will bring us extended democracy, personal liberation, enhanced powers of organization and coordination, renewal of community, information transmuted into wisdom, education freed from the grip of pedagogical tyranny, a new and wondrous complexity arising from chaos—and much more. Can any gift prove dangerous while acting as such an extraordinary magnet for every conceivable ideal?

It is at least curious, given the bright light of idealism focused upon the Internet, that its actual development should have proceeded largely according to a dim, scarcely conscious, technical logic. The "intrinsic necessities" of its growth seem to derive as much from the technical machinery's insistence upon its own, natural articulations as from any choosing on our part:

- Often hailed as an unparalleled weapon against the establishment, the Internet actually grew out of a scheme for making military communications more secure.

- The Internet's original purposes were centered on the exchange of technical data. Its functions were so thoroughly equated with calculation and computation in the narrowest sense that, until these last few years, any distinctively social activity (courting, political activism, the formation of communities) was considered sensationally newsworthy. Today, on the other hand, many observers routinely promote the Internet as a means for salvaging the primacy of personal relationship and community in a depersonalized society.

- Now feared by some as a perfected instrument of commercialism and regimentation, the Internet was, until quite recently, a daytripping playground for hippies reincarnated as engineers—a playground governed, for example, by the sort of anti-commercial spirit driving the Free Software Foundation.

"Again and again," writes Howard Rheingold, "the most important parts of the Net piggybacked on technologies that were created for very different purposes," yielding what he calls "the accidental history of the Net."[1] Huge corporations have fallen from grace because they did not foresee the twists and turns in this strange, unpredictable evolution. And, of course, *foreseeing* is all most of us can hope for. Marketing departments try to steal a glimpse of what may happen one or two years ahead, and find little reason to consider what *ought* to happen. The underlying technical trajectory is what it is. High-tech firms hire consultants as prognosticators, not as wise counselors assessing the human condition and its needs.

So the Internet (or, simply, "the Net") grows like wildfire, and everything just seems to happen. Net surfers rejoice and give ritual thanks for the exhilarating monthly growth figures—so many new sites, so many new users, so many new accesses to popular databases—apparently taking all this "success" as evidence that the gods of cyberspace are with us.

But if there is indeed some sort of embodied wisdom at work in the machinery of growth, one wonders exactly whose wisdom it might be.

---

1. Rheingold, 1993: 67.

Are *our* ideals being realized? It is hard to imagine any truly human aspiration whose fulfillment "just happens." Surely every ideal worthy of the name can be realized only through some sort of *conscious struggle and achievement*. Ideals arise in thought—our very highest, morally fervent thought—and thereby become goals toward which we can strive creatively. Only a machine realizes its aims automatically, and therefore its aims are not ideals.

If, on the other hand, the Net develops by a mechanistic and distinctly nonidealistic logic of its own, one might expect its evolution to follow neatly predictable lines. Logic, after all, is supposed to yield predictability. But this is not true; the logic may, in the first place, prove too complex to grasp. And it may also be the case (I believe it *is* the case) that what we have been imparting to the Net—or what the Net has been eliciting from us—is a half-submerged, barely intended logic, contaminated by wishes and tendencies we prefer not to acknowledge.

This book is an attempt to bring those tendencies to the full light of consciousness, so that we can choose our future rather than compute it automatically and unawares. Not that freedom to choose brings predictability; it most certainly does not. It only makes us responsible. But out of that responsibility we can impose a worthy *meaning* upon the future. The alternative to our doing so—the alternative to freely embraced meaning—is the abstractly patterned, manipulable emptiness of the informational machine. This, too, *derives* from the human being—but only from those places within us where we have long been adapting ourselves to the machine's relentless and increasingly subtle imperatives. No ideals can survive there.

Fatalism and hope

There is more than one way to poison the soil in which profound ideals might otherwise flourish. The most obvious blight, perhaps, results from the kind of cynicism or fatalism that prevents germination in the first place. This shows itself, for example, in the frequent assumption that powerful commercial interests—corporate "big money"—must

3

unavoidably subvert the Net's liberating potentials in favor of the crass profiteering whose results are so vivid in the television wasteland. On such an assumption, how you and I manage our choices (whether as corporate employees or as consumers) counts for nothing at all.

But ideals can be destroyed by excessive hope as well. The plant oversupplied with artificial fertilizer may show rapid, impressive progress, but its growth is rank, weak, and unsustainable. The first good rain will lay it flat. Similarly, much of the enthusiasm for the Net as an agent of desirable social change betrays an artificially reinforced hope.

The following paragraphs, which circulated on the Net in 1994, illustrate this enthusiasm in an extreme form. They were part of a recruitment campaign for a movement calling itself DigitaLiberty.

> DigitaLiberty believes that technology can set us free. The economies of the developed world are now making a major transition from an industrial base to an information base. As they do, the science of cryptology will finally and forever guarantee the unbreachable right of privacy, protecting individuals, groups, and corporations from the prying eyes and grasping hands of sovereigns. We will all be free to conduct our lives, and most importantly our economic relations, as we each see fit.
>
> Cyberspace is also infinitely extensible. There will be no brutal competition for lebensraum. Multiple virtual communities can exist side by side and without destructive conflict, each organized according to the principles of their members. We seek only to build one such community, a community based on individual liberty. Others are free to build communities based on other principles, even diametrically opposed principles. But they must do so without our coerced assistance.
>
> Effective communities will thrive and grow. Dysfunctional communities will wither and die. And for the first time in human history, rapacious societies will no longer have the power to make war on

their neighbors nor can bankrupt communities take their neighbors down with them.[2]

Ideals in the abstract. Whatever one makes of the obvious naiveté in this discarnate utopianism, it must be admitted that the notions strung together here have become Net commonplaces: we're entering an information age; cryptography for the masses will guarantee a universal right of privacy; community is moving online; the Net prevents social coercion and conflict; and somehow what is best in cyberspace always survives, while the inferior withers away.

There are two things to say about the DigitaLiberty appeal. First, it extrapolates the human future from purely technical considerations. "Technology can set us free." Respect for the privacy and individuality of another person is, on such a view, captured in the idea of an uncrackable code given by the tools of communication. Likewise, the boundaries of community can neatly be traced in Network diagrams. And social evolution is patterned after technological development, wherein newer, better, more sophisticated products inevitably replace older, more primitive ones.

Second, such a recasting of social issues as technological ones points to a thoroughgoing habit of abstraction. *What can be mapped from the human being to a machine is always and only an abstraction.* One cannot embrace a *device* as the midwife of freedom without having lost sight of the living, ambiguous reality of freedom as an experience of alternative, *inner* stances. All that is left is an abstract shadow of these stances, in the form of external, machine-mediated "options." Where freedom once required the fateful exercise of an enlightened, heart-warmed will, it is now enough to play with clickable choices on a screen.

This habit of abstraction shows up clearly in a thinking that reconceives privacy as something like a technically shielded anonymity. Such thinking notwithstanding, the fact remains that we must *have to do with each other* in the normal course of our lives—we must know each other—and therefore any genuine privacy can only be rooted in a deep

---

2. Net announcement posted by cpsr-announce@sunnyside.com on December 6, 1994.

5

and sensitive mutual respect. No technical gadgets can underwrite this sort of intimate respect; they can easily make it more difficult.

The alternative to intimate respect—already suggested by all-too-visible tendencies—is to isolate ourselves ever more from each other, taking refuge behind uncertain, shifting personas, remote forms of communication, and anonymous transactions, which we then call "human freedom." This can only lead to an abstract "society" of automatons, inputs, and outputs. It may not matter whether you and I are really there, behind the machinery of interaction, but at least we will know ourselves to be free!

We yield to automatic side effects. I have spoken of both fatalism and breathy idealism, and I have pointed out that at least some of the idealism currently suffusing cyberspace is linked to (1) an anthropomorphism that confuses technical capabilities with human qualities; and (2) a habit of abstraction through which inner qualities such as personal respect disappear into mechanisms.

The interesting thing is that these two characteristics of Net-centered idealism apply just as well to the fatalistic view that big, self-interested corporations must necessarily co-opt the Net's promise of a better society. For this fatalism arises, however questionably, from an incontestable fact: the large corporation today, recognized in law as a kind of nonpersonal person, operates rather like a computer. That is, it mechanically calculates and maximizes the bottom line, without particular reference to anything other than mathematical (monetary) "values." Here again we see both anthropomorphism (the corporation as person) and a highly abstract, mechanical reflection of a distinctly human activity—in this case, the activity required for embodying the *values* of truth, goodness, and beauty through productive activity.

Optimists, of course, assume that higher values will somehow arise from purely commercial, computational activity as an automatic side effect, much as computation proper is supposed to deliver on the ideals of freedom, privacy, and the rest. The pessimists, on the other hand, simply

6

read the automatic side effects differently: power and wealth will be concentrated in the hands of a few; morality, esthetic concerns, the environment, and health will be sacrificed for profits; the alignment of big business and big government will squeeze out the "little guy"; and so on.

But the important thing for the moment is what both optimists and pessimists agree upon: the corporation is a mechanism operating with a life of its own, delivering its freight of good or ill independently of the inner qualities, the choices—the ideals—of its larger human constituency. And the decisive fact is this: such automatic side effects, whatever their nature, can *only* be destructive in the long run, since they testify to an abdication of consciousness.

This abdication is the characteristic temptation presented by the intelligent automaton—whether the automaton is a computer, an unreflective business organization, or the intensifying computational bias within *us* that first made possible the computer's invention. We are, in matters large and small, increasingly given the option of "running on automatic." This is true in our financial affairs (ATM transactions), our personal relationships (email supported by automatic document processing software), our vocations (which now, with ever greater subtlety, we can reduce to unconscious algorithm-following), and our purely stimulative, reflex-based entertainment (video games, shock-value movies).

To run on automatic is, for the human being, to sink toward instinct, unfreedom, and statistical predictability. It is to give up what sets us most vitally apart from our material environment and our tools. It is to remain asleep in our highest capacities.

Whether our ideals can survive depends—beyond all pessimism and optimism vested in automatic processes— on whether we can consciously take hold of the mechanisms around us and within us, and raise them into the service of what is most fully human because most fully awake.

The first prerequisite is to recognize the severity of the challenge.

The scattered self

Anyone who has been in a position to observe the brief, intense history of the Internet will certainly have noticed the wild swings of online senti-ment, from utopian fervor to crashing disillusionment and back again. When a few agitated email messages leaked out of Russia during an abortive coup, the Internet became, by most accounts, an irresistible weapon to save the world for democracy. (Presumably, the Chechens whose deaths graced this morning's newspaper were too late getting their Internet accounts). On the other hand, let the United States government pass a law to permit wiretapping in everyone's beloved cyberspace, and immediate visions of a worse-than-Big-Brother begin dancing through our heads.

This ping-ponging between extremes does not suggest that much work is being done at the realistic level where ideals can be furthered. Every ideal demands a persistent, long-term work upon my own nature, as I stand embedded in society. The difficulties of this social immersion— for example, the personal frictions, antagonisms, and frustrations—are the occasion for most of the work. Anyone who has understood and accepted this work cannot be moved very much by the technological and political shifts that alternately bring ecstasies of hope and paroxysms of fear.

The vacillating, ungrounded idealism of the Net points us toward an important fact: *the correlate of the mechanism or automaton is the scattered self.* To understand this, it may help to think of the psychoanalyst's couch. It is just when the patient abandons his conscious functioning in favor of the most automatic, reflexive responses, that his "output" becomes helter-skelter, scattered, irrational, yet predictable in the merely associational terms characteristic of a lowered consciousness

In other words, the level where we act most mechanistically and unconsciously is the level where coherent meaning is shattered into those suggestive shards that the analyst (from a higher and more conscious view-point) must painstakingly try to reassemble into a meaningful story. The effort is not always successful. And even if it is, it does the patient no good

8

unless he, too, can eventually arrive at something like the analyst's higher understanding, begin to integrate his life around it, and then choose his future in full responsibility.

A failure to digest things. It is hardly novel to comment on the personal scattering so readily induced by modern culture. Daily newspapers present my sweeping glance with a collage of the most dissonant images and stories imaginable, each allocated a few inches of space, a few moments of my time. The suffering in some African war immediately yields to an overjoyed lottery winner, who in turn gives way to a dispute in the city council, followed by survey results on American sexual habits. The weather, comics, sports, book reviews—scanning all this is how I prepare to meet the day ahead. My attention, rather than engaging problems at hand in a deepening meditation, is casually, almost unnoticeably dispersed.

In a similar way, the television sound bite has become notorious; so, too, the dizzying succession of images in movie and music video. Magazines and billboards, the chatter of boomboxes and the endless miles of retail aisleways heaped with a fiendishly beguiling array of merchandise— all compete for a moment's subliminal notice from an otherwise absent subject, so that someone else's intentions can have their way with me. Everything is calculated to prevent my standing firmly within myself, choosing my own way in conscious self-possession. Left helpless to digest much of anything in particular, I have no choice but to let go and move with the flow, allowing it to carry me wherever it will.

The critical law at work here is that whatever I take in without having fully digested it—whatever I receive in less than full consciousness— does not therefore lose its ability to act upon me. It simply acts from beyond the margins of my awareness. Nothing is forgotten; it is only neglected. This is as true of Muzak as of the film image, as true of sound bites as of retail advertisements. To open myself inattentively to a chaotic world, superficially taking in "one damned thing after another," is to guarantee a haphazard behavior controlled by that world rather than by my own, wide-awake choices.

The correlate of scattered "input," then, is scattered "output." Car, telephone, and television collaborate in this scattering by affording a "freedom" of action that tends to enslave me. It becomes so easy to *go* somewhere else—whether via screen, phone lines, or gasoline-powered engine—that the whirl of ceaseless goings substitutes for the hard work of inner attention to the fully dimensioned present. Encouraged to veer off wherever I wish with scarcely so much as a moment's forethought, I am never fully *here*—or there, or anywhere.

All this is, as I have noted, a conventional criticism of modern culture. (Which isn't to say that we shouldn't occasionally remind ourselves of it so long as nothing changes.) But my current topic is the Net—this at a time when the networked computer is widely assumed to counter the cultural trends just cited. By means of the Net, it is supposed, I can extend, concentrate, and enhance my mental powers. Where I am inattentive, ever-alert software running on my computer will be attentive for me. Where I am scattered, the computer will execute precise, almost maniacally focused behavior, deterred by no passing whims. Where my personal reach falls short, I can draw upon the nearly unlimited resources of a vast, electronic community.

Empty receptacles. It is not a happy task, in the face of such optimism, to have to argue that computers and the Net have become the most highly perfected means yet for the scattering of the self beyond recall. This is already hinted by the common experience of Net converts—those many newcomers just now discovering the Internet, who find themselves enthralled by the Walmartlike aisles of cyberspace, stocked with a glorious surfeit of information. It reminds one of the stories a few years back about Russian immigrants making their first, overwrought excursions to American supermarkets. Some of them became frantic and unhinged by the incomprehensible abundance. But in the online world, it seems, being overwrought never has to end.

The relevant symptoms run far beyond the mall syndrome. They are visible, for example, in a remark by Vinton Cerf, one of the Internet's designers: "It will become critical for everyone to be connected. Anyone who doesn't will essentially be isolated from the world community."[3] One particular form of this false urgency shows up in a scarcely questioned conviction within online circles regarding scholarly journals. As one Net contributor writes:

> Print journals are now valid as historical records rather than as the primary source of new information. If a particular field does not have ejournals [electronic journals], I believe that the researchers in that field are falling behind. The immediacy of the research in these fields could be questioned. Many fields are moving so quickly, that anyone not involved in electronic exchanges on their research would be out of it.[4]

This is arrogant nonsense, however often repeated. In what disciplines will the contribution of the next Galileo or Einstein or Darwin depend upon researchers having this month's data rather than last year's? That the "latest information" should have become such a shrill concern is itself evidence that efforts to grasp new and deeper *meaning*—to see the world more *profoundly* and with new eyes—are giving way to a mindless accumulation of data and opinion.

The frantic concern for recency illustrates, despite protestations to the contrary, the computer-aided triumph of the "empty-receptacle" view of the mind. *Date*-able knowledge is at the same time *data*-ble knowledge—something we collect and store in our heads, like bits of information in a database. The computer database, in fact, has become the overwhelmingly dominant metaphor for the knowledgeable mind. It is also, I would suggest, an excellent metaphor for the scattered mind—the mind that feverishly gathers glittering trinkets here and there, convinced that, somehow, a big enough pile of such notions will magically coalesce into one of those new paradigms said to be taking shape all around us.

---

3. "US data highway gathers speed," *The Boston Globe*, 26 December 1992.

4. From a contribution to the "ipct-l" list (ipct-l@guvm.ccf.georgetown.edu), 16 November 1993.

The truth of the matter is that the mind *contains* nothing of enduring value. Its assets—and the very substance of its achievement—reside in its own, rigorously disciplined, revelatory shape, its flexibility, its strengthened vividness, its powers of attention and concentration, its self-awareness, its capacity for reverence and devotion.

But these qualities of the self-possessed knower, of the understanding consciousness, are exactly what, over the past five hundred years of scientific tradition, we have taught ourselves to ignore. As a result, the knowing self has disappeared into a vague sort of insupportable subjectivity—a ghost in the machine—now finally ready for its ultimate exorcism in favor of a denatured, mechanized reflection of intelligence. The scattered self is a disappearing self.

Additional symptoms of scattering. Needless to say, the scattered and disappearing self may have difficulty recognizing its own condition, for that would require moments of quiet contemplation and self-reflection. Consistent with the empty-receptacle view of mind, the "infonaut" finds great honor throughout cyberspace for his computer-mediated acquisition of data, but little encouragement for the mind's attention to its own activity. It is no wonder, then, that the age of the computer network should be greeted with the utterly false and unself-aware conviction that, having finally halted the attenuation of consciousness toward a vacuous and isolated subjectivity, we are now entering a new era of computationally supported Superconsciousness.

I have already mentioned a few reasons for seeing things otherwise. The reality of its scattering effects can, in fact, be traced in virtually every aspect of the computer's presence. Here are some examples:

- Among those whose work gives them full and unrestricted access to the Internet, the daily flooding of mailboxes often assumes legendary proportions. Many of us take pride in the speed with which we can dispose of messages—faster, perhaps, than we take in the three-inch story on the newspaper page. To contemplate the speaker behind the words—who is he, what is my connection to him, and what do I owe him in the form of attention and concern?—is hardly realistic. Persons fade from view, and words become more important than their human source. Increasingly, our "business" is found in the words alone.

- Closely related to this is the almost universal habit of scanning induced by certain forms of Net access. USENET newsgroups and high-traffic email discussion lists particularly encourage this habit. Few computer users seem to realize the damaging effects of scanning, which forces a superficial, abstract, associational reading of disjointed texts (if their contents are consciously noted at all). Over the long term one understands far more by thoroughly absorbing and then reflecting upon a very few messages—or a few paragraphs in long, sprawling messages—than by racing through endless kilobytes at top reading speed. I suspect that many people sense this, but nevertheless find it nearly impossible to counter the insistent urge (seeming to come from without) toward a kind of hyper-browsing.

- Again closely related is the difficulty many Net users have in resisting the continual intrusion of incoming messages. The moment a message arrives on their system, a bell sounds or an icon lights up, and they interrupt whatever they are doing to see what has come in. The workday—already tending toward fragmentation in the modern office—is finally reduced to electronically zapped smithereens.

- The potential advantages of hypertext are, in actual practice, a powerful invitation to scattering. It requires a tremendous inner discipline to sink oneself deeply into the thoughts represented by any given text, rather than to set off in grand, superficial pursuit of all the imagined delights behind the "doors" showing up as hypertext links on the screen. Clearly, a generation raised on *Adventure* and video games—where every door conceals a treasure or a monster worth pursuing in frenetic style—has its own way of appreciating the hypertext interface. And society's experience with television—where the "links" are buttons on a remote control device—doesn't suggest

13

positive things about our ability to use hypertext rather than be used by it.

• Many features of electronic word processing software tend to promote automatic, reflexive activity in the composition of our own texts.[5] This is evident enough in the texts themselves. The message dashed off "without a second thought"—and often copied with equal thoughtfulness to a distribution list—is the message that determines the tone of the Net. We find ourselves immersed in a sea of words produced much too easily, without depth or weight, and saying nothing in particular.

• The programming task requires one to abstract from a problem just those elements that can be embedded in a mechanism. Apart from a conscious, countervailing effort, this means *inattention* to all the human dimensions of the problem that cannot be mechanically captured. For example, group support software is typically designed to assist in the transformation of a set of initial "inputs" into a set of eventual "outputs." That this entire effort is merely a transient reflection of the *real* purpose of any productive group—which is, or should be, for the individuals to work creatively together, and thereby to foster mutually the development of their human capacities—hardly figures in the design of most software engineering projects. So the lives of both programmer and program user are filled with inherently unrelated tasks—unrelated because lacking connection to enduring purposes.[6]

• Even the much-discussed "hacker syndrome" is related to the scattered self. The obsessiveness of the socially cut off, out-of-control programmer can only arise as the complement of a lost center. While this obsessiveness represents a kind of concentration and attention, it is an attention that rules the self rather than being at the self's disposal.

---

5. See especially chapters 15, "Dancing with My Computer," and 16, "The Tyranny of the Detached Word."

6. See chapter 10, "Thoughts on a Group Support System."

That is, having failed to gain an ability to direct himself in conscious purposefulness, the hacker becomes subject to compulsions acting from unhealthy places beneath consciousness.

Beyond these brief suggestions, the television may have a few things to tell us about the potentials of the computer.

A prison window. If the television has proven an ideal instrument for scattering and weakening my powers of attention and my ability to be fully present, the networked computer promises to challenge me more radically still. Where television leads me through an endless kaleidoscope of passive experiences without any possibility of my being "all there" in any of them (I cannot react in any normal way to the accident shown on the screen, so I learn to blunt my powers of presence and response), the computer invites me to carry out even the active business of my working and social life without being all there.

I may revel in the fact that all of cyberspace, offering all its manifold transactions, is available through this small window on my desk. It is well to remember, however, that until recently most windows mediating the world to us in such a restrictive fashion had steel bars in them. Not many welcomed the prison. Some prisoners, it's true, have reported sublime experiences when catching a rare moment's glimpse of a bird through a narrow slit open to the sky. But it seems enough today if the window is glazed over with phosphors, so that we can divert ourselves unremittingly with the wonders of 3-D graphics, imagining that we are free to go wherever we wish.[7]

No doubt we *can* structure our lives and society so as to conduct all important business upon the surface of this small window. In outward terms, Vinton Cerf's claim may then become true: anyone disconnected from the Net will be isolated from world community. But even then, we must hope there will remain someone for whom the world hidden behind the glossed-over window is not altogether forgotten. Someone for whom

---

7. For discussion of common issues presented by computers and television, see chapter 14, "Children of the Machine," and chapter 25, "What This Book Was About."

the bird-shaped collection of illuminated pixels invokes the faint memory of a living creature with seeing eyes and beating heart—and for whom the difference between image and reality has not yet faded into mistiness. Someone for whom a routine financial transaction can still be an expression of trust. Someone for whom strong feeling has not finally been reduced to the vacuity of an email flame.

One reason the computer's invitation to scattering—like television's—is so strong, is that everything appearing on the surface of this small window remains an abstract representation of the unseen world beyond the window. When the world is presented to us at such a great remove, we require a heroic effort of imaginative reconstruction to avoid slipping by degrees into a habit of treating the representations on the window surface in the half-conscious, reflexive manner typical of the video game player. There is good reason for thinking that television has made this effort of imaginative reconstruction more difficult. The computer, by letting us enter a gamelike world even while conducting our business, may be making the effort nearly impossible.

False comparisons. Many people assume that computer technology is leading us out of the television wasteland, "because now everything is interactive." But this overlooks almost the entire significance of interactivity, which enables us to put the video screen to extensive new uses. We couldn't do our banking or coordinate our engineering projects by television; with the computer, we can.

The important thing about interactivity is not that it redeems old forms of entertainment (it doesn't), but rather what it does to the new activities now being adapted to the video screen. Making sitcoms interactive will not lead to cultural transformation, but there's every reason to expect, for example, that moving local, face-to-face politics online will tend to change the character of those politics *in the direction of* what we've already seen happen to televised politics.

Interactivity, in other words, does not salvage the preexisting wasteland, but it may well reduce huge tracts of once-thriving adjacent territory to semiaridity. The argument based on interactivity would have us say, in effect, "Look how much greener than the desert this new, semi-arid land is!" Meanwhile, by means of the computer, concrete human activity itself is invited toward passivity, automatism, and lowered consciousness. This is a momentous development.

The sleight of hand in the argument about interactivity is repeated on many fronts. To cite one other example: the informality of much computer-mediated communication is often seen as a recovery of the direct, the personal, the participatory, the emotionally expressive. Many observers, contrasting this "new orality" with formal or "literate" communication, see the computer carrying us back to earlier, more vivid and personalized forms of human exchange.

But the relevant comparison is not between oral and literate. It is between the genuinely oral communication that once took place face-to-face, and the "secondary orality" now electronically replacing that communication. Here we see the computer's influence running exactly counter to the usual thesis: informal communication is tending toward the abstract, disengaged, and remote, with feeling conveyed indirectly through the artifice of written expression, and participation unavoidably constrained by the narrower channel.

I should add that the ease with which this sleight of hand succeeds—and anyone willing to spend time perusing a selection of Net discussion groups can quickly verify the success—is itself testimony to an idealism loosed from reality.

Ideals cannot be engineered

The ideals sought by the scattered mind are empty ideals, abstract ideals, ideals without grip—hovering uselessly in the air above earth rather than *ennobling* earth. Much of the appeal of cyberspace appears to be its clean, dematerialized, conceptual nature, born of the programmer's and engineer's schematizing, ungrounded and therefore uncontaminated. That many Net enthusiasts see this as a strength—as an opportunity to realize our highest ideals—testifies to the absence of the concrete human being from the idealist's aseptic calculations. He has forgotten that the improvement of the human being is a messy, lifelong undertaking, inseparable from suffering.

What, then? *Can* human ideals survive the Internet? Surely they can, but the main reason for thinking they are not *in fact* surviving lies in the much too easy, much too widespread conviction that they will naturally take root in the etherealized soil of cyberspace. The Net's idealistic (or, equally, its fatalistic) depiction evidences a loss of awareness about where ideals may find (or fail of) their fulfillment.

The fulfilled ideal is never anything other than an extended human capacity—for generosity, for sympathetic understanding, for forgiving, for the imaginative projection of a better future . . . . Our having forgotten this fact suggests that the issue today is whether we can come to ourselves in the presence of our intelligent artifacts, and therefore whether there is any future for human ideals.

The computer, like so many tools, is a specialized and one-sided expression of what we have become, and therefore requires an effort of self-mastery. It requires the restoration of a disrupted internal balance. We benefit from this, for in mastering new tools we strengthen our own capacities. In this sense, every tool paradoxically offers us one gift above all others: it gives us something to work against. We turn it to our own use—overcoming it in the process—not primarily in order to gain some *thing* as a result, but in order to have accomplished the overcoming. It is always ourselves we work on, whether we realize it or not. There is no other work to be done in the world.

And today the needful work is to distinguish ourselves from our machines. It is to rediscover, for example, that all knowledge is knowledge of man, and that nothing worth calling an ideal can be found in the engineered world, but only in ourselves.

All this has a simple and inescapable implication. If the computer's gift is a landmark one in human history—and I believe it is—it can only be so because it poses a landmark danger. We can, after all, fail in the required self-mastery. If we are asked to come to ourselves over against our machines, we remain free to shun this extremely difficult work. So far, there has scarcely been an acknowledgment that the challenge even exists, let alone engagement with it.

A place for hope, and a place for doubt. I am not a fatalist, but my pessimism about our immediate prospects in the "age of information" could scarcely be greater. At the same time, some will find my underlying hope, rooted in the reality of human freedom, difficult to tolerate. Given these contrary tendencies of my thought, it may help to differentiate the two contexts in which my pessimism and hope come to expression:

- When I am speaking to the individual as he sits at his computer, I cannot point and say either "good!" or "bad!" We're not in that universe of discourse. All I can say is, "Enliven the word! Work at enlivening the word! If you cannot do so, you will lose yourself! Like it or not, the computer is with us to stay. So far as you are required to use it, you must redeem it or you will become like it." Where the individual's sovereign freedom rules, I speak of choices, and cannot prescribe.

  There is hope. The mere exchange of written words between two human beings *can* lead—for persons with extraordinarily developed sensitivities—to a more intimate knowledge of each other and a more substantial bearing of each other's burdens than most of us will ever achieve, say, in a lifetime of marriage. There have been some truly remarkable correspondences over the course of history.

  In some ways, the computer may be helping to call us toward exactly such deepened perceptions of each other. Wherever there is a word, there is a little frozen piece of the interior of a human being. It can, through painfully difficult effort, be thawed and enlivened. It can bring the other person alive for us. Moreover, the computer's inert manipulation of the word drives us to seek, by contrast, how we can speak out of our full humanity.

19

- If, on the other hand, I am addressing policy issues or social prospects, then current responses to the imperative just described become the basis for my assessment. Here the facts are whatever they are, and there is no necessary balance between hope and despair. We can, at a particular point in history, be quite as evidently headed toward disaster as once we were headed, say, toward World War II. Our task is to read the evidences and draw whatever conclusions we must.[8]

My own conclusion, given voice in the following chapters, is stark: if we continue assimilating our lives to computers according to the tendencies already broadly active in society—and those tendencies show every sign of retaining their grip upon us—then we will finally lose ourselves.

It is in this second, *policy* context—where, for example, we choose to inflict the computer upon millions of schoolchildren who have not asked for this reductive assault upon their higher capacities, and where we rush to assimilate every aspect of society to the computer's programmed necessities—that a spirit of judgment reigns most uncompromisingly in me. I say this confessionally, for I would rather it were not so. I would prefer to state the computer's challenge from a wholly positive inner stance. Fear and judgment in an author do not encourage the reader's awakening to himself; yet a book is justified only insofar as it serves this awakening.

Some sort of "full disclosure statement" is therefore advisable. I conclude with two such statements: the first relates to the two preceding contexts, and the second to my own journey in writing this book.

We must see what is at risk. As I was finishing work on *The Future Does Not Compute*, a friendly critic referred to my "jeremiad" against computers and wondered whether a more balanced approach might increase my effectiveness. It was then that I first made the distinction

---

8. For an overview of some of the social forces directing society's adaptation to the computer, see Iacono, Suzanne and Kling, Rob, "Computerization Movements and Tales of Technological Utopianism" in Kling, 1995. Numerous other papers in the same volume provide useful background.

between personal responsibility and social policy. And I went on to reply as follows:

"You claim that I grant no possibility for 'real and important kinds of online community.' That's not true. I accept both the reality and the importance.

"The online community is *real* because every medium that passes a 'word'—by which I mean an expressive gesture, an act with an inside—will bear some kind of human community. As I remark in chapter 6, community will even take hold of the asphalt highway and the television talk show. The online community is also *important* because, given its inevitably deepening hold on society, everything rides on our learning to master it—to make it as fully human a community as possible.

"Similarly, some readers seem convinced that, because in the policy context, I see little positive hope for certain computer uses, I must be telling them, 'it's wrong for you to use these things,' or at least 'it's impossible to do anything worthwhile or genuine or personally authentic with these things.' As a *policy* matter, this may be close to the current truth: those institutions being adapted to the computer will almost certainly continue to be drained of their remaining human dimensions. That's the way we are employing the computer. It has a lot to do with our abstracting and computational bent, under development now for several centuries. The computer requires a frightfully intense effort on our part if we're to overcome its downward pull.

"But as a way of addressing the individual facing his computer, this reading is almost the opposite of the truth. Not only *can* we do worthwhile things with computers, not only are worthwhile things being done every day, we *must* learn how to bring our computerized interactions fully alive, so that they represent more than just the hopeless loss of something. This is true regarding *all* the terms of human exchange, in whatever medium.

"So another way I could state the relation between the two contexts is this: so far as I *must* deal with the computer—because it is ever less escapable in modern society—or so far as I feel it my personal necessity to take up the challenge of the computer, to that degree I confront the urgent need to discover how to make the computer an instrument of human ends. But this is *not* the same as choosing to thrust the computer ever more deeply into a society that already looks like failing the challenge badly.

"This, then, brings me to the central matter. I said above that I haven't really learned yet how to speak about the computer's promise. I am hoping you will grant at least the possibility that there are some good reasons for this—perhaps, in the first place, the 'simple' reason that computers present a vast and complex challenge that few of us are yet well positioned to take on. Considering that the real terms of the challenge still go almost completely unacknowledged in social debate, I think this explanation is reasonable.

"It is, moreover, related to a second point. Can anyone seriously accept the grave personal responsibility to *enliven the word* without first having an inkling of what is at risk—that is, without first recognizing the perilous place to which we have come as *homo computandus*? I do not believe it is possible. We are not going to sweat the necessary blood over something that hasn't become desperately, threateningly important to us.

"Bear in mind where we are, as I have pictured it in PART THREE, 'The Electronic Word.' In the line that runs from orality to literacy to the printed book to the computer, we find the computer bringing to near completion the severing of the word from its live source in the individual. Not only that, but the programmed computer now sets the words in motion, mimicking (and, by common understanding, duplicating or replacing) the speaking human being in many and expanding circumstances.

"You and I will not adequately embark upon our individual labors without seeing the scale of the threat, and we cannot see the scale of the threat without . . . seeing it. What I have basically attempted to do in this book is to sketch the threat. I have also tried to make clear that the only reasonable place the sketch can lead is to a kind of inner awakening whose content I'm in no position to prescribe for others.

"For the general undertaking of the book, I can only believe that what you call my jeremiad is a true and 'balanced' representation. Perhaps it is not the most effective approach. I am trying to discover others. But the difficulty of starting with the positive potential of the computer is, I am convinced, a Herculean one.

"Personally, I would indict the book on two counts: it does not lead over into a strongly positive vision (because the vision is as yet beyond my ken); and it does not adequately depict the desperation of our current circumstances.

"It's not inconceivable to me that the computer in our society will prove a kind of 'necessary disaster,' rather as one might think of World War II as having been a necessary prerequisite for some more distant good. At the point where World War II loomed large, a wise person might have accepted the prospects and given himself over to planting seeds for the future amidst the enveloping chaos. But no wise person will speak casually of the 'good' in such things as wars—even though good does somehow emerge from the rubble. I myself have just recently been chastised—with some justice, I fear—for speaking too lightly of the good in illness.

"But isn't it even less wise to speak lightly of the good in something that promises to bring suffering on the level of a pestilence or a war, and yet is widely embraced as if it were a savior?"

If a question of balance can be asked of the book, it can also be asked of the author . . . .

This book is a symptom

This book is not full of solutions. In fact, it is itself a symptom. When I write about the dangers of computerized technology, I find that I have sketched my own one-sidedness, much as the police artist sketches a criminal from a victim's description. An editor wrote alongside one of my more computer-phobic outbursts, "How can you say this when it's your own life you're describing?"

It *is* my own life; that's why I can say it. I work on a concrete basement floor at home, isolated in front of a large screen and surrounded by a high-powered computer, modem, laser printer, telephone, and fax machine. I'm an editor for a publisher of computer books. For the past thirteen years my job has included programming responsibilities in addition to technical writing. In order to produce this book, I have sat for much-too-long days—and weekends—in front of my terminal, eyes glassy, spinal nerves in my neck going bad, general health and fitness deteriorating, my family neglected, the equipment around me dictating the terms of my existence.

I do not now wish I had done differently. But I will never again live with technology in quite the same way. To be imbalanced is one thing; to fail to change and grow is another. I have changed. Or, at least, I have *started* to change. If nothing else, this book has forced it. It has required me to look technology in the eye, and begin deciding what to do about my own relation to it.

One thing was done even as I wrote: I moved with my family to a strongly rooted rural community—a sort of unintentional intentional community—where the attempt to find a human-centered stance toward technology is much less a matter of theorizing than a deeply committed way of life. There is irony in this, however: my telecommuting is what made the move possible.

I have also begun to manage my exposure to technology. But this does little good as a purely negative process. I have recognized, as Robert Sardello puts it, that I must discover the *soul* of technology, and work toward its redemption.[9] Among other things, this requires that I find the counterbalance within my own life to the relentless pressures—issuing from within as well as from without—to compute the terms of my humanity. The computer, after all, symbolizes a society in which the head

---

9. Sardello, 1992.

has been severed from heart and will. I have learned the hard way that when my head runs on by itself—automatically, according to its precious, insulated logic—it is controlled by subterranean impulses of heart and will that I can never be fully aware of.

Art and nature, I have begun to glimpse, can play a healing role here—hardly a revelation to those less one-sided than I. So, too, can such simple acts as scheduling my time harmoniously and paying a more concerned attention to my immediate environment. There is also the need for a disciplined exercise of perception and thinking—certainly as important as exercising the physical organism. And then, for me—self-contradictory as the effort turned out to be—there was the writing of this book. These pages, you might say, record the conversation I had with myself as I sought a way out. The self-contradiction is part of the story.

If I had wanted a book that was not a symptom, I would have had to wait until I possessed all the answers. There would never have been a book. No one will find a solution to the problems of technology—or to any other human challenge—except by first coming to terms with himself and moving personally toward wholeness. But to capture something of the move toward wholeness is to capture an unfinished—and therefore still symptomatic—enterprise.

You may read the symptoms as you wish. If you think that I have "intellectualized" too much, I will not quarrel with you. I may even reply under my breath, "Yes, that's part of what I mean—that's the one-sidedness of our age, from which only now do I nurse any timid hopes of eventual escape." If you find my view of technology overly negative, I can only acknowledge that I have not yet been able to recognize what a redeemed technology might look like. I am absolutely convinced that redemption—sometime, somewhere—is possible. But I also know that a society can choose to make a pact with the devil. Even *such* a pact may perhaps be redeemed; but I do not know the way.

I have striven in this book to *understand*, so far as I am able, the encounter between man and computer. If understanding is not itself a solution, it is at least an essential prerequisite for any solution. Anyone

who demands *from others* something more than understanding—for example, an "answer" or a "program"—is himself driven by the computational
paradigm. What he really wants is mechanically effective "information"
and an escape from personal responsibility. It is, in fact, the great blindness
imposed by the technological spirit to believe that we can safely ignore
ourselves—as if all we needed were a proper, technical plan of action.

Really, there never can be solutions in human affairs. There are only
passages. By contrast, the computational paradigm is the final
crystallization—in "hard logic"—of our efforts over the past few hundred
years to recast the issues of human destiny as questions of technique. But
your destiny and mine are not technical problems to be solved; they are
meanings to be entered into, and possibilities for personal growth.

This book is written for those who seek escape from everything anti-
human, and who would reclaim their own destinies. It's just that I cannot
tell you exactly what the escape is, and I certainly cannot point you to
your destiny. I can only try to contribute, within this broader, human
context, to an understanding of the problems.

Perhaps, at least, the display of my own symptoms will aid the effort
to understand. If I remain one-sided, it is precisely with the one-sidedness
of the computer-in-the-head. I still struggle to apprehend—or be apprehended by—those soft-breathed, inner gestures that, like the patient
caress of wind and water, can dismantle the frozen, logical perfection of
the most adamantine crystal.

Man, Computers, and Community

2

THE MACHINE IN THE GHOST

THE INTELLIGENCE OF COMPUTERS is delivered upon tiny chips made of silicon—just about the most homely and earthy material known to man. Silicon amounts pretty much to sand. Apply a few volts of electricity to some duly prepared slivers of silicon, and—if you are like most people—there will suddenly take shape before your eyes a Djinn conjuring visions of a surreal future. It is a future with robots who surpass their masters in dexterity and wit; intelligent agents who roam the Net on our behalf, seeking the informational elixir that will make us whole; new communities inhabiting the clean, infinite reaches of cyberspace, freed from war and conflict; and lending libraries of "virtually real" experiences that seem more sensational than the real thing—all awaiting only the proper wave of industry's well-proven technological wand.

As you probably realize, not all of this is idle or fantastic speculation—even if it is the rather standard gush about our computerized future. Something *like* this is indeed coming—in fact, has already arrived. And few observers can see any clear limits to what computers might eventually accomplish. It is this stunning, wide-open potential that leads some people to wonder what the Djinn will ask of us in return for the gift. After all, any potential so dramatic, so diverse, so *universal*, can be taken in many directions. That is its very nature. Who will choose the direction—we, or the Djinn?

Tools get under our skin

As far back as human traces go, man has used tools. But tools are slippery things—exceedingly hard to define. Everything from a hand-held stone to language has been seen as a tool. Tools are, by most definitions, extensions of ourselves, and are both the result of and the means for our acting in the world. Even our own limbs may be used as tools. In fact, we can readily view our limbs as "archetypes," or primary examples, of what it means to be a tool.

But haven't I lost my way if I can't tell the difference between a tool and myself, or even between a tool and my own, word-borne thoughts?

Well, maybe not. At least, there's a truth here worth going after: When we talk about tools, we are, one way or another, talking about ourselves. There's a depth of meaning in the old saying, "To someone who has only a hammer, everything begins to look like a nail." We not only shape things with our tools; we are shaped by them—our behavior adapts. This has been recognized in many different arenas. You may, for example, have heard the expression, "the medium is the message"—that is, the tools we use to communicate a message affect what we say. One consequence is that you will probably find yourself putting on a different "personality" when you compose an electronic mail message, from when you write a note on stationery. Somehow—rather uncannily—tools always seem to get "under our skin."

The unconscious as steam engine. One other thing is undeniable about tools: over the course of history they have become increasingly complex. This is a fascinating study in itself, for there seem to be certain thresholds of complexity—or, perhaps, thresholds in our own minds—beyond which the character of the tool is mightily transformed. There were, of course, various mechanical devices far back in history—for example, looms and hoes and catapults. But during the Scientific and Industrial Revolutions, the cleverness embodied in *mechanisms* changed with extreme rapidity, entailing a kind of systematic, rationalized intricacy not seen before. A modern offset printing press or harvesting combine is as far removed from the loom of an ancient Greek household as—well, as we feel ourselves to be from ancient Greece.

Since a radical transformation of tools implies a parallel transformation of the tool user, we are not surprised to learn that the age of great mechanical invention was also the age during which our ancestors of a few hundred years ago began to "feel" as if they inhabited a clockwork universe. Here's how Owen Barfield describes the matter:

> I recall very well, when I was writing my early book, *History in English Words*,[1] being astonished at the ubiquitous appearance of the *clock* as a metaphor shortly after it had been invented. It turned up everywhere where anybody was trying to describe the way things work in nature . . . . Coming a little nearer to our own time [the student of words] finds the psychology of the unconscious, in which the first half of the twentieth century felt so much at home. Strange how squarely it seems to be based on an image of "repression," which is much the same as *com*pression! Was it after all just the steam-engine in disguise?[2]

Barfield was writing before the computer age. If he were penning those words today, he would have to cite, not just another "contraption," but something strangely transcending all the products of the machine era. For now we seem to have crossed another threshold—one carrying us far beyond the most impressive achievements of the Industrial Age. Computers offer us an entirely new order of complexity, intelligence, flexibility. They achieve what we could scarcely imagine an old-style mechanism achieving. These modest, unimposing devices on our desks demonstrate a remarkable capacity to *emulate*—that is, to become *any* tool. Need a

---

1. Barfield, 1986. First published in 1926.

2. "The Harp and the Camera," a lecture subsequently published in Barfield, 1977b: 73–4.

calculator? Typesetter? Mailbox? Pencil and paper? File cabinet? Library? Tape recorder? There they are, sitting in front of you, awaiting your command. A computer can even become, in its own way, a tornado or ocean wave, modeling these things in such a compelling manner that some theorists now believe the essence of the tornado or wave really is *in the computer.*

But this new threshold is even more momentous than I have so far suggested. The truth that we cannot talk about tools without talking about ourselves, now becomes stunningly literal. Not only do our tools reveal things about us, they promise to *become* us! That, at least, is what many people think is happening through research in artificial intelligence. Other people worry that, because tools inevitably work their way under our skin, we are in the process of becoming "mere computers." Does our enthusiasm for computerlike models of the mind reflect our firm grasp of the computer, or rather the computer's firm grasp of us?

We meet ourselves in our computers

How do we begin assessing the computer as a human tool? The claims and counter-claims easily become tiresome. For every benefit of the computer you cite, I can point to a corresponding threat; and for every alarm I sound, you can herald a new opportunity. This slipperiness, in fact—as I have already suggested—must be our starting point. Part of the essence of a computer is its flexibility, its emulative ability, its diverse potentials. It is a *universal machine.* Given a technology of almost pure, open-ended potential, the machinery itself is, from a certain point of view, scarcely worth discussing. It is a template, a blank screen. Everything hinges upon what we bring to the technology, and which of its potentials we choose to realize. The one sure thing about the computer's future is that we will behold our own reflections in it.

Even the "computer-human interface" people—who have contributed so much to our understanding of machine design—have failed to probe adequately the implications of the fact that we're really dealing with a human-human interface. Those were software engineers who designed that obstructive program you struggled with last week. Computer scientists conceived the languages that constrained the programmers. And certain academicians first recognized, or thought they recognized, the quintessence of their own mentality in a transistorized logic gate. Could they have done so if they had not already begun to experience themselves as logic machines? Could I, for that matter, allow the hammer in my hands to run riot if there were no answering spirit of aggression within me?

This is why I find naive rhapsodizing about computers so disconcerting. It expresses the very sort of blithe unawareness that converts the technology into a profound threat. Machines become a threat when they embody our limitations without our being fully aware of those limitations. All reason shouts at us to approach every aspect of the computer with the greatest caution and reserve. But what incentive has our culture provided for the exercise of such caution and reserve? It's more in our nature to let technology lead where it will, and to celebrate the leading as progress.

Of course, every invention, from television to nuclear power, tends to incarnate the will (conscious or unconscious) of its employer. And if that will is less than fully conscious, the invention wields us more than we wield it. Can anyone really doubt that we have become the tools of television far more than the reverse? But the computer ups the ante in a game already extremely perilous. It relentlessly, single-mindedly, apes us even in—or perhaps especially in—those habits we are not yet aware of, for it is endowed in some sense with a mind of its own.

- Have we been learning to view the human being as a cipher in a political calculation? The computer will refine those calculations beyond our hopes.

- Are we content to employ our educational system as a tool for shoveling "information" into child-receptacles? The computer offers endless databases from which to do the shoveling—and entertainment to "help the pill go down." (First, parents turned their children over to a television screen; now we can give teachers the same right.)

33

- Have our businesses been converting themselves into computational machines geared to a purely quantitative bottom line, disconnected from considerations of human value? Computers not only can assist such businesses, they can *become* such businesses; all they need is an appropriate program. (Computers on Wall Street, trading in financial instruments, are already profitable businesses pursuing "clean," mathematical values.)

- Has ours become an age of meaninglessness? The computer asks us to betray what meanings we have left for dessicated information. The complex, qualitative, metaphorical nature of meaning only gets in the way of the easy, computational manipulation of numerically cast information.

All of which is to say that we have been progressively distilling into the computer certain pronounced tendencies of our own minds. These tendencies are certainly related to that entire several-hundred-year history by which our culture has gained both its technological triumphs and its horrors.

But is the computer really just a blank screen reflecting our own natures? Doesn't it invite—even encourage—a one-sided display of human traits? It seems undeniable that what the computer asks from us is above all else "what computes." It asks us to abstract from human experience a quantity, a logic, that it can cope with. And yet, we must acknowledge that during the past several centuries we have shown, quite independently of the computer, a strong passion for reducing all of human experience, all knowledge, to abstraction. The computer is a perfected result of this urge. Can we blame the computer for this?

The will toward artifice

On the one hand: the machine as an expression of the human being. On the other hand: the machine as an independent force that acts or reacts upon us. Which is it? I am convinced there is no hope for understanding the role of technology in today's world without our first learning to hold both sides of the truth in our minds, flexibly and simultaneously. The relationship between human being and machine has become something like a complex symbiosis. We who devise "thinking machines" cannot escape our own most intimate responsibility for the planet's rapidly crystallizing, electromechanical nimbus, nor can we escape the prospect of its increasing—and potentially threatening—independence of mind and self-will.

In sum: if machines do not simply control society, neither can we claim straightforward control of their effects. We and our mechanical offspring are bound together in an increasingly tight weave. To substantially modify the larger pattern—rather than simply be carried along by it—requires profound analysis of things not immediately evident, and a difficult effort to change things not easily changed. If it is only through self-awareness and inner adjustment that I can restrict the hammer in my hands to its proper role, I must multiply the effort a millionfold when dealing with a vastly more complex technology—one expressing in a much more insistent manner its own urgencies.

But that is not quite all. We are not—yet, at least—bound to our machines by a perfectly rigid symmetry of mutual influence. The willfulness we encounter in technology, even where it has long since detached itself from us, nevertheless originates in the human being—a fact some of the severer critics of technology overlook.[3] So long as we can document the nonneutrality of technology—as these critics so effectively have— then we do not live in absolute thrall to it. For understanding is the basis of our freedom.

Freedom is admittedly a risky business. We *can* choose to ignore the sound warnings of these critics; we *can* continue giving full rein to the half-conscious impulses we have embedded in our machines even while abdicating the kind of responsibility the critics plead for. We *can*, that is, finally descend to equality with our machines. This would be a fearful

---

3. See chapter 5, "On Being Responsible for Earth."

symmetry indeed, precluding the sort of understanding from which freedom arises and sealing off the escape from pure, mechanical determination.

Throughout the following pages my arguments will retain a double edge. At one moment I will emphasize the determining influence we have already given to our machines; the next moment I will urge the burden of freedom. There is no essential contradiction here. A recognition of what has been determining us is the only basis for a responsible freedom.

Nor does either side of this double truth require me to call for a mindless rejection of technology. I will, in fact, have little to say about technology as such in this book. What I really fear is the hidden and increasingly powerful machine within *us*, of which the machines we create are an expression. Only by first coming to terms with our own "will toward artifice" can we gain the freedom to use wisely the artifices of our creation.

3

THE FUTURE DOES NOT COMPUTE

COMPUTERS ARE TOOLS OF THE PAST. They are perfectly designed to aid our understanding precisely insofar as it is a past-understanding. For example, if we want to know when lunar eclipses will occur in the year 2053, there's no better tool for figuring it out than a computer.

"But wait a minute. 2053 isn't in the past. That's a prediction of the future."

Well, yes, in a trivial sense. More reasonably, you might say it's the past simply projected into the future. And the projection involves nothing new; it's *nothing but* the past. Everything in the "prediction" was already fully implicit in the celestial configuration of, say, 1857. All we're saying is, "Here's what the past looks like when projected onto the year 2053."

What happens when we *really* turn our computers toward the future—or try to? All too often, disaster. Disaster, for example, in the form of decision support systems wrongly applied. Human decisions clearly are (or ought to be) matters of the future. We make decisions in order to choose a future different from the one now approaching us. No analysis of what *is*, and no set of previously calculated questions or

37

heuristics, can remove the burden of choice. When I choose a future, shall I reject 1% of the analysis—which is to say, 1% of the past—or 99%? What is to guide me—more analysis of the past?

How shall I choose my wife?

Ask yourself about the critical decisions in your life. How did you choose your present vocation? There are, of course, very sober ways for doing this. Begin by taking a few psychological tests to inventory your skills and aptitudes, personality type, likes and dislikes, character, stability, financial requirements, geographic preferences, physical characteristics (strength, endurance, handicaps), and so on. Then align this inventory with a similar analysis of all the possible vocations (basic skills required, profiles of the most successful people in each vocation . . .). Finally, identify the closest fit and (presto!) there's your future—presumably a well-adjusted, profitable, and happy one.

But, no, something's not right here. Have you, or has anyone you know, *ever* made an important decision by weighing all related factors, adding them up, and then obeying the sum? This is not really your future we're talking about; it's your past. The real question is, what do you choose to become—despite what you are now? What future not already embodied in the past will you embrace? Of the great figures of history, where would they be if they had merely hewed to a reasonable future? Joan of Arc. The first black in a white Mississippi college. The first woman doctor. The soldier who dives on a hand grenade to protect his comrades—what sort of a future is that? Yet we honor him.

The psychologist, Alfred Adler, went so far as to make a rule of the fact that outstanding people typically work *against* their profiles and their past.[1] He tells us of various painters who had eye problems, and claims that 70% of art students were "found to suffer from some optical anomalies." Musicians, he notes, have often suffered from ear afflictions—leading to deafness in the case of Beethoven and Robert Franz. Clara

---

1. Adler, 1964: 21–43.

Schumann reported hearing and speech difficulties in childhood. And then there's Demosthenes, the stutterer, who became the greatest orator of Greece. What sort of decision support system might have been useful—or destructive—to these people?

Or take marriage. Shall I choose a wife reasonably, because all the indicators point to our being well-adjusted and happy, or shall I plunge into a future I cannot fully see, but that I am strangely, mysteriously, drawn to, dimly recognizing something of myself (but not *yet* myself) in my partner? Is there really a choice to be made between the perfectly compatible marriage of the inventory-takers and the reality cited by Adolf Güggenbuhl-Craig? Marriage, he says, is

> a special path for discovering the soul . . . . One of the essential features of this soteriological pathway is the absence of avenues for escape. Just as the saintly hermits cannot evade themselves, so the married persons cannot avoid their partners. In this partially uplifting, partially tormenting evasionlessness lies the specific character of this path.[2]

Surely we may as well accept this from the start (and you can see such acceptance in every good marriage), for that is the way it will turn out in any case. Can I gain anything truly worthwhile in life without suffering (and discovering) the unexpected? But how shall I program into my computer the unexpected, or the equation of suffering and reward?

Every question about the future—every human question—is like this. We strike out into the unknown, with a hope and a vision perhaps, but without an adequate "basis" for our decisions. After all, a *perfectly* adequate basis would mean the decision was trivial, because divorced from questions of human destiny. Unfortunately, however, broad areas of our lives have fallen under the spell of the computational approach, where we imagine the computer—the past—to hold the secret of a future that is, therefore, no longer a future.

---

2. Güggenbuhl-Craig, 1971: 41.

Computing to work

Look, for example, at business. In many contexts we take it for granted that our businesses should be managed as matters of the past. Analyze the market precisely enough, design the product to fit the analysis, and the bottom line is guaranteed—because it is already implicit in the past. At least, that is the ideal of "perfect analysis and planning" toward which we strive, and we measure our success against it.

What has fallen out of this picture? Just the entire meaning of *work*, just the whole *human* reason why people band together and direct their creative energies toward productive ends. *Ends*—things worth pursuing. Goods that are good, services that serve. The corporation has divorced itself from questions like "What task do I wish to take up in the world?" and "What is the future we wish to create?" We form our companies only to learn that they no longer embody *our* ends, but somehow have a neat, predictable logic of their own. We choose a future only to find it taken out of our hands, exchanged for a permutation of the past.[3]

The computer, one might almost say, was invented as an inevitable refinement of the corporation. Much of the early work in artificial intelligence came out of schools of management, and there was a great deal of excitement—this was back in the 1960s—about how computers would soon take over all the business manager's hard decisions. And make a better job of it. Computers didn't bring anything essentially new; they were just going to be better machines than we had yet managed to be.

Weighing the past is critically important, in business as elsewhere. It helps us to see the current playing field, identify constraints, compare options against an established framework. For this, computers are immensely valuable. But they do us no good if, in the process, we lose the future—if our thinking becomes so shaped to a knowledge of the past that our courage fails us when it comes time to break the machine and declare for the unjustifiable.

---

3. Chapter 8, "Things That Run by Themselves," explores these necessities in considerable detail.

THE FUTURE DOES NOT COMPUTE

When judges are computers

There is a strong case to be made—although I have not made it here—that our acquired skill in analyzing the past has largely hidden the future from us. This is hardly surprising when you consider that our past-knowledge is commonly held (at least in academic and scientific circles) to imply that there *is* no future—no future of possibility, no future not already determined by the past.

The horror of such a view—once it links up with the computer's ability to preserve the past as our future—echoes through a query by one of the pioneers of artificial intelligence. John McCarthy asked, "What do judges know that we cannot tell a computer?"[4] The question is grotesque. Some theorists may, after all, have succeeded in reducing their own tasks very substantially to mere computation. But a judge must forever be asking: by what metaphor can I understand this person before me? How does he differ from anyone I have seen before? How may I grasp the difference, and what decision may I impose, consistent with law, that will give him the best chance of coming to himself?

There remains one convenient thing about an impoverished, ossified future: it computes. Of course it computes—it is exactly what the computer was designed to give us. Our true future, on the other hand, can never be computed—so long, that is, as we retain the courage to call it into being at all.

---

4. Quoted in Weizenbaum, 1976: 207.

4

SETTLERS IN CYBERSPACE

HOWARD RHEINGOLD IS THE SORT OF GUY you'd feel safe with even among the most disreputable, unshaven denizens of what he, like everyone else, prefers to call cyberspace. That is just as well, for occasionally he seems particularly drawn to the shadier haunts, where he introduces us to offbeat—even threatening—characters of the Net, and takes delight in surprising us with their gentle and positive side. An ever genial and informative guide, he ushers his readers[1] on a bracing, personalized tour of the online world. While unabashedly playing "cheerleader" for the new networking technologies, he also calls up lucid visions of danger. And those who find his outlook insufficiently one-sided will still enjoy contented hours mining his wealth of historical narrative, anecdote, and observation to support their own utopian or apocalyptic predilections.

As one whose slightly alarmed imagination runs toward the apocalyptic, I am a little disappointed that Rheingold's critical eye is much more

---

1. Rheingold's book is *The Virtual Community* (Reading MA: Addison-Wesley, 1993). An earlier version of this commentary on the book appeared in the electronic journal, *Interpersonal Computing and Technology*, vol. 2, no. 2 (1994).

intent on discerning the human future in the networked computer than recognizing the origin and future of the computer in the increasingly computational bent of the human being. Surely it is only when the latter inquiry complements the former that we can begin to assay the dangers we face. But Rheingold's geniality elicits an echoing geniality of my own, so I am more inclined to begin with our common ground as children of the Sixties.

It was, for me, a surprise to learn from *The Virtual Community* just how rooted in the Sixties counterculture many of the earliest, person-to-person computer networks were. Stewart Brand, who founded the WELL (Whole Earth 'Lectronic Link), asserts flatly that "the personal computer revolutionaries *were* the counterculture." Several of the early leaders of the WELL were alumni of the Hog Farm commune, and Rheingold—a WELL veteran in his own right—seemed to find himself soul-sharing with other children of the Sixties wherever he went to investigate the early history of computer bulletin boards and conferencing systems. "Personal computers and the PC industry," he notes, "were created by young iconoclasts who had seen the LSD revolution fizzle, the political revolution fail. Computers for the people was the latest battle in the same campaign" (p. 48).

Lost in the counterculture

I, too, grew up with that generation, and I, too, see in its passion and indignation and arousal a glimmering hope for the future. But here I am obligated to meet Rheingold's confessional journey with a disclosure of my own. I never really signed on with my generation. When, in 1968, I made the required, ritual visit to Haight-Ashbury, the scene there struck me as too silly to take seriously. Of course, I had already sealed my status as a generational outsider when, four years earlier (the year I entered college) I acted as a Chicago poll watcher on behalf of the Goldwater campaign.

Something of the outsider has driven my restlessness ever since. When, in the Seventies, I ran an organic farm for several years, I found myself comfortable neither with the alternative food network nor with the buttoned-down bankers from whom we received operating funds. The social politics of the alternative types seemed too absurdly wrong-headed and unrealistic. (I found it vastly more edifying—not to mention *fun*—to listen to William F. Buckley in debate than to endure the naive ramblings of those who saw themselves saving the world.) Meanwhile, the conventional types—just so far as they registered no discontent with the social institutions to which they submitted—seemed to have lost their souls.

It shocks some of my friends—for whom my behavior is the height of irresponsibility—to learn that I have never voted in a public election. (I was too young to vote for Goldwater.) I never felt I had enough of a handle on the *real* historical processes to make the act of voting meaning-ful. I couldn't see how any of the things that really mattered were ever touched upon by politicians. The gyros guiding the human passage upon earth, I thought, spin invisibly within us, where our nascent moral suspicions and imaginative understandings first shape themselves; everything about the political system, so far as I could tell, served only to obscure what was important. I couldn't help thinking that my "statement" in refusing to vote was much more likely to have some minuscule awakening effect upon myself and others than the weight of a thousand votes in the pollsters' and sociologists' rude calculus. So I have spent twenty-five years standing apart, watching, and trying to understand.

This is not an apologia—or, at least, not only that. I am not proud of the fact that I have been so thoroughly cut off from extended community for these twenty-five years. I see it more as a personal symptom than a cultural indictment. And yet, my relative isolation has taught me a few things—above all else, to recognize the same symptoms in the larger society. And one thing has become painfully, vividly clear to me: very few in our society—not even those who most passionately cultivate community—quite know what it is they seek, or where they might obtain it, or how to grasp hold of it when it is actually offered to them.

45

It is as if a certain isolation of self is built into the structure of the human being today. I am convinced that much of the "community" we experience is more an effort to bury the loneliness than to reckon with its causes. And I suspect that the causes have a lot to do with our failure to acknowledge, let alone to have any useful language for grasping, the spiritual self whose cut-off condition is at issue. More and more, we try to lay hold of this self in the intelligent machinery that reflects a vague shadow of it—which only accelerates our loss, even while temporarily anesthetizing us against the pain.

I now find the larger social and political processes beckoning for the first time. This book is one of my responses. Another has my family, as I write, preparing a move—to a rural community centered around an organic farm, a school without computers, an intentional village for the mentally disabled, and an intellectual and artistic life that rivals many a university town's. Whatever the future may actually hold, this move *feels* like the first step across a lifetime's continental divide. For me it is, finally, a step toward community—and one for which I fear my computer is more likely to prove a distraction than a help.

Pioneer days

I am not the only person to live through these twenty-five years. One hopes that the impulses that gave rise to the Hog Farm will be found, now matured and transformed, in the new virtual communities. In any case, Rheingold makes it clear that we can understand the early history of virtual community only in the light of these impulses.

The WELL—which is at the center of Rheingold's story—was a kind of intentional community. Its founders deliberately seeded it with discussion leaders who passionately believed in its potential for transforming society. Its success was purchased, in part, by giving free accounts to journalists, who discovered in it a source for unusual, future-oriented stories. Given this publicity, the WELL began to draw from a national and then international pool of idealistic computer networkers, sociologists studying the new virtual communities, participants in the first online Grateful

Dead discussion groups, and, eventually, anyone and everyone. "People who were looking for a grand collective project in cyberspace flocked to the WELL" (p. 43).

All this newness and idealism accounts for many of the positive things Rheingold sees in the early virtual communities. Of course, as he himself points out, marked antisocial tendencies have also surfaced. John Perry Barlow—one of Rheingold's subjects and a co-founder of the Electronic Frontier Foundation, as well as a former Grateful Dead lyricist—captured both sides of the truth in a distinctive way:

> Cyberspace . . . has a lot in common with the 19th century West. It is vast, unmapped, culturally and legally ambiguous, verbally terse . . . . hard to get around in, and up for grabs. Large institutions already claim to own the place, but most of the actual natives are solitary and independent, sometimes to the point of sociopathy. It is, of course, a perfect breeding ground for both outlaws and new ideas about liberty.[2]

The thing to take to heart, I think, is that neither the blatant outlawry nor the sheen of idealism tell us a whole lot about the future shape of the territory once it is settled. They do remind us, though, that what we'll finally have to face is ourselves. This is critically important. Many are intoxicated with the wild freedom, the self-determination, the escape from tyranny, the unbounded opportunities for unchaperoned contact and association they discover in the Net. It all becomes a "new paradigm." New paradigms may indeed arise, but we should not forget the old realities that remain.

One of those realities is the social requirement for structure and reliable sources of information. Currently, many avoid the Net's more boisterous districts because the signal-to-noise ratio is too low. Surfing the Internet with an ear for the endless saloon gossip, the avalanches of self-published papers, announcements on every conceivable topic, uncertain news modulated through obscure channels, promotions of all sorts—it's a

---

2. Barlow, 1990.

47

notorious time sink (not to mention a rich source of hopelessly mixed metaphors). You quickly begin to look for the kind of established structure that enables you to make educated guesses—much as you say, "Yes, I know what to expect from this magazine, and it's likely to contain something of interest." As Michael Heim remarks, "the need for stable channels of content and reliable processes of choice grows urgent."[3]

And just because our society *is* organizing itself around networking technology, those channels *will* take form. We, who work and play, will impose our structured preferences upon the new media, just as we have imposed our preferences upon the printing press, television and every other technology.

The self-absorbed Net

Besides the idealism of a kind of pioneering counterculture, a second factor powerfully affects what Rheingold finds in virtual communities: the historically inbred or self-referential character of the Net. Many of those who are most enthusiastic about its possibilities are the same people who develop the enabling software and hardware, or who write about cyberspace, or who study it (the flood of sociologists and anthropologists let loose upon the Net is legendary), or who are trying to make policy for it, or who—like so many schoolteachers—have been told that it is important for their future, so they're desperately trying to figure it out.

Rheingold relates, for example, how he was invited to participate in a (face-to-face) Washington conference. Before attending, he opened a discussion on the WELL. After spending a few minutes a day there for six weeks, he possessed "more than two hundred pages of expert advice from my own panel." The topic of the conference he had been invited to: *communication systems for an information age* (p. 59).

This self-referential use of the Net colors much of Rheingold's book. Whether it's organizations like the Electronic Frontier Foundation or Computer Professionals for Social Responsibility, or online activists who

---

3. Heim, 1993: 104.

48

are convinced computer networking will reinvigorate democracy, or other activists who believe computer networking will redeem education, or yet other activists who are attracted by an almost mystical vision of electronic culture ("cyberculture," as they are likely to call it)—in most of these cases Net success stories occur for a good reason: not only do these people *use* the Net in their work, but their work is *about* the Net; often it is even aimed at *promoting* the Net. One hopes that the Net would "succeed" at least for them. Their experiences, however, may offer little insight into broader social issues.

The settling of cyberspace

Rheingold is particularly impressed by the "enormous leverage" the Net can give ordinary citizens at relatively little cost—"intellectual leverage, social leverage, commercial leverage, and most important, political leverage" (p. 4). I find this notion of leverage rather hard to understand against the backdrop of a future in which the Net has become as ubiquitous as everyone expects—that is, when the promotion of the Net itself is no longer a primary function of the Net.

Rheingold cites a successful political campaign by online activist Dave Hughes, who stunned his local city council by mobilizing 175 citizens to turn out for a council meeting. They won their case, and Hughes credited a computer network with making the organizational effort possible. The credit was no doubt well deserved; the council members were presumably baffled by this invisibly conjured turnout.

Yes, the practiced gunslinger in the Old West had a decided advantage—but only until law and order was established. What becomes of the activist's differential advantage—his special leverage—when the political process has fully adapted itself to networked communication and *all* campaigns are Net campaigns? Will the individual citizen then find it easier to affect the political process, or will the sheer, inundative bulk and sophistication of machine-assisted, well-financed activism put politics even more out of reach than the TV-driven juggernauts of our own day?

The same sort of question applies in many arenas. There's a race now by investors to "guarantee" themselves an incremental advantage in the financial markets by employing computerized trading programs. Some of these programs are created in think tanks employing Ph.D. mathematicians and economists who bring the newest and most esoteric statistical theories to bear upon their task. The aim of the programs: to manage sometimes massive transactions on a split-second basis in order to secure a marginal leg up on mere chance. Such investment mechanisms are in continual flux, for the discovery of a winning formula quickly changes the probabilistic and psychological matrix upon which the formula was based. How is the "little guy" to compete?

Similarly, all the talk about individual empowerment through electronically accessible information really has more to do with the differential advantage for a few players early in the game than it does with any fundamental social change. It's rather like the pyramid scheme: those who are quickest off the mark win big; the rest must hope eventually to climb back to the break-even point in a game that is now speeded up and very likely more demanding than it was before.

The common response to these observations is that the individual— the "plain citizen," small investor, modest entrepreneur—can use the new technology to counter the advantage of the big players. I will be able to send "knowbots" roaming the Net in search of information useful to me. I can buy my own software to do programmed trading. I can tie into the world Net and become my own activist. But this gets ridiculous fast. Every new leap of technology simply cranks up the speed of the game another notch. What improves my efficiency does the same for the millions of other players. As Langdon Winner has pointed out,

> the availability of low-cost computing power may move the baseline that defines electronic dimensions of social influence, but it does not necessarily alter the relative balance of power. Using a personal computer makes one no more powerful vis-à-vis, say, the National

Security Agency than flying a hang glider establishes a person as a match for the U.S. Air Force.[4]

Trying to find a calculus of advantage in the spiraling competition between the machine-assisted individual and the machine-assisted System strikes me as a fruitless pastime. Eventually, we will have to step back and realize that there are only two things in this picture: on the one hand, increasingly powerful, machine-assisted machines, and, on the other hand, you and I. If you and I are looking for "empowerment," for an advantage over the next person, then that's the sort of society we will create, and that same spirit is what we'll encounter in the machinery—only here it will harden into a volition substantially independent of our own wishes. If, on the other hand, we are truly and wisely seeking human community, then we will eventually figure out the right uses for machinery—however drastic our change of direction must be—and our human focus will prevent our embedding further anti-human tendencies in that machinery. Either way, the future shape of society is to be sought, finally, within the human being, not in technological assessment.

Who threatens the Net?

Rheingold makes many bows in the approximate direction of this truth. He certainly understands that the human future requires, not an endless drive for competitive advantage, but rather a spirit of cooperation. It is one of his virtues that he repeatedly returns to the truth that it is you and I who must make our virtual communities hospitable places; the issue, he says more than once, still hangs in the balance. And in discussing leverage, he cautions us:

> But the technology will not in itself fulfill that potential; this latent technical power must be used intelligently and deliberately by an informed population. More people must learn about that leverage and learn to use it while we still have the freedom to do so . . . . The

---

4. Winner, 1986: 112.

odds are always good that big power and big money will find a way
to control access to virtual communities . . . . (p. 5)

But here and throughout the book he shows a tendency—perhaps
carried over from the counterculture—to finger anonymous and institu-
tional antagonists: the "big boys" who "divide up the power and loot";
"malevolent political leaders with their hands on the controls of a Net";
the "governments and private interests" who turn the media away from
democratic debate toward talk shows and commercials (pp. 279, 289).
This is justified so far as we have tended to invest certain institutions with
a life of their own. One thing to realize here, however, is that the computer itself will "receive" these unconscious tendencies even more eagerly
than the corporation.[5] A second thing is that, ultimately, even these institutionalized and mechanized projections of our nature must be traced
back to ourselves. It is we who watch the shows, we who populate the
massive government bureaucracies, and we who, day by day, transact the
nation's corporate business.

When Rheingold says that "the most insidious attack on our rights to
a reasonable degree of privacy might come not from a political dictator-
ship but from the marketplace" (p. 292), he is doubtless correct. But the
citizens who determine the character of the marketplace are the same citizens who will make the Net whatever it becomes. When we're all in the
electronic marketplace together, will our enemy be any less ourselves than
when we were all in the industrial marketplace together? When the Net
subsumes all social functions, will the balance of healthy and destructive
forces be more positive than we already know it to be?

Seeing the future in ourselves

Rheingold passes along many touching stories, such as that of Lhary, a
participant in the WELL's Parenting discussion group. Lhary came down
with leukemia and moved to Houston. When he checked into a Houston
hospital, he continued to log onto the WELL from his hospital room.

---

5. See chapter 8, "Things That Run by Themselves."

Some of the Parenting group "got together and personally tie-dyed regulation lab coats and hospital gowns for Lhary to wear around the hospital corridors."

By such acts true community is indeed nourished, and it is heartwarming to find an online group so generous in spirit and so committed to the cultivation of community. It is also an important signpost for the future: this is one way we *can* use the Net. That stories like this tell us a whole lot about how we *will* use the Net—how we will shape it and it will shape society—nevertheless seems to me doubtful. The overall effects of the telephone upon community are probably not explained very well by the fact that people can and do extend acts of generosity toward friends or strangers over the phone. I think Rheingold would agree that this points us only to a range of possibilities, not likelihoods.

Where, then, do we look for the likelihoods? When I think of a leukemia patient in a hospital, the first thing that occurs to me is how inhospitable that environment is likely to be—and how much it might drive *anyone* to a network terminal for support. Why have our hospitals become what they are? How is it that we have the most technically sophisticated medicine in the world, and yet have largely expunged the human element from it? There is nothing more intimately human than the healing process; in it we must come to terms with ourselves, our destiny on earth, our deepest human connections. Healing is, in the true sense of the words, a ministry, a laying on of hands. If there is a place where community ought to have formed, it is here. And yet, given what hospitals have already become, and given the promise of new technologies we are even now embracing—remotely executed surgery, computer-generated diagnosis, ATM-dispensed medications—what are the prospects for medical communities of healing?

In sum: I would, as far as possible, take the Parenting group over the hospital, and that is one reason I am pessimistic about the high-tech future. The medical establishment has been precipitated from the numerous currents and countercurrents of a complex society, and tells us much more about the kind of meaning we assign to technology than any pioneering experiments on the WELL. We may hope the more successful of those experiments will begin to shape the future, in however small a way. But if we plunge into that future without being realistic about the social forces of the present—if we give free rein to whatever the engines of technology spew out—we can only provoke disaster.

Some of this is, I think, implicit in Rheingold's comment about sharing over the Net:

> Reciprocity is a key element of any market-based culture, but the arrangement I'm describing feels to me more like a kind of gift economy in which people do things for one another out of a spirit of building something between them, rather than a spreadsheet-calculated quid pro quo. When that spirit exists, everybody gets a little extra something, a little sparkle, from their more practical transactions; different kinds of things become possible when this mind-set pervades. Conversely, people who have valuable things to add to the mix tend to keep their heads down and their ideas to themselves when a mercenary or hostile zeitgeist dominates an online community (p. 59).

The only thing to add is that the technology of networking does nothing to implement a charitable spirit. In fact, it appears to add a new level of challenge, since it's easier to mask one's selfishness or disinterest in a world of electronic exchange than it is where sharing is supported and encouraged by a more tangible and present community. The Net demands a higher order of communal awareness from a society that has already failed badly at the "easier" levels. Our potential for a descent, under the Net's influence, from bad to worse is chilling—and all the more likely at a time when so many are hailing the Net as a nearly automatic cure.

The mechanisms of our future

If, as I noted at the outset, the computer has its origin in the computational bent of humans, we must look there for its future as well. Rheingold's caution notwithstanding, it seems to me that the most ominous symptom of what lies ahead is found in the ease with which so many Net enthusiasts argue directly from patterns of technology to emerging social realities. The resulting analogies are often strikingly naive. Does the Net give everyone a chance to type into a terminal? That spells democracy. Does the Net put people in touch with each other? That spells community. Does the Net make information databases available? That spells a more educated and cultured society. Such leaps from a purely mechanical or formal set of relationships to the specifically human are breathtaking.[6]

All of which brings me back to the Sixties flower children. At some deep level they knew their challenge to society was both radical and founded upon a yet-unrealized potential in the human being. Sticking flowers down the barrels of the pigs' guns truly was an earth-shaking gesture. Like the lone Chinese standing in front of a tank on Tienanmen Square, it symbolized the fact that something in the human being—some remaining spark of innocence and hope and bravery—held more promise for the future of society than all the mechanisms of raw, earthly power. This remains just as true when those mechanisms have become largely informational.

I am not sure whether the more sophisticated, electronic "counterculture" of our day has kept a grip on this truth. There are some encouraging recognitions in Rheingold's book, and yet one senses in the electronic culture as a whole that a critical balance has shifted, and that the main hope today is felt to lie in the technology itself. If this is true, then no doomsaying can adequately capture the horrors of the future.

Perhaps that is why I warmed so much to Rheingold's genial guidance. One naturally hopes to stand within a "magic circle," shielded by largeness of spirit from what is to come. And largeness of spirit *is* a shield—but it will no longer prevail if we as a society incarcerate it within the forms of our technology.

---

6. For an elaboration of these thoughts, see chapter 6, "Networks and Communities."

5

ON BEING RESPONSIBLE FOR EARTH

JERRY MANDER THINKS we should trash computers, along with much of the rest of modern technology. He is, I think, as close to being right as one can get while being crucially, tragically wrong.

Mander's *In The Absence Of The Sacred—The Failure of Technology and the Survival of the Indian Nations* is a profoundly important book, and I would give much to guarantee its broad dissemination throughout our society. One can scarcely participate responsibly in contemporary discussions of technology while willfully ignoring Mander's broad thesis.

We need to see ourselves

Technology, Mander tells us, is not neutral; it has a mind of its own. The same goes for businesses; the corporation, which Mander rightly likens to a machine, is driven by an unconsidered compulsion to grow, and is biased toward the profitable employment of new technology, regardless of the social consequences. Those consequences—whether we're talking about the telephone, the television, or genetic engineering—are rarely visible during the early stages of development. Nor is there any realistic public discussion about the effects and desirability of new technologies.

> By the time the body politic becomes aware of problems with technology, it is usually after they are well installed in the system and their effects are too late to reverse. Only now, four decades after the introduction of computers, are there any rumblings of discontent, any realizations of their full implications. By the time the alarm finally goes off, technologies have intertwined with one another to create yet another generation of machines, which makes unraveling them next to impossible, even if society had the will to do it.

> As the interlocking and interweaving and spawning of new technologies take place, the weave of technology becomes ever tighter and more difficult to separate . . . . Technological evolution leads inevitably to its own next stages, which can be altered only slightly. (pp. 188–89)

When a society is trapped in a pattern it does not even think to escape, the important thing is to offer viewpoints outside the pattern, enabling people to see themselves from new and unexpected angles. Mander does this in two ways. First, he shows us modern society in a historical context. Considering that much of his sketch spans only a few decades, it is surprisingly effective in giving us fresh eyes. He mentions, for example, how, during the Fifties, his neighborhood would gather around the only available television set at certain times during the week:

> Viewing was a group event, with socializing before and after. Soon, however, each family had its own set, or sets. Programming extended to all hours, day and night. A community event was transformed into an isolated experience: at first, families watched alone; then soon each individual was left alone in his or her own room, silently watching. (p. 16)

The entire neighborhood changed its character, yet no social assessment, no decision to embrace or modify such effects accompanied the change. It just happened—it was "the nature of things"—and so was accepted as part of life's inevitability.

Mander's second strategy for getting us to see ourselves is to confront us with wholly incompatible cultures—the various American Indian nations, as well as native peoples on other continents. Nothing could be more dramatic than the collision between our own cultural steamroller and those indigenous races that might have opted out of our mad technological rush, but whose options were taken away from them. At its worst, this collision leads to the almost overnight destruction of family, tribe, and spiritual conviction under an inexcusable and continuing policy of cultural extinction. It is worth the price of the book just to learn something about what happens when private land ownership and the ballot, for example, are forced upon a people whose connection to the land is much more profound than the laws of economic ownership can ever recognize, and whose tradition of consensus building, rooted in the unhurried contemplation of an enduring tribal wisdom, may have much to teach *us* about social governance.

Computerized technology is not a fixed quantity

Mander's critique seems to me unassailable in broad outline: technology now runs out of control, and prominent among the consequences of this fact is the unprecedented destruction of human cultures. However, a penchant for reckless commentary mars his exposition. A few examples:

- Mander repeats uncritically the wholly uncertain claim that we face crises of ozone depletion and global warming. It would have been better merely to point out that we are playing Russian roulette with our environment.

- He asserts—probably wrongly—that computers give large companies competitive advantages over smaller ones.

- He swallows the absurd, if oft-repeated, opinion that the Judeo-Christian religion desanctifies the world and places mankind in oppressive domination over it. To fail to distinguish between the sources of Judeo-Christian belief and their perversion within certain strands of Western culture is like seeing a propensity toward alcoholism in the religion of American Indians.

• In his ill-advised singling out of Ronald Reagan ("the television president"), Mander notes various "Orwellian" pronouncements of the former chief executive, such as when he "unabashedly claimed that massive rearming was the way to disarm." But to leave it at that is to push the ejection button, fleeing the dilemmas and necessities of the human condition. There is, after all, a case to be made that Reagan was right, and that he succeeded. There has long been too much silliness and conformity in the political orthodoxies of the various cultural reform movements; one hates to see so effective a contrarian thinker as Mander following along blindly.

These peccadillos do not vitiate the main argument. But Mander does neglect one critical fact: what we have embodied in technology are our own habits of thought. Yes, our artifacts gain a life of their own, but it is, in a very real sense, *our* life. We too easily ignore the ways in which we infuse these artifacts with the finespun web of our own, largely subconscious habits of thought. The need is to raise these habits to full consciousness, and then take responsibility for them.

This is most clearly true for the computer. Everything we might complain about in the computer—its insistence upon dealing with abstractions, its reduction of the qualitative to a set of quantities, its insertion of a nonspatial but effective distance between users, its preference for unambiguous and efficiently manipulative relationships in all undertakings—these computational traits have long been tendencies of our own thinking and behavior, especially as influenced by science. Trashing the current technology therefore gains us nothing if we ourselves do not change—we will, out of habit, simply invent a new prison for ourselves using whatever materials are at hand. But if we *can* change our habits of mind, then Mander's argument that many technological products have a fixed, irremediable bias and should therefore be shunned loses its validity.

To destroy or to create

In his crusade against technology and its enabling mindset, Mander dismisses all human exploration as a quest for "economic gain, military advantage, the satisfaction of the ego, and satisfaction of technological society's intrinsic drive to expand" (p. 139). Similarly, he can see in the human hope to fulfill "nature's evolutionary design" only a covert extension of the doctrine of Manifest Destiny (pp. 140–41). He is right this far: there is no denying our wholesale abuse of our trust as stewards of earth. But we have already been given, by Mander's own testimony, the godlike authority to destroy the earth. To refuse to accept the equally godlike task of redirecting that authority toward healing and the fulfillment of earth's potentials is to guarantee ultimate ruin.

It may be nearly unthinkable that, in our present state of sleepwalking subservience to technology, we could begin to tame the monster, to make it the obedient servant of truly human ends. But (as Mander acknowledges) it is equally unthinkable that we should simply turn our back upon technology in the manner he advises. The one course does not seem to me more difficult or less likely than the other.

What is tragic about Mander's admirable book is that, by flatly rejecting the computer and other forms of technology, it invites us away from exactly that sense of deep, positive *responsibility* for technology without which we can have little hope for the future. There is no true responsibility that is not a *creative* responsibility, requiring human art and artifice.

To put it differently: another word for responsibility is "dominion" —not the dominion of raw power, but of effective wisdom. The human task, however much we have botched it to date, will remain decisive for our planet. The earth is in our hands.

Much in the Western tradition—in which Mander seems to find few redeeming qualities—is requisite to our inescapable responsibilities. This includes all that is best in the uniquely Western development of scientific discipline: the habit of rigorous, detached observation, the finely tuned mental machinery of analysis, the requirement that theories *work*. But Mander is right when he claims that, in the name of this discipline, we

61

have lost our bearings and spawned technologies that now run amok through the countryside. The glimmers of hope here and there—increasing acceptance of biological pest management and other techniques of the organic farmer; sensitive ecological studies of the environment; the nascent effort to understand the principles by which indigenous peoples have cared for the earth; the slowly growing awareness that technology threatens to make us as much as we make it—none of these can come to fruition within a science still stubbornly determined to exclude the human spirit.

We are indeed caretakers of our planet. But even the most reverent gardener must invent, contrive, fashion clever devices, and discover how to foster rebirth amid the most extensive decay and failure. This exercise of a devout, wise, spirit-connected authority over the earth is surely what the earth craves—today more than at any other time in our history.

True, current technologies express our disastrous abdication of this authority. Our machines begin to run by themselves, and to serve their own ends, and we ourselves are carried along. Mander is right in this. But that is exactly why human responsibility must be taken seriously—even to the point of "redeeming" technology. For I think it is fair to say that we can no longer stop or even redirect the engine of technological change by brute, external force. Such force is the principle of the engine itself, and only strengthens it. We must tame technology by rising above it and reclaiming what is not mechanical in ourselves. And if we can manage somehow to do that—I do not say that we *will* do it—who knows what the technology of the future may become?

6

NETWORKS AND COMMUNITIES

IT IS NOT SURPRISING that in a culture widely cited for its loss of community, the word "community" itself should come in for heavy use. The more we lack something, the more we may be fascinated by fragmentary glimpses of it. A starving man will discover food where the well fed see only garbage.

One doesn't, however, expect the starving man to pretend his meal is a catered banquet. And yet, the magical delivery of precisely such transformed goods seems to be what many expect of the electronic network. For example, the publisher of *The Internet Business Journal*, Michael Strangelove—articulating the faith of a thundering host—is sure that "the Internet represents a return to the fundamental dynamics of human existence: communication and community."[1]

I need not remind you of the special affinity wanderers on the Net seem to have for this word "community." We hear about online

---

1. Net announcement posted by Strangelove Press (mstrange@fonorola.net) on November 18, 1993.

communities, the Internet community, global electronic communities, virtual communities, and so on. There are senses in which this usage is perfectly reasonable: human community in *some* form or another will naturally take hold of whatever mechanisms we create for expression and communication—whether car and road, telephone, computer network, or even the television talk show.

In most cases, the physical media are not likely to become identified in our minds with the very substance of community itself. But have you noticed how easily "network" now seems almost to imply "community"—as if a set of electronic connections automatically *consti-tuted* community? The phrase "net communities" captures this well, for its meaning slides effortlessly between "a matrix of communication chan-nels" and "communal human exchange."

There is no doubt that physical networks will dramatically affect the forms of our communities. But if we fail to distinguish radically between such networks and the personal *sources* of community, then the only sure thing is that we will continue to degrade what community remains.[2]

Technology is not community

What is true of community holds for democracy as well, for democracy is a set of human institutions (and, for that matter, styles of community) rather than a group of technical tools. And yet, even as sensible an observer as Howard Rheingold was tempted into remarking that "if a BBS (computer Bulletin Board System) isn't a democratizing technology, there is no such thing."[3]

The assumption that networks constitute some sort of positive realiza-tion of, or at least predisposition to, community and democracy is extraordinarily widespread. One repeatedly encounters the thought that (in the words of one Internet contributor) "the Net is fundamentally

---

2. For purposes of discussion, I will take "community" in the broadest possible sense as "the meaning we find through our life together."

3. Rheingold, 1993: 131.

democratizing and leveling."[4] Apparently, the fact that a Net connection may reach into each home substitutes in this thinking for any consideration of how people will actually *relate* to each other over their connections. The relation is somehow thought to be given by the connecting technology itself.

Another Net voice agrees:

> While I'm not forecasting Utopia, I think networks of the future will be the most incredibly egalitarian technology ever invented. It will transform our entire societies. Imagine that homeless people or single parent children can "interconnect" with anybody who is willing to talk to them in the *world*. The possibilities are rather dazzling. Sure, there might be even cyberspatial outcasts, but the point is that we will be doing *at least* as well as we are now, which is not something to "write home" about.[5]

What seems so obvious to this speaker as to require no defense is that giving Net connections to the socially isolated will at least *tend* to lead them out of their isolation in happy ways. It's a stunning leap of faith. Who constitutes the society that isolated them in the first place—persons different from those who will make the Net whatever it becomes? Did the telephone—bringing with it the ability to call anyone in a city of five million people—move the city toward more intimate community, or has it merely enabled us to hunker down within our separate castles, talking, perhaps, to more and more people while cut off from community more than ever before?

I take all this to be part of the general tendency to substitute thoughts about technology for thoughts about the actual terms of human exchange. Given this substitution, a community is no longer, in the first instance, a group of people bound together by certain mutual concerns, interests, activities, and institutions (which find expression through whatever technical and nontechnical means are at hand). Rather, a community becomes

---

4. From a contribution to the "irvc-l" list (irvc-l@byrd.mu.wvnet.edu), 19 October 1993.

5. From a contribution to the "irvc-l" list (irvc-l@byrd.mu.wvnet.edu), 9 October 1993.

the mere "instantiation" of a network diagram that shows the available technical means for interaction.

It's rather as if you traced on a map a set of automobile routes, and then focused upon this "community" of roads. You certainly could learn something about the people who use these roads by analyzing traffic patterns; and all roads provide, to one degree or another, a *site* for expressions of community. But you are hardly likely to conclude that the asphalt network itself is decisive for *constituting* community.

Now, it's true that many so-called Net communities do find almost their sole expression across certain electronic links. Describe the online traffic, and you've quite neatly characterized almost everything that distinctively binds these people together. This neat characterization, however, results precisely from the extraordinarily restricted nature of the community, by any traditional standards.

Gilded vision

The commentator who seems most determined to read one-sided social implications into networking technologies is George Gilder. He comes very close, as we will see, to reconceiving a network's distributed intelligence as the very substance of an ennobled society.

Gilder's head is abuzz with facts and figures about the technologies that will "come blindingly to the fore" during the next few years. His central conviction is that peer-to-peer communication will replace broadcast (radio/TV) and centrally switched (telephone) communication. "Whether offering 500 channels or thousands, television will be irrelevant in a world without channels, where you can always order exactly what you want when you want it, and where every terminal commands the communications power of a broadcast station today."[6]

The reason for this is that "fiber optics is going to render bandwidth and hertz virtually free." We will no longer have to choose from among communication channels dictated by others. Rather, we will simply sit at

---

6. Quotations in this section are from Gilder, 1993a, and Gilder, 1993b.

our terminals and tune in to whatever we wish, anywhere in what Gilder calls "fiberspace." One thread of glass the width of a human hair, he tells us, can carry one thousand times the content of today's entire radio spectrum. So we will all have access to everything, and can speak to everywhere.

From couch potato to mogul. Gilder's technical vision may, for all I know, be accurate, but his prediction of the social consequences is startlingly naive. Noting the "100,000 acts of television violence" watched by the average thirteen-year-old child, and citing the "obtuse denial that such a diet could affect behavior," he goes on to indict the television industry, which

> ignores the fact that people are not inherently couch potatoes; given a chance, they talk back and interact. People have little in common with one another except their prurient interests and morbid fears and anxieties. Aiming its fare at this lowest-common denominator target, television gets worse year after year.

And what does Gilder believe will save us from television? The fact that, instead of five hundred channels to choose from, we can choose *anything*—and can talk back if we want. When intelligence and control are embedded in the devices at our fingertips, it means that "technologies are much more servants than rulers of [our] life."

Moreover, we can be assured that "confidence in the new paradigm . . . does not spring only from the desire for a better culture, and it cannot be stemmed by some new global plague of passivity and tube addiction." Why? Because "propelling the new order is the most powerful juggernaut in the history of technology: an impending millionfold rise in the cost-effectiveness of computers and their networks." Somehow this apparently means that the new, whizzy devices will also have a power of psychological and social healing.

Gilder was asked about the "utopian" ring of his hope, since "anything complex self-organizes into nested hierarchies, just in order to manage itself"—a patently false assumption by the interviewer, incidentally, since it doesn't apply to living organisms. But Gilder's response couldn't be more telling:

> You need nested hierarchies, but the real miracle of microelectronics is that these extraordinarily complex hierarchies can be incorporated into individual silicon chips, with virtual supercomputer capabilities . . . . So hierarchies do indeed exist, but they are ubiquitously distributed, *which renders them an egalitarian force.* When everybody commands a supercomputer, you give the average owner of a work station the power that an industrial tycoon commanded in the industrial era, or that a TV station owner commands in the age of broadcasting. *In other words, the hierarchy is in the silicon rather than in the human organization.* So you have this incredible distribution of power. [Emphasis added.]

So where the industrial tycoons and TV station owners blew it, unaccountably tempted by crass gain, the rest of us—once we can grab power for ourselves—will save the day. If we have intelligent and discriminating devices at our fingertips, we will use them intelligently and discriminatingly. If we can address anything we wish to anyone we wish, we will speak with a previously unwonted maturity. We're no longer going to let those TV moguls keep us down and reveling in smut.

Gilder cites the Internet, with its distributed intelligence, as "an exciting kind of metaphor for spontaneous order." Dumb the Net down by eliminating the central, controlling intelligence, distribute that intelligence to the periphery where it is under control of a hundred million users, and wondrous patterns of human beauty will take shape within the flexible, receptive, glass palace of fiberspace.

Yes, order arises from complexity, but it arises through complex laws, not magic. And in all social affairs the *nature* of the order depends upon the nature of the human being. We have discovered that we could not create a healthy order in televisionland when the task was as simple as clicking a button to register our preference for decent programming. Will we now find it easier to impose healthy order upon the Internet by redirecting our proclivities toward a vastly more diffuse and challenging task?

We already have in the corporation (including the entertainment corporations Gilder chastises) an example of emergent, humanlike behavior arising from myriad, complex, unanalyzable interactions. Is that behavior somehow more automatically responsible than the individual entrepreneur's? Will it become so as soon as every employee has an intelligent terminal?[7] Did the old-fashioned neighborhood gossip network, with its extensive, peer-to-peer connectivity, automatically generate reliable news?

Wake up and smell the waste products. It is precisely *because* a complex order of one sort or another will emerge from the new technologies that we must be cautious. The order is not given in advance, and is not inherent in the technology itself, which only defines a range of possibilities. The form we give to those possibilities will reflect ourselves. At the same time, we have to acknowledge that the order *is* substantially biased in advance, because the forms of the basic technology *already* reflect what we have become—and it happens that what we have become can be read in our existing, television-centered culture.

Any thinking person has to ask: If the computer is about to merge with the television screen, is it because our society feels compelled to redeem television, or is it rather because the cultural forces behind television—the most irresistible communication medium in history—are extending their reach in dramatic, new ways.

Fiberspace is a glass mirror. The only question is whether we will struggle through to what is highest in us, or instead give way to those same, subterranean, overmastering currents that seemed always to have the last say when we clicked the remote control. The latter path is as easy as remaining passive—as easy, that is, as believing the Net is only a force for good and will therefore "take care of itself."

It is not a matter of bewailing everyone's bad taste and trying to protect people from themselves. It's a matter of realism about the challenges ahead of us. Gilder—mesmerized, I suspect, by glamorous formulations

---

7. For discussion of this issue, see chapter 8, "Things That Run by Themselves."

of chaos and complexity theory; by the naive promises of artificial intelligence; by dreams of a new, bioengineered Genesis; and by the undeniable
appeal of other enticing motifs in a grand myth of automatic, evolution-
driven (and now also technology-driven) Progress—fails to reckon with
this truth: the more complex and indirect the mechanisms through which
human actions come to expression, *the more you and I must be masters of
ourselves*. Putting it the other way around: the more degrees of freedom
we have in expressing ourselves—in projecting ourselves every which way
into our environment—the easier it is for the emergent social pattern to
be taken over by unruly collective, or subconscious, powers—easier, that
is, unless each of us manages to be uncommonly *awake*.

Far from being able to relax about what emerges from complexity, we
are being asked today to take conscious responsibility in one domain after
another that our ancestors could not even have named, let alone have
thought about. From the environment to the rule of law among nations,
from genetic engineering to virtual realities, from failing social structures
to failing value systems, the message is unambiguous: "You can no longer
remain unconscious where you slept before; one way or the other, you are
creating your future. Wake up before you find that the devils within you
have done the creating."

Characteristically, Gilder dismisses some of these latter-day concerns
with remarkable optimism: "It's utter garbage to say that our grandchil-
dren won't live as well as we do. People who say this just don't see the
technology. They live in this bizarre world of thermodynamics, where
entropy rules, and we're dominated by our waste products. It is very
short-sighted."

Gilder is right, to the extent that our waste products are not the *first*
concern. The first concern is the state of mind that allowed us to treat
Nature as a toxic waste disposal site, and then to view ourselves as having
exhibited nothing more than a technical defect. That the polluting stance
itself may entail great suffering for both mankind and the earth; that the
inner ugliness and loss of meaning from which this stance arises may lead

to crises quite apart from the externally poisonous ones—such possibilities apparently do not occur to Gilder.

Making contact

It is a useful exercise to look at how intelligence has been impressed upon the machinery of communication, and then to ask yourself what social functions this automated intelligence is filling in for. There is, for example, the extremely subtle intelligence of the many layers of digital switching hardware and software upon which the Net is built. One consequence of this is captured in a well-known observation: "The Net treats censorship like a malfunction, and routes around it." That is, issues of propriety, formerly decided by competing values and opinions within a community, are now turned over to an automatic mechanism.

Looking more directly at the switching machinery itself, we can say that it enables each of us, in the most remarkably efficient manner, to make contact with individuals and groups around the world. But what does *making contact* really mean?

It all depends. As an intermediate case, the telephone can help us see the range of possibilities. Telephones, too, are based on impressive switching technology, and they allow me to call almost anyone I wish. But telephoning retains at least some of the human significance of *making contact*—as expressed, for example, in that "loaded" initial moment when I must declare myself to someone I have called out of the blue. Such a moment tends to mobilize the character—the *presence*—of the two personalities involved, whether they happen to be rude or considerate, shy or daring, clever or dull. Even so, the telephone conversants will likely remain far less fully engaged than they would in a face-to-face meeting.

With the Net's intelligence, however, I can direct my message to a single stranger, or to a thousand at once, with scarcely so much as an interruption of my reveries. It is not that the Net forces such detachment; it doesn't. But the Net is more than willing to assume the whole burden of *making contact*, if I am willing to leave it at that. I am free to skip the loaded moment altogether. One mailbox gets in touch with another. To

71

make anything more of the movement toward contact—to bring more of myself to it—I must consciously exert myself where, in face-to-face encounter, the effort occurred more naturally and could be more fully expressed.

Nothing requires this effort of me. In fact, I can't help feeling a bit uneasy in talking about the sort of *inner work* one might do when preparing to fire off an email message to someone else. It seems slightly affected.[8] What, after all, *is* such work? But if the answer has become hazy for me, it is because the immediate realities of personal exchange have become hazy. I have been losing sight of the various aspects of myself called up by the human being before me—the insecurity and invitation to rashness when I must think and respond "on my feet" (very different in quality from the rashness of Net flaming); the need to be receptive to every unexpected signal from the other, and to recognize something of myself reflected in it; my immediate like or dislike of traits extraneous or relevant; the obscure promptings of will from hidden places within me, perhaps too sudden to disguise; the various defenses of an ego that must present itself on all fronts rather than through words that have wholly detached themselves from me; and, above all, the underlying moral and esthetic coloring of each moment, the respect or disregard for the delicate conditions in which words of wisdom may thrive, the extraordinary challenge in honoring the other person's autonomy and potential.

The list could go on. But it all *does* seem a little pretentious as I type the words here onto my screen, and that is what worries me. When someone stands in front of me, the issues are much more immediate—I do not need to "recall" them from quite the same distance, or with quite the same affectation.

Shielding ourselves from intrusion. The alternative, of course, is simply to put such issues out of mind. To all appearances, Gilder does this when he attempts to soothe the prevailing fears about invasion of privacy. He

---

8. I discuss some related issues in PART THREE. See, in particular, chapter 18, "And the Word Became Mechanical."

tells us that "what is really an invasion of privacy is a telemarketer who gets you out of bed or the shower. They don't have any idea who you are, no notion of what you want." Those who possess a thorough database of information about you, on the other hand, can "call you and try to solve your problem. That is much less of an invasion than [is] an intrusion by a company that doesn't know anything about you."

The idea is that we should be glad when companies have more complete information about us, because then they can serve our needs better. Gilder will doubtless have a harder time selling this view than he will some of his others. More important, however, than his conclusion are the premises underlying it:

> So a lot of the so-called invasion of privacy will be a positive experience for most people. Computer communications can be sorted through, and you can keep what you want and kill what you don't. Increasingly, as your communication is channeled through computers, you will increase your control over it. It's the dumb terminal, the phone, which is the model of the violation. It violates your time and attention because it's dumb. If you have a really smart terminal that can sort through the communications and identify them, you can reject anything you don't want.[9]

The truth in this, setting aside the larger contention about privacy, is in the difference between the phone and the Net's intelligent terminals. If the Net saves us from unwanted intrusions, it is because it easily saves us from the other person altogether. *Making contact* becomes a matter of software "that can sort through the communications." What Gilder calls our "control" over these communications is—as in all efforts to control others—a matter of shielding ourselves from people.

On the Net, the kind of control Gilder welcomes is unavoidable, lest we be drowned. We have no choice. I said above that the Net doesn't actually *force* our detachment. That wasn't quite true, for in a way it does. The more we form society around the Net, the greater the percentage of

---

9. Gilder, 1994: 47.

our daily business we cannot help transacting without making personal contact. How much of the personal is there in a credit-card transaction? We don't really *have to do with* the people we have to do with. They are largely extraneous to the main transaction, and carry out a mechanical function. Or, rather, the main transaction has itself become a mechanical function.

This, then, is what I am saying must be countered by a new, conscious, and *inner* striving. For my part, I hardly know how to begin. And yet, the movement to dissolve society and reconstitute it on the Net moves forward at a ferocious pace. My pessimism becomes most acute when, as in Gilder's case, the problem—let alone its extremity—is not even acknowledged.

A fragmentation of community? There seems to be a great difficulty in holding onto the truth—as obvious as it is—that ease and flexibility of switching do not constitute ease and depth in making human contact. Certainly the connectivity makes communication "easier," but it achieves this precisely by rendering *contact* more incidental, more shallow.

I suspect that every major technical advance in communication since the invention of writing has marked the path away from community rather than toward it.[10] Community is, in the first instance, something to be salvaged from information technology, not furthered by it. There is surely a case to be made (and many have made it) that the telephone, automobile, radio, and television have all contributed to social fragmentation, personal isolation, and alienation from both self and other.

In any event, one of the Net's attractions is avowedly its natural susceptibility to being shivered into innumerable, separate, relatively homogenous groups. The fact that you can find a forum for virtually any topic you might be interested in, however obscure, implies fragmentation

---

10. This has to do with the relation between accuracy of communication and fullness of meaning, discussed in chapter 23, "Can We Transcend Computation?" Technical improvements, almost by definition, facilitate accuracy rather than the expression of meaning.

as its reverse side. There may be advantages to this "principle of infinite cleaving," but the cultivation of community is not one of them.

To establish community in any deep sense is much more a matter of coming to terms with differences than merely matching up similarities. But it is not clear that the Net encourages our *coming to terms with* each other in this sense at all. If that were the real possibility opened up by the Net, we would hardly be excited about it, since most of us already have vastly more opportunities to interact with the people on our block, in the office, at church, and in our volunteer associations than we could take advantage of in a hundred years. Exactly what is the *new* thing we're celebrating?

Powers of heart and soul

Historically there have been any number of village societies in which the physical means of communication were evenly distributed in the form of a common airspace. Each person was physically enabled to communicate with all the others. I am aware of no evidence that this equality of access predisposed such villages any more to democratic forms of community than to other forms.

The fact is that the qualities of community—whatever its form—are, in essence, *soul qualities*. They can only be expressions of our own inner life. The view that a technology can be "democratizing and leveling" testifies to a radical alienation from everything that constitutes both the inner life and culture.

It is highly disturbing to hear technology debated as if the forms we need for building community were somehow inherent in the technology itself. When we take such a stance, we confirm that we have lost sight of our own creative responsibility for the substance of community. In that case, the technology truly *will* become the remaining substance of community—for we will have given up everything in the human being that cannot be embedded within the machine.

All this, I hope, will make clear why I find the following statement so unsettling. It is a clause taken from the opening line of a proposed

75

"Charter of Communication Interdependence of the global nongovernmental movements for peace, human rights, and environmental preservation," and it refers to the creation of various electronic networks, such as the PeaceNet.

> WHEN IN THE COURSE OF HUMAN EVENTS it becomes possible to dissolve the communication frontiers that have divided peoples one from another . . . . [11]

What hope is there for peace and human rights when I conceive the barriers separating me from my fellows to be mere obstructions on a network technology diagram rather than the powers of darkness shadowing my own heart?

---

11. Frederick, 1992.

7

AT THE FRINGE OF FREEDOM

IT IS STRANGE that in a society founded so centrally on the creative initiative and freedom of the individual, we should today find this same individual so utterly helpless before the most urgent social problems.

Or so it seems. If you are troubled, for example, by the drug problem in our cities, what can you actually *do* about it? The educational system, family structure, mass media, organized crime, international commerce, welfare system—all affect, and in turn are affected by, the culture of drugs and violence. It is not easy to see where you and I might step into the picture and make a discernible difference. It is all too easy to see how we might throw our lives away.

Similar perplexities arise if you think about the famines regularly scything millions of people, or the massive human assaults upon mother earth, or the stranglehold with which the indifferent imperatives of technological development now direct the evolution of social forms. The problems have gone so systemic, the causes become so tortured and inaccessible, the interrelationships grown so intricate, that we cannot imagine how to fix one thing without fixing everything. That, of course, seems impossible, so paralysis sets in.[1]

"What can I do to change things?" has become as much a prelude to resignation as a declaration of hopeful intent. Which is to say that the forces at work seem ever more impersonal, more disconnected from individual human activity, more autonomous. Perhaps (although I do not believe it) this is the inevitable result of increasing social complexity. In any case, you and I will most likely continue to take our places within a scheme of things whose larger outlines are already given, and amidst processes of change that seem elemental, inescapable, overwhelming. When a "new world order" is proclaimed, the new realities are not what we saw and planned for—not what we carefully ushered into place—but more like something that happened to us. We can only react, and wait for the next set of realities. Oddly—or perhaps not so oddly—our sense of personal helplessness coincides with historically unsurpassed technical powers.

Our apparent inability to mend things has a perverse flip side: the things we *can't help doing* seem unavoidably to worsen matters. Every action sets in motion endless, outward-flowing ripples, some of which are

---

1. To say all this is not merely to say that social problems have become almost intractable. Presumably, ancient Rome and many other societies have faced intractable social problems. The point I am making lies in the *relation* between evolving human responsibilities and evolving social problems. One sees in this relation two things: (1) We unavoidably feel a growing sense of *individual* moral responsibility in social domains previously (but no longer) ordered by instinct and by a kind of subconscious, collective, social wisdom. For example, the various contemporary questions of sexual morality, the global challenge of representational government, and our problematic dealings with the environment all have become matters of conscious moral awareness where once they were wholly unconsidered (in any explicit sense). (2) Certain personal moral obligations, at one time clearly in view, have "disappeared" into the impersonal texture and structure of society. (See, for example, the mention of insurance below.) And yet, we still know ourselves to carry these responsibilities, even if the means for dealing with them appear lost to us. This is the main issue for the current chapter. (2), incidentally, does not contradict (1). To say that certain personal moral obligations have "disappeared" into impersonal social structures despite our still "owning" those obligations is to say that these social structures—previously unconsidered and governed by a social wisdom transcending individual consciousness—are now susceptible in a new way to our conscious and unconscious choices, and therefore confront the individual as moral challenges.

undeniably destructive. The smallest and most essential purchase, for example, may well entail unhealthy consequences for the environment. If I have the means to live in a community where my children will receive a first-class public education, I must ask what effect this choice has upon other children in other districts. The politically naive hand that offers food to a starving Somali child may call down death and destruction on an entire village. Even in paying taxes or contributing to a charitable organization, I take on my own share of responsibility for certain things I find inexcusable. The moral conflicts so fiendishly calculated in the modern dictatorial state—involving thousands of small complicities on the one hand, and, on the other, unbearable threats to self and loved ones (what would become of us if we strictly followed our consciences?) —remain a constant, if more muted, feature even of democratic societies.

"The System"—a negatively tinged and historically recent phrase —captures something of the impersonality and moral ambiguity I'm talking about. The System is something we try to beat, and fear becoming trapped in. Vaguely allied with the devil, it is a power we nevertheless must employ—or at least outwit—if we are to succeed in doing good.

There's no avoiding the System. Not even Henry David Thoreau at Walden Pond could pretend to an immaculate escape from participation in, and responsibility for, the larger society. As a result of our "complicity," either of two pathologies may be reinforced: neurotic self-condemnation, or a dulled conscience. Both are fully enough in evidence. But perhaps most pervasively, we find a vague, persistent sense of collective guilt, without which the more absurd, guilt-driven expressions of political correctness could never have surfaced.

Institutions take form within the human being

Some fifteen years ago Alexander Bos wrote a remarkable little booklet commenting on some of these matters. It's called *Nothing To Do With Me?* He describes, for example, the history of insurance in Europe. "Before 1600 it had almost exclusively the character of mutual help. In small communities there was an unwritten right to receive help. If someone had had a fire, for example, he could go round with an urgent letter, collecting money to restore his burned house. Of course people gave generously, knowing that in their own time of need they could count on the other for a contribution" (pp. 22–23).

Over time, however, the desire for individual freedom militated against this sort of mutual dependence, leading to the payment of premium and interest. "B, having obtained credit from A, pays interest, to buy off any obligation to help A when he needs it." Banks and insurance companies eventually came to insulate the one who needs from the one who helps, so that the entire system was depersonalized. One *bought* security. Or tried to—for Bos points out that the resulting independence was illusory. How many of us feel any profound security before the faceless bureaucracies that hold our welfare in their hands? Quite apart from the threat of inflation and the unforeseen revelations in the small print at the back of the insurance contract, I am still helpless "if, by the time I am pensioned off, there isn't anybody who is willing to do anything for me" (pp. 23–24). In the humblest terms: who will open the jar of food that an arthritic hand cannot manage? And the nursing home, with all its terrors for the elderly, stands as an apt image for the final stages of an institutionally nurtured helplessness.

This is not to say that the old system always worked, or that the new does not offer dramatic changes we have come to identify with progress. Bos is merely trying to make clear that there is a *connection* between what human beings choose to become in their own hearts, and the social structures that grow up around them. In this particular case, the issue is whether our historical abandonment of institutions based on personal trust has led to independence, or instead to a more thoroughgoing—if also a more diffuse and unaccountable—dependence upon a system over which one has almost no control at all.

Hungry dragons. The subtle threads linking the interior of the individual to prevailing social forms extend beyond economic matters. Bos mentions, for example, our obsessed fascination with sensational news—sex

80

scandals, grisly murders, embezzlements, the spectacular downfall of public figures. Here, too, he searches within the individual for the essential, enabling gestures leading to social problems:

> Such news is food for a particular kind of feeling and emotion. By the time this morning's paper comes out, yesterday's food has long been used up. There is an emptiness left behind, and the soul is hungry for a new injection. It is like the dragon in the fairy tale, that must have a young maiden every year, otherwise it will break out and destroy the whole neighborhood.... Is it only actions that are real; and do feelings and thoughts actually have no effect? If millions of hungry little dragons are all clamoring for a young maiden, isn't there one who is really bound to be eaten up? When so many people are anxiously on the look-out for the next murder—with "sincere" moral indignation—does the desire not create a potentially magnetic field to attract just such a deed? Most of us will think we could resist an impulse of that sort, but the chain of humanity has weak links in it. There will be people who from whatever cause ... are predisposed to such action.... There has to be copy for tomorrow's edition. (pp. 13–14)

We know too much about mass hysteria and other aberrations of the collective psyche to dismiss these remarks out of hand. Only recall the Los Angeles freeway shootings, which came in a bizarre, well-publicized wave. Having witnessed such a pronounced form of the dragons' hunger, we cannot reasonably ignore the likelihood of more subtle and pervasive predations.

• • •

All these inner choices have their social costs, incalculable though they be: in the legal and penal systems we have erected to protect our contractual relations with each other, in the medical and psychiatric consequences of mutual alienation, in the dissipation of human resources by the industries of mindless and sensational entertainment.

Technology can distract us from ourselves

There may be, then, discernible connections between my individual behavior and the particular social forms and institutions that grow up around me. This is true even in the case of those strange outbreaks that seem, at first, wholly foreign to my own life. To recognize the uniting threads, however, requires me to look beyond the external and mechanical relationships; it requires me to look within myself, and to learn a most delicate skill: how to identify my own reflection in society and society's reflection within me. Upon such a basis I can perhaps *begin* approaching social problems as meaningful issues to work upon.

Not that it will ever be easy. There is no denying the almost personal "wish" of society to wrench itself free from the human individual, and to tear along as a self-driven mechanism determining its own future. We see this in the corporation, we see it in all those academic disciplines framing a purely mechanistic view of the world, and we see it above all else in the largely self-determined and insanely accelerating evolution of technology. Crowning it all is the computer. With computers we construct our models of society. All good models "run by themselves." But if society runs by itself, I do not need to worry about *my* contribution.

It now almost seems to us as if all social forms are merely side effects of technical developments. When a problem arises, our first thought is, how can we bring technology to bear upon it? The furthest thing from our minds may well be: what does this problem tell us about ourselves and about how we should change?

Nor is this surprising. For in a society built to "run by itself"—a society in which the idea of individual choice brings to mind, first of all, the "mechanisms of the market"—technology truly does offer the only immediate, apparent change. And so we draw its weave ever tighter. Once the terms of human exchange have been reduced to the "transactions" of a *transaction processing system* (as a common type of software is called) will we know how to work on society other than by tinkering with the computational processes? And what, then, becomes of the human potential for *inner* development?

Ask yourself: in all the public discussion about the Net—in all the debates about carriers and content; telephone, cable, and broadcast companies; technical standards and configurations; universal access and privilege; privacy; productivity and unemployment; telecommuting and corporate redesign—how many people have discussed what you and I need to learn about dealing with the burden of technology that we carry inside us and project into our society? (For surely every newly invented machine and technical process is first imaged within its creators.) There is not much evidence that we are paying heed to the peculiar dragons of technology.[2]

Between helplessness and freedom

For reasons that should appear at the end, I have intended for this chapter to be frustrating—although I hope *constructively* frustrating. You may in any case be asking, "Are we free to change things or not? And if the individual does still make a difference, by what means?"

I would answer yes to the first question, even if it's a rather complicated yes:

- Our society more and more runs along by itself like a machine.

- This, however, does not mean we should abdicate our freedom, although nearly irresistible forces in society are asking that of us. Rather, it summons us to discover and exercise our freedom. The need is to recognize ourselves in our machines, and our machines in ourselves, and begin to raise ourselves above our machines. A society running on by itself, out of control, points to processes in ourselves running on without conscious control.

I began by citing the paradox of individual freedom in an era of individual helplessness. It is indeed a paradox, but not an insurmountable one.

---

2. Which is not to say there aren't plenty of things to worry about in purely external terms. For a sourcebook on substantiated dangers posed by computers—ranging from physical injury due to robots running amok, to the abuse of information stored in databases, see Neumann, 1995.

We could not seek freedom if we did not experience constraints. To recognize constraint is to assert a free capacity; a wholly unfree creature would know nothing of constraint, which can only be felt as a hindrance to some existing potential. Neither the wholly unfree nor the wholly free could experience what freedom *means*.[3] Freedom, you might say, is not a state, but a tension, a name for the process of becoming free.

So the paradox of apparent individual helplessness in an era of unprecedented social challenge is exactly the sign we would expect if the promise of freedom now stands brightly before us. Our dilemma is not really a paradox so much as it is an invitation. Our freedom remains nascent, sometimes perverted, often trivialized. But the prevailing spirit of helplessness is both a challenge to what freedom we have and the proffered means for its further development. Precisely there, where our experience of unfreedom is most painfully acute, we are being prodded, invited, to enter into freedoms not yet discovered.

This brings me to the crux of the chapter. Don't ask me for a program, an action plan, a list of things you should do. That is exactly what almost everyone else is trying to tell you, and what I cannot. To ask for a program is already perilously close to asking for a "machine" that will take care of the problem. It is already to be looking for a technical solution. If what I would *do* must be set out in a list—an algorithm—then I have yet to take hold of my freedom. And I will finally and fully have declined the invitation to freedom if the day comes when I can no longer even conceive my responsibility for society except in technical terms.

So the first thing is more a knowing and a being than a doing. If the thin threads connecting my freedom to social problems are becoming ever more tortuous and obscure, the first connection I must look for is precisely the one between myself and the increasingly detached, self-willed character of society.

But I do not wish to avoid the question. There *is* something you and I can do. It is to recognize that the logic of the problem "out there" is also

---

3. Kühlewind, 1984: 76.

a logic "in here." The failure to see in this recognition a real doing—a necessary lifetime of doing—is itself the problem. *The doing required of us is a refusal to continue seeing all problems as the result of a doing rather than a being, as technical rather than spiritual.* Blindness at this point is exactly what allows the the problems to detach themselves from us and run on according to their own logic. They run on because we do not confront them within ourselves. Where, on the other hand, we recognize ourselves in the world and then take responsibility for ourselves—well, I cannot say what additional doing will result (for the doing will be in freedom), but it will be a real doing, issuing from deep within, and therefore the only doing that counts.

*

8

THINGS THAT RUN BY THEMSELVES

THE PEER-TO-PEER CONNECTIVITY we celebrate on the Net is not a recent invention. Within groups of restricted size—small companies, intentional communities, old-fashioned neighborhoods—it is common to find individual communicating freely with individual across the entire group.

As communities grow larger, however, the significance of peer-to-peer connectivity becomes uncertain. We cannot simply extrapolate from the small group. After all, the telephone gives us near-perfect connectivity across the entire country. But if we were all to begin calling each other, chaos would ensue. That is why structure is inevitably imposed: conventions and etiquette, social boundaries, personal interests, connection costs, privacy laws, time constraints—innumerable factors lead to patterns of network use that look quite different from any naive ideal of peer-to-peer connectivity. Try reaching the CEO of your telephone company. (Or just try penetrating the computerized, automated answering system to reach a customer-service agent.)

The need, then, is to develop some sense for the social structures likely to take shape around large-scale networking technologies. A good place to start is with the corporation. Corporations are dynamic entities, often multiplying many times in scale over several years. Here we can watch the efforts of integral, highly networked communities to continue functioning integrally as they expand. We can observe their unaccountable transformations. And when we do, we begin to see the extraordinarily difficult *human* challenges posed by expanding networks of interaction.

It has been an oddity of the Internet's early phases that it evoked such a rush of unqualified optimism about the inevitable benefits of raw "connectivity." The Net was going to free the individual from the System. That optimism has already darkened a bit, if the Net discussions going on as I write are any guide. But the corporate experience suggests more than a few peripheral shadows around the earlier hopes. As we consider the evolution of networking technologies, we also need to consider the evolution of totalitarianism. By means of networks, the System has a remarkable ability to take hold of us in an ever more absolute—and ever more invisible—manner.

From start-up to behemoth

One of the dramatic features of the past two or three decades has been the prominent role of the start-up venture, particularly in what we call "high-tech" industries. Of course, every company has to have started at some time. But this recent period has seen an unprecedented surge of new ventures, many of which have contributed to the technological re-shaping of society we are now witnessing. And the phenomenon has been pronounced enough to yield—in high-tech at least—a distinctive "start-up culture." Many engineers have learned to thrive on the peculiar rush they derive from these intensive efforts, abandoning their company as soon as it becomes an established success and moving on to a new initiative. Others, of course, have learned the meaning of burnout.

Remarkable energies are poured into the high-tech start-up (crystallizing—once the company grows old and tired—into the inevitable tales about the wondrous accomplishments of the Heroic Era). The founding employees *identify* with the new business. The company is something they helped form, an instrument for carrying out their purposes, for realizing their particular vision of the future. The company is simply . . . *them*. This explains why they are willing to invest such extraordinary time and energy in the undertaking. Their own interests and goals find expression through the company.

There is something of the organic principle in these organizations. The organs of the human body do not primarily relate to each other mechanically and externally, but rather bear within themselves the imprint and the functioning of the whole, while at the same time the whole embodies the health and fulfillment of each organ. So, too, the individual employee in the well-honed start-up internalizes the principles and aims of the entire "organism," freely bringing them to bear upon her own tasks without outside coercion. But at the same time, the organization as a whole is an integrated expression of the will of its employees.

The result is an uncommon flexibility and a knack for intelligent improvisation. In a strong start-up you often find every employee prepared to leap into whatever breach opens up, without regard for job description, status, or explicit marching orders. Motivation is high, and the creative juices flow. Since everyone knows everyone and has at least some familiarity with all aspects of the operation, the whole organization fluently and intelligently adapts itself to the changing shape of its competitive world.

Little fish become big fish. No wonder such organizations often outperform rather dramatically their huge, established brethren. But then they join the brethren. It seems as inevitable as the law of gravity. One subtle reversal in particular marks the crucial, if long and drawn-out, transition from vigorous young start-up to well-fed, bureaucratic behemoth. Where initially "we had a vision"—and the company was the instrument for realizing it—now the company's separate existence is the given, and management begins asking itself how it can mobilize employees on behalf of the company. The very form of the question betrays the underlying problem: employees have become instruments for realizing the now wholly independent, self-justified goals of the company.

A second symptom accompanies the first. The aim of the entire effort is no longer a good or service, the achievement of which requires, among other things, economic discipline; rather, the economic "bottom line" itself becomes the controlling focus of the company. But this is to turn things upside down and inside out. It leads to episodes like the one James O'Toole reports:

> I once asked a PepsiCo vice president if anyone in that corporation had ever raised the issue of the morality of promoting junk food in ghetto areas where kids weren't getting enough basic foods. He answered, "If anyone would ever be so foolish as to raise the question, he'd find himself out on the street."[1]

Needless to say, employees sense this reversal of ends and means, this loss of human purpose, and come to see the company as competing against their own goals and interests. To ask, *why am I doing this work?*—what human vision of the future are we as a company striving to realize?—is hereafter to sound a rather uncomfortable, dissonant note within the organization. It is easier to say, "I just work here," and to seek one's deeper satisfactions elsewhere.

I should mention in passing that the transition we're talking about seems inevitable, given the structure of the corporation—particularly the ownership structure. Just consider: when it dawns upon the employee that he and his fellows and their entire purposeful undertaking can be sold off to the highest bidder without any input from all those who made the beautifully efficient start-up venture purr—well, that's when everyone begins referring to the vaguely defined corporate string-pullers as "they." Which is certainly no surprise. Can any meaningful human endeavor

---

1. O'Toole, 1985: 301.

today remain meaningful when the "bottom line" is that the participants must operate as chattels?[2]

The computer's new-venture virtues

It is not my purpose here, however, to analyze corporate structure. What I want to point out immediately is that the virtues of the high-tech start-up company closely resemble the advantages offered by computer networks. The freedom of peer-to-peer relating throughout a network; the immediate access to information from all network nodes; the way in which a single node, organlike, can present itself and its influence to the entire "virtual organism," while in turn being guided by the state of the whole network; the potential informality and blurring of functional divisions; the distribution of intelligence and responsibility throughout a network—all this suggests that the computer network is a technological reflection of the healthy, effective start-up venture.

And so I believe it is. But now another issue stares us in the face: this strange difficulty in carrying the strengths of the start-up into the maturing organization. Despite the blood oaths of those early heroes—owners, managers, and employees alike—"not to let it happen here, because we're different," the stiffening of the organization and the alienation of its personnel always seem to happen. And whatever the aforementioned role of the underlying corporate structure in this inevitability, much else is at work. The company gains a life of its own. It is experienced—by owners as well as employees—as the resistance that must be overcome in order to achieve human purposes, rather than as the natural instrument for those purposes.

This is extraordinary, given the strength of the original desire by all parties to avoid precisely such an outcome. What "independent" forces are at work here, sabotaging the wishes of everyone involved? But before

---

2. Peter Drucker's contention in *The Post-Capitalist Society* that employees own corporate America through their pension funds is quite irrelevant here. Such abstract ownership has no bearing on the critical issue: the concrete relations of responsibility between employees and the organizations in which they invest their creative and productive lives.

attempting an answer, we need to look more closely for a moment at the structure of the behemoth—the organization going through what Bernard Lievegoed calls the second phase, or *phase of differentiation*.[3]

Where the pioneer (start-up) phase acquires a certain organic character, the differentiated phase (corresponding to traditional "big business") shifts toward mechanism. Every task is analyzed into its subparts, and these parts are placed in well-defined external relationships to each other, so that the workplace becomes the rationally organized sum of its aggregate parts. A flexible structure based on personal relationships yields to a strict hierarchy of delegation and control. Lievegoed lists a number of traits of such organizations (some of which were more prominent in large corporations at mid-century than they are today):

- Mechanization: people are replaced with machines wherever possible.

- Standardization: every thing and every process is reduced to a precise, uniform standard.

- Specialization governs both the departmental and managerial functions.

- The organization "gives the impression that it can be contained in a deterministic or stochastic model in which the human being is reduced to a predictable factor which reacts to economic stimuli."

- The coordination required throughout the ramifying organization is achieved by "formalizing relationships and interconnections. The informal and personal pioneer style, which continues for some time in the second phase, for instance in the style of management, ensures that the negative sides of the formalizing process do not become apparent immediately. *In a certain sense the informal organization makes it possible for the formal organization to exist*" (p. 72).

---

3. Lievegoed, *The Developing Organization*. This book was first published in 1969 (before the onset of the computer's transformation of work). Throughout this chapter I draw upon Lievegoed's analysis of organizational phases, in addition to my own, ten-year stint with computer manufacturers.

- Whereas the focus of management in the pioneer phase was on the market, it now turns inward. "Administering and controlling the internal structure of the company becomes the most important task of management" (p. 69).

You may already have said to yourself what I'm now going to point out: if you wanted to "perfect" precisely this sort of organization, pushing it as far as it could possibly be pushed, you would want a network of computers. The corporate network offers unprecedented powers of monitoring and control, exquisite standardization enforceable through software, extensive replacement of human functions by machine, and an effortless way to concretize the organizational chart—by simply engraving it upon the computer network.

The computer, it seems, has a split personality. It is no accident that we see a flood of books either celebrating the computer's power to usher in a new era of democracy, teamwork, and creative ferment, or else bemoaning its reinforcement of centralized, hierarchical power. But in reality the computer has no personality at all. It all too readily accepts *our* personality.

A new totalitarianism?

Personally, however, I am not persuaded by those who greatly fear the computer-reinforced, hierarchical organization. That style of organization *is* on its way out—not because of the computer, but because for the past few hundred years Western society and the evolving shape of individual consciousness have made the principle of centralized control steadily less tenable. The movement toward political democracy and, in business, toward employee participation, antedate the computer revolution. It is not that a network makes us participatory, but that our will to participate takes hold of the network.

This explains a certain confusion. Many observers—especially those who actually *use* the Net—are convinced that "cyberspace" is an intrinsically egalitarian, democratizing, community-intensifying medium. But this is to project the historical truth just stated onto the technology, while at the same time betraying a poverty of imagination. Feeling in their bones the untenability of old tyrannies—and exulting in the prospects for their demise—these observers simply cannot picture to themselves the future triumphs of a metamorphosed spirit of oppression. Sauron, they seem to think, knows only one form.

If you really want to see the multiple faces of the computer's split personality—or, as I have been arguing, its split potentiality—then you need to look toward the peculiar opportunities and temptations of the future. It is conceivable that we are witnessing the twilight of the familiar dictatorial state. But if that is so, then the proper question—the only historically justified question—is: "What new forms will the totalitarian spirit be likely to assume in our day?" And I will argue that the answer to this question serves just as well for a second question: "What hitherto uncontrolled forces smother the promise of the start-up venture once it reaches a certain size and maturity?"

The problem we're up against in both cases is hard to put a dramatic name to. In fact, this very difficulty partly defines the problem. But I will attempt to name it anyway. We're talking about the danger of *things that run by themselves.*

The dangerous face of oppression today is the faceless one, the nameless one, the one for which none of us seems to be responsible. So we pay it no attention—which is exactly what lets it go its own way.

Who can any longer be said to *run* the U.S. government or any of its departments? Or the large corporation? In the words of a director and president of Shell Oil when asked how it felt at the top of his company, "It's like sitting on the back of a huge brontosaurus and watching where he's going."[4] Jokes about oil and old dinosaurs aside, one senses this same incomprehension and helplessness throughout all our institutions today. The politician's ritual promise to take charge and *move* the System is taken by the rest of us with resigned good humor.

---

4. Quoted in Bos, 1983: pp. 14–15.

What has become of the great political and business leaders of the past few centuries who, by force of their (sometimes despotic) personalities, placed their own imprint upon government and business? First they became organization men, and then they became the passive tools of their own media images. *So, now, even the strongly hierarchical organization runs by itself.* Which is to say that, effectively, the hierarchy isn't functioning as a hierarchy. It's not really directed from the summit. Something else is going on.

That's why the only way you can reach the top of the pyramid is by becoming faceless. The hierarchy runs under a power that can never quite be pinned down. Who really knows who "they" are? To hear everyone talk, "they" are everywhere, and yet no one you actually speak with seems to be one of "them."

A more potent somnambulism? The answer is not to look for strong leaders of the old style. It's no use going backward. The task ahead is to learn how we, as a community of human beings, can take responsible hold of our organizations, making them an expression of our life together. This must involve neither the extinguishing of the many by the tyrannical dominance of the few—a by no means dismissable threat—nor the disappearance of the community into an organization that runs by itself.[5]

It is this latter threat that most of us fail to recognize clearly enough. There must be, as I said, a *reason* for the heretofore inescapable conclusion of the new venture's exciting start. Whatever that reason is, it is powerful enough to defeat the most concerted will of the most intelligent and well-meaning people—and to do so time and again, despite all the hard-earned lessons of the past. It is just a fact today: the organization takes on a life of its own; it begins to run by itself.

---

5. As to the computer's reactionary usefulness: Joseph Weizenbaum, referring to the conviction of some that computers came along "just in time" to reinforce institutions like banking, welfare, and credit reporting, claims that this misses the point. "These institutions . . . may have needed to be transformed, perhaps in revolutionary ways. I believe the computer has not worked to revolutionize the world as we know it so much as to shore up existing, decaying systems." (Weizenbaum, 1986.)

Furthermore, *here* is where the computer menaces us with a chilling potential. For while the mechanical devices of the Industrial Age also ran by themselves—endowing us with fantasies of a clockwork universe—the computer runs by itself *with an attitude*. It not only runs like a traditional machine, but also receives a dimmed-down, mechanical—yet *technically* effective—shadow of our inner life, and then sets *that* to running by itself.[6]

And so the power of the computer-based organization to sustain itself in a semisomnambulistic manner, free of conscious, *present* human control—while yet maintaining a certain internal, logical coherence—is increased to a degree we have scarcely begun to fathom. We are rapidly fashioning a diffuse "body" that far exceeds the traditional corporate dinosaur in its ability to incarnate an autonomous and anti-human spirit.

The human community has yet to make itself master even of the moderate-sized corporation. But already we are hailing the Net for its *globalizing* tendencies. The question is whether we are recasting an unsolved problem on a scale that leaves us altogether without hope.

Engineering teamwork

The successful high-tech start-ups have left traces in the mature organization. Sometimes much more than traces, for you can occasionally find whole corporate departments that function very much like a start-up. This is true particularly of engineering departments. (I will return to this in a moment.)

But our aim cannot be to preserve the start-up. Organizations must be allowed to mature. The need is to raise the start-up—or the differentiated organization into which it has evolved—to a higher level. Relationships, functions, and tasks that have become mechanical must now be

---

6. The chapter "Incomprehensible Programs" in Weizenbaum's *Computer Power and Human Reason* is an effective, if frightful, characterization of computer programs "that run by themselves." Weizenbaum also deals with the implications of such programs within an organizational context.

made organic—but more consciously, and at a more complex evolutionary stage than in the start-up.

If the start-up can be considered a collection of loosely cooperating cells, the *integrated organization* (as Lievegoed calls it) is more like a higher organism with major subsystems ("organs"). Where functions of the pioneer phase overlapped and were not clearly delineated (and then became rigid and isolated in the differentiated company), they must now be carried out by complex, interpenetrating functional centers. Where coordination was achieved by direct and informal personal contacts, it now requires sophisticated networking and horizontal cooperation. Where the organizational structure was flat, it must now be exceedingly intricate —yet ever-changing in form, and flexibly adapting to shifting needs. Where individual effort was decisive, now the company depends upon teamwork. In general, the pioneering, seat-of-the-pants style, which gives way to detailed planning and organization in the differentiated phase, must now evolve into the clear formulation of policy (principles) and the management of innovation. After-the-fact evaluation of performance against policy replaces before-the-fact control.[7]

Those who have worked, as I have, in the sizable and effective engineering departments of computer manufacturers will find this description familiar. Given the competitive pressure upon them, software and hardware design teams *must* work this way, or they'll soon be out of business. These teams have a lot to teach us, not only about how computers might be used in the integrated organization, but more generally about the human shape of such organizations, with or without computers.

One hopes that the thriving start-up ventures of the past couple of decades, and the successful engineering teams inside mature businesses, both signal the beginning of an effort to take the company consciously in

---

7. Increasingly in our day the challenge is to move directly from the pioneer to the integrated organization—or (in the case of large start-ups) actually to *begin* with an integrated style. The differentiated organization holds steadily fewer attractions for us—a hopeful sign.

hand and mold it into an instrument for accomplishing the purposes of its human community.

The schizophrenic organization. Unfortunately—and despite these promising potentials—the signs so far are not good. I have already pointed out the failure of start-up organizations to realize their visions of maturity. And what is most immediately noticeable about the engineering teams within established companies is the extraordinarily narrow, technical nature of their tasks. This narrowness is the very evident prerequisite for their success. The tasks have all the advantage of being precise, logical, humanly unproblematic. What would happen if the human resources function—or the strategic marketing function—or finance—were brought into a truly integrated organization?

But it is nearly unthinkable. When the layoff or the merger comes, can we have Human Resources operating on the basis of teamwork that arises from, and penetrates back through, the entire company? Hardly so, for the layoff and merger are only possible in the first place (in their common forms) because the company *as a human commmunity* has already been discounted.

Take, for example, the "humanly unproblematic" nature of the hardware and software engineering task. That is exactly the problem: the human being has largely been removed from both the engineering cycle and the finished product. The product is conceived as something that stands complete and objective by itself, quite independently of the human expression going into it. The terms of that expression are therefore narrowed down to the strictly technical.

A complementary consideration applies to those who purchase and use the computer-based product. This product has now become a kind of intelligent, empty template with the active power, in running by itself, to shape a human community to its emptiness—that same expressionless emptiness governing its manufacture.

Such, then, are the results when the engineer coding away at her terminal considers her task a technical one only, and when there are no means within her own work life for integrating broader issues of purpose and value.

I discuss elsewhere what can happen when decision support software is misused within the corporation.[8] But it will almost inevitably be misused so long as it is being designed by engineers who see it as consisting of so much "logic," and who themselves are functioning within their companies solely as technicians. All attempts to mend this situation will amount to the most scanty patchwork until—well, for one thing, until Human Resources can interact meaningfully with Engineering in a single, integrated organization. And until the task of writing software becomes *at least* as humanly problematic as managing the Human Resources department.

Looking realistically ahead

It is simply fatuous to believe that computers and the Net are one-sidedly biased toward the encouragement of a richly communal business organization. No doubt they *would* be biased that way if we ourselves were. But there are many signs that we are inclined rather to let things run by themselves, as the whole, broad, technical thrust of our society already does.[9]

Moreover, within the corporation, computer networks readily transform interpenetrating, organic relationships into a web of outer, mechanical ones. Human interaction within these networks easily verges upon the exchange of data that a computer can manipulate. What *looks* like a resonant pattern of personal exchange is often less notable for the unlimited "connectivity" it embraces than for the way it painlessly and unnoticeably filters a deep, personal dimension out of the corporation's functioning—exactly the dimension that must be brought to uncommon clarity if we are to overcome the smothering powers of the inertial organization and preserve its youthful hopes.

It is easy, when caught up in the excitement of an inchoate, miraculously growing, ever-surprising, global electronic network, to revel in the

---

8. See chapter 10, "Thoughts on a Group Support System."

9. Jacques Ellul makes this point in great and persuasive depth in *The Technological Bluff.*

"play" and unexpected freedoms it allows. But this enjoyment of the untamed, experimental, and still largely unproductive Net tells us no more about its mature potentials than the small, freewheeling start-up venture tells us about the corporate behemoth. If the Net is to become as useful in our major undertakings as so many expect, then it *will* be mapped into our highly elaborated organizations. And only if we have made those organizations our own, learning to express ourselves through them, will we succeed also in expressing ourselves through the Net.

On the other hand, if we persist in the cultivation of a purely technical stance toward our work and our technology, we will find that, like the corporation, it takes on a life of its own, which is at the same time our life—but out of control and less than fully conscious. In an age of universally distributed, technically intelligent tools, this autonomous life may exercise a totalitarian suppression of the human spirit that will be all the more powerful for its diffuseness and invisibility. We might, in the end, find ourselves wishing for the "good old days" of strong, dictatorial rule. At least then we knew where the enemy was.

Stirrings of hope. Rather than end on such a pessimistic note, I would like to suggest where we might look for a more hopeful future.

Probably not in any of those giant, self-propelled—and mostly high-tech—industries commonly thought to be carrying us into the future. I would look first of all in small, out-of-the-way places—businesses where the aim is not growth, but rather to provide products or services that a particular clientele seeks as a matter of belief or principle. There are, for example, those who value healthy food, free of poisons, grown within a healthy human community, and distributed and sold through healthy enterprises—all linked together by a consciously shared and worked out set of *intentions*. The costs will be greater, some may say, but that is foolishness, for you can only measure your costs against what it is you want to create and obtain. The question is, "what do we find important?" and the businesses I have in mind will be driven by this question.

There are such businesses now, some of them thriving—and not only in food production. There are many small publishers who will accept a manuscript, not simply because the book will sell, but because they believe the book is important for mankind's future. There are personal care and health product companies whose businesses are guided, not by glamorous images and celebrity endorsements, but (radical as it may seem) by deep convictions about *what is healthy*. There are environmental services that are an expression of love for the natural world.

I have heard it said of a group of telecommunications executives meeting to discuss the "national information infrastructure" that *these folks are in business; they're not in it for their health*—a strange truth when you think about it. There is hope for a business only when its officers and employees *are* in it for their health.

Success and growth for such a business can be measured solely by the *achievement of its purposes*, not its quarterly stock price gain. One hope for the future is that we may learn to see more of our lives governed in this way by our own, meaningful purposes. The esthetic and functional design of home and workplace (architectural and building trades); the balance between man and machine in our activities (virtually every occupation); the varieties of recreation that can truly revitalize us—these and many other domains may become fields for the conscious attempt by businesses to achieve *what matters*.

I would also look toward the nonprofits—what Peter Drucker calls the third, or social, sector. In many of these a social purpose is the whole *raison d'être*, and the idea of stewardship is therefore successfully substituted for the idea of plundering the market. This largeness of purpose provides fertile ground for growing an organization that is fully an expression of, and controlled by, its wide-awake human constituencies.

I would look for the expansion of "socially aware" banking and investing. The hope here is not that more politically correct businesses will be supported, but rather that *any* business will be supported only by those who are specifically concerned about its overall goals, its use of resources, its internal organization and treatment of employees, its effect upon the environment, its role in its immediate neighborhood, and every other aspect of its operation.

This hope applies not only to our investing, but also to our consuming. In a growing number of markets people are buying products with a "social conscience"—from ice cream to cosmetics to toys. That the real social value of some of these choices remains controversial does not matter, for unanimity of opinion is not the goal. What is important is the free expression of conscience. Indeed, where the social issues are complex and not fully understood (and one can hardly imagine social issues to be otherwise), the proposed solutions had *better* be controversial. But this concerned and free expression is a prerequisite for the emergence of any true solutions.

We can, therefore, welcome the efforts to certify and label products, so that the consumer has some basis for his choices. For example, an effort is underway to begin identifying timber grown by sustainable methods. Many other products, from tuna fish to computers, have been labeled with respect to various environmental concerns. Although we can expect such practices to be employed cynically and misleadingly by some—and there are no easy standards in any case—these beginnings at least point in the right direction.

I would look for organizations able to take a playful, "nonserious" attitude toward any new technological device: taking the time to get to know it, to "massage" it and be massaged by it, and finally determining whether and how they can shape it to their own will rather than yielding to its will. This, of course, is the truly serious stance, for it implies respect for the powers embedded in every tool.

I would *not* look toward businesses that leap into a market opportunity just because it's there—letting themselves grow explosively as the opportunity allows, until the whole market suddenly collapses (as tends to happen when you are dealing with artificially created "needs") or changes its character. Then the company is left with thousands of orphaned employees, not to mention a huge inventory of wasted resources. Large companies can aim to be nimble and adaptable—and this is surely good—but the first rule of adaptability should be: adapt yourself to a real human need, involve those whose need you are meeting in your own planning, and let your production be guided as much as possible by the expectations and long-term commitments of this entire community.

All this, of course, requires that in my roles both as consumer and as employee, I be willing to participate in the fashioning of business. In this regard, the consumer movement of the past few decades is a positive development, but it needs to enter into a more intimate, cooperative, and productive relationship with the *producers* of goods and services. Businesses seeking to produce enduring value for consumers can only succeed to the extent that consumers accept a responsibility to support them.

One can, incidentally, see at least a distant hint of such a collaborative relationship in the X Consortium, which is responsible for some of today's most important and most "open" networking and graphics software. A group of high-tech companies support the Consortium in its development of new products; these products go through a phase of public review, and then, upon completion, they are placed in the public domain. The participating companies—and anyone else who wishes—use the public-domain software as the basis for their own, enhanced, commercial products. One reason companies support the Consortium is that, by participating in the early phases of product development, they get a head start on developing their own, improved versions of the software—this in a market where a few months can make the difference between profit and loss.

Personally, I suspect the time will come—however remotely—when the idea of racing to market in order to beat a competitor by a few months will seem terribly odd. I cannot readily imagine any human need that is served by such a race. In fact, the race seems to indicate a process that is running on by itself, without reference to need. If the slightest slackness on my part means that someone else is going to beat me to market, then clearly there's no reason for *me* to worry about the supposed need remaining unmet! So I must in fact be worrying about something else: keeping up with the treadmill. If I must bend my entire organization—and huge financial resources—toward being first on the market by a few months, then I've devoted my organization to a margin of good that is so infinitesimally thin as to be meaningless. I've also almost guaranteed a margin of bad somewhere down the road—in the form of corporate "restructuring" when the product directions that once seemed so important lose their relevance or appeal. And in the meantime my employees will recognize, consciously or not, that they are participating in a mechanism of cancerous growth from which meaning has largely been eliminated.

Most of the signs of hope I've listed above imply at least a partial detachment from the pressures of an economic treadmill running under its own power. I have no doubt that these signs must seem like folly to many. And so they *would* be folly in most "normal" business contexts. But I never wanted to suggest that our future lies in what is now normal business. As things come to run more and more by a logic of their own, any *human* alternative can only look more and more like illogic and folly.

9

Do We Really Want a Global Village?

Referring to our wired planet as a "global village" makes about as much sense as calling multinational companies "global craft shops": it works fine so long as you attach meaning only to the first word of the phrase. In the case of "global village," however, nearly all the emotional freight is delivered by the second word. Given how few of us can claim any direct experience of a traditional village culture, one wonders what it is we're really saying.

No one can doubt that the world's wiring reflects the imperatives of business. To a first approximation, the global village *is* the global "craft shop"—which only adds to the perplexity, since the patterns of community we have built into our corporations are not widely felt to be village-like.

On the other hand, we have fed for some years now on certain images of electronic, transnational, people-to-people contact. A few well-publicized faxes and Internet messages from Tienanmen Square and coup-threatened Russia greatly encouraged our already eager sentiments. Somehow we can't help ourselves: all this opportunity to pass messages around just *must* lead to an era of peace and neighborly understanding. At the very least, we cannot deny that the communication itself is a good thing!

There are strange juxtapositions here. Many of those societies in which the village has until now remained central—societies where networking is as easy as saying hello to a neighbor—are busily dissolving themselves in the cauldron of their own unrepressed fury, villager pitted mercilessly against villager. Surely *this* is not the community we wish to globalize! Where then, one asks, *is* our model? Perhaps it is merely a ghastly sense for the ironic that prompts us to hail the birth of the global village just as villages around the world are self-destructing. But the unwelcome thought nags: could it be that what we so eagerly embrace, unawares, are the powers of dissolution themselves?

Legacy of the colonial village

The current ethnic strife forces at least one self-evident lesson upon us: there are ways to bring diverse peoples together—to give them common institutions, a common currency for cultural exchange, common purposes and undertakings on the world scene—while yet failing utterly to bridge hellish chasms dividing human being from human being. It is not just that the Soviet experiment and the colonization of Africa failed—as they did even in their most benign manifestations. More than that, they were gigantic incubators for future misunderstanding and strife. And no one can doubt that the transcultural nature of the experiments—the tendency to globalize and rationalize human interaction without a proper foundation within the depths of the human being, without a true meeting of persons across the superficially breached cultural barriers—has contributed to the massive regional disasters that have afflicted former colonies in recent decades. In this context, the global village looks all too much like a convenient means for universalizing the conflicts already so evident in the "colonial village."

You may wish to dismiss ethnic hatreds as resulting from the very sort of oppressive domination our global networks will hereafter make impossible. The political power of the fax and all that. I don't doubt that particular styles of domination *may* eventually pass from history's stage—or even that electronic communication may play a part in the passing. What concerns me is the likelihood of our expressing within a new social and technological landscape the same spiritual vacuity that gave rise to the old tyrannies.

Can we claim to have composed the elusive melody that brings neighbor into harmony with neighbor? Whatever that melody may be, it was woefully unsung in the villages of Bosnia, where the people had long been able to talk to each other unimpeded. The grounds are tenuous indeed for thinking that proper electronic links were the critical, missing elements in villages subsequently shattered by the shrill dissonance of a hatred long inaudible even to its owners.

Giving in marriage. These observations may seem overwrought in the context of the Internet. That, in fact, is precisely what worries me. In dealing with the titillating prospects of a new electronic culture, we naturally find ourselves talking about human beings who have become manageable abstractions of themselves. Sharing information and cooperating in purely technical undertakings too easily figures, in the electronically adapted imagination, as "village paradise regained." Yet the global peace and understanding of this levitated discourse are only pale shadows of the peace-giving powers we must summon if we are to assist the transformation of an all-too-real village where the inhabitants rape, mutilate, and kill their neighbors. Moreover, the widespread substitution of an abstract, "information-rich" discourse for a more muscular and humanly *present* interaction may be very much part of the formula for mutual alienation, the consequences of which we are now seeing in the world.

I am not saying it is impossible to express deep human concern to another person in an email message. There's no need to tell me how you met your spouse over the Net, or how you participated in a successful, electronic fund drive for a charity. I know about these things and am glad for them. So, too, people were happily given in marriage throughout Bosnia, until a few years ago. But to leave matters there is to refuse to probe the subtle weave of shaping forces from which an unexpected future may crystallize.

A global electronic culture can, in one sense or another, bring about a union of peoples. The question is whether this union only offers a less visible—and therefore more insidious—communal dissociation than was effected by the failed political unions of the past. Recognizing such things is painfully difficult; how many Yugoslavs in 1990 could have looked into their own hearts and the hearts of their neighbors and descried the conflagration to come? And it may be precisely *this* sort of recognition that an online culture suppresses more effectively than any external authority possibly could. Many indeed—by their own testimony—have seized upon the Net as an opportunity, not to face what they are, but to live out their fantasies.

Technology transfer

The global village is by all accounts a technological creation. Many would-be village architects are inspired by the endless potentials they discern in a satellite dish planted among thatched-roof houses. This techno-romantic image calls up visions of information sharing and cooperation, grassroots power, and utopian social change.

What it ignores is the monolithic and violently assimilative character of the resulting cultural bridges. Jerry Mander and many others have given us a hair-raising account of the effects of technological imperialism upon native peoples around the world.[1] A global village that leaves no place for native or alternative cultures seems uncomfortably like the old colonialism in a new guise. But this statement requires some elaboration.

Sources of satisfaction. We in the West have distilled the abstract essence of logic and mathematics from our former worlds of interest (for example, from the behavior of the night sky). Unfortunately, we have proven less adept at recovering the possibilities of meaning in the original subject matter once we have conformed our thoughts to its abstract distillate. The

---

1. Mander, 1991. Also see chapter 5, "On Being Responsible for Earth."

light of mathematics may have descended into our minds from the circling stars, but how many students of mathematics still look to the night sky with wonder?

Our loss becomes an acute problem for others when we apply our now disembodied rationality (often in the form of computer programs such as expert systems) to the concrete needs of developing nations. This rationality, detached as it is even from our own former sources of meaning, is doubly alien to the people we would help. And what meaning we do invest in software and technology remains, for the most part, unconscious.

Doris M. Schoenhoff, in *The Barefoot Expert*, points out that expertise—the kind we export to other nations—is always "embedded in a community and can never be totally extracted from or become a replacement for that community."[2] When we attempt the abstraction and apply the result across cultural boundaries, the logic and assumptions of our technology can prove bitterly corrosive. Worse, the kind of community from which Western technical systems commonly arise is, for the most part, *non*community—typified by the purely technical, one-dimensional, commercially motivated, and wholly rationalized environments of corporate research and development organizations.

Within our own society, even food is subject to technological manipulation. We can produce various artificial foods, supposedly nourishing, and the inevitable temptation is to bring such products to bear upon the problems of hunger in the world. But this meets surprising resistance. As Jacques Ellul puts it,

> We must not think that people who are the victims of famine will eat anything. Western people might, since they no longer have any beliefs or traditions or sense of the sacred. But not others. We have thus to destroy the whole social structure, for food is one of the structures of society.[3]

---

2. Schoenhoff, 1993: 115.
3. Ellul, 1990: 53.

What has for us become a merely technical problem may well remain for other cultures an intricate nexus of profound meanings. The wonderful rationality of our solutions easily destroys the only things that really count. "It is discomforting," writes Denis Goulet,

> for a sophisticated technical expert from a rich country to learn that men who live on the margin of subsistence and daily flirt with death and insecurity are sometimes capable of greater happiness, wisdom, and human communion than he is, notwithstanding his knowledge, wealth, and technical superiority.[4]

This is not to justify the continued existence of poverty, but only to point toward the inner world from which alone meaning can arise. When technology arbitrarily destroys inner worlds, its logically compelling aspect begins to look like a grotesque, mechanical sneer. And given the aggressively self-driven, uncontrollable nature of Western technology today, it almost certainly *will* destroy the inner world—which is to say, the culture—of the recipient societies. It will likely do so much more rapidly, even, than it has been uprooting the culture of the originating nations.

Technology in place of culture. Schoenhoff remarks that what we export today is no longer simply the various products of Western expertise. "Western expertise itself has become the [exported] technology"—for example, in the form of expert systems.[5] But this holds true for much more than expert systems. The entire technical infrastructure, including the computer networks upon which everything is increasingly founded, enforces an imperial "wisdom" of its own. Ellul speaks, for example, about the centralizing character of even the most distributed networks. It is a centralization without need of a center: a governing logic, a systematic requirement for interaction, a necessary rationalization of all the parts within a huge, incomprehensible, but perfectly coherent and compelling totality. This rationalization is just "in the nature of things." The uncounted fragments of logic continually being added to the system

---

4. Quoted in Schoenhoff, 1993: 80.
5. Schoenhoff, 1993: 75.

through millions of separate processes that no one can fully comprehend or even know about—all these demand their own, mutual rationalization, and we ourselves are unavoidably pulled along by the grand pattern.[6]

In this sense, even if in no other, the global village is a kind of global totalitarianism. And one thing it asks of us is clear: in attacking any local problem we must yield first of all, not to the meanings inherent in the problem, but to the constraining necessity of the global system itself. The village farmers in Nepal may not feel any need of a satellite dish, but they will receive one nevertheless; it is a prerequisite for "development."

But, as I have already pointed out, this willy-nilly imposition of technology destroys the fabric of meaning by which communities are knit together. Our bafflement over conflicts in the global village reflects a forgetfulness of the fact that human life can be sustained only within a sea of meaning, not a network of information. When we disrupt this meaning with our detached logic and unrooted information, we cast the villagers into the same void that *we* have been able to endure only by filling it with endless diversions. Not everyone has access to our diversions—and many of those who do are not so quickly willing to sell their souls for inane stimulations. Religious fanaticism—to pick one alternative—may prove more meaningful.

Philistine technology. Our rush to wire the world will some day be seen to have spawned a suffering as great as that caused by this century's most ruthless dictators. There is no doubt about what we are up to. Our quest for a global village *begins* with the implementation of physical networks and accompanying technology. Then, of course, the local communities must adapt to this global, culture-destroying machine they have suddenly come up against. This sequence is vivid proof that the global village has absolutely nothing to do with culture, value, or meaning—nothing to do with the traditional significance of community, with democratic values, or with anything else that grows up from the healthy depths of the human

---

6. Ellul, 1990: 162–63.

being. It is, purely and simply, the extension of a technical and commercial logic implicit in the wires already laid down.

If we really wanted a global village, we would *start* with the local culture, learn to live in it, share in it, appreciate it, begin to recognize what is highest in it—what expresses its noblest and most universal ideals—and encourage *from within the culture* the development and fulfillment of these ideals. Only in this way can *any* culture enlarge itself.

Technological change should be introduced only so far as it serves the natural, consciously chosen evolution of a people. "What is important," says Schoenhoff, "is that development, including technological and economic development, must proceed from a vision of the human person and the purpose of life and not simply from a theory of production and consumption"[7]—not even, I might add, from a theory of the production and consumption of the empty commodity we now call "information." In a healthy society, technology would emerge from the cultural matrix; it would not arbitrarily destroy that matrix.

We can hardly play a positive role in the development of other cultures without first ennobling our own behavior to the point where we are no longer content to exploit those cultures for a strictly economic benefit. The real "meaning" of the world's wiring is in fact little more than the exploitation of commercial opportunities—the purest philistinism—in which nearly all of us are implicated. Enabling cultures around the globe to transform themselves from within is hardly part of the picture.

When cultures collapse instead of transcending themselves through their own best elements, only chaos can ensue. This is the whirlwind we have been reaping for some time. The current, furious attempts to assimilate every society to the inhuman imperatives of the information age will only intensify the maelstrom.

---

7. Schoenhoff, 1993: 82–83.

The lie

It wasn't long ago when we smiled to ourselves at the reports of Russians and Chinese buying up blue jeans and dancing to rock music. Somehow we knew that this meant we were winning. No doubt our confidence was justified—and all the more as we penetrate our "enemies" by means of commercial television, cinema, and, finally, the fully integrated logic and the virtually real images of a brave new world. And yet, we are only now beginning to sense, with a restless foreboding, the slowly emergent effects of these images upon our own culture. What if it turns out that "winning" is the worst possible outcome?

The obvious lie should already have alerted us to the dangers. A culture that has largely succeeded in eradicating the last traces of its own village life turns around and—by appealing to a yet further extension of the eradicating technology—encourages itself with Edenic images of a global village. This is Doublespeak. The television, having helped to barricade the villager behind the walls of his own home, will not now convert the world into a village simply by enabling him to watch the bombs as they rain upon Baghdad. Nor will we suddenly be delivered from ourselves by making the television interactive and investing it with computing power. (Interactivity allows, among other things, the hand to guide the bomb to its target.) In none of this do we see a healing of the terms of human exchange. Nor do we see evidence of escape from the inexorable, despotic logic already responsible for the fortification and isolation of our own inner-city "villages."

10

Thoughts on a Group Support System

Decision support systems have come a long way since the Sixties and Seventies. Time was when Nobel Prize laureate Herbert Simon could announce with a straight face: "There is every prospect that we will soon have the technological means, through [heuristic programming] techniques, to automate all management decisions."[1] From battlefield strategy to commercial product development, machines would increasingly take charge.

While I suspect there is more truth to Simon's prediction than most observers allow—after all, only a person whose own thinking processes were already largely "automated" could have ventured such a statement—history has contravened his expectation. Now, some thirty years later, neither the battlefield commander nor the CEO is in foreseeable danger of obsolescence.

We still hear about decision support systems, of course, but they mostly attempt to offer a relatively humble suite of logistical services to

---

1. Simon, 1965: 47.

the human decision maker. The buzzwords flitting about the research publications tend toward the more modest end of the spectrum: electronic meeting systems, groupware, computer-mediated deliberation, and so on. What these denote can range from simple electronic extensions of the chalkboard and the paper memorandum to ambitious, if relatively crude, gestures in the direction of Simon's original vision.

Brainstorming, analyzing, and voting

I will look briefly at reports of one particular "group support system." Developed by researchers at the University of Arizona,[2] this system was designed to facilitate meetings. The meeting room contains a microcomputer for each of four to ten participants, and a large projection system for displaying either an individual's work or the combined results of group work.

The typical meeting under this system has three phases. Using *Electronic Brainstorming* software and typing at their separate terminals, all members of the group record their ideas regarding the questions posted on the meeting's agenda. Although these contributions are anonymous, everyone can see the complete and growing list of ideas. Next, a vaguely described *Issue Analyzer* helps the group "identify and consolidate key focus items resulting from idea generation." Information from other sources can be imported during this phase. Finally, a *Voting* tool provides various methods for prioritizing the key items. Again, voting is anonymous, but the results are easily displayed for all to see.

The Arizona researchers report on the experimental use of this system at IBM. In one case a manager, frustrated in her attempt to identify certain problems in shop-floor control through conventional meetings, employed the group support system with apparent success. "At the end of the brainstorming session, the manager reflected that for the first time she was able to get meaningful answers" to her questions. Immediately following this, the group prioritized a list of "focus items," held some face-

---

2. Nunamaker, Vogel, Heminger, et al., 1989.

to-face discussion, and voted. The result? A high degree of satisfaction among the participants, who felt they had successfully addressed the problems.

This system can clearly provide low-level, logistical support. Ideas, once entered into the computers, are part of a meeting record that can be recalled at any time. Complete "minutes" of the session are available immediately upon its conclusion. Votes can be taken and recorded in an instant. Not surprisingly, the *Issue Analyzer*, designed to help structure the actual problem analysis, came in for criticism as "clumsy." It appears that this was where the face-to-face discussion proved most important.

Overall, the system produced large time savings "strongly correlated with the degree to which the group's task was stated clearly and concisely." One participant cited "the preciseness of the process procedures" as an advantage. The researchers note in a later publication that "process structure helps focus the group on key issues and discourages irrelevant digressions and unproductive behaviors."[3]

Paradoxically, the anonymity of the process won praise for "knocking down barriers" between people One user mentioned the "openness of the process and its lack of intimidation. This was because of the anonymity." A second was impressed by "the way the personalities are taken out of the process so that the process becomes more rational." And a third remarked how "the anonymity of the input allows participants to change positions on an issue without embarrassment."

In a related experiment, a Hughes Aircraft manager offered a similar observation: "I noticed that if someone criticized an idea of mine, I didn't get emotional about it . . . . No one knows whose idea it is, so why be insulted?"

---

3. Nunamaker, Dennis, Valacich, et al., 1991: 41–61.

Are there no risks?

The general literature on group support systems yields a mixed and confusing set of conclusions, leading the Arizona researchers to emphasize the importance of context. For example, the size of a group, the complexity of its task, and the prevailing corporate culture will all help determine the effectiveness of electronically supported meetings. Also, electronic support does not always have to take the same form. The system described here can be combined with any degree of "traditional" group interaction; it can be adapted to asynchronous use and distributed throughout several offices; and presumably—although the researchers do not mention this—the anonymous feature could easily be turned on or off, according to a group's wishes.

The University of Arizona developers claim a number of benefits for their electronic meeting system. In their own words, it

- enables all participants to work simultaneously (human parallel processing);

- provides an equal opportunity for participation;

- discourages behavior that can negatively impact meeting productivity;

- enables larger group meetings which can effectively bring more information, knowledge, and skills to bear on the task;

- permits the group to choose from a spectrum of structured or unstructured techniques and methods to perform the task;

- offers access to external information; and

- supports the development of an organizational memory from meeting to meeting.

On the other hand, they identify no risks or liabilities, although in a general discussion of electronic meeting systems they mention in passing the potential for depersonalization by the electronic medium, together with the necessarily limited "view" offered at any one time by a video display screen. Having listed these as theoretical concerns, they do not go anywhere with them.

Another researcher describing this same work manages to come up with two potential disadvantages: most people cannot type as fast as they speak, so the meeting is slowed down unless there are approximately eight or more participants (in which case the advantages of parallelism more than compensate for slowness of typing); and the system is useless for "one-to-many" forms of communication, such as lectures.[4]

There is something disconcerting about this peculiarly limited range of assessment—a limitation, incidentally, that seems quite typical of efforts in this field. The adaptation of the group task to a kind of computable algorithm seems just a little too easy, and the world of possibilities outside the algorithm just a little too neglected. This neglect is only more disturbing when set beside the authors' claim that the technology "is fundamentally changing the nature of group work."

It is not that it is *wrong* to assess one's tools and methods against criteria such as the external flow of information, the precision of procedures (as indicated by faithfulness to a step-by-step, procedural outline of the way things ought to proceed), and time-to-solution. It is just that if these considerations do not take place against a larger and more meaningful backdrop, they easily begin to oppress, a fact generally ignored within the engineering and research worlds giving birth to the new software tools.

This is not to say that supporting software is inherently threatening. Much depends on the awareness of the group using it. That is exactly why the restricted vision of the researchers and their test subjects is disturbing—the cultivation of a wider awareness is exactly what does *not* seem to be going on.

The risks are not trivial. For one thing, the work group may begin to conceive and carry out its tasks mechanically, simply following the prescribed format for its own sake. Such prescription can cramp any human relationship—particularly where creativity is desirable (and where isn't

---

4. Aiken, 1993.

it?). Even to write things down at too early a stage—so that the things written confront one as a kind of objective, already achieved "reality"—*can* in some cases stifle any further, freewheeling, imaginative thinking.

My own experience of meetings suggests that critical insights often crystallize unexpectedly at the end of a long and meandering journey—and they may even nullify everything that preceded them. And yet, the journey was essential to the insight. Any effort to make the later stages grow too systematically out of the earlier ones may discourage profound revisualization of a problem in favor of a pedestrian "solution."

Group work does require structure as well as freedom. But when the structuring tools contain embedded intelligence, one needs to assess carefully just how intrusive and coercive their influence might be. For such intelligence is aggrandizing: it not only increases the range of capability and the adaptability of the tools, but for these very reasons it also invites users passively to abdicate some of their own responsibility for shaping group processes.

The development of human capital

The issues here pierce to the essence of the business undertaking. *Is the corporation a human activity in the service of human needs, or not?* It is remarkable how easily and subtly the human-centered view slips from our grasp. Indeed, just so far as the corporation is viewed as an enterprise designed to score a profit, rather than to serve worthwhile ends under the discipline of economic controls, to that extent the entire organization has already been cut loose from its human justification and reduced to something like a computational machine.

But suppose we answer, "Yes, the corporation is a human activity in the service of human needs." What then? The first thing we realize is that the individual and group activities within the company are more than a means to some external end; they are themselves a primary justification for the company's existence. After all, prominent among human needs is the need to work, to create, to cooperate, to solve problems, to struggle against the solid resistance of the world. In this striving, the individual and the working community grow, and such growth is—or ought to be—a good part of the reason for binding these human efforts together in the first place.

In this context, every problem is a gift—part of the company's inventory of "raw goods"—and invites the production of new, human "capital." This is far different from seeing a problem merely as something to be gotten rid of by the most efficient means possible.

All of which indicates that meetings we support electronically cannot be assessed solely in terms of productivity, time-to-solution, precision of procedures, and so on. A manager must balance many different concerns, in addition to getting the product out the door. Is each member of the group being stretched so as to gain new skills and exercise a more mature judgment? Does the distribution of tasks reckon appropriately with the different ages and experience levels of group members? Is there a way to call upon this or that contributor's intense personal interests? What do the frictions between Jane and John suggest about their future assignments? In what ways can the group internalize and make practical the larger organization's commitment to meeting human needs?

The potentials of age. Consider, for example, the effect of age upon a worker's role. A twenty-five-year-old will typically approach life far differently from a fifty-year-old. Youth is full of biological energies, invincibility, and an expansive, I-can-do-anything optimism. In later years, this refreshing, energetic, I-centered, immediate-task-oriented style shifts toward the more reflective and communal. Here's how Bernard Lievegoed puts it in *The Developing Organization*: "At 35 a man will ask in a certain situation: 'How can *I* solve this problem?' A man of 55, if he has weathered the crisis in the right way, will ask . . . 'Who is the most suitable person to solve this problem?' or even 'How can I delegate this task so that the person concerned can learn something from solving it?'"[5]

---

5. Lievegoed, 1973: 152.

As Lievegoed points out, some will not make this transition success-fully, but instead grow more rigid with age, hewing to petty rule, defend-ing their own turf ever more jealously, and generally proving a headache to the larger organization. In this case, management must ask,

> What mistakes have *we* made so that *he* has become like this? When he was between 40 and 50 did we not profit from the fact that his department ran on oiled wheels? Did we leave him there because we could not be bothered to make a change? Did we overlook the symptom that no promising young men emerged from his depart-ment ready to move on to higher levels?" (p. 153)

When a manager is prepared to ask such questions, and then, with the questions in mind, to facilitate the deeply organic interrelationships within a group—all in service of the values and purposes governing the larger organization—will the group support software help her or hinder her? I don't believe there is any direct answer. There is only a complex set of issues we haven't really begun to address yet.

Using software as a foil. Or, again: in any group committed to human ends, the issue of anonymity mentioned earlier would present itself as a problem and an opportunity. Here, in fact, one can imagine a judicious and constructive employment of computers. If I were a manager with access to the system described above, I would use it to the hilt in tackling a specific issue. Then I would hold a follow-up meeting in which the electronically supported session became a foil for assessing the group's cur-rent state and performance. Why did participation improve when anonymity was guaranteed? Am I—or is someone else—behaving in meetings so as to squelch the free exchange of ideas? What are the various strategies of intimidation at work in our group? How can we function more openly, without intimidation?—for surely a group cannot be at its most productive if its members do not have the maturity to deal forthrightly with each other!

And so the distortions and constraints of an electronic support system, used as a kind of foil, can help to answer the question, "What distinguishes a human-centered organization from a mechanism?" But the prerequisite for this is, unfortunately, just what is missing in the current literature: an ability to step back and look for the distinctly human potential in social institutions. Nor is the failure here surprising. What should the programmer look for, if not what is programmable? And yet, if we were not thinking in mechanical terms, we would train our engineers to think first of everything about a task that *cannot* be programmed. Only when they had fully lived their way into the specifically human—and therefore never fully capturable—dimensions of the task would they consider what supporting role their software might play.

Approached in this spirit, software engineering would prove a discipline of continual revelation by clarifying the boundaries between man and machine.

11

In Summary

Our ever more intimate embrace of technology—which now means especially *computerized* technology—is hardly news. At the same time, anyone who claims to discern in this embrace a crisis for humanity risks becoming mere background noise in an era of rhetorical overkill. Nevertheless, something *like* such a claim is the main burden of this book.

The qualities of our technological embrace are admittedly difficult to assess. It's not just that we cannot buy things without participating in financial networks and contributing ourselves as "data" to consumer databases; nor that companies are now refusing to work with suppliers who lack "network-compatibility"; nor that in order to compete in most markets today, you must adapt your business to the computational landscape; nor that "knowledge" increasingly means "computer-processed and computer-accessible information"; nor that our children's education is being shifted online with a stunning sense of urgency; nor, finally, that our chosen recreations are ever more influenced by the computer's remarkable ability to frame alternate realities.

Clearly, these are important developments. But on their surface they don't tell us what *sort* of embrace we're caught up in.

Perhaps more revealing is the fact that we can no longer envision the future except as an exercise in projecting technological trends (with computers likely to be doing at least some of the projecting). Questions about the future of community, of social activism, of education, of liberty and democracy—even of religion—now threaten to become debates about the evolution of technology.

The same truth emerges even when we express our fear of technology, for it is often the fear of what "they" will do with technology to rob us of privacy or access to information—and "they" turn out to be conceived as impersonal mechanisms of government and corporate business: machines running by themselves and largely beyond anyone's control. Nor can we imagine remedies without appealing to these same organizational mechanisms. One way or another, we seem convinced, the Machine cradles our future.

This helps to explain the advice I've heard too often for comfort: "technology's penetration of our lives will continue in any case; why resist? Why not find the pleasure in it?"—the rapist's plea, but now applied against ourselves on behalf of our machines.

All of which raises a question whether the difficulty in characterizing our embrace of technology results partly from the fact that technology is embracing *us*, the squalid terms of the encounter having largely been purged from our traumatized consciousness. While I would answer a qualified "yes" to this question, I do not take the answer to imply a rejection of technology. Rather, it implies a need to understand both the logic of the technological assault, and the inner qualities of our submission. For the fact is that we are locked within a complex, *mutual* embrace. Only in accepting this fact will we begin to discover the nature of the crisis now facing us.

Who—or what—holds our future?

As I write these words, John Perry Barlow's article "Jackboots on the Infobahn" is circulating on the Net. Barlow is cofounder and vice-chairman of the influential Electronic Frontier Foundation, and his piece is a counterattack against government plans to standardize the encryption technology based on the "Clipper" chip. He sees in Clipper "a last ditch attempt by the United States, the last great power from the old Industrial Era, to establish imperial control over cyberspace." His conclusion?

> If they win, the most liberating development in the history of humankind [that is, the National Information Infrastructure] could become, instead, the surveillance system that will monitor our grandchildren's morality.[1]

This peculiar sentence bears within its brief span nearly all the unresolved tensions afflicting the current assessment of high technology. If the Net is the most liberating development in the history of humankind—but evil forces may somehow snatch this incomparable gift from us at the last moment, turning it into an instrument of unsurpassed oppression—then, it seems, the Net can be neither liberating nor oppressive in its own right. It's all a question of what we *do* with it. It's not the Net we're talking about here; it's you and me. And surely that's the only place to begin. Neither liberation nor oppression can become living powers in any soil except that of the human heart.

As soon as we put the matter this way, however, we *can* begin to talk about the "nature" of the Net. Not some absolute, intrinsic nature, to be sure, but an established character—a kind of active willfulness—that ultimately derives from *our* character. Our technological expressions, after all, do exhibit certain tendencies, patterns, biases, and these can, to one degree or another, be read. But it remains true that what we are reading—what we have expressed through the technology—can only be something of ourselves. We should not ask, "Is technology neutral?" but rather, "Are *we* neutral in our use of technology?" And, of course, one

---

1. Barlow, 1994.

hopes we are not. No striving for what is good, true, and beautiful—or for their opposites—can reasonably be called neutral.

On the other hand, we see an apparent compulsion to treat our machines as objective crystal balls in which we can discern the human future. This is part of a broad willingness to anthropomorphize the machine—to transfer everything human, including responsibility for the future, to our tools. It is easy to forget that such anthropomorphism is a two-way street. If we experience our machines as increasingly humanlike, then we are experiencing ourselves as increasingly machinelike. The latter fact is much more likely to be decisive for our future than the former.

Are we giving up our freedom? What complicates the issue is that we are free to hand over something of our humanity to our machines. We can refuse our own responsibility for the future, and machines will readily fill the void. They will make our decisions on the battlefield or in the board-room; they will imagine a deeply falsified subatomic world for us; and they will supply us with the words we write.[2]

Therefore one can talk about the "nature" of the Net in a still more troubling sense. For the proclivities to which we have given expression do, after all, take up a kind of *independent* life in our technology. This has always been the case, but its truth is hugely amplified in computer-based technology. It is precisely the distinguishing feature of computers that they can act as independent agents. What we express in a programming language—and such languages already bias our expression, if we are not extraordinarily alert—becomes the self-sustaining law of the now autonomous, mechanically intelligent agent.

And yet, even here we should not lose sight of the fact that this autonomous life is, finally, our own. We confront its agency, not only in the computer, but in our organizations, in the functioning of our econ-omy, in politics—and also in ourselves just so far as we "run on

---

2. See, respectively, chapter 10, "Thoughts on a Group Support System"; chapter 13, "Impressing the Science out of Children"; and chapter 16, "The Tyranny of the Detached Word."

automatic" and enter unconsciously, or with only a technical consciousness, into those domains where history is so loudly demanding we take hold of our destiny. We confront it wherever seemingly insoluble human problems arise through no one's apparent fault—much as an individual's conscious intentions can be subverted by split-off, independent fragments of the psyche ("complexes") for which he does not seem to be responsible.

All this, I hope, suggests the need for sensitive balances in our thinking—quite a different matter from weighing piles of "facts" or "information" in crude opposition to each other. In particular, we must hold the balance between two poles:

- Emphasizing human freedom, we can call the technology neutral, since we are free to use it for good or ill. (It remains to ask: how *are* we using technology to shape ourselves and the world?)

- Emphasizing established human proclivities, we can deny the neutrality of the technology in which those proclivities have been embedded. (There can be no positive outcome in this case, for if we are governed by our own existing tendencies, whatever they are, then we have renounced human freedom, and an inhuman future awaits us.)

As an absolute conclusion, neither statement is tenable. But as poles marking the movement of thought, they are both essential. I believe strongly in the decisive potentials of our nascent human freedom, and therefore my appeal is to the reader's understanding and powers of choice. To that extent, I keep to the pole of freedom. But my fears, and the urgency of my message, derive from the second pole. For I am convinced that, paradoxical as it may seem, we are strongly tempted to use our freedom in order to deny freedom, pursuing instead the mechanization of life and thought. Such a course is open to us. We can forsake the responsibility of choice and put the machine in charge. We can let ourselves be driven by all the collective, automatic, unconscious, deterministic processes we have set afoot in the world and in ourselves.

A crisis of awakening

Opening today's electronic mail, I find an announcement circulated to all members of the Consortium for School Networking discussion group. (The group is aimed primarily at teachers and administrators in grades K–12.) The announcement solicits contributions to a book, and begins in this admirably straight-shooting fashion: "The Texas Center for Educational Technology is committed to producing a publication that reports successful uses of technology in education." A little further down—with no hesitations voiced in the meantime—the message continues:

> The purpose of this book is to help other educators justify to their school boards and school administrators the purchase of expensive computer-based technologies. We want to hear from you about positive changes in student achievement, student behavior, or teacher/administrator productivity that are a result of the implementation of technology. We also want to hear from you about improvements in student test scores, attendance, tardiness, attitude toward subject matter, and/or self-esteem that are attributable to the use of technology.

These people seem to know what they want. Surely they will find it. Just as surely, one can reasonably complain about the imbalance of their enterprise. Most teachers haven't yet figured out what to do with the computers and the online access being shoved at them, and already this educational center is prepared to assume that only good can come of it all?

But asking for balance is admittedly a tricky matter. The obvious thing is to tally all the "good effects" of computers in the classroom, and all the "bad," and then to hope that the good outweigh the bad. One encounters exactly this approach, not only in education, but in all fields where computers are used. The skeptic is typically met with counterbalancing testimonials about how "my daughter had a wonderful learning experience with such-and-such a computer program"—much as critics of television have become used to the ritual observation that "there are some good programs on TV." And so there are.

There is no argumentative sum. Such assessments can, in fact, be worthwhile. The challenge for the critic is to avoid disparaging them while pointing gently toward a deeper set of issues. After several decades of a massive social experiment with television, there are finally signs that we are taking more concerned notice of the medium's underlying effects, whether expressed through "good" programs or "bad": what is happening to nervous systems, habits of attention, moral and esthetic judgments, the structure of the family, thinking processes?

I am not sure we will be given this many decades to become properly aware of our computers. For what is directly at risk now—what the computer asks us to abdicate—are our independent powers of awareness. Yet these powers are the only means by which we can raise ourselves above the machine.

The more intelligence, the more independent life, the machine possesses, the more urgently I must strive with it in order to bend it to my own purposes. Here, then, is the fundamental level at which I need to strike a human-centered balance between myself and the machines around me. "Balance," however, is too mild a term; I need to experience a *crisis*—a kind of turning point that prepares the way for healing. The word "crisis" was classically related to a decisive act of *distinguishing*, and the necessity today is that I learn to distinguish my own humanity from the subhuman. I cannot do so without a fearful, morally tinged struggle toward consciousness.

This is a very different matter from seeking balance in the usual sense. It will not do simply to cultivate as many socially beneficial effects of computers as possible—whether we count elevated student test scores, or participation in electronic elections, or the analysis of scientific data, or cross-cultural communication as "socially beneficial." For one can imagine a brave new world in which we have eliminated all but the desired effects, yet in which we steadily descend to the level of our machines. The deeper question is: how do our desires already reflect our adaptation to our machines, and how can we rise above that adaptation?

The very attempt to sum the advantages and disadvantages associated with computers is itself a sign of how far we have already succumbed to the computational paradigm. For there is no such sum. There is no absolute advantage, and no absolute disadvantage. *Everything* depends upon what happens within you and me—and we can change that. Therefore, even to argue that there is a threat from computers—if that threat is seen as fixed and objective—is only to further our descent. This is my own greatest challenge, for where my strong predilection is to *argue the facts*, I should instead seek to *awaken*. Awakenings prepare the way for a new future, and for different facts.

I can put all this in a slightly different way. The experts in human-computer interfaces are working hard to design computer programs that "cooperate" more fully with humans and mesh harmoniously with our natural capacities. These undertakings are valuable. But they are not enough, for they do not yet address what it is, with all our capacities, we have so far become, or what we may yet become. What if the human being to whom we so beautifully adapt the computer is the wrong sort of human being? What if our efforts really amount to a more effective adaptation of the human being to the machine, rather than the other way around?

After all, it is we who first conceived those refractory machines now being redesigned. *Something* in us harmonized with the original designs. That is, something in us was already inclined toward the mechanical. Unless we can work on that something—master it—our remedial efforts will lead to ever more subtle, ever more "successful" expressions of the same tendency.

That *work* is what I have been referring to. Only a crisis within the individual can summon unexercised, forgotten, or future human capacities. "There is no birth of consciousness without pain" (C. G. Jung). If, in our technological experiment, we are to know who is adapting to whom—who is embracing whom—we must first gain a clear experience of both human and machine potentials, and how they differ.

But a great deal in our recent cultural history—and almost the entire thrust of the ongoing technological effort—has consisted of the attempt to bridge or deny any such difference. We have learned to regard ourselves as ghosts in the machine, awaiting a proper, scientific exorcism. It should hardly surprise us if this habit of thought has affected our actual capacities. We have more and more *become* mere ghosts in the machine.

On being awake. "Civilization advances in proportion to the number of operations its people can do without thinking about them."[3] While echoing current notions of progress, this is nevertheless the momentous opposite of the truth. Everything depends today on how much we can penetrate our activities with a fully conscious, deeply felt intention, leaving as little as possible to the designs that have "escaped" us and taken up residence in the impersonal machinery of our existence.

I am not decrying our ability to walk or drive cars without the crippling necessity of thinking about every detail of our behavior. But it *is* important to gain a conscious grasp of the meanings inhering in such activities. This requires an ability to enter at will into them with imaginative thinking. What is the difference between crawling on all fours and striding forward in an upright position? That we try to understand the relation between man and animal without having gained a conscious experience of this difference testifies to a science driven by purely external and reductionist approaches. It is a science that would explain consciousness without ever bothering to enter *into* it.

Similarly, we need to grasp the difference between driving a car and walking, or between viewing a two-dimensional, pespective image and participating in the world itself, or between interacting with a computer and interacting with a person. But these are exactly the inner distinctions we have been training ourselves to ignore. It is no surprise, then, that many can now readily conceive of dealing with computers that are, for all practical purposes, indistinguishable from persons.

---

3. I have not succeeded in tracing this quotation—attributed to Alfred North Whitehead—to its origin.

I am not claiming any easy or automatic distinction between comput-ers and people. If what we have been training ourselves to ignore—and may therefore lose as capacity—is what distinguishes us from machines, then we must expect that over time it will become more and more plausi-ble to program our machines to be like us.

This brings us back to the crisis of awakening. Our relation to com-puters is more a matter of choice, of the direction of movement, of inner experience and discovery, than of unalterable fact. This is not to say, however, that the choices will remain open indefinitely. Critical choices never do. The growing child, for example, must develop certain human capacities, such as speech, when the time is "ripe," or else risk remaining incapacitated for the rest of its life. There can be no stasis at such times; one either moves forward, or else loses much of what one already has.

There is good reason to believe that all of human life is governed by this principle. Personal crisis, then, is the only saving response to modern technology—a crisis of consciousness provoked by the oppressive resis-tance of mechanized intelligence, much as the child's first, faltering steps are a crisis of "uprightness" in response to the downward pull of gravity.

The child takes those steps in obedience to a wisdom calling from "without," a wisdom not yet grasped as conscious understanding; our task as adults today is to make the deepest human wisdom fully our own. Where, as a child, I differentiated myself from the animal, now I must learn to differentiate myself from the machine—and this differentiation lies in the deepening of *consciousness*. It is therefore not only a matter of pointing to established human nature; it is also a matter of *realizing* human nature in its movement toward the future.

That I do not *feel* this task a real one, pressing upon me daily, may be the surest sign of my growing comfort with the rule of the machine, whose purely technical evolution, running comfortably along lines of least resistance, lets me sleep.

PART TWO

Computers in Education

12

Net-based Learning Communities

ENTERING A CLASSROOM, the sixth-grade girl sits down at her terminal and composes an email message to her "Net pal" in India. The two of them are comparing notes about efforts to save endangered species in their separate localities, as part of a class project. Their messages, discharged across the Internet, reach their destinations within minutes. Each child's excitement about making contact is palpable.

In later years, these children may even chance to meet, and their email exchanges will have prepared them to accept each other on equal terms, rather than to be put off by cultural barriers.

An attractive picture? I once thought so. But even assuming this sort of thing to be one of the bright promises of the Net, I doubt we will see its broad realization any time soon. Why? Because the promise is being overwhelmed by sentimentality, uncritical futurism, and the worship of technology. We're seeing an unhealthy romanticization of the Net.

The world is disappearing from the child

Allow me a brief flanking movement here. It's now routine for social critics to bemoan the artificial, fantasy-laden, overstimulating (yet passive) environments in which our children grow up. I'm not sure the bemoaning helps any, but I believe the concerns are largely justified. The problem is that they too rarely strike through to the heart of the matter. For if the child must fill up his existence with "virtual" realities and artificial stimulation, it is because we have systematically deprived him—not to mention ourselves—of the real world.

Link together in your mind a few simple facts, many of them commonplaces:

Schools have become ghettos for the young. Perhaps for the first time in history, our century has seen children strictly cut off from meaningful connection to the world of adult work. That work is hidden away behind the walls of the industrial park, or else has disappeared into the remote, intangible, and opaque processes magically conducted through the screens of computers. Likewise, all the once-local functions of government have become distant, invisible abstractions, wholly disconnected from what the child observes going on around him. The evening news concerns events he must find hard to distinguish from last night's movie. The ubiquitous television serves in addition to cut him off from meaningful interaction with his own family. Even the eternal inevitabilities have become invisible; sickness and death are but the rumors of a sanitized mystery enacted behind closed doors in the hospital—grandmother will not utter her last groans and die untidily on the couch in the living room. And perhaps most importantly (but this receives little attention), the science he encounters at school is increasingly a science of abstractions—forces and vectors, atoms and equations. And so he is deprived also of his living connection to trees, rain, and stars. The world recedes behind a screen, a veil of unreality.

I do not pine for the particular forms of a lost past. The question, rather, is how to replace what needs replacing, and with what. As things stand, the picture sketched above leads to a crushing conclusion, first elaborated so far as I know by the Dutch psychologist Jan Hendrik van den Berg at midcentury. Can we rightly complain, van den Berg asked, when the child grows up and somehow fails to "adjust"? Adjust to what? Nothing is there—everything is abstract, distant, invisible! And so the modern outcome seems inevitable: the child is forced to live within an inner fantasyland, cut off from the nurturing, reassuring matrix of structures and authorities that once constituted community. No wonder the surreal world of the video game is his natural habitat. Nor will it do any good to trash the video games, if we find no way to replace them with a real and appealing community.

How can we knit a community together?

To turn such a child over to the Net for instruction is not an obvious good. Can we structure the bewildering, abstract, gamelike maze of possibilities into healthy learning experiences, appropriate to the child's age? Or will he be more inclined to find here only a yet more glorious video game landscape?

The "interface" between the young girl and her Net pal is undeniably thin, one-dimensional, remote. As valuable as it may nevertheless be, it is not the missing key for redeeming the learning community. Even as a tool for promoting global understanding, it scarcely counts beside the much more fundamental—and deeply threatened—sources of social understanding. The girl, of course, will learn whatever she does of friendship from peers who sweat, bleed, taunt, curse, tantalize, steal, console, and so on.

If I need to find out whether she will become a good world citizen, don't show me a file of her email correspondence. Just let me observe her behavior on the playground for a few minutes—assuming she spends her class breaks on the playground, and not at her terminal playing video games. Unfortunately, the assessment is not likely to turn out positive so long as the schoolyard is hermetically isolated from any surrounding, multidimensioned community. And to see the Net as an easy remedy for *this* kind of isolation is, at best, simplistic.

The danger of the Net, then, is the very opposite of the romantic pic-ture: it invites further de-emphasis of the single, most important learning community, consisting of people who are fully present, in favor of a con-tinuing retreat into communal abstractions—in particular, retreat into a community of others whose odor, unpleasant habits, physical and spiritual needs, and even challenging ideas, a student doesn't have to reckon with in quite the same way her neighbor demands.

An instructor in advanced computer technology for a Midwest high school wrote to me that "students who think it is cool to have a pen pal in Malaysia won't talk to the black students who locker next to them." He went on,

> Where I teach we have the ESL [English as a Second Language] pro-gram for the whole district, butting right up against the TAG [Tal-ented and Gifted students] program. I have run a telecom project for students in TAG classes for the last two years and I have yet to see any of the TAG students, who spent weeks "talking" with students in Kuala Lumpur, say so much as a word to the Southeast Asian stu-dents in the ESL program.

When are we together? The most bothersome thing in all this is the ten-dency to leap rather too easily from raw technology, or from simple images of its use, to far-reaching conclusions about extraordinarily com-plex social issues. There is, after all, one absolutely unavoidable fact: tech-nologies for "bringing people together" do not necessarily *bring people together.*

Before the news media went gaga about the information superhigh-way, there were asphalt superhighways. In many ways these did bring us closer together. The whole transportation revolution was no puny thing, even beside the computer revolution. It remade society. We now brush up against each other in ways unimaginable in earlier eras. Few of us would want to give up all the new possibilities. But, still, the uncomfortable question remains: is that the spirit of "community" I feel as I peer over the edge of the superhighway at the dilapidated tenements below? And when I turn to the Net for my commuting, will I lose even the view from the asphalt?

Actually, the rhetorical question is unnecessary. I telecommute from my suburban basement, and rarely have occasion to venture very far out. I blame no one else—nor any technology—for this; the choices are my own. But one still needs to ask: how will technology play into the kinds of choices society (that is, we) are already tending to make? *Here* is the sort of question we should be asking when we gaze into the future. Some technologies naturally tend to support our virtues, while others give play most easily to our vices. I am dumbfounded that so many fail to see how the spreading computer technologies—in education as in many other arenas—not only offer distinct hopes but also tempt us with seductive overtures at a most vulnerable moment. It would be much easier to welcome an exploration of the computer's uncertain promise if one didn't see so many eyes firmly shut against the already existing tendencies.

The things that count

Perhaps my single greatest fear about the growing interest in networked learning communities is that we will further undermine the human teacher. The most critical element in the classroom is the immediate presence and vision of the teacher, his ability to inspire, his devotion to truth and reverence for beauty, his moral dignity—all of which the child observes and absorbs in a way impossible through electronic correspondence. Combine this with the excitement of a discovery shared among peers in the presence of the actual phenomenon occasioning the discovery (a caterpillar transforming itself into a butterfly, a lightning bolt in a jar), and you have the priceless matrix of human growth and learning.

The email exchange between the young girl and her Indian counterpart, added to *such* an environment, might be a fine thing. But let's keep our balance. Surely the problems in modern education stem much more from the rarity of the aforementioned classroom milieu than from lack of student access to such Net "resources" as overseas pen pals.

Many people in our society are extremely upset—justifiably so, in my opinion—with the current educational system. That gives some hope. But a dramatic and ill-advised movement toward online education may well be the one smoke screen fully capable of preventing an aroused public's focus upon the issues that really count.

Yes, the student eventually will have to acquire Net skills, just as she will have to learn about word processors and the organization of reference materials in the library. But this is not a new model of learning. The most evident new model—not a very desirable one—lies still half-understood in the Net's undoubted potential for dispersing energies, distracting attention, reducing education to entertainment, and—above all else—leading the television-adapted student ever further from human community toward a world of fantasies and abstractions, a world too artificially plastic and manipulable, a world desperately removed from those concrete contexts where she might have forged a sturdy, enduring character.

Let's give our teachers a realistic sense of the possibilities and the challenges of the Net, so they can soberly assess how it might further this or that teaching goal. Let's *not* subject them to a tidal wave of blind, coercive enthusiasm that adds up to the message: "Connect as soon as possible, or be left behind."

13

IMPRESSING THE SCIENCE OUT OF CHILDREN

THE SCIENCE AND ENGINEERING TELEVISION NETWORK (SETN) would
like to help science teachers. In a draft Internet announcement,[1] SETN's
president, Gary Welz, talks about the moving pictures that scientists and
engineers create, ranging from "dazzling supercomputer animations produced by mathematicians and physicists to the video images of living cells
shot by biologists through powerful microscopes." Teachers lack access to
this "exciting visual material"—which he thinks a shame, for "it is precisely the stuff that could stimulate a greater interest in mathematics and
science." His proposed solution? Employ the Internet's video capabilities.

The assumption here is dead wrong. Video images, of course, will
have their worthwhile uses. But high-tech dazzle is not what stimulates
interest in math and science. Such a notion nevertheless seems implicit in
much of the push for online science lessons today. Unless nature comes
packaged with cinematic drama and slick technology—unless we find

---

1. Net announcement, "Science and Engineering Television on the Internet: Scientific
Publishing in a New Medium," posted by SETN (SETN@mitvma.mit.edu), September 15,
1993.

some way to capture the most remote and astounding phenomena (so our fears seem to run)—we'll lose the kids.

Yes, supercomputer animations of subatomic transactions and video images of strange, unseen interiors possess a certain wow factor. But they do not foster in the child either an understanding of the world or a more eager pursuit of scientific discipline. One doubts, in fact, whether these productions are received in any different spirit than Saturday morning cartoons and Hollywood's special effects. What they *are* likely to do is create a demand for the next advance in our ability to deliver a high-impact image. Most of us probably need only refer back to our own experience in order to satisfy ourselves that television nature programs—presumably much more impressive than the city park or the woods out back—offer no particular encouragement for children to become naturalists.

The fact is that efforts to impress children into science are more likely to do the opposite. The crucial requirement is not that the child receive maximal impact from some display, but rather that he *actively discover within himself a connection to the phenomena he is observing*. In this connection —arising from a properly engaged imagination and not from a surfeit of stimulation—are to be found both the need to understand and the terms of understanding. But the supercomputer animations and strange videos visited upon him by technology preempt the imagination and operate at an abstract remove from the child. Just as he may have few grounds for distinguishing the evening news from the ensuing movie—and therefore little cause for personally engaging the issues over which the reporters seem so distantly exercised—so, too, he may find himself quite unrelated (other than incidentally and passively, via the jolt level) to images presented in the name of science.

Two-minute science lessons

Science museums have come a long way in technological sophistication during the past several decades. We pour great sums of money into exhibits designed to impress. Have these high-tech exhibits brought greater teaching effectiveness? Donald Norman is skeptical:

If the people stick with an exhibit for as long as two or three minutes, the curators are delighted. Two or three minutes? How on
earth can anyone ever learn anything in two or three minutes? It
takes hours. Recall the estimate of five thousand hours to turn a
novice into an expert (and even this isn't really enough). Granted,
we don't expect the science museum to produce experts, but two or
three minutes?[2]

The director of a major science museum explained to Norman that
"visitors don't want to read lengthy descriptions or to hear the details of
science. We have done our job if we can get them excited by the phenomena of science." So the excitement need no longer be the excitement
of a penetrating sympathy and an aroused *understanding!* Just entertain the
visitor, and hope the impact will lead to active interest sometime later.

Oh, yes, these museum experiences may create a thirst for more. But
this particular thirst will most likely be quenched in a theme park, virtual
reality game, or high-tech movie. If these latter are any guides—and, in
our society, they are already perhaps the dominant custodians of childhood imagination—one can receive an impression without its provoking
an increased desire to understand. Furthermore, it seems to me that anyone who directly observes the impressions made upon children through
technical artifice and the media of artificial vision can only conclude that
these are more likely to kill off the world than to bring it alive. Certainly
there seems to be a growing consensus that the sustained assault of televised images tends to induce apathy, hyperactivity, inability to concentrate,
and various antisocial effects in young children.

Where does wonder come from?

How, in this context, can we naively extrapolate from a child's fixation
upon captivating images to his pursuit of science? The child who has just
watched *Jurassic Park* may be obsessed with dinosaurs; he may want you to
buy every plastic, stuffed, and inflatable dinosaur within sight; he may, if
he is young enough, delight in a visit to a fossil site where he can scratch

---

2. Norman, 1993: 39.

around for real bones. We can only hope, however, that the scratching does not prove, over the long run, a sadly unvisceral experience compared to watching the movie.

Of course, it need not—not if we have given the youthful explorer the ability to bring a fragment of bone alive, discovering in it a lost world of mystery; not if, peering through the eye sockets of a skull, he becomes a lithe, four-legged hunter prowling a wondrous, alien landscape, skirting the shadows of imagination in an endless, hungry quest; not if he senses within himself something of this same instinctive prowess, both honoring it and finding appropriate expression for it; not, finally, if he is encouraged during each passing year to fill in this world of his explorations with an ever deeper and truer imagination.

If, on the other hand, his imagination has been co-opted by the incessant bombardment of artificial images, forced upon him in excruciating and dazzling detail, with little of his own creative participation, then the outcome is indeed doubtful. With each fresh assault we deprive him of one more opportunity, before his psyche is wholly distracted and scattered, to develop a sense of wonder and reverence before the mysteries of the real world—the world he can directly perceive and bring to life from within. In no other way can the world live.

There is a difference between "special effects wonder" and the true wonder that leads toward a devout scientific curiosity. The latter, as I have already indicated, grows from an awareness of one's immediate connection to the phenomena—from a sense that the inner essence of what one is looking at is somehow connected to the inner essence of oneself. But this connection—despite all the academic *talk* of how we ourselves "construct" the world—is something scarcely experienced any longer. The world has become alien and our science a basket of abstractions—equations and particles, fields and statistical distributions.

It would be ironic if the scientist, having given up the phenomenal world for these technologically effective abstractions, should then try to reengender public interest in science by embodying the abstractions in a kind of docudrama—a "dramatic reenactment" of nature (with technical enhancements, of course). In this would be an admission that it is only to phenomena—not to equations and metaphysically conceived particles—that we can find a connection. And yet, those dazzling supercomputer animations of subatomic realms are—as phenomenal displays—not merely "virtual"; they are almost totally false, as any respectable physicist will insist. To extract their modicum of abstruse, mathematical truth is hopelessly beyond the primary-age student (and perhaps the rest of us as well).

Furthermore, these false phenomena of our technological creation are even more remote from the child than the equations by which we conjure them, for they now stand at *two* removes from nature: first there is the reduction to mathematics, and then the reembodiment of the mathematics in an unreal and deceiving model. All this, however, is extraordinarily difficult to convey to a person raised on artificial images and alienated from the surrounding world.

The loss of nature

Imagine the delight of a very small child, upon whose finger a honeybee or butterfly has just alighted. Butterfly and child are not then two unrelated creatures. The child is not looking *at* a butterfly. He and the butterfly have, for the moment, found themselves sharing destinies in a suddenly transformed world. This world speaks to the child, but only because he has plunged into it, and does not know it as disconnected from himself. Moreover, an unbroken thread links his delight to the mature awe of the most detached, far-seeing scientist.

In the video image, it is *not* the world that speaks, except indirectly, by means of abstractions wholly beyond the child's ability to understand. The child, who can be wonderfully at home in nature, is most definitely *not* at home amid the complex techniques of the film and computer laboratories—nor amid the unapproachable images mediated by those techniques. The images are unanchored, floating free of the world.

An anecdote may help here. A correspondent, upset by my views on the use of computers in education, wrote that "with computers, you can watch a caterpillar become a butterfly. You can just as easily watch it become a cow, a stegosaurus, or a basilisk." On this basis he claimed that "the message of electronic media is true—to the imagination."

This is horrifying. Has the imagination nothing to do with nature's truth? By what law does my computer change a caterpillar into a cow, rather than a butterfly? To be sure, both metamorphoses look equally "lawful" on my display screen. But that is the horror, for the child will have no reason to differentiate the one from the other. In nature, however, one would be beautiful, and the other a grotesque nightmare. Pity the children in whom we plant such nightmares as if from the hand of nature herself!

But even the video image of a caterpillar changing into a butterfly may be a nightmare, for it pretends to be "the world," and yet the little boy's living excitement is no longer there. He has been robbed of it in favor of a different, more passive fascination—one implicated, moreover, in the destruction of imagination. Nor can he preserve a sense for the inner truthfulness of the caterpillar's transformation when he finds it arbitrarily juxtaposed with feverish hallucinations. Abstractly, there is no difference; in the computer animation everything is lawful, which is to say that natural law—nature—has disappeared. And even where the images are "real" ones, these realities are now abstract—no longer rendered by the true fire of imagination flickering between child and butterfly—and they do not cause the finger to tremble. By subjecting the child to these distant reflections of truth prematurely, we risk destroying his living connection to the world.

A child raised in deep communion with nature will later gain an adult ability to deal properly with abstraction. But even for the adult, abstraction wholly divorced from its matrix of origin leads only to effective power shorn of understanding or meaning. That is why the equations governing subatomic "particles" have landed any who bother to consider their meaning in a metaphysical quagmire. The equations have become so utterly detached from the phenomena of the world that we cannot find our way back.

The physicist may *choose* the lostness of her abstractions. But for the healthy child this lostness is truly a nightmare, and we are criminal to inflict it upon him, unasked.

14

CHILDREN OF THE MACHINE

ONE WANTS SO BADLY to *like* what Seymour Papert has done. In his book *The Children's Machine* he deftly limns the stiff, repellent, institutionalized absurdities of conventional education. His emphases upon the child's natural proclivities, informal classroom settings, the integration of education with life, and the sheer fun of learning all bear on what is wrong with education today. He condemns the idea of teacher-as-technician. And best of all, he repeatedly stresses a "central theme" of his book: the "tendency to overvalue abstract reasoning is a major obstacle to progress in education." What we need, he tells us, is a return to "more concrete ways of knowing" (p. 137).

Papert made his reputation in education by introducing computers in the classroom—and, particularly, by creating the Logo language, which enables young children to learn through programming. That may help us understand why he places the computer at the heart of his educational program. But it does not ease our perplexity, verging finally on incredulity, as we read that computer technology is to be the primary instrument for overcoming abstraction, reintegrating education with life,

151

and embedding the student in concrete learning situations. Yet this is precisely Papert's thesis.

It is true that the computer is a concrete object—a magnetic focal point around which the schoolchild may happily revolve. It is also true that we can, if we choose, assimilate innumerable learning activities to the computer, interest the child in them, and thereby enable him to learn "concretely," in the course of pursuing his interests.

But it is a strange definition of "concrete" that places all its stress upon the student's active involvement, and none at all upon whatever it is he is involved with. The only fully concrete thing a computer offers the student is its own, perhaps enchanting presence. Beyond that, it hosts a mediate and abstract world. The image on the screen, the recorded sound, the "output behavior" of a program—but not the world itself, apart from computer technology—constitutes the universe of the student's learning.

It is rather as if we decided to make an encyclopedia the basis of the child's education. Except that the computer, as Papert points out, can be much more engaging than an encyclopedia, appealing as it does to more of the senses, while also inviting the child's interaction. This makes it easier for the child to remain caught up in the computer's presentation of "reality"—and therefore inserts a more distracting, more comprehensive veil between him and the world into which he was born than an encyclopedia ever could.

Unfortunately, many schools *have* relied upon what one might call the "encyclopedia model of education." In decisive ways—although they are not the ways he has considered—Papert's employment of computers in the classroom strengthens this model.

How do children learn?

Because Papert's views are highly influential both in the United States and abroad, it is worth the effort to track the painful contradiction running through his book. In order to do that, we need to begin with some of what is most right about his approach to education:

The unity of knowledge. The pursuit of a single interest, if allowed to ramify naturally, can lead to all knowledge. Papert cites his own adult experience with the study of flowers, which led him to Latin, folk-medicine, geography, history, art, the Renaissance, and, of course, botany. This potential unity, however, is destroyed as if deliberately by the traditional, rigid division of subjects and the fragmented schedule of the school day.

School should develop a child's capacities, not fill him with facts. This is the cry of every would-be reformer. Nevertheless, in our day it is a conviction remarkably hard to honor under fire in the classroom. Somehow we can't shake the feeling in our bones that knowledge is something we can collect and regurgitate (what else is the "information" everyone lusts after today?) rather than a discipline of our faculties and character. Papert, however, with his personal commitment to lifelong learning, does seem to grasp in quite a practical way that the classroom must *engage* the student if it is to develop capacities rather than bury them.

We learn through immediacy and direct exploration. Opposing a one-sided doctrine of scientific objectivity, Papert argues that schools distance the child too much from the object of study. Children, he says, "are at risk because they do not have access to a wider immediacy for exploration and have only very limited sources to which they can address questions" (p. 11). When we teach them mathematics, we should encourage them to draw on their own interests, as well as their direct experience of number and space. (He illustrates how cooking leads to a practical facility with math.) "Geometry is not there for being learned. It is there for being used" (pp. 16–17). Even more pointedly, he chides an imaginary critic this way: "The reason you are not a mathematician might well be that you think that math has nothing to do with the body; you have kept your body out of it because it is supposed to be abstract, or perhaps a teacher scolded you for using your fingers to add numbers!" (pp. 31–32)

Abstract reasoning is overvalued. Papert dismisses as "perverse" the effort to give children a facility for abstraction as early as possible, and tries instead to "perpetuate the concrete process even at my age. Rather than pushing children to think like adults, we might do better to remember that they are great learners and to try harder to be more like them" (pp. 143, 155). By concrete learning Papert means learning that is inseparable from some activity, as "kitchen math" is embedded in cooking. He claims that "it is not natural, even if it is possible" to teach practical mathematics as a separate subject. In sum:

> The construction that takes place "in the head" often happens especially felicitously when it is supported by construction of a more public sort "in the world"—a sand castle or a cake, a Lego house or a corporation, a computer program, a poem, or a theory of the universe. Part of what I mean by "in the world" is that the product can be shown, discussed, examined, probed, and admired. It is out there.

Other principles. Papert has much else to say that is valuable. For example, he appreciates the importance of humor in learning. He does not believe teachers should be bound by rigorous, standardized curricula. He wonders whether the "opacity" of modern machines might discourage learning. And he rejects uniformity among schools, preferring instead the "little school," the principle of diversity, and the opportunity for "a group of like-minded people—teachers, parents, and children—to act together on the basis of authentic personal beliefs" (p. 219).

Seeking a counterbalance to abstraction

Papert writes with grace and good humor, effectively combining anecdote with exposition as he circles his subject. From his own experience and that of others, he searches out the sort of "intuitive, empathic, common-sense knowledge about learning" that he says we all possess, and that a wise teacher relies upon when trying to help a student. "Perhaps the most important problem in education research is how to mobilize and strengthen such knowledge" (p. 27).

He embraces "concrete science," contrasting it with the highly rigorous, formal, and analytic ideology "proclaimed in books, taught in schools, and argued by philosophers, but widely ignored in the actual practice of science." This ideology badly prejudices education against concrete constructions, play, serendipity, and the pursuit of direct interests. We need to give our children "a more modern image of the nature of science" (p. 150).

Papert is no doubt right about this. Or, rather, half-right. If a false picture of science as immaculately formal and analytic proves tenacious in its grip on us, it tells us something important about ourselves. The falsehood is not so easily correctable precisely because it represents an entrenched ideal toward which many of the sciences—and certainly the "hardest" ones—continue to strive. So even when the scientist recognizes the qualitative, intuition-ridden, serendipitous daily reality of his work, this recognition has little effect upon his theorizing, which is driven toward the extreme of formality, abstraction, and analysis by all the acknowledged principles of his discipline. Few physicists, in their published papers, are about to downplay traditional, abstract modes of analysis in favor of some new manner of qualitative description. And those published papers are the purest statement of the reigning ideals.

Which is to say that the "false" picture is not so false after all; it is the goal toward which a great part of science continues to move according to a necessity few have managed to escape. (Incidentally, the computer— logic machine, number cruncher, and formal system—was originally conceived as not much more than the perfect fulfillment of the urge toward calculation and analysis.)

So it is not merely that we must give children a more modern image of the nature of science. First, science itself—and our culture, in all its habits of thought—must change. Otherwise, scientific practice will progressively approach the established ideal, and there never will be a "more modern" picture to give our children.

How fundamental are differences in programming style? Papert's own arguments suggest how sticky it can get when one attempts, with less than radical resolve, to break with the ruling canons of abstraction. He tells about a class of teachers who were learning to draw with Logo. This programming language allows one to construct increasingly complex images from a few simple, geometrical shapes. At the most primitive level, for example, a house could be drawn by placing a triangle on top of a square. This, in fact, was how the class began. But at a certain point, one of the teachers discovered how to combine very small-scale geometric constructs so as to produce a squiggly-looking set of lines that served well as the smoke rising from a chimney. Subsequently this became the model for a variety of softer effects. Papert goes on to discuss how the teachers began to appreciate different programming styles, two of which he dubbed the "hard-edged" and "smoky" styles.

> The hard-edged style is closer to the analytic, generalizable ways of thinking valued by the traditional, "canonical" epistemology . . . . Moving from the hard-edged to the smoky style involved a step away from an abstract and formal approach to one that invites all the words that Piaget (taken as representative here of a far wider span of psychological thinking) would attach to the thinking of younger children: concrete, figural, animistic, and even egocentric.

This, however, is misleading. It may be true that the hard-edged/smoky distinction represents a significant difference of style. It may also be true that different types of people will consistently be drawn to one or the other approach. And it may even be true that the stylistic differences are in some respects fundamental. But there is something else to notice here: Logo is requiring that, at bottom, both styles be conceived identically. That is, both hard-edged and smoky programmers must think of their artistic constructs, in the first place, as *programs*. Whatever result they visualize at the start, they must analyze it so as to derive a step-by-step ("algorithmic") method for producing a higher-level effect from a series of almost perfectly abstract, lower-level ones—all hung out on a Cartesian grid.

What this means is that the attempt to create a smoky style at a high level reduces to a hard-edged undertaking at a lower level—the level of actual implementation, which is to say, the level at which the student is directly engaged. The smoke, analyzed closely, is seen to be manufactured in much the same way as the house fabricated from square and triangle; it's just that the scale of the effects has changed.

My point, however, is not how the drawing *looks* (presumably it will be easy to make the scale of analysis so small as to conceal the basic drawing elements completely), but rather what is asked of the artist in order to produce it. Given an image he wants to create, he must break it down conceptually into geometrical "atoms," and then assemble these atoms in a logically and mathematically articulated structure. *He operates primarily in an analytical mode* that gives him numerically defined, quality-less constructs for manipulation. It is with such analysis—and not with an eye for imaginal significance—that he is encouraged to approach every image.

What has happened here is that the artistic task has been embedded within a programming task. While it may be legitimate to speak of the hard-edged and smoky *effects* the programmer aims at, the programming itself—which is the child's immediate activity—possesses a fundamental character that remains the same regardless of the style of the effects. The programmer may start with an interest in some aspect of the world, but the act of programming *forces* him to begin filtering that interest through a mesh of almost pure abstraction. To draw a figure with Logo, the child must derive a step-by-step procedure (algorithm) by which he can construct the desired result: tell the cursor to move so many steps this way, so many that way, and repeat it so many times. For example, the following Logo code draws an equilateral triangle with sides fifteen units long:

```
FORWARD 15
RIGHT 120
FORWARD 15
```

RIGHT 120

FORWARD 15

This is a long way, on its face, from a triangle! The mental algorithm bears only a highly abstract relation to the actual figure. As programmer, the child is encouraged away from a direct, qualitative experience of form, entering instead a web of mathematical relationships. These relationships are exactly what count when it comes to teaching algorithmic thinking and the nonqualitative aspects of mathematics itself. But, as we will see, they are not what the younger schoolchild needs.

Papert sincerely wants to escape the one-sidedness of an overly analytical, abstract approach to learning. But his discussion of hard-edged and smoky programming styles at least raises the question whether—for all his appeals to the intuitive, the concrete, the personal, the immediate—he has indeed found the proper counterbalance to abstraction, or whether abstraction has consolidated its triumph by assimilating the proposed remedies to its own terms. I ask this with some trepidation, since Papert's own urging against overreliance on abstraction couldn't be stronger. He cautions us at one point to be "on the lookout for insidious forms of abstractness that may not be recognized by those who use them" (p. 146).

The only reasonable course here is to honor his counsel by turning it respectfully upon his own work.[1]

What is immediacy?

Papert believes that computers afford the child a "wider immediacy for exploration." He takes every opportunity to show how children plunge into this immediacy, propelled by their natural interests. They even give rein to their fantasy as they interact with the world on their screens. But how immediate *is* this world?

All re-presentations of the world must be, to one degree or another, abstract. Representing requires selectivity—an *abstracting* of particular

---

1. Much that I will say here depends for its positive force upon a familiarity with the general pedagogical approach outlined in appendix C, "Education Without Computers." The reader is encouraged to review that appendix in conjunction with the current chapter.

features from the broad "given" of experience—as well as a translation into some sort of representational language. For example, a photograph reduces the landscape to a two-dimensional pattern of pigments on a flat surface. This pattern approximately captures certain color relationships of the landscape, while also encoding some of the mathematical relationships given by the laws of linear perspective. Despite the limitations, we can learn to see the reduction *as if* it were the real thing. But, of course, it is *not* the real thing.

The same holds true for a computer. Only the illuminated screen itself—along with the mouse, keyboard, and other physical apparatus—is an immediate reality for the student. Papert repeatedly celebrates the concrete presence of the apparatus, and the student's active involvement with it. No one will deny him this. But the virtue of immediacy possessed by the technical device as such is *not* a virtue of the content mediated by that device. The difficulty so many have in making this distinction—or in finding it significant—is remarkable, and suggests that the computer's greatest danger may lie in its power to alienate us from the world, unawares.

All this merits elaboration, which I will attempt by considering the primary uses Papert envisions for computers in the elementary school classroom. These are three, having to do with the computer as an interactive repository for knowledge, as a programmable device, and as a controller for "robots" built with Lego blocks. The first and last of these receive attention in the following section; computer programming, already touched upon, is taken up again later in the chapter.

Education by hypermedia

Jennifer, a four-year-old preschooler, asked Papert where a giraffe puts its head when it sleeps. "My dog cuddles her head when she sleeps and so do I, but the giraffe's head is so far away."

The question sent him scurrying through his books for information about the sleeping habits of giraffes. But then he wondered why Jennifer could not conduct this kind of investigation herself. Obviously, she couldn't do so by reading treatises on wildlife. It is in our power, however, to create a "Knowledge Machine"—a computerized database that would give her "the power to know what others know."

> Such a system would enable a Jennifer of the future to explore a world significantly richer than what I was offered by my printed books. Using speech, touch, or gestures, she would steer the machine to the topic of interest, quickly navigating through a knowledge space much broader than the contents of any printed encyclopedia. (p. 8)

The Knowledge Machine can certainly be built. Doubtless one of its strongest points would be its incorporation of film footage of the sort now appearing in the best televised nature programs. Jennifer could call up moving images of a giraffe in all the glories of its natural environment—and, if she were lucky, perhaps even catch sight of a giraffe sleeping. That such images are the most frequently cited benefit of television may signify just how far immediacy has departed from us.

Snakes—real and onscreen. Addressing these issues in the Net's "waldorf" discussion group, Barry Angell wrote:

> Yesterday my 11-year old son and I were hiking in a remote wood. He was leading. He spotted [a] 4-foot rattlesnake in the trail about 6 feet in front of us. We watched it for quite some time before going around it. When we were on the way home, he commented that this was the best day of his life. He was justifiably proud of the fact that he had been paying attention and had thus averted an accident, and that he had been able to observe this powerful, beautiful, and sinister snake.

Angell then asked exactly the right question: "I wonder how many armchair nature-watchers have seen these dangerous snakes on the tube and said 'this is the best day of my life.'" And he concluded: "Better one rattlesnake in the trail than a whole menagerie of gorillas, lions, and elephants on the screen."

Jennifer's teacher, of course, could not respond to her inquiry by taking her on a safari. Neither can most of us encounter rattlesnakes at will—even if we want to. But this is hardly the important point. The issue has to do with the nature of immediacy, *whatever* we happen to be experiencing. In this regard, any emphasis on dramatic, "footage-worthy" content is itself questionable. In the words of Kevin Dann, another contributor to this same Net discussion:

> As an environmental educator leading field walks for many years, I found I often had to wrestle with the fact that kids (and adults) who had been raised on lots of this programming expected the same sort of visual extravaganza to unfold before their eyes; they expected a host of colorful species to appear and "perform" for them.

And a third contributor, high school teacher Stephen Tonkin, added:

> I have precisely the same problem with astronomy. The kids no longer seem to want to learn about the movements of the stars and planets, but want to get onto the small end of a telescope as soon as possible. They are then disappointed when the somewhat blurry image of Jupiter, although optically many times better than what Galileo saw, does not match up to the space-probe shots they see on the goggle-box or in encyclopedias.

It's not just a matter of unrealistic expectations and consequent letdown. The real question about the Knowledge Machine—as also about television—is whether the expectations it induces, and the experience it offers, have anything to do with a healthy, knowledge-producing participation in the world. For the world mediated by the screen simply is not the world. The skills needed to navigate the technical device are not at all the skills needed for a discipline of nature observation. Nor is the experience and understanding that results from the one context equivalent to the experience and understanding that results from the other. What takes shape upon the screen is reduced, translated, abstract, and therefore remote from the child, however entrancing it may nevertheless be.

Papert is correct in saying that the student learns through involvement. But surely an essential part of this truth is that the learning relates to the nature of the thing one is involved with, and the mode of involvement. It is simply backward to immerse the elementary school student in an artificial, computerized environment before he has learned much at all about the world. How can he translate the terms of artifice, the language of representation, back into a reality he has never known?

When the Scientific Revolution began, practical experience of the world tended to be extensive, while theory was making its first, tentative conquests. The need was for more and better theory. Today the situation is quite otherwise: we tend to be full of theoretical knowledge, and only weakly familiar with the world our theory is supposed to explain. The greatest need is for direct experience.

This sort of concern applies to more than just theory. Almost the entire range of computer use is characterized by one degree or another of *virtual* reality, wherein the computer is thought to give us, not a theoretical model of the real, but some sort of parallel experience *virtually like* the real. Yet, how will we continue to make the judgment, "virtually like," once we have fully exchanged the world for virtuality? We will have nothing from which to distinguish the virtual.

Lego constructions. Early on, the Logo programming language was married to the Lego building block. With embedded computer chips, Lego toys can be controlled, robotlike, by Logo programs.

The main burden of what I want to say about Papert's enthusiasm for computer-controlled Lego robots will follow shortly. Here I will only point out that these plastic Lego blocks, compounded of various geometrical shapes, stand at a considerable remove from the branches and stones, reeds and burrs, with which a child in more immediate contact with nature might play. The child's imaginative use of the blocks is already constrained—if only by their shapes—toward "engineering" applications. The pursuit of design is nudged toward artificial regularity.

The difference between a sand castle and a Lego fortress; between a carved, wooden boat and a computer-guided, motorized, Lego boat; between a puppet of stick, cloth, and stuffing, and a Lego figure—these differences are worth reflecting upon. That natural objects might speak to the child in a rich, sympathetic language foreign to more sterile (even if more "realistic") objects is something we today have a hard time appreciating. It remains true, however, that our ancestors knew the world as ensouled, and certainly the younger child still today has something like the same experience. We should at least ask what developing capacities of the child feed upon the forms and substances of nature before we casually substitute for them our latter-day artifices.[2]

In any case, there is no doubting that the regularly shaped, plastic Lego blocks fit particularly well with Papert's emphasis upon the algorithmic and programmable. There is no neat algorithm for either carving or sailing a little wooden boat in the usual, childlike manner—and yet these activities offer a great deal of worthwhile experience, from which a later appreciation of mathematics and engineering can most healthily arise.

· · ·

The upshot of all this is, I think, that the Knowledge Machine, Logo programming language, and robots *do* involve children in a concrete learning environment possessing genuine immediacy—but they do so only when the "subject" is the most abstract: mathematics and the quantitative aspects of engineering, science, and computing. All other subjects are approached either indirectly through these primary abstractions (just so far as the emphasis is on programming) or through a complementary, televisionlike abstraction (just so far as the emphasis is on the computer as a knowledge resource).

Of course, children, being irrepressible, will tend to make of *every* context a concrete one—whether this involves playing "ball" with Lego blocks, creatively crashing their elaborate constructions, or simply focusing on the immediate construction process. My argument here has to do only with the distinctive claims made for the programming experience and for the computer as a knowledge resource. These claims, after all, are

---

2. See appendix C, "Education without Computers."

central to Papert's book, and are one reason for the widespread pressure to introduce computers into the primary school classroom.

Insofar as the proponents of Lego/Logo are simply advertising the benefits of concrete learning environments, I have no quarrel with them. But, as every good teacher knows, there is little difficulty in getting children to work concretely and creatively with whatever materials are at hand! The expense of computers is hardly necessary for this. And when computers *are* imported into the classroom, then we need to recognize that their *distinctive contribution* is to move the child's experience away from the concrete, and toward the abstract.

The remainder of this chapter will, I hope, fill out this statement.

How fast is zero?

Dawn, a kindergarten student, was playing with a computer program that made objects move across the screen at a speed determined by a number she typed. Papert relates her excitement upon realizing that zero, too, was a speed. She had recognized, as he puts it, that "standing still is moving—moving at speed zero" (p. 126). He sees in this a replay of the Hindu discovery that zero could be treated as a number. Moreover, he tells us that many children make the discovery on their own—without aid of a computer—when they hit upon the familiar joke, "Are there any snakes in the house? Yes there are, there are *zero snakes*." So

> this is not a strange oddity about computers; it is part of the development of mathematical thinking. The computer probably contributes to making the discovery more likely and certainly to making it richer. Dawn could do more than laugh at the joke and tease the teacher and her friend: Accepting zero as a number and accepting standing still as moving with zero speed increased her scope for action. A little later she would be able to write programs in which a movement would be stopped by the command SETSPEED 0. Even more interesting, the joke can be extended. [An object] will obey the command FORWARD −50 by going backward fifty steps. (p. 127)

Dawn's experience may not be "a strange oddity about computers," but Papert's satisfaction in it definitely testifies to an extraordinary, if unexamined, urge to push the child's learning toward abstraction. Two things need saying about this particular anecdote:

First, Dawn was being trained to see a moving object as a purely abstract quantity—what we call its speed. Why abstract? Because, for the sake of her revelation, the nature of the object itself had to fall completely out of the picture; whether it was a light bulb or a zebra made no difference to the numerical speed she was learning to "see in her mind." Nor did it matter much whether the object moved up or down, in a curve or a straight line, to the left or to the right. And, finally—which is Papert's main point—it didn't even matter whether the object was moving or resting.

This is the height of abstraction. It turns this kindergarten girl's attention away from everything but a certain quantity. It starts her on the way toward that pure "head world" that is almost the entire world of our era. But, apart from the sheerest abstraction, rest is *not* movement. It is more like the *source* of all movement—a fact attested to not only by the ancient notion of an unmoved mover, but by our own physical and psychological experience of the various meanings of "rest" (experience that will rapidly become irrelevant to all Dawn's theorizing about the world). Nor is vertical movement the same as horizontal movement, or circular movement the same as straight movement, or movement to the left the same as movement to the right.

Are all these distinctions meaningless, or at least irrelevant to Dawn's intellectual growth? Certainly the ancients would not have thought so, for their qualitative cosmos was thick with felt differences between rest and movement, right and left, up and down. And surely every modern dancer and every artist still has a direct experience of these differences, finding in them material for expression. Children themselves *live* in their movements, and can readily be taught to bring the various qualities to fuller awareness—if, that is, they are not instructed early and systematically to ignore these qualities, which we have long been convinced have no place in scientific descriptions.

Second, as to the claim that Dawn's computer was simply assisting and making "richer" a discovery frequently occurring to children without computers: this is just not true. The "zero snakes" business—so typical of the wordplay children love—centers on peculiarities about the meaning of "zero." These, however, are not normally elaborated by the child as ruling abstractions. In a natural learning environment, the joke is highly unlikely to result from a systematically trained observation in which one learns to look past the immediately given object and see in its place an abstract, numerical property. A child so trained will indeed pick up an early ease with mathematics, but will not know the world to which she subsequently applies her mathematics—an imbalance that admittedly may fit her well for the adult society into which she will move.

In actual fact, I suspect that the joke usually occurs when the child is scarcely thinking about particular objects at all. She is simply struck humorously by the discovery that people use "zero" like other numbers—which is a long way from any profound grasp of their theoretical reasons for doing so. The usage wouldn't be funny if she wasn't fully aware of the real, qualitative differences between zero and other numbers—the differences Dawn is being trained to lose sight of.

Cybernetics

Papert introduces cybernetics by distinguishing between an artillery shell and a smart missile. The shell rides upon a single explosion, all the conditions for which must be precisely calculated in advance. As the distance for the shot increases, it is harder to allow correctly for temperature and wind conditions.

A smart missile, on the other hand, operates on the principle Papert calls "managed vagueness." Launched just roughly in the right direction, it relies on continual feedback to make midcourse corrections. In this way it can home in with extreme accuracy upon the remotest of targets—as those who watched television coverage of the Gulf War are vividly aware.

Papert sees in this cybernetic principle of feedback an opportunity for children "to invent (and, of course, to build) entities with the evocatively lifelike quality of smart missiles" (p. 181). He tells us of one eight-year-old girl who constructed a "mother cat" and "kitten" from Lego blocks. When the kitten "wanted" the mother, the girl would make it beep and flash a light on its head. The mother was programmed to move toward the light. That is where smart missiles come in:

> The Lego cat never "knows" at all precisely where the light is located; all it "knows" is vaguely whether it is more to the left or more to the right. The program makes the cat turn a little in the appropriate direction, move a little forward, and repeat the cycle; turning one degree or ten degrees on each round will work equally well. (p. 20)

Papert's conclusions from all this are dramatic. The cybernetically motivated cat is "more in tune with the [child's] qualitative knowledge . . . than with anything precise and quantitative. The fact that it can nevertheless find its way to the exact destination is empowering for all qualitative thinkers and especially for children. It allows them to enter science through a region where scientific thinking is most like their own thinking" (p. 20). Or, again, the shift to cybernetics "widens the focus from prototypes of behavior with a primarily *logical* flavor . . . to include prototypes with a more *biological* flavor." It even encourages fantasy, he says, since children describe many of their devices as dragons, snakes, and robots (p. 182).

All this needs emphasizing. Papert is not simply engaged in the questionable task of teaching this eight-year-old the mathematical principles of cybernetics (for which there could hardly be a more fit tool than Lego constructions harnessed to Logo). He is seizing upon the claim that this kind of programming gives the child a first, scientific approach to biology. The robot engages in "purposeful" behavior (he puts the word in quotes), and provides "insight into aspects of real animals, for example, the principle of 'feedback' that enables the Lego cat to find its kitten" (pp. 19–20). Indeed, he considers the biological realism here sufficient to require a kind of semidisclaimer about reading anything metaphysical into the devices:

> The pragmatic discovery that the [cybernetic] principle can be used to design machines that behave as if they are following goals is basic to modern technology. The fact that the thermostat seems to have the goal of keeping the temperature in the house constant does not stir me particularly. But however much I know about how such things work, I still find it evocative to see a Lego vehicle follow a flashlight or turn toward me when I clap my hands. Is my reaction a streak of residual metaphysics? Is it because the little thing seems somehow betwixt and between? I know that it isn't alive, but it shares just enough with living beings to excite me—and many others too. Whatever the reason, such things are intriguing and making them is an exciting way to engage with an important body of knowledge. (pp. 194–95)

Motherly solicitude? There is no denying the body of knowledge to which Papert refers. It finds expression in all those disciplines striving to understand the human being as a mechanism—albeit an extremely complex one. It is no surprise, therefore, to find that here—as in the matter of hard-edged and smoky programming—the attempted leap toward more flexible (biological, qualitative, imprecise) strategies turns out to be a heightening of the original (physical, quantitative, precise) approach.

If the programming of explicit trajectories requires an abstraction from real objects and real propelling forces, the programming of "smart," cybernetic objects is a yet more extreme abstraction. For now it entails the attempted reduction even of purposive behavior to a simple, quantitative algorithm. The child, far from gaining any immediate experience of directed attention (whether of a mother cat toward a kitten, or a human mother toward her toddler), is taught to make the translation, "this attention is captured and expressed by a numerical algorithm governing motion in space." Shall we wonder if a child so instructed grows up estranged from her own directing will and motherly solicitude?

I am not denying that the use of cybernetic principles yields any gain. In their apparent *results* (as long as we look with reductionist eyes and are willing to deal in quantitative approximations) the new programs are in some sense "better" than the old ones—"more lifelike." This is obvious on the face of things. What is not so obvious is that—because it remains within the sphere of analysis and abstraction—the gain comes at a price. Yes, we manage—in an external way—to simulate a higher function (purposive activity), but we achieve the simulation only by first having reconceived the function in stilted, mechanical terms. We change in a profound way what "doing something purposefully" *means*, draining it of everything the child knows directly, which is then replaced by a patina of abstraction.

It is no wonder Papert likens his children's efforts "more to what has recently been called 'artificial life' than to artificial intelligence" (p. 182). The flourishing discipline of artificial life is based on the most remarkably pure abstraction imaginable. Chris Langton, perhaps its leading theoretical guru, has surmised that "life isn't just *like* a computation, in the sense of being a property of the organization rather than the molecules. Life literally *is* a computation."[3]

Finally, as to the exercise of fantasy in constructing "dragons, snakes, and robots": of course, children being children, they will employ their computerized devices in the service of an irrepressible fantasy. The question is whether, as they do so, they will find their fantastic impulses progressively darkened, obscured behind the brittle compactions of logic with which they are forced to play.

Respecting the child

It is appealing to see how naturally Papert accepts the child as his partner in learning. But acceptance means little unless we accept the child *for who he is*. Papert seems willing, on many counts, to take children for small adults. Quite apart from his passing remark that "seventh-graders are

---

3. Quoted in Waldrop, 1992: 280.

scarcely children" (p. 174), he shows himself eager to let even the very young child establish her own educational agenda. There is, in this, an intimate mixture of truth and potential disaster.

The disaster is uncomfortably close to the surface. In discussing four-year-old Jennifer and the Knowledge Machine, Papert observes that children of this age combine "a remarkable capacity for making theories with a nearly helpless dependence on adults for information that will test the theories or otherwise bring them into contact with reality" (p. 7). But children of four do not make theories and test them, if by those activities one means anything remotely like the logically sophisticated, intellectually centered activity of the adult. The child is not looking for what *we* tend to think of as "relevant facts," but rather for a coherent image. And the coherence is experienced, not as explicit logical consistency, but rather as a pictorial unity of feeling and meaning.[4]

Furthermore, the child's "nearly helpless dependence" upon the teacher is not something to be scorned or avoided. It is, rather, the natural order of things, whereby the adult bears a grave and inescapable responsibility to help the child enter as fully as possible into her own nature. The fact that the era of dependence for human offspring is vastly longer than for animals is not a disability; it is the prerequisite for development of our general, "nonhardwired" capacities. The child is not born already adapted to a specialized niche, but must gradually develop the universal potentials of her freedom.

In today's world, the critical thing is to *slow down* the child's accrual of information and facts derived from sophisticated adult intellects. These facts fit too closely together—like the geometrical "atoms" of the Logo programmer—in a rigid mesh that causes the child's thought processes to crystallize into fixed forms prematurely. The child loses—never having fully developed it in the first place—that fluid, imaginative ability to let experience reshape itself in meaningful ways before she carves out of it a set of atomic facts. Even the creative scientist requires this ability, if she is

---

4. For an elaboration of this point, see appendix C, "Education Without Computers."

ever to escape current theories and see the world afresh. Otherwise, all she can do is to recombine the basic terms already given to her. The ability to reimagine those terms themselves—as an architect might reimagine a building to harmonize with a different setting—disappears.

The heart of the matter, then, is nearly opposite to what Papert makes it. The information that the child can receive from a Knowledge Machine—or any other source, including the encyclopedia—is hardly what matters. What counts is *from whom she receives it.*[5] The respect and reverence with which a subject is treated, the human gestures with which it is conveyed, the inner significance the material carries for the teacher—these are infinitely more important to the child than any bare, informational content. Her need is not to gather facts, but to connect imaginatively with the world of the adult—which is necessarily to say: with the person of the adult—and to find that her own lofty fantasy (which makes an animate toy of every stick or scrap of cloth) can progressively be instructed and elevated so as to harmonize with the adult's wisdom even while remaining true to itself.

To lose sight of the child's healthy dependence upon the teacher is to forget that all knowledge is knowledge of the human being. It is true that we've tried to structure many fields of knowledge *as if* their content were wholly unrelated to the human being—but not even in physics has this effort succeeded. As to the child, her need is not for facts or information of the sort a machine can convey, but for seeing human significances. And she is given these in the person of a teacher whose broad compassion, devotion to the truth, inner discipline, and imaginative reach embraces and creates a fitting home for whatever new things approach the questioner—a home that can be shared.

It is, however, painfully difficult for most of us to accommodate the child's need, if only because we are no longer possessed of her imagination, and have striven to eliminate the very terms of imagination from our science. We may bask in the child's evident need for *us*, but we fail to

---

5. I discuss this further in the section, "Beyond Shoveling Facts," in chapter 25, "What This Book Was About."

realize that this need is the very heart and hope of her education. It places a grave responsibility upon us to become like little children, so that we can guide her like an elder child leading a younger.

Because a logic of intellectual questioning is always *implicit* in the inquiries of childhood, we can choose to construe those inquiries as if the child's mind were actually puzzling over a bit of missing information, rather than over the picture-coherence and drama of an imaginative content. Moreover, we can train the child to put her questions in the form *we* find most natural, and can even force her to mimic us in her own thinking at an exceptionally early age. But this is also to force her abandonment of childhood, while at the same time depriving her of her richest potentials as an adult.

Fun and authority

Papert argues that, by comparison with a Knowledge Machine or video game, "school strikes many young people as slow, boring, and frankly out of touch."

> Video games teach children what computers are beginning to teach adults—that some forms of learning are fast-paced, immensely compelling, and rewarding. The fact that they are enormously demanding of one's time and require new ways of thinking remains a small price to pay (and is perhaps even an advantage) to be vaulted into the future. (p. 5)

He asks why schools don't fasten upon the ways children learn most intensely outside the schoolroom. And he suggests that schools may soon have no choice in the matter, for the explorers of the Knowledge Machine "will be even less likely than the players of video games to sit quietly through anything even vaguely resembling the elementary-school curriculum as we have known it up to now!" (p. 9)

I am no defender of the established curriculum and teaching methods. But my first impulse is to respond by offering the parallel reading, "will be even less likely than children raised on television to sit quietly . . . ." What is obviously right about Papert's argument is that there is never an excuse for education that does not captivate the child and give full reign to her developing capacities. What is just as obviously overlooked is that the mere fact of sparking a child's enthusiastic assent does not prove an activity healthy. Will the computer-trained child be as bored as the television-trained child when it comes to the struggle to understand and constructively interact with the less predictable, less yielding, less algorithmic, and therefore less programmable real world?

Papert cannot help liking the impact of Logo in the primary school classroom because he sees children gathered around their computers and Lego creations, absorbed, guided by their own interests, doing things in a self-directed way—and no longer under the tyrannical thumb of a technician-teacher. Much in this picture *is* good, but I hope you can see by now how it might add up to an extremely worrisome whole.

Surely the child is *not* sovereign in the sense that her own preferences can reasonably define the educational agenda. Her interests are there to be engaged by the teacher, not to replace the teacher. And if the teacher has misconceived his task to be that of information shoveler, we do not save the situation by exchanging the shovel for a computer. There simply is no solution for inadequate teachers except to help them become adequate. To think otherwise is like believing the child of failing parents would be better off raised by machines—it misses the essence of what education is about. The problem can only be fixed where it occurs.

The authority of the teacher, like that of the parent, must issue from a recognition of the child's emerging self and a wise devotion to her needs. Such a wisdom is what the child longs for. To make of the child an adult is to place a burden upon her that she cannot rightly carry. On the other hand, to treat her as an adult-in-the-making—bearing potentials we can scarcely hope to honor as fully as she deserves, and for which we must sacrifice something of ourselves—this is to create a *human* environment in which she can belong and blossom.

In search of imagination

I suggest in a later chapter that true imagination seizes upon the qualitative and phenomenal rather than the abstract and theoretical.[6] Imagination is a profound power of synthesis which, at the most fundamental level of its operation, gives us the "things" of the perceptual world—trees and clouds, streams and rocks. It is also the means by which we apprehend new meanings and obtain our most basic, revelatory insights regarding the world, for these insights always require us to see the world with new eyes. Operating at an unconscious level, the imagination is responsible for those different ways of "carving up" the world that we all inherit, based on the languages we speak. But the imagination can also be disciplined and employed consciously—as we all must at least begin to do when we undertake the sensitive understanding of a foreign language.

Papert seems to glimpse the real challenge of imagination when he writes that

> the deliberate part of learning consists of making connections between mental entities that already exist; new mental entities seem to come into existence in more subtle ways that escape conscious control. (p. 105)

Unfortunately, he nowhere pursues the second part of this statement, apparently setting the matter aside as unapproachable. Such reticence is understandable, for the puzzle of imagination (and its correlate, meaning) resists solution in our day. And yet, so long as we lack any approach to this problem, we inevitably reconceive the imagination's true operation—that is, we reconceive this fundamental, world-creating principle of synthesis—as nothing more than the discursive synthesis of *ideas* upon a framework of logic. This is to lose the imagination in favor of those rational and analytical operations by which (quite properly, as far as they go) we are in the habit of articulating complex ideas.

---

6. Speaking of Owen Barfield's work; see chapter 23, "Can We Transcend Computation?"

So it is that the promise of Papert's "relational, concrete thinking"—which might have employed the imagination centrally—dissolves, as we have seen, into logical, analytical thinking. His "emergent explanations" are simply the other side of higher-order abstraction. He applies both these quoted phrases to the cybernetic programming style, where the child must "imagine" herself inside the object, and where the object's performance does not seem, in any direct way, to be "what the computer was told to do" (pp. 194, 200–1). However, this cybernetic programming simply places another level of computational abstraction between the child and the phenomena she is supposedly coming to understand. The distance between visible output and algorithm is even greater than in the more direct, less flexible sort of programming. There is no true imagination directed at the behavior itself as sentient or conscious activity (speaking of the mother cat/kitten example), but rather an analysis of it in one-dimensional, mathematical terms. This is the assimilation of imagination to analysis with a vengeance.

I believe we will remain indebted to Papert for his respectful stance toward the child, and for his richly conceived learning environments, among other things. As to the problem of imagination, one hopes for exciting results should Papert seek to explore further his dangling allusion to those "more subtle ways" by which "new mental entities" are formed. The task is urgent, for one thing is certain: we will not manage to preserve the imagination of childhood until we at least make a start at recovering it in ourselves.

Stalking the wild kitten. We *can* discover occasional pointers toward imagination, even if in odd places. What immediately occurs to me regarding the cat and kitten—via a few associational links—is the work of the remarkable tracker, scout, and wilderness expert, Tom Brown, Jr. Brown spent some twenty years of his youth in the outdoors, honing to an almost unbelievable pitch his animal tracking and other survival skills. He learned to romp playfully with many wild animals, and allowed deer to scratch themselves, unawares, against his outstretched fingers, as if against hanging branches. Over the past two decades, he has been demonstrating his skills and teaching many thousands of students to develop similar—if more rudimentary—capabilities of their own. Law enforcement agencies have employed his tracking prowess against criminals.[7]

But the point is this. Under the tutelage of Stalking Wolf, the Apache scout who was his childhood mentor for 10 years, Brown was set numerous tasks of the imagination. Above all else, he was taught a penetrating and participative awareness of his surroundings. He had to understand them so well *from the inside*, and to merge so completely with them, that he passed through the woods without leaving the slightest ripple—even while taking in the significance of every disturbance on the breeze for miles around. He remarked of his advanced tracking exercises that, finally, he had to forget all the technical details (he studied literally scores of minute "pressure points" in each fragmentary track) and *become* the animal. In the end, he says, it was a matter of "tracking the spirit"—knowing the animal so well, and entering so deeply into the meaning of its tracks, that he could say what it would do next even where no physical evidence of the track remained.

Needless to say, "what it would do next" varied greatly from one species to another. The fox, the deer, and the raccoon each had its own way of being. Would the animal head upstream or downstream in a particular circumstance? Go around or over a barrier? Move toward its "home" or away—or execute a pattern of complex indirection? To grasp the individual animal's character, to take hold of its "archetype" in such a way as to predict its behavior in a previously unobserved circumstance—this is indeed to employ the imagination as an instrument of knowledge. And such knowledge, such training, appropriately framed, can engage even the small child in a wonderful way.

I wonder: once we have seen a child so engaged, could we ever again tolerate the reduction to a "cybernetic algorithm"—or any other algorithm—of the cat's motherly approach to her kitten?

---

7. For more on Tom Brown's story, see, for example, Brown and Watkins, 1979, and Brown, 1982.

PART THREE

The Electronic Word

15

Dancing with My Computer

I WRITE FOR A LIVING—painfully, line by line, word by word, endlessly revising under an intense compulsion until finally, by clarifying the words on paper, I succeed in clarifying my own thoughts. And it's true, some of the revising does occur on paper. But I quickly enter the edits on my computer, which is the primary venue for this excruciating "trial by composition." I can scarcely imagine producing a lengthy manuscript on an old-fashioned typewriter—every time my revisions got too thick on the pages, I'd have to retype the entire thing. With a computer, I simply enter the changes and print out a fresh copy of the whole. There's something reassuring about this prodigal issuance of clean drafts. After all, scribbling edits on top of edits on top of edits quickly becomes demoralizing—not to mention illegible.

You might ask, however, whether by now I'd have gained a more disciplined mind if my writing tools were simpler. I might have less editing to do. Necessity would constrain me to think carefully *first*, and only then commit the words to paper. My thought processes would be more clearly detached from the automatic reflexes of my fingers.

Well, I'm not so sure . . . . The question troubles me. For the moment, I will let it pass. But it does usefully remind me of something else.

How to make music at the keyboard

Have you noticed the typing habits of computer engineers—a great number of them, anyway? They type a sequence of characters in a convulsive burst, backspace through half of what they typed, then retype, pause, launch into another convulsive burst, backspace . . . . And so they create their software, lurching spasmodically from "if" to "then" to "else." Nor is it just their fingers that betray this cramped style. The whole body picks up on the messages from the fingers, becoming tense, rigid, fixated. One can easily imagine this rigidity leaking into the psyche—perhaps, in fact, we hear its faint overtones in many an email flame. More tangibly, there's the rash of carpal tunnel syndrome cases.

It is, of course, the obscenely compliant backspace key that encourages these habits. I, too, have suffered its consequences. But I've also wondered: can my computer, which echoes back and magnifies my nervous state with such maddening consistency, become thereby a kind of tutor leading me toward new inner disciplines? That is, if I listen to it with the right sort of alert detachment?

In particular, when I notice the deterioration of my typing, what is to prevent me from executing an about-face and approaching my keyboard like a pianist? Slow the pace down. Cultivate an easy, flowing, gentle rhythm. *Relax.* Let that graceful rhythm permeate my whole being. A bit silly, you say? Only if dancing to a Strauss waltz and to a jackhammer amount to pretty much the same thing. But I can vouch for the difference, for I have made exactly this experiment (not on the dance floor with piano and jackhammer, but with my computer), even if the trial is not yet anywhere near complete. It's taken two years to *begin* overcoming—what? The sly temptations of the machine? Or the tendencies of my own organism? (Where is the line between me and my computer?) Whatever the case, there is no question that the Strauss approach is more fun.

Our changing relation to language

When it comes to email, a great percentage of Net users don't even bother with the backspace key. People who are fully capable of composing articulate, pleasing text are content when at their terminals to send off scruffy messages they would never commit to stationery. Messages riddled with grammatical errors, typos, non sequiturs. Given the pressure of our urgent schedules, the attempt to do better hardly seems justified.

It is undeniable that our relationship to our own words has gotten looser and looser—just as it is well known that earlier peoples were bound much more intimately to language. Go far enough back, and the word exerts what now seems to us an almost magical influence. Word, thing, and self were bound together in a mystical unity. The penalty for blasphemy was not so much externally imposed as it was a direct inner experience of the disastrous consequence of one's own words.

The philologist Owen Barfield remarks somewhere that we can only begin to understand such otherwise incomprehensible events as the Inquisition by realizing that the medieval mind could scarcely distinguish between a man's words and beliefs on the one hand, and his innermost, essential being on the other. Language was participated in more fully, so that the distinction between speaking a monstrous untruth and *being* a monstrous untruth was nowhere near so clear-cut as it is today.

This is not to justify the Inquisition. Nor is it to say that we no longer participate in our language at all. When we speak, we still inhabit our words—and they take possession of us, even if only in more external ways. This extends right down to the distinctive embodiment each sylla-ble achieves within our physical speech apparatus. These formations, as gesture, extend throughout the entire body. (I've heard the claim made that, with fine enough observation, one can distinguish different ethnic groups by the ways they open a door or shake hands, because the spoken language lends a recognizably distinct character to all physical acts.) Even when we read silently or imagine someone speaking, our speech organs perform rudimentary, mimicking movements. Moreover, our dances to language begin early: researchers have found that the prenatal infant moves in rhythmic response to the words and sounds impinging upon the womb from outside.

Nevertheless, it's a long way from the Inquisition to the flame wars of the Net—despite occasional outward similarities! The restraints have been lifted, our intimate connections to our own meanings have dissolved, and we find ourselves free to speak any conceivable words that occur to us, with little thought for the consequences. But the crucial thing about every freedom is what we do with it. Could it be that here, too, our computers are inviting us to undertake a new discipline?

Can we make words our own?

Let me draw a picture, however one-sided: I sit at my keyboard and produce all letters of the alphabet with the same, undifferentiated, unexpressive, purely percussive strokes. Words, phrases, endless streams of thought flow effortlessly from me in all directions, with so little inner participation that I have reached the opposite extreme from the ancient word–self unity. I spew out my words easily, unthinkingly, at no psychic cost to myself, and launch them into a world already drowning in its own babble. The swelling torrent threatens to engulf every deeply considered word, every moment of attentive listening, every initiative emerging as a tender shoot from a timid heart. (Pity the unborn child who must dance to the frenetic tunelessness of this incessantly aggravating assault!) In too many of my words there is no serenity, no lucent depth of meaning, no set purpose—but only the restless discharge of random surface energies. And as I produce my own words, so I will likely judge those of others, discounting them as the superficial *disjecta membra* they too often really are.

We are, perhaps above all else, creatures of language. What effect does it have on us when we immerse ourselves in a sea of cheapened words? On the few occasions when I have spent a couple of nonstop hours reading USENET newsgroups, I have found my head almost hurting—a very different experience from, say, spending the same couple of hours reading a well-written book. A lot of this no doubt has to do with the difference between screen and paper, or between scanning and systematic reading.

But some of it, I suspect, also has to do with the rootlessness and disorder of the words themselves.

This line of thought quickly threatens to become snobbery, so I had better make an end of it. But not before asking whether our computers, networks, and bulletin boards, by mirroring and magnifying certain of our tendencies, are pointing out something important to us. Just when our words have become so easy and careless, so loose and aimless, so wedded to superficial logic while detached from the persons conversing—just, that is, when our words have become so *computerlike*—it seems a good time to consider what model of the human speaker we would embrace. And if we finally come to declare for a new, inner discipline of words, our computers—by faithfully magnifying our failures—will act as worthy disciplinarians.

16

THE TYRANNY OF THE DETACHED WORD

I CARE ABOUT THE WORDS I write, and that is where the danger begins. Just when I am most taken with their sound and rhythm, their logical articulation, their imagery and meaning—then the risk is greatest. For words always come from the past, whether from the previous moment's thinking or the earliest genesis of the race. The word's greatest gift—which is to preserve the thought and meanings that preceded us—is also its greatest threat, for this enshrined life of the past easily tyrannizes the delicate tracings of fresh thinking.

I'm sure most writers have had experiences like mine: I write a paragraph that "clicks," and then begin to feel pride in it. But as the larger text evolves, the "inspired" paragraph may no longer fit quite so well. Rather than throw out the valued words, however, I now seek to preserve them by wresting the context into a compatible shape.

Or, what is worse, at every step I allow my thinking itself to be controlled by the direction of the preceding words, so that a train of thought is always rigidly determined by what has gone before. I live in the pleasure of—and in obedience to—the word of the past. In this way, I conspire against the eruption of new meaning, the unexpected shift of perspective, the subtle nuances that might require me to junk all that fine writing I've just produced. Words now disconnected from any current thinking—dead words, alien words—suborn my writing to their own purposes.

We see something similar in group discussion. Over time, every group puts a distinctive spin upon its language, establishing god- and devil-terms, creating a rich background of word associations and, with its cognitive habits, gouging out familiar and comfortable ruts through the receptive terrain of meaning and inference. It is a useful exercise to observe how group discussions are governed by influences from the past. Once topic X or phrase Y comes up, does everyone seem to know instinctively where things are "supposed" to be headed?

Word processing

The computer as word processor strengthens the independent power of the words we have already produced. I sit, transfixed before a video screen, watching the cursor as it slides along and ejects one word after another—*my* words—almost as if it were acting under its own power. I easily find myself waiting half-consciously to see what words come out next. And they do come. When my thinking crystallizes so quickly and effortlessly into a finished, limiting structure of words, I am tempted to abandon further thinking prematurely, deferring to a kind of automatic thinking encouraged by an existing, visible word-structure that wants nothing more than to extend itself in a too-obvious, shallowly consistent, or unconscious manner. Then I no longer summon my words; they summon me.

Even the word-processing capabilities that might favor my more active involvement all too readily serve other ends. For example, the ease and rapidity with which I can cut and paste text enables my hands to keep up more closely with my mind, but also encourages me to reduce my thinking to the relatively mechanical manipulation of the words I see in front of me. To edit a text, then, is merely to rearrange symbols. Existing symbols and their "self-evident" relations—not the thinking that *makes* symbols—become almost everything.

Of course, no two people work in just the same way, and temptations vary. On my part, I had, until recently, thought myself relatively immune to these coercions, for I tend to linger over a paragraph, continually revising it until I am satisfied. But now I recognize how "broken up" and fragmented this process has been. I play with my verbal constructions piece by piece, shuffling words and matching incomplete grammatical forms until the whole finally comes together and seems right. My computer readily abets such a disjointed approach.

This working from the part to the whole substitutes for a sustained and intense thinking that grasps the whole before struggling to articulate it in a particular manner. I try to build a whole from parts rather than allow the parts to be determined by the whole. But this is precisely to give the already achieved and incompletely vested word veto power over my thinking.

Often, for example, I will type the first phrase of my next sentence without having any idea how that sentence will end—or even what it will say. Clearly, then, this opening phrase is determined more by the "natural flow" of the preceding words than by the integral requirements of my current thinking—which I haven't thought yet! And now what I *will* think is substantially constrained by the words I have already written. I may indeed work upon this process until the results seem fully satisfactory. But this domination of the word and fragmentation of my thinking—to one degree or another inescapable with or without a computer—is exactly what I need to work *against* if I would realize thinking's highest potential.

Thinking and physical activity. I have just recently been trying to write some of my briefer texts by hand, away from the computer. But I find within myself a surprising resistance to the experiment, even as another part of me senses its healthiness. My continual urge is to abandon the difficult effort to think through the matter at hand, and revert instead to the muscular *action* of typing. It feels like this would be to *get on more quickly with the job.*

But, of course, this is not true. If anything, there is a natural antagonism between thinking and physical activity. We tend to purchase our thoughts *at the expense of* activity. Vigorous activity—culminating in "fight or flight" at the extreme—throws us into instinctive, automatic behavior. The natural pose of intense, concentrated thinking, on the other hand, is found in a body held alertly still—almost turned in on itself (Rodin's sculpture has become a stereotypical image of this)—or else in gentle, rhythmical activity that calms the mind.

It is easy to observe how, as an important thought begins to take hold of us, we often pause for a moment, stopping whatever we were doing. It is as if the energies that might have gone into physical movement are diverted toward the emerging thought.

Original thinking is always difficult; it requires a discipline of will to quiet the body and summon the powers of attention necessary for cognitive exploration. It is much easier to grasp at the thoughts that "come naturally," mediated in less than full consciousness by physical activity. The computer, as we have seen, cooperates with us in this.

Words given by eye, ear, and hand. To *see* my own words visibly forming even before my thinking has consummated its creative embrace of the truth is to threaten with abortion the fruit of that union. For, of all our senses, the eye helps us most to freeze the world into finished "things." These things easily become "mere givens" due to the eyes' passivity: we do not feel or consciously participate in the touch of the light upon the sense organs. And so the visible words I type onto the screen tend all the more to penetrate me with established meanings, whereas any genuine *thinking* I am engaged in must work in the opposite direction, struggling through to the right meanings and even finding a way to invest its words with new meaning. To be fully conscious is to be master of one's words, not their pawn.

The word ringing in my ears—whether spoken by myself or others—is not quite so easily frozen; its "ringing" is not only the aural shuddering of its outer body, but also an inner resonance of meaning not yet reduced to a single, mathematically pure tone. To hear a word—this was true, at least, until the advent of recorded speech—was to hold it in a quivering, semantic balance while one read inflection and facial expression, timbre and gesture, rhythm and breathing—and through all these, the intention of a Self. We knew instinctively the multivalence of all meaning.

So, also, the word I write with my own hand may well correspond to a thought more rounded and fully gestated, for the difficulty of editing words once committed to paper requires a more careful and complete inner activity to *precede* the outer act of writing. And somehow the "analog" motions of writing make the words more intimately and expressively my own than the efficient, drumlike repetition of nearly identical keystrokes. It is not at all the same experience to write (or speak) the words "ugly" and "fair," whereas little difference can be found in typing them.

Such matters become insignificant only when one forgets that *expression*—in matters great and small—is what distinguishes and shapes all human life for good and ill. Nothing is fully human that is not word-like, and every word we express, whether through speech or gesture or coherent pattern of action, either augments or diminishes our life. If the stage actor must be aware of the significance borne by every minutest detail of movement or speech, then we who "act" our own lives should not forget the same truth.

From words to information

The computer is becoming ever more sophisticated in its drive to detach the word from thinking. Outliners mechanically reshuffle for us whatever words already happen to be there, never tiring of their labor, and minimizing the requirement for us to *think* our way through to the "best words in the best order." When a machine does the shuffling, our subdued attention need only recognize when something reasonable has "clicked into place."

More aggressively, new, experimental software actually guides our writing by continually offering up words and phrases to extend the last thing we typed. This generosity is made possible by an analysis of our previous patterns of use. (One hopes we really *were* thinking back then . . . .) But the analysis works only upon the external *form* of our words, not their shades of meaning; it trains us in the repetition of familiar forms that do our "thinking" for us.

Reflecting afterward upon a friend's gesture or word, I may suddenly realize with a jolt: "Oh, so *that's* what he meant!" I finally see through a certain surface meaning with which previously I may have been content, and thereby grasp a meaning that was not at all evident before. Something like this *seeing through* is required in every apprehension of new meaning.

But seeing through is exactly what the computer's active intelligence cannot do. The information processor *demands* text in which outer form and intended meaning are as predictable as possible.[1] The unprecedented use of a word, the unexpected metaphor, may lay bare for the first time a sublime truth—but it will only cause the information processor to stumble. For the information processor classifies, stores, links, and searches text based solely on surface appearance—the "shape" of the words—and is programmed on the assumption that these shapes can be mapped to a set of preestablished meanings.

Only as our language approaches perfect formality (exemplified by pure logic or mathematics) does the form of a text become an absolutely reliable key to its meaning. Unfortunately, however, this perfection is achieved precisely because the meaning has finally disappeared altogether—a formal language is all form and no content. It waits to be

---

1. I am not speaking here of the information processor's passive reception of words typed by the user, but rather of its abilities to "read," "understand," and "intelligently manipulate" text. Such abilities, currently under intense development, will become increasingly central to the computer's role in society.

applied to something—but once it is applied it is no longer formal, and no longer so easily processed by a computer.

Where is the thinking self? In general, the more abstract and empty (that is, formal) our thought and language become, the easier it is for us to sound off in superficially cogent verbal emptiness—and the easier it is for a computer to manipulate the text. The *thinking self* disappears behind a cloud of words, and is carried along passively by the words themselves in conventional combinations—the subconscious syntax of one's cultural milieu, mechanically executed, and therefore mechanically readable.

This is not surprising when you consider that the programming languages specifying what a computer can *do* are themselves formal; by design they exhibit no meaning except what is on the surface, where the only "meaning" is the external form. That is why the computer can read and compile them without ambiguity. It will not find itself betrayed by original and unpredictable meanings shining *through* the words. There is no danger that a metaphorical *do, begin,* or *continue* will slip into the program's stream of instructions, pregnant with new and unanticipated meaning.

Many researchers in cognitive science think they spy the essence of intelligence in the formal shuffling of symbols. They have become so used to the detached word that they find it natural to set words in motion and then to take the result as thinking itself. The separation of the word from thinking becomes final, with the now-mummified life of the word substituting for thinking. No wonder cognitive scientists spend so much time grappling with the question whether meaning "means" anything at all.

Word and image

It is clear enough that computers have other potentials for the human speaker beside those mentioned here. What the screen and keyboard elicit from me will not be what they elicit from everyone else. But one notes with a touch of anxiety how difficult it may be to resist the pull of the computer away from active thinking and toward mere association, convention, and formal abstraction. One's fears only increase upon seeing

191

how naturally and harmoniously the computer and television appear to have conspired. Sven Birkerts, who teaches writing to freshmen at Harvard, tells how

> I read through their first papers—so neatly word-processed, so proudly titled with the bold-faced curlicues that the technology makes possible—and my heart sinks. The writing is almost always flat, monotonous, built up of simple units. Immigrant prose. But no, immigrant prose, clumsy though it may be, is often alert to the textures and imagistic possibilities of the language. This writing is bland and slippery, unpressurized by mind. It shows, if anything, the influence of rhetoric and televised banality. The prose has little or no musicality and lacks any depth of field; it is casually associative in movement, syntactically inert, and barren of interesting reference. Complexity is nonexistent.[2]

Ironically, technology that was supposed to liberate us from the "tyranny of linear, rationally structured words" in favor of image, intuition, and pattern, is guaranteeing that whatever words remain are as linear and, in a superficial sort of way, as rationally structured as possible. After all, the essence of linearity is not that words should be stuck in a fixed order, but rather that their *meanings* should be stuck, so that all ordering possibilities are precisely defined and mechanically executable from the start. This is exactly what the programmable and information-processing computer asks of us. We must leave our words alone—sleeping—and may bestow no imaginative kiss upon their inert forms, lest they waken and dance free of the predictable structures in which the machine has snared them.

But debase the word and you have debased the image as well, for the image only "speaks" through its word-nature. What is becoming of this nature is evident enough in the prevailing conviction that it is more important for images to make an impact than to possess meaning. "If you catch people's attention, at least you have a chance to say something meaningful. Fail to catch their attention, and you lose your opportunity."

---

2. Birkerts, 1992.

And so the image, too, becomes in its own way a matter of calculation, influencing us from without rather than coming alive as new revelation within.

How many images assaulting us today are intended to reveal a more exalted truth—to lead upward to comprehension—and how many instead lead downward to instinct and mechanism, where "intuition" degenerates into the sort of gut feeling that coerces our buying choices, and where the kind of distracting, pleasurable sensations one feeds on at the cinema are all we can hope for?

• • •

Yet, in the end, the computer performs an invaluable service for us. In displaying the detached word and bringing it into a kind of lifelike motion, the information machine challenges us to discover within ourselves the place of mastery over words. What are the sources of our meanings, and how can we consciously draw upon those sources to shape a technology that, unguarded, would destroy meaning (and therefore also destroy the world)?

The word's dreary passage through the information machine may enable us to recognize the dessication of meaning, and the mechanization of thinking, to which we ourselves are liable. It is we who have invested the machine with its computational prowess, which we skillfully abstracted from our own patterns of thought. Now we must choose: to submit our future to these automated abstractions, or else to exercise our own thinking capacities in a way that threatens to disfranchise the highly capable devices sitting on our desks.

But the choice need not be posed quite so grandly. Everything hinges on how I receive and work with those "inspired" words on my screen, staring at me from out of the past.

17

THE GREAT INFORMATION HUNT

IT REALLY IS AMAZING, this odd acquisitiveness with which hordes of academics, engineers, cyberpunks, and self-advertised "infonauts" roam the Net looking for treasure troves of information, like so much gold. They hear the cry—"There's information in them thar nodes!"—and the rush is on. Who knows what they do with this gold when they find it, but for now most of the excitement seems to be simply in discovering that it's there—*on the Net!* It's almost as if the "electrons" themselves exuded a certain fascination—a kind of spell or subliminal attraction.

So-called Netsurf discussion groups and publications have been created for the sole purpose of identifying and sharing Net "finds." An announcement reached my screen a short while ago, advertising a new forum of this sort and promising experiences comparable to the great world explorations of the past or to the adventures of a fantasy novel.

The dissonance occurs only when one tries to imagine these same adventurers standing in a library, surrounded in three dimensions by records of human achievement far surpassing what is now Net-accessible. Would there, in these surroundings, be the same, breathless investigation of every room and shelf, the same shouts of glee at finding this collection of art prints or that provocative series of essays or these journalistic reports on current events?

It's hard to imagine such a response. But then, if the excitement is not about actual encounters with expressions of the human spirit, what *is* it about? One gets the feeling that a lot of it has to do with a futuristic, almost religious vision of what the Net is becoming—and all these interim discoveries are more valued for the progress they indicate than for themselves. Signs for the faithful. Epiphanies.

Just what the essential vision is, however, remains obscure. To all appearances it has something to do with a peculiar sort of insularity or privacy paradoxically cast as openness to the All. I can "touch" all these resources from *right here at my desk*—almost while remaining shut up within myself. There's no need to go out into the world; I participate in an alternative universe, all of which maps into my own corner of "cyberspace." It's a kind of return to the womb, promising both self-sufficiency and universal, solipsistic powers.

But perhaps there's an element of the video game here as well—the adventurous quest to rack up points for booty captured. (The nature of the booty in a video game never counts much for itself; it's for scoring points, and "information" works just as well.) In the best case, this is a team game, not a competition among individuals; we can all take pleasure in the latest finds, happily reporting our discoveries to each other while sustaining ourselves amid the common euphoria. The euphoria seems only too justified, for no one can doubt that the treasures will grow ever richer—and in tantalizingly unpredictable ways. So the doctrines of endless Enlightenment and Progress become the compelling subtext of a universal video game few can resist playing.

Nor can one dismiss the drug analogy. If cyberpunks, the electronic underground, and the science fiction writers celebrating cyberspace all suggest such an analogy, they're not alone. Few surfers disguise the rush they get from their Net fixes, and the terms of a new, psychedelic vision are now common currency within the Net culture as a whole. Michael Benedikt puts the vision to words:

> The design of cyberspace is, after all, the design of another life-world, a parallel universe, offering the intoxicating prospect of actually fulfilling—with a technology very nearly achieved—a dream thousands of years old: the dream of transcending the physical world, fully alive, at will, to dwell in some beyond—to be empowered or enlightened there, alone or with others, and to return.[1]

As Geoff Nunberg remarked, "it's not surprising to find Timothy Leary on the editorial board of *Mondo 2000*, having decided to drop in again now that things are once more getting interesting."[2]

And, finally, television offers a more suggestive model for understanding the Net than is usually appreciated. Window-based user interfaces together with innovative software design make it increasingly easy to fill one's screen with a kind of busy, ever-changing clutter. Watching the screen as things happen—even if it is only text scrolling—readily induces a semiconscious, "coasting" mental state not too different from the half-hypnotized passivity of much television viewing. Partly as a result of this, the entertainment, novelty, and "impact" quotient of Net content is often emphasized—and will be more so as the competition for attention grows slicker and fiercer.

Even the fate of whatever active consciousness remains is precarious. The computer's information-processing tools substitute an easy, automatic activity for higher forms of conscious control. This can be seen, for example, with the emergence of hypertext navigation on the Net. The navigator is invited toward that same, distracted, associational manner he may already have learned in front of the television screen. (The hypertext "button" is close cousin to the remote control button, and the joltingly syncopated rhythms of channel surfing prove equally apt for Netsurfing.) Hypertext, in the absence of a determined discipline, can discourage any

1. Benedikt, 1991: 131.

2. Geoff Nunberg, language commentary for *Fresh Air*, National Public Radio, 6 July 1994.

sustained attention to another's train of thought, substituting a collage of impressions for concentration, and a flaccid openness for the muscular reception of new and difficult meaning.

If the Net's information riches are less daunting than those of the library, perhaps it is because we don't really have to *deal* with them; we need only yield ourselves to the information-processing software.

All these surmises aside, the one thing everyone seems to agree on is that the Great Information Hunt is now under way. Putting information online, buying and selling information, unearthing the decisive informational nugget in an out-of-the-way place, massaging information more effectively with software, adapting the labor market to an information economy, giving everyone equal access to public information, preventing violations of private information—all these concerns testify to how many aspects of society have been assimilated (rhetorically, at least) to the imperatives of information.

One might have expected the craze for information to be qualified by judgments of reliability, accuracy, relevance, helpfulness, and so on. But somehow this peculiar word, "information," has escaped the constraints hindering all merely mortal terms.[3] This is shown by the fact that no one who hails the Age of Information would be equally ecstatic about an Age of Opinion, or Age of Gossip, or Age of Random Bits. Apparently, *information as such*—anything storable in a computer—is now felt to possess an objective value sufficient to underwrite the New Age. This aura of objectivity is partly owing to the development of a mathematical theory of information—a theory from which, as it happens, all considerations of meaning are intentionally excluded. That is, the objective aura is achieved by eliminating from view everything related to the *content* of information. This raises the question whether the coming age might actually be the Age of No Content, or the Age of Meaninglessness.

---

3. This is a point Theodore Roszak makes in *The Cult of Information* (p. 8). Roszak's book contains a valuable treatment of the "cult" from many different angles.

Descent from wisdom

There are occasions in our lives when we come upon something priceless—something, to be sure, that we might also have encountered on the Net. For example, a transforming work of art, an author whose insights mark a turning point in our own development, or a rare friend. But, of course, we don't simply *find* the pricelessness; we must live our way into it. If an author profoundly alters the course of my life, his influence will almost certainly arise from my long, intense, and perhaps disturbing contemplation of his writing.

It is clear enough that one doesn't go surfing the Net for *such* experiences—and a good thing, too, since only a fool spends his days looking for deep transformation or the turning point of his life. One must attend to the tasks of the moment—hoping, perhaps, for the unexpected visitation, but content to let the day's work yield a day's harvest. Here, in the "uneventful" expression of discipline and devotion, is where wisdom, growth, and transformation take hold of us. They can take hold only from within.

Such wisdom cannot be embedded in the Net (or in the library), either as distributed information or as anything else. Wisdom is a capacity, a quality of one's activity, a gift for seizing meaning from life. Because it knows itself and is moved only by its own necessities, wisdom is the very substance of freedom.

Virtually everyone acknowledges the distinction between information and wisdom. It is regarded as a truism. An anonymous formula circulating on the Net captures a common reading of the distinction:

DATA
    organized is
        INFORMATION
            made meaningful is
                KNOWLEDGE
                    linked to other knowledge is
                        INTELLIGENCE
                            granted experience is
                              WISDOM

This runs under the heading, "Data to Wisdom Chain," and it shows how easily the truism can be read as a lie—exactly the lie, moreover, that helps to explain the Great Information Hunt. *Data and information are the raw materials of wisdom.* That is the lie.

Your wisdom and mine—such as it may be—arises from a meeting between ourselves and the wisdom speaking from our surroundings. Only when, as knower, I confront the world itself, can I make its wisdom my own. I do not manufacture wisdom from bits and pieces; I call it down, out of the not-yet-comprehended, through an inner union with it. Data, on the other hand, are the final, abstract precipitate of a fading wisdom—a lifeless and meaningless residue. There can be no reconstitution of wisdom solely from this residue.[4]

I do not confront the world through my computer, any more than I confront it through a tape recorder, television, or book. And when I start with data—the bits and bytes, the pure, computational elements of the computer's own shadow-cogitations—I have removed myself as far from the world as it is humanly possible to do. Given the most extensive data set imaginable, I cannot reconstruct the world from it. First I have to know what the data are *about,* and this forces me inexorably back toward a new starting point in wisdom. Data that contained their own meaning would not be data.

On converting ourselves to information

The Chain and the Great Information Hunt are of a piece, for the conviction that information leads to knowledge and wisdom is what justifies the Hunt—or would justify it if the conviction weren't patently false. "Many people believe," Edward de Bono has observed, "that if you collect enough information it will do your thinking for you and that the analysis of information leads to ideas. Both are wrong."[5]

---

4. I discuss this matter more extensively in chapter 23, "Can We Transcend Computation?"

5. Quoted in Calamai, 1993.

To see what the Great Information Hunt is really telling us, we need to recognize one thing: the Net is the most pronounced manifestation yet of our tendency to reconceive the human interior in the manner of an exterior, and then to project it onto the external world. Look at almost any inner aspect of the human being, and you will find its abstracted, externalized ghost in the Net. The outer substitutes for the inner: text instead of *the word*; text processing instead of *thinking*; information instead of *meaning*; connectivity instead of *community*; algorithmic procedure instead of *willed human behavior*; derived images instead of *immediate experience*. At the same time, by means of a ubiquitous metaphor of mentality, popular discourse levitates the Net somewhere between mind and abstraction—and not infrequently strikes toward mystical heights.

Two truths of analytic psychology bear on this. The first is that we can only project those inner contents of which we have more or less lost awareness. It is the progressive dimming of our interior spaces that enables us to to imagine them out there, objectified in some sort of global, electronic, "central nervous system."

The second truth is that when we project aspects of ourselves, we are driven to recover them—often madly and in inappropriate places. Surely at least part of the reigning excitement over the Net's informational riches has to do with this felt possibility of completing ourselves "out there." If the infatuated lover is convinced that to lose his beloved would be to lose the most important part of his own life, so, too, the compulsive Netsurfer knows that the potentials of his intelligence, the drama of deep discovery, his hopes for mastering life, all lie somewhere out on the Net—if only he can get the proper software and hardware tools for conquering cyberspace.

I said above that "only a fool" spends his days looking for deep transformation or the turning point of his life. Yet, projection and infatuation make fools even of the best of us. The most satisfying explanation I'm aware of for some of my own experiences on the Net and for those of many I see around me is that, having been more or less alienated from the sources of our own wisdom and selfhood, we hope somehow to gain renewed life by "electrifying" our sensibilities from without. The currents of raw data and information on the Net, coaxed upward by software toward an *appearance* of wisdom, serve the purpose well—not altogether unlike the drug trips of the Sixties.

And yet (as so often happens with those who speak of projection) I may be in danger here of missing the more literal truth. It is, after all, *true* that I can find more and more of my self out on the Net. My concern, for example, about the privacy of information, reflects the fact that I have become "indexable" by Social Security number, credit checkable by bank account number, morally judicable by expenditure record, and intellectually measurable by academic transcript.

In an earlier era, the knowledge anyone else might have about me was largely *personal* knowledge—knowledge of my character—and the prevailing form of privacy invasion was gossip (or physical coercion). The invasion was something people did to each other, whereas now it looks more and more like a mere manipulation of abstractions in cyberspace. But, then, abstractions in cyberspace must be what we are becoming.

There is no question that the human being today (like the world itself) is increasingly re-presented as a collection of information, and that this abstract representation can be "out there"—on the Net—in a way that I myself cannot be. Or, rather, once could not be. This points toward a consideration similar to one I have already submitted elsewhere in this book: if we choose to reduce ourselves more and more to bodies of information, then it will eventually become true that we can reside on the Net and discover all there is of each other there. Our projections of ourselves will have replaced ourselves. Then it really will be the communion of human beings—whatever husks are left of such communion—that we conveniently gauge in bits per second.

What does the computer see?

When I send an email message to a correspondent, it is quite obvious that the computer and network perform a service similar to stationery and the postal service. My words appear on my correspondent's screen, as fully available for inspection as if they had been set down on paper. And, of course, he *can* print them on paper, or forward them to any number of others, or edit them for incorporation in something he is writing, or store them for retrieval five years from now, or combine them with many other texts and then subject the whole to some sort of programmed analysis.

Why, then, should one speak derogatorily of the "reduction to bits" or the re-presentation of ourselves as abstractions, when we now have *at least* the capabilities for effective communication that we had previously?

The question is reasonable as far as it goes. It just doesn't go far enough. *Nowhere* is the computer employed simply for its ability to reproduce the function of earlier technologies. Or, if that is how things typically start, it is not how they end. Seymour Papert does not import the computer into the classroom so that young children can read books on the screen instead of on paper; he wants them to *program* the computer, and thereby to harmonize their minds with the computer's algorithmic intelligence. The Wall Street brokerage firms do not pour millions into computer programming merely to duplicate their old trading systems; the new software packages execute sophisticated trading strategies of their own devising. Nor are the global databases, now expanding at lightspeed, just miniaturized filing cabinets and libraries; they are libraries reconceived as informational structures—raw material for the computer's logic.

The computer has not ushered us into an age of information; we already lived in one. What the computer gives us is the age of *automated* information *processing*.

While I am enjoying all the novel ways to perform old, familiar tasks (such as exchanging messages with a friend), it is easy to ignore how the computer insinuates new elements into the picture. It may not seem important that personal correspondence must be translated into ones and zeros for transmission, and then translated back again—and for my reading of a friend's message it really doesn't matter. But the necessity for the translation tells me something important about the nature and limitations of the computer—which is also to say, the nature and limitations of the "nervous system" upon which we are reconstructing society. When it comes to the things this nervous system can do in its own right—the human and social functions we entrust to it—the limitations are exactly what matter.

In sum: the computer's miming of older, simpler ways is hardly the decisive point. Or, you might say, the *miming itself* is the decisive point. None of the earlier technologies exhibited this sort of independent, logical, imitative capacity. The computer acts in its own right, and the quality of its actions—or, rather, the strictly quantitative and logical basis of its actions—challenges us in a way that the familiar activities it now mimes did not.

To say that the message I see issuing from my computer consists "merely of ones and zeros" is a common misunderstanding. What I see are the words of my friend. The complementary—and far more dangerous—misunderstanding occurs when I claim that the computer itself transcends a logic of ones and zeros. It does not. What the computer sees issuing from me is *information.*[6] And everything it does is founded on *this* kind of seeing.

A dream of alchemy

The computer willingly places its mimicking intelligence at our service. All it asks of us is one small thing: that we allow it to start with information or data, and to proceed from there by means of mechanized logic. In working with the computer's distinctive capabilities, we must not start with our experience of the world, but with "facts" conforming to a database. We must not start with our own perception or thinking, but rather must develop tools (as one Net voice put it) "to explore vast information spaces in search of matching data or objects"—the objects, of course, being such things as huge arrays of searchable text strings. In

---

6. According to the theory of information, fathered by Claude Shannon in the 1940s, the amount of information in a message is a measure of the message's "statistical unexpectedness." Lincoln's Gettysburg address might have exactly the same quantity of information as a few statements of arithmetic addition or subtraction. In its standard form, the theory makes no claim to reckon with content as meaning. This is perfectly legitimate. The problem occurs, as I suggest in chapter 23, when the attempt is made to leap upward from the mathematical treatment of information (taken as the more fundamental level) to meaning.

general, we must not start with our *selves* as knowers, but only with those informational re-presentations of self and world distributed throughout the Net.

What the computer asks of us, in short, is that we trust it to pull us up along the Data to Wisdom Chain. The theorists of information are more than happy to encourage us in thinking this possible. Philosopher and cognitive scientist Fred Dretsky opens his book *Knowledge and the Flow of Information* with the words, "In the beginning there was information; the word came later." The hope resounding through the rhetorical atmosphere of the information age is that, having submitted our lives and society to a logic of ones and zeros, we can ascend again to meaning—and not only meaning, but unheard of and glorious meanings, suitable for a New Age of Information.

This optimism—as irrepressible as it is misguided—finds an infinite variety of expressions. For example, a message with the following signature block[7] made its way into my email box only a few minutes ago:

> "The shortness of life, the frailty of reason, and the dull routine of senseless activity do not allow us to gain much knowledge, and what we do learn we all too soon forget." (N. Copernicus, Astronomer and Scientist)

> "Give me enough speed and memory, & I'll outrun life, out think reason, zap routine, gain on the brain, and forget NONE of it." (Greg Stewart, Computer Artist and Small Business-man)[8]

"Gain on the brain." Once the human interior has been reimagined as brain function, there is no difficulty in picturing the Net as a kind of extension of human mentality. What naturally follows, as I have already suggested, is the hope of recovering the self out on the Net. And just so far as this hope is vested in computational activity, it entails a naive faith in

---

7. It is part of Net culture to include quotations or other text, along with the sender's name and identifying information, at the end of messages. This concluding section of the message is called the *signature block*, or the *.sig*.

8. Used by permission of Greg Stewart (overyoured@aol.com).

the computer's ability to transmute information into meaning. The modern forty-niners panning for informational gold are chasing a dream of logically programmed alchemy.

From information to power

Given the inflated expectations for Net-enhanced minds, one wonders where all the new Supermen are to be found. Not, apparently, on the Net. There, one typically encounters a culture of stunning illiteracy—by which I mean not only an unfamiliarity with the broad literature of human understanding, but also a chronic inattention to those subtle shifts of meaning that can radically transform the "bits and bytes" of any discussion. As Peter Calamai, an editor of the *Ottawa Citizen* newspaper, remarked to the 1993 International FreeNet Conference,

> The level of public discussion on the Net is appallingly shallow .... The ability to communicate instantaneously seems to discourage reflection. You can see how far we have to go by looking at the minutes from the Mechanics Institutes that flourished in many 19th century rural towns in Canada .... The level of discussion—the insight into the human condition, the recognition of underlying values—recorded in those Mechanics Institutes minutes is far more profound than anything I've yet seen on the Net.[9]

Presumably those earlier generations still realized that understanding is not a collection of things or "knowledge constructs," but rather a way, a path of personal growth. It is experience illumined from within by careful, sustained reflection. It is a habit of observation and a discipline of thinking given penetrating force by a trained imagination. If information is truly something we can collect—gathering it to ourselves like squirrels hoarding acorns—if it can be made into a commodity with a price and subjected to trading in a futures pit, then it is not food for the human spirit. What ennobles and gives wisdom cannot be sold, and will never yield itself to a Boolean search.

9. Calamai, 1993.

What *can* be sold is "empowerment," and that is the real significance of the passion for information. Within a technologically influenced culture fascinated by the means of invisibly effective constraint, the field of information justifies its advertisement in at least one regard: it readily yields to appropriate wizardry, congealing into instruments of power.

So we encounter another paean to information—one sung even more loudly and more insistently than the hymn of Enlightenment. The following "information sheet" about the respected quarterly journal, *The Information Society*, offers one of the more prosaic variations on the paean's text:

> An "information revolution" is clearly underway. The exponential growth in computational capability per unit dollar will continue at least for the next several decades. Communication bandwidth is undergoing simultaneous exponential growth. Connectivity among individuals, companies and nations is forming what some are calling "worldnet", "cyberspace", "global grid" or "the matrix." These combined trends are leading us into an Information Society in which wealth, power and freedom of action derive from access to, and effective use of, information.

We might have thought it strange that wisdom and freedom should cohabit so easily with wealth and power upon a couch of information. This is no traditional marriage! It was once claimed that "the truth will make you free," but surely *that* freedom has little to do with wealth and power—as little, in fact, as truth has to do with information. Freedom is what took hold of Aleksandr Solzhenitsyn when he first stepped into the Gulag and resolved to die toward all those human ties, possessions, and interests that had formerly engaged him, and to embrace his new life for whatever it might offer. As bereft as anyone can be of information, wealth, or power, he remained freer than his captors.

Loss of the self

But none of this explains *how* information and the Net lead to empowerment. We can understand this connection only by first appreciating a
paradox: the computer's cleanly logical necessities tend to induce seizures
of chaotic arbitrariness.

We have, of course, already seen hints of this. The Great Information
Hunt, for all the impressive rationalism of its software tools, stands for the
scattered, distracted mind, impelled by automatic reactivity. It stands for a
half-awake, association-based consciousness flitting from one Net link to
another and dissipating mental energies in a formless, curiosity-driven
excursion. Most of all, it stands for the dissolution of the sovereign self.
The effort to recollect the self from the Net's perfectly well-behaved envi-
rons results only in a further dispersal of the self—a loss of coherence.

It is not particularly odd that this should be so. A sheen of orderly
information and logical discipline all too readily masks an utter irrationality. The figure of the fool in literature sometimes illustrates this well, as
when he interprets conversation in an absurdly literal, yet perfectly "logical" manner.

Michael Heim is, I think, pointing in this same direction when he
notes how "logic can move like a juggernaut adrift from any personal
engagement with its subject matter. Someone with a great deal less experience, for example, can make us feel compelled to accept a conclusion
we know instinctively to be wrong." The compelling power arises precisely from operating in a vacuum, where everything *must* be just so. The
advantage of a vacuum is that the meanings and complexities of the world
cannot muddy things—or can do so only in carefully controlled ways.
"We can be perfectly logical," writes Heim, "yet float completely adrift
from reality."

Heim sees this characteristic in the Boolean operators with which we
search through information, sifting out "hits" by keyword. "Through
minute logical apertures, we observe the world [of information] much like
a robot rapidly surveying the surface of things. We cover an enormous
amount of material in an incredibly short time, but what we see comes

through narrow thought channels."[10] These narrow slits present us with a collection of discrete fragments, but never with a *view*, nor even with fragments of the world itself. We receive, rather, bits of informational abstractions: data, derived images, vagrant text wrenched free of any speaker.

This floating adrift from reality is, I think, one of the preeminent symptoms of the information age. It is possible only when we do not possess ourselves with any firmness. The glittering glass shards of information can absorb my attention, drawing me this way and that, only when I lack self-mastery and so must attempt to recollect myself from the Net. But the attempt inevitably fails. The Net's distributed information does not enable me to "pull myself together," for it provides no principle of coherence. All the intricate, informational linkages of cyberspace notwithstanding, an inescapable arbitrariness rules.

The upshot of all this is that the clear, bracing air of a well-delineated "information space" is never wholly purified of its more fetid and murky double. The two belong together. One can, in this regard, venture a fairly safe prediction: over the coming years, fringe Net phenomena such as flame wars, weird impersonations, the more bizarre forms of underground culture, pornographic commerce, manifestations of psychosis . . . will grow increasingly pronounced and erratic, while at the same time the reasoned mechanisms for filtering "strict business" from the more chaotic background noise of the Net will steadily gain in effectiveness.

We have already long been witnessing a kind of rationalization of social processes (business, government, scientific research, warfare, education) against a backdrop of meaninglessness, alienation, pathology, disintegrating social ties, a permanent underclass—rather as science preserves an elegant, mathematically clean, probabilistic theory erected upon the dark, chaotic substrate of quantum randomness. Our ruling abstractions abandon the world to chaos in favor of "systems thinking" and schemas for the

---

10. Heim, 1993: 20, 22.

effective manipulation of things. And the Net gives us the best opportunity yet to construct an entirely new world of sterile abstraction, superimposed upon the demons of our subconscious.

And, finally, empowerment. Neither you nor I nor anyone in the world can exercise power over someone who is fully in possession of himself. The self-possessed individual moves only according to his own necessities, even as he serves the needs of others. *This* is what we should hope to celebrate: the end of empowerment. We do not need power, whether over others or over the world. We need wisdom, and the ability to connect with our own destinies.

If the Net empowers, it is by subverting our self-possession, substituting for it a compelling yet arbitrary and fundamentally irrational show of logic—a fool's logic—ultimately related to the logic that says, "buy this car because of the beautiful woman lying on it." To be sure, each of us recognizes the absurdity of the logic—but it is exactly this strange combination of recognition on the one hand, and submission to the absurdity on the other (the ads do, after all, work) that testifies to the loss of self. Television has taught us much about this loss. The interactive Net, by rendering even our conscious *activity* passive and automatic, promises to teach us a great deal more.

The Net's empowerment is the correlate of a dimmed consciousness, which in turn allows the outward scattering of the self's inner resources. On the one hand, the scattered self lacks sufficient presence of mind to resist the arbitrary impulses that serve power; on the other hand, it seeks to exercise its own power, since the experience of power has always substituted easily for a genuine coming to oneself.

The dimmed consciousness itself has two sides, answering to the Net's double potential. There is a contraction, by which we adapt our thought life to those narrow slits, surveying the world with the cold, piercing logic of the dragon's eye. Then there is what remains outside the circle of this contraction—a world of meaning unattended to, and therefore sunk into the subconscious, where it moves us according to a shadow "logic" now beyond our reach.

These two aspects of the dimmed consciousness—a visible but creatively impotent logic, and its invisible, irrationally potent shadow—cooperate quite well in subjecting us to the appeal of the beautiful woman. Like the "clear-toned sirens" of the *Odyssey*, she offers wisdom and the knowledge of "all things that come to pass upon the fruitful earth."[11] Only such a temptress could beguile us into this madly compulsive pursuit of information and the technological innovation it brings, with no one stopping to ask what any of the gadgetry has to do with the fulfillment of the human task.

Warned of the sirens' threat by a goddess, Odysseus stopped the ears of his comrades with wax to block out the deadly song. Then he had himself bound to the ship's mast, so that he could listen freely without danger of being overcome. By no means immune to temptation (upon hearing the subtle harmonies, he fought fiercely to be loosed from his bonds), he was able to prevent disaster only by virtue of this inspired forethought.

Such insistence upon wakeful experience, combined with resolute preventive measures to compensate for personal weakness, remains the appropriate response to the seductive promise of informational omniscience. We must somehow contrive the sturdy mast and the restraining ropes from within ourselves. The discipline may be difficult, but in finding an answer to the enticing song of self-extinction, we will have contributed far more to society than by adding our bones to the sirens' mouldering heap on the forlorn shores of cyberspace.

---

11. Homer *Odyssey*, 12.184–91.

18

And the Word Became Mechanical

ON A BLACK NIGHT in the early 1980s, a fierce scream congealed the darkness deep within MIT's Artificial Intelligence Laboratory. The late-working engineer who went to investigate discovered Richard Stallman—one of the nation's most brilliant programmers—sitting in tears and screaming at his computer terminal, "How can you do this? How can you do this? *How can you do this?*"[1]

The image is no doubt provocative, revealing as it does a striking urge to personify the computer. And yet, perhaps we make too much of such occurrences. After all, the computer is hardly unique in this respect. Don't I curse the door that jams, implore my car's engine to start on an icy morning, and kick a malfunctioning TV with more than just mechanical intent? The fact is that we manifest a strong tendency to personify all the contrivances of our own devising. The computer simply takes its place among the numerous other objects to which, with a kind of animistic impulse, we attribute life.

---

1. Cobb, 1990.

This may be the point worth holding on to, however. Once we acknowledge our anthropomorphizing compulsions, we must immediately grant that the computer is ideally designed to provoke them. Whatever our considered, philosophical understanding of the computer and its intelligence, we also need to reckon with this "animistic" tendency—at least we do if we seek self-knowledge, and if we would prevent our own subconscious impulses from infecting our philosophical inquiries.

The embodiment of intelligence

Anyone can write a program causing a computer to display stored text and stored images on a screen. So, at a bare minimum, a computer can do anything a book can do—it can present us with a physics textbook, provide road maps, entertain us with stories, exhibit art reproductions, and so on. It's true that few of us would choose to read *War and Peace* on our terminal screens. Nevertheless, much of what we experience from a computer, ranging from the individual words and icons that label a screen window, to the content of email messages, to the text of Shakespeare, is in fact the computer's "book" nature—that is, its relatively passive ability to display stored text. The only intelligence here is the same, derivative intelligence that books may be said to possess.

Lacking any better term, I will call this wholly derivative intelligence of the computer its *book value*. However, the notion extends to other sorts of stored material in the computer besides text—for example, voice recordings and video images. Just as a book displays "someone else's" intelligence and not its own, so also do the tape recorder and television. In what follows, I'll use "book value" to include all such derived content.

No one would claim that its book value represents what the computer itself *does*. Those who talk about how computers will be able to think and converse are not merely referring to the way tape recorders and books "speak." They have in mind an autonomous *activity* of the computer—an activity directly expressing intelligence.

So I will use these terms—"book value" and "activity"—as rough markers capturing the distinction I'm after. While I have had, and will have, a great deal to say about the logical or mathematical character of computational activity, here I propose to look at certain peculiarities of book value in our culture. It is a curious fact that, today, book value—the detached word—readily takes on a life of its own, whether or not it is associated with the computer. At the same time, we seem strongly inclined to adopt an anthropomorphizing or superstitious stance toward this detached word.

Getting computers to think the easy way

Several years back I spent some time monitoring the USENET news-groups dealing with artificial intelligence (AI). Most of those who participated in the discussions were engineers or academics pursuing professional work in AI. One contributor described his undertaking this way:

> I am currently writing a program that allows the user to build a net-work consisting of thoughts and relations. The user starts by building a thought node. Each thought node contains a pointer to a list of relation nodes. Each relation node contains a pointer to another thought node. Every time a new thought is created, a relation node is added to the relation list of the current thought . . . .

What are we to make of this language? A few innocent-sounding sentences and suddenly we have a computer dealing with "thoughts" and relations—all in the context of discussion about artificial intelligence! One easily overlooks the fact that the speaker is apparently talking about nothing more than a tool for creating a cross-referenced outline or net-work diagram. The computer itself is no more dealing in thoughts than does a typewriter.

Despite his loose language, this contributor may just conceivably have had properly humble intentions when he submitted his ideas for consideration. The same cannot be said for the writer who informed his colleagues that he had hit upon just the ticket for giving computers free will. It requires that we write a program for a "decision system with three agents":

The first agent generates a candidate list of possible courses of action open for consideration. The second agent evaluates the likely outcome of pursuing each possible course of action, and estimates its utility according to its value system. The third agent provides a coin-toss to resolve ties.

Feedback from the real world enables the system to improve its powers of prediction and to edit its value system.

So much for free will. So much for the problem of values—"ought" versus "is." So much for the question of who these "agents" are that consider possible courses of action, understand likely outcomes, and apply values. It is all beautifully simple.

This same contributor rebuts the notion that computers cannot experience feelings. His appeal is to diagnostic messages—the words of advice or warning that programmers instruct the computer to print out when, for example, a user types something incorrectly.

A diagnostic message is a form of emotional expression. The computer is saying, "Something's wrong. I'm stuck and I don't know what to do." And sure enough, the computer doesn't do what you had in mind.

One wonders: are we up against an exciting new understanding of the human mind here, or an animistic impulse of stunning force? Do we confront theory or superstition? The USENET discussions in which such observations as these are launched continue month after month in all seriousness. The messages I have cited here were selected from hundreds of similar ones. We might hope that this is no more than the all-too-frequent descent of electronic discussion groups to a lowest common denominator. But there is evidence that the problem goes far beyond that.

Natural ignorance

Professor Drew McDermott, himself an AI researcher, published an essay in 1981 entitled "Artificial Intelligence Meets Natural Stupidity." In it he remarked on the use professional researchers make of "wishful mnemonics" like UNDERSTAND or GOAL in referring to programs and data structures. He wondered how we would view these same structures if we instead used names like G0034. The programmer could then "see whether he can *convince* himself or anyone else that G0034 implements some part of understanding." In a similar vein, he describes one of the early landmark AI programs: "By now, 'GPS' is a colorless term denoting a particularly stupid program to solve puzzles. But it originally meant 'General Problem Solver', which caused everybody a lot of needless excitement and distraction. It should have been called LFGNS—'Local-Feature-Guided Network Searcher.'" He goes on to say,

> As AI progresses (at least in terms of money spent), this malady gets worse. We have lived so long with the conviction that robots are possible, even just around the corner, that we can't help hastening their arrival with magic incantations. Winograd . . . explored some of the complexity of language in sophisticated detail; and now everyone takes 'natural-language interfaces' for granted, though none has been written. Charniak . . . pointed out some approaches to understanding stories, and now the OWL interpreter includes a 'story-understanding module'. (And, God help us, a top-level 'ego loop.')[2]

I once sat in a conference where the head of a university computer science department was asked how a computer could possess a selfhood and a knowledge of itself. He immmediately replied that it is easy enough to create a program variable giving the computer a name for itself, and to cause the computer to associate the record of its past activity with this name. Thus, "since [the computer program] has a term for itself, it can remember what it did, and can tell you what it has thought about." So much for the nature of memory, personal experience, and selfhood.

These stories show that it is not only casual users who are liable to mistake book value for what the computer itself *does* or *understands*. If a word flashing on the screen suggests to our cooperating minds a native intelligence within the machine, sophisticated engineers appear similarly susceptible to the name of a variable in a program listing. One is

---

2. McDermott, 1981: 145–46.

reminded of the word's powerful evocations during ancient times. As we are often told, our ancestors did not always distinguish clearly between word and thing. The word bore within itself some of the inner, spiritual significance of the thing to which it referred. But this only makes our own behavior all the more puzzling, for we are certainly inclined to reject what we take to be the superstitions of the ancients. And we do not believe—or at least we *say* we do not believe—our machines to be possessed by spirits.

What, then, can we make of a technically trained person who casually attributes thoughts and feelings to a computer on the basis of its diagnostic messages? Has he become pathologically superstitious about machines, or has he instead become pathologically separated from his own world of thoughts and feelings, which he reduces to a collection of vague abstractions of the sort he can easily attribute to a computer? Or are these two sides of the same phenomenon?

Computerized therapy

One of the classic, if now hackneyed, episodes in early AI work occurred in the mid-1960s, when Professor Joseph Weizenbaum of MIT wrote a language analysis program called ELIZA. He initially designed the program to imitate a Rogerian psychotherapist—a relatively easy task, he tells us, because much of the therapist's technique "consists of drawing his patient out by reflecting the patient's statements back to him." In ELIZA's case, the patient would type comments on a typewriter, and the computer would respond in kind. One conversation between ELIZA and a young lady went like this (ELIZA's responses are in capital letters):

Men are all alike.

IN WHAT WAY

They're always bugging us about something or other.

CAN YOU THINK OF A SPECIFIC EXAMPLE

Well, my boyfriend made me come here.

YOUR BOYFRIEND MADE YOU COME HERE

He says I'm depressed much of the time.

I AM SORRY TO HEAR YOU ARE DEPRESSED

It's true. I am unhappy.

DO YOU THINK COMING HERE WILL HELP YOU NOT TO
BE UNHAPPY

I need some help, that much seems certain.

WHAT WOULD IT MEAN TO YOU IF YOU GOT SOME HELP

Perhaps I could learn to get along with my mother.

TELL ME MORE ABOUT YOUR FAMILY

My mother takes care of me

WHO ELSE IN YOUR FAMILY TAKES CARE OF YOU

My father.

YOUR FATHER

You are like my father in some ways.

WHAT RESEMBLANCE DO YOU SEE

You are not very aggressive but I think you don't want me to
notice that.

WHAT MAKE YOU THINK I AM NOT VERY AGGRESSIVE

You don't argue with me

WHY DO YOU THINK I DON'T ARGUE WITH YOU

You are afraid of me.

DOES IT PLEASE YOU TO BELIEVE I AM AFRAID OF YOU

My father is afraid of everybody

WHAT ELSE COMES TO MIND WHEN YOU THINK OF
YOUR FATHER

Bullies.

DOES THAT HAVE ANYTHING TO DO WITH THE FACT THAT
YOUR BOYFRIEND MADE YOU COME HERE

As Weizenbaum points out, the computer's language analysis was very primitive. Its programming reflected a single context—that of the therapeutic dialog—and its "understanding" consisted substantially of keying in on certain words and drawing on a set of stock responses. (Of course, it also had to do some basic grammatical parsing of English text.)

Nevertheless, Weizenbaum reports on the "shock" he experienced upon learning how seriously people took the program:

> Once my secretary, who had watched me work on the program for many months and therefore surely knew it to be merely a computer program, started conversing with it. After only a few interchanges with it, she asked me to leave the room. Another time, I suggested I might rig the system so that I could examine all conversations any-one had with it, say, overnight. I was promptly bombarded with accusations that what I proposed amounted to spying on people's intimate thoughts . . . . I knew of course that people form all sorts of emotional bonds to machines . . . . What I had not realized is that extremely short exposures to a relatively simple computer program could induce powerful delusional thinking in quite normal people.[3]

There is a sense in which we must agree with Weizenbaum—a sense that is central to my own argument. Yet I suspect he would acknowledge another side to the issue. How delusional is it to assume an intelligence behind the use of language? Language, as we all learn in school, is one of the chief distinguishing features of man. We simply never come across language that has not issued, in one way or another, from a human mind. If I find a series of words neatly impressed upon the sand of a desert island, I will conclude—no doubt correctly—that I am not alone. There is another human speaker on the island.

Furthermore, we have become fully attuned to mechanically mediated human communication. While telephone, radio, or TV might hopelessly disorient a time-traveling Roman, we take it as a matter of course that these devices put us in touch with other people. Weizenbaum's secretary, quite undistracted by the mechanical contrivances she was dealing with, immersed herself from habit in the meaning of the text addressed to her, and she felt (with good justification) that this text originated in another mind, *one that had considered how to respond to just the sorts of comments she was making.* What she was most likely not doing was considering explicitly whether she was speaking with the computer itself, or a

---

3. Weizenbaum, 1976: 3–4.

programmer, or some other person. She was simply *conversing with words.*
Who was behind them didn't matter. The episode may say more about
the pervasive and accustomed anonymity of our society than anything
else.

Words in the void

The word has increasingly detached itself from the human being who
utters it. This detachment received a huge impetus with the invention of
the modern printing press in the fifteenth century. The phonograph, telephone, radio, and TV encouraged an ever more radical separation. Today,
even in live musical performances, lip-synching is common—who knows
whether it is a recording or a human larynx from which the sound arises?
(Actually, with or without lip-synching, the *immediate* source of the sound
is a loudspeaker rather than a larynx, which is why the controversy over
lip-synching is mostly irrelevant.)

If a phone connection puts me at one mechanical remove from my
conversational partner, a recorded phone message more than doubles the
indirection, for here there is no possibility of interaction. But, no, that's
not quite true. As phone systems become ever more sophisticated, I am
allowed to push buttons in an increasingly articulate manner. At the same
time, the spliced-together snippets of recorded speech manage to respond
in an increasingly intelligent manner. And, like Weizenbaum's secretary, I
follow along with all the seriousness of someone conversing with a real
person, even if I am more or less aware of the arrangement's limitations.
This awareness will no doubt attenuate with time, even as the mechanical
devices gain in deftness.

Many in our society have only recently experienced the shock that
comes when one first realizes that the "person" who rang the phone is
really a recording. But those among us who are already accustomed to
recordings will readily acknowledge a certain process of acclimatization:
as the collage of recorded and "real" voices becomes more and more
intricate, and as the underlying programming responds more and more
flexibly to our needs, we make less and less of a distinction between the

various levels of genuineness. We are comfortable doing business with the words themselves.

The System speaks

We have, it seems, long been training ourselves to disregard the distance between the verbal artifacts of intelligence and their living source. The words themselves are source enough. Little of the day goes by without our being assaulted on one side or another by disembodied words speaking for we know not whom. Street signs, billboards, car radios, Walkmans, newspapers, magazines by the grocery checkout stand, televisions in every room, phone callers we have never met, movies, video games, loudspeakers at public gatherings, and—if we work with computers—a Noachian deluge of electronic mail, news, network-accessible databases, and all the other hidden vessels of the *information* that is supposed to empower and liberate us.

We live out much of our lives under the guidance of these words-as-artifacts. How can we do otherwise? How can I pierce behind the intricate *mechanism* mediating the words I hear, so as to discern the true *speaker*? How can I discover more than a few fragments of the individuality of Peter Jennings or Tom Brokaw behind the formulas and technology of the evening news? (Think how different it would be to watch and listen as the cameras inadvertently picked up a half-hour's off-the-air conversation between Brokaw and one of his colleagues. And how different again to participate in a face-to-face exchange with them.)

We are so used to words that have become disconnected from their human source that we scarcely notice the peculiarities of our situation. But we *do* notice on at least some occasions, as the unflattering stereotype of the bureaucrat makes clear. When I quibble with a disenfranchised clerk over some irrelevant regulation, with whom am I speaking? Not the clerk himself, for he has no authority to speak on his own account. (That is probably the main cause of my frustration; I *thought* I was going to converse with a person.) But if my conversation is not with the clerk, who *is* it with? Nobody, really—which is why I quickly begin to blame the System.

The fact is that, like Weizenbaum's secretary, I am merely *conversing with words*, and these words are produced by a vague mechanism neither I nor anyone else can fully unravel. Yes, the words somehow originate with human beings, but they have been subjected to a kind of organizational/mechanical processing that renders them simplistic, too-logical, slightly out of kilter. They are impossible to trace, and so I don't try. Why try? It is the disembodied words that determine my fate. They are the reality.

One way to think of the challenge for our future is this: how can I work toward a society in which every transaction is as deeply *human* a transaction as possible? To make an exchange human is to reduce the distance between words and their source, to overcome the entire mediating apparatus, so that I am myself fully present in my words. Even when stymied by a bureaucracy, I can at least choose to address (and respect) the human being in front of me. This will, in fact, encourage him to step out of the System in some small way rather than retreat further into it as a defense against my anger. On the other hand, I support the System just so far as I give further impetus to the automated word.

Superstition

I began this chapter by asking what stands behind our "animistic" urge to personify mechanical devices. I then distinguished between the *book value* of the computer and its native *activity*. The remainder of the chapter to this point has focused upon book value: the ease with which both user and programmer attribute book value to the computer as if it were an expression of the computer's own active intelligence, and the degree to which the word has detached itself from human beings and taken up an objective, independent life within our machines, organizations, and systems.

There may appear to be a paradox here. On the one hand, the increasing objectification of what is most intimately human—our speech;

on the other hand, an anthropomorphizing liaison with our mechanical contrivances. But, of course, this is not really a paradox. When speech detaches itself from the speaker, it is indeed objectified, cut off from its human source. But it still carries—if only via our subconscious—some of its ancient and living powers. And so its association with machinery readily evokes our personification of the machinery.

We may think ourselves freed from superstition. But if we take superstition to be a susceptibility to the magical effects of words, then it would be truer to say that ours is the age in which superstition has come into its own. Having reduced the word to a dead abstraction residing outside ourselves, we subject ourselves to its invisible influence. Our single largest industry, centered on Madison Avenue (but also operative in every corporate Marketing Department) is dedicated to refining the instruments of magical control. *Seeming* to be alien, a hollow physical token and nothing more, approaching us only as a powerless shape from without, the word nevertheless has its way with us. We detach the word from ourselves and it overpowers us from the world.

Nor is it an accident that the great social and political ideologies have arisen only during the last couple of centuries. These elaborate word-edifices, detached from their human sources, sway and mobilize the surging masses. The passionate believer in an *-ism*—what is it he believes in? An idea from which all human meaning has been purged, leaving only an abstraction and the controlling passion of belief itself. That is what makes the ghastly, inhuman contradictions possible: a communist workers' paradise to be achieved by disfranchising or massacring the workers; a capitalist common good to be achieved through the universal cultivation of selfishness.

Religion and ideology. Religion, too, has doubtless taken on a more ideological character over the last few centuries—as suggested, for example, by sectarian fragmentation. But the more "primitive" phases of religion contrast strikingly with the genesis of modern *-isms.* The prophets spoke in similes, images, koans, symbols, and parables; their words were accessible only to those "with ears to hear." The words had to be meditated upon, slowly penetrated by means of an answering word within the hearer. And the believer was ever driven back to the human source for understanding; the words of the prophet were inseparable from his life. They were not written on the subway walls, nor on religious billboards.

It is quite otherwise with ideology. For Communist revolutionaries around the world, not much depended on the person of Marx or Lenin, or on the authenticity of words attributed to them. Faith was vested in empty generalities—the proletariat, the revolution, the classless society. Words that change the course of the world are no longer bound to their human source. Unlike the symbol and parable—and much more like scientific descriptions—they have become abstract and capable of standing by themselves, for they are nearly contentless. They are automatic—fit to be spoken by the System—and therefore the human subconscious from which the System has arisen is invited to supply the real meaning.

Some people believe we have seen the end of ideology. My own fear is that we are seeing its perfection. The disembodied word no longer requires even the relatively impersonal support of the activist's cell, the political movement, the faceless bureaucracy, the machinelike corporation, the television evangelistic campaign. The machine itself, uncannily mimicking the human being, now bears the word alone—and we call it information. Our -*ism* is declared in our almost religious devotion to a life determined, not from within ourselves, but by divine technological whim.

• • •

It is easy enough to see a danger in the reaction of Weizenbaum's secretary to ELIZA. For despite it being an *understandable* reaction in view of our culture's detachment of the word, it is clearly not a *healthy* reaction. She evidently proved blind to the laughable limitation of her therapist and the essential artificiality of the exercise, because she could not distinguish properly among book value, mechanical activity, and human presence. And having lost her ability to trace word to speaker, she must have lost as well some of her ability to deal truly with human beings in general; for the human being as *productive spirit*, as the source of the word, had at least temporarily escaped her reckoning.

We may scorn her for that, but it would not be wise. Better to note that the test she failed becomes daily more subtle, and that the rest of us, too—whether in passively absorbing television commercials, or beating our heads against petty bureaucracies, or allowing electronic mail to put us into "automatic mode"—fail it every day.

19

LISTENING FOR THE SILENCE

THE NOTORIOUS SLOPPINESS of computer-mediated communication is often attributed to its being more like conversational speech than like traditional writing. The idea seems to be that sloppiness works fine in conversation, so why shouldn't it work just as well in online communication? But perhaps the premise here sneaks within the gates just a bit too easily.

There are several elements of effective conversation:

The ability to listen. I mean an active sort of listening—the kind that enables and encourages, eliciting from the speaker an even better statement than he knew he was capable of producing. The kind that enters sympathetically into the gaps, the hesitations, the things left unsaid, so that the listener can state the speaker's position as effectively as his own. To listen productively is to nurture a receptive and energetic void within which a new word can take shape. Such listening is half of every good conversation, perhaps the most creative half.

Needless to say, listening expresses a deep selflessness. And, if my own experience is any guide, the discipline required is far from natural. In fact, it usually seems impossible. But this does not prevent our working toward it, as toward any ideal.

What about computer-mediated communication? Clearly, listening is still more difficult here. The speaker is no longer physically present. He no longer demands so insistently that I attend to his words, nor is my listening immediately evident to him. If I wish, I can more easily conceal my disinterest.

However, the situation is not hopeless. Even in face-to-face communication I must "overcome" the physically detached word if I would find my way to the mind of the speaker. So it's not as if the computer confronts me with an altogether new challenge. It's just that I must make a more conscious effort of attention, actively seeking out the speaker behind the words on my screen. When I do this well, my response can still convey a quality of listening. Listening is in any case more than a mere visible blankness. It is a receptive participation that colors all aspects of the conversation.

Silence. Silence is implied in listening, but also in speaking. It is the place where the right words can come together. Without silence, the torrent of words becomes coercive for both speaker and listener. The words are automatic, unconsidered, expressing thoughts and feelings the speaker himself is not fully aware of. They run in ruts, responding in the same old ways to the same old triggering remarks. Silence is the dark soil through which the seedleaves of a new understanding may push through to the light.

Silence is essential to the proper management of a conversation. Only when I am silent can another contribute in a balancing way. Only when the whole group regularly punctuates its discourse with silences is there a chance for the conversation to be formed consciously as a communal work of art instead of running on wildly under its own power.

How does an electronic discussion group incorporate a discipline of silence? I'm not sure to what extent it is possible. But each contributor can at least exercise such a discipline within himself, weighing each remark before submitting it. The familiar advice about writing a response, then waiting a day before mailing it, is often appropriate. So, too, one can give place to silence in contemplating the shape of the conversation as a whole—as one would a painting before adding a new stroke. Admittedly, online discussions are so often utterly random and shapeless that it hardly seems worth the effort. This is not surprising, since creative silence is a rare thing even in our deeply personal conversations. Nevertheless, there is a goal we can work toward here.

Respect for the word. The word is the instrument of our *meanings*. Only with words can a human being mean something. In this sense, every meaning-gesture is a "word." There is no activity we can properly call human that is not a kind of speaking—whether it occurs in a conversation, on a ballet stage, or in a sports stadium.

Our ability to convey meaning depends on two things. We need an established, shared vocabulary of some sort. And we need to employ that vocabulary in a distinctive way, impressing our meanings—which is to say, ourselves—upon it. To whatever extent this latter effort is superfluous, we are passing along empty information.[1] For meanings are not simply given in our words, as if those words were containers; meaning arises dynamically in the gaps between the words—but does so in part because of the particular words we have used.

That is why machine translation only works (to some extent) with highly formalized (that is, relatively empty) vocabularies typical of certain sciences and scholarly disciplines. Such languages are designed to eliminate all meaning, to squeeze out every contaminant that might infect the spaces between the words.

Computers, so far as they act in their own right, are exchangers of information, not meaning. They do not learn from the gaps between words. So there is no need for a computer to apply the disciplines of listening and silence. There is nothing to listen for, no human meaning to

---

1. See chapter 23, "Can We Transcend Computation?"

take form in the silences. The transactions are automatic, given solely by what is "contained in" the words—which is a purely formal emptiness.

As we embrace the age of information and all the tools for processing information, it is well to keep asking: where in all this is the listening? Where is the silence and the meaning? In all the discussion of information, one rarely hears a clear distinction articulated between automatic processing and human conversation. The distinction matters.

Attention to the larger human context. Conversing is the way we are human. We are not machines exchanging data; rather, we should expect that our every meeting is fated; that the way we handle ourselves may help someone else along the way, or else cause him to stumble; that we have something important to learn from the encounter—all the more so if we find ourselves irritated, angry, or otherwise derailed from constructive response.

Online flame wars have attracted much attention, leading some to ask whether electronic communication encourages undue emotional outbursts. The question is worth asking, but I wonder whether the more dangerous symptoms lie at the other end of the spectrum. Anger is at least an indication that there is something *personal* at stake, even if we are not fully conscious of it. What if we lose the personal altogether?

One can imagine businesslike networks of communication that verge increasingly upon the "ideal" of pure, automatic information exchange. One might even suspect that this is the required direction of movement, since, for reasons of efficiency, we must transfer responsibility for more and more of our business communication to software. We who must merge our own efforts with those of our machines cannot help feeling ourselves pulled toward the machines. How do we pay attention to the person on the other end when it's unclear who that person is—if he is anyone at all—amid the mechanisms?

To respond to a system as if it were a person becomes downright silly. (Do I apologize to the software for my mistakes?) We *can*, however, read every system as the human expression that it ultimately is, and then act accordingly. This could mean refusing to reply to a computerized suite of telephone recordings, opting instead for the human speaker. It could mean recognizing that a particular computer-based system expresses so fundamental a denial of the human being that the only acceptable response is to unplug one's connection—or even to carry out some strategy of "technological disobedience."

I am not being facetious here. Any such reactions will necessarily be highly personal—which is not another way of saying they are unimportant. Quite the contrary; from the sum total of such reactions we will determine the future shape of technological society. And the more radical responses at least have this merit: they take the system *seriously*, rather as we must take people seriously. These responses are vivid testimony to the presence of a human being at some point in the system. Our need for such reminders may become acute.

Filtering out the human being

Such, then, are a few features of conversation: listening, silence, respect for the words that make communication possible, and attention to the larger human context of all meaningful communication. Of course, the contrast between "good practice" and reality can be painful. I have lately been asking myself about the effects of the peculiar *scanning* mode I find myself reverting to when perusing a much-too-full electronic mailbox or discussion folder. Not only is it uncomfortable to eyes and head, but it reminds me of the state I can fall into when listening to a rather dull lecture: I drowsily follow the words and phrases at a certain superficial level (so that I would immediately perk up if the lecturer interjected a wholly absurd sentence), and yet engage in no creative interaction with the speaker's *meaning* at all. I just track along with the surfaces of the words—behaving rather like an electronic search tool, paying attention to mere word sequences rather than meanings.

Can I even make it an *ideal* to listen attentively when, as happens so often, I must sift through masses of half-considered words on my computer screen—many of them uninvited, of little interest, and from unknown sources? Full attention would sap my energies and prevent "getting the job done." And yet, this habit pretty well encompasses a denial of every principle discussed above. To receive *any* language this superficially damages us, I suspect. Penetrating the thought of another requires an active ability to recreate within one's own consciousness the inner life of the other. It's an ability implying the utmost in attention and conscious effort, and can only be learned over a lifetime. Every time I attend to someone's words in a merely mechanical fashion, I degrade what is most fully human in both of us.

Could it be that the "necessity" I feel for superficial scanning tells me something important about what I have allowed my job to become? Isn't it really under my control? Why do I call down upon myself so much "half-important" material, if not to satisfy some sort of profitless information greed? These questions lead directly to one of today's hottest topics on the Net: information filtering.

Fading conversations. The information glut is not new. Long before the Net's burgeoning it was impossible to keep up with more than a tiny fraction of the journals, books, conferences, and discussions bearing on one's professional field, let alone those relating to avocational interests. No one with any sense tried to take in *everything*, for that could lead only to the intellectual shallows. Far more important was deep interaction with those colleagues one did encounter in person or in writing.

Now, however, there is almost a frenzy of concern for "filtering." Software tools for selecting, categorizing, filing, and analyzing information—and even for responding automatically to personal messages—are under intense development. A primary reason for this, quite evidently, is that computers give us our first automatic scanning and processing abilities. Somehow it seems that we can "get at" much more information than we could in the old-fashioned library.

This is no doubt true in some sense. But two cautions seem necessary. First, no more today than yesterday does breadth of acquaintance substitute for depth of contemplation—even if the available tools make the temptation to spread wide almost irresistible. And second, we need to realize the subtle nudges these new information-processing tools administer to us. Just consider: in conversation with a friend or colleague you would most definitely *not* apply a rigidly pre-set filter to his remarks—not, at least, if you were interested in learning from him rather than imposing your biases upon him.

Tools for filtering make it clear that human exchange is becoming less conversational. The human context of the word is ever less important, which is to say that what the words mean is defined within a relative vacuum. This necessarily leads to our taking them more abstractly, for concreteness derives from a particular human milieu. Without such a milieu, we can only talk about what the words might mean "in general."

Half of every conversation consists of what meets me unpredictably from the other side. Half of learning is achieved by the world, working upon me at its own initiative. The aim of the filter is, at one level, to eliminate unpredictability—to select my "input" according to criteria *I* can fully control. Of course, it's also true in direct conversation that I can choose my partners, but certain human constraints prevent my simply walking away as soon as a "wrong" turn is taken or one of my "filter this out" keywords is spoken. I have to deal with the person, whose presence alone grants him a certain claim upon me.

The frightening prospect is that cyberspace will fade into a mere disjunction of subjective universes as each of us encases himself within a solipsistic cocoon. The paradox here is that reduction of knowledge to "objective" information is precisely what prepares the way for this triumph of subjectivity. But, then, in all things a perverse subjectivity is the unavoidable correlate of a perverse objectivity.

Am I advising you to avoid all use of software filters? No. The only thing I would state in such absolute terms is the most general principle: we must do whatever we find necessary to preserve our fullest humanity in the presence of our machines. But it does seem to me that the comparison between online communication and conversation proves useful in focusing our thinking about the choices. Certainly it is true—to retrieve our starting point—that if we take the requirements for conversation seri-ously, then the demands placed upon us by the "orality" of computer-mediated communication are at least as stringent as the demands embod-ied in traditional standards of writing, even if they are somewhat different.

PART FOUR

Owen Barfield, Computers, and the
Evolution of Consciousness

20

AWAKING FROM THE PRIMORDIAL DREAM

The whole world reaches in man
its own consciousness.
—Goethe

CARL JUNG, GAZING upon a timeless African landscape, found himself momentarily absorbed, dreamlike, into a world not yet fully awake:

> From a low hill in the Athi plains of East Africa I once watched the vast herds of wild animals grazing in soundless stillness, as they had done from time immemorial, touched only by the breath of a primeval world. I felt then as if I were the first man, the first creature, to know that all this *is*. The entire world around me was still in its primeval state; it did not know that it *was*. And then, in that one moment in which I came to know, the world sprang into being.[1]

I imagine most of us have had some such experience, at least to the extent of finding ourselves lost in the hypnotic scene before us as in a reverie. We find ourselves enmeshed, or "caught up," in the world. Our minds seep outward into our surroundings, so that we no longer stand apart from the tableau we contemplate. The psyche, having momentarily escaped the self's constraining will, lives outside the self. Once that loss of

---

1. Jung, 1968: 95–96.

boundary occurs, it requires a certain inner wrench, or pulling away, to extract (recollect) ourselves from the world. Only then do we regain our previous separate existence.

In Jung's case the wrench was also a moment of revelation. He not only recollected himself, but he was struck by the nature of the transition. He knew he had experienced two radically different relationships to the world, and in moving from one state to the other he felt that not only he, but also the world itself, had changed. Something in the world *depended* on the birth of awareness in him. It was not only he who had "come to himself," but the world had come to itself through him.

Living in a dream

You may well ask, "What exactly was this change of awareness Jung describes? Surely he maintained full awareness of the world even during his reverie. He was, after all, conscious throughout, and his senses were registering the scene. His ability to describe the episode in retrospect proves as much."

There are, however, differing levels of awareness. When I awake in the morning, I may recall my dreams—proving that I experienced them with *some* sort of consciousness—but I nevertheless wake *up* to a sharper awareness. My dream consciousness, however powerful its feelings, is in some regards duller, less focused than my waking consciousness. It lacks conceptual clarity. And above all, it is less aware of itself. In the hierarchy of awarenesses, each higher state may "know," or be awake to, the lower ones, while the lower ones remain asleep with respect to the higher. Freud could only have written his *Interpretation of Dreams* while wide awake.

Jung spoke of *that one moment in which I came to know.* This knowing is not, in the first place, a matter of gaining additional facts. The spellbound Jung could not "know" any facts at all. His consciousness was temporarily dispersed in his environment, without awareness of self; his coming to himself was a return to a more centered awareness. Such a centering must precede the apprehension of fact.

There are infinite gradations of consciousness. We can demarcate a "lower" end of the spectrum by imagining the wholly dreamlike, instinctual consciousness of animals. The gazelle and lion upon which Jung gazed, and the eagle circling overhead, do not ever "come to themselves." They may see with eyes far sharper than our own, distinguish smells we will never know, and give ear to distant chords hidden in our silences. Yet, while they live *in* these experiences, they do not *apprehend* them. They glide through the primeval landscape in a dream.

Ancient man—myth-making man—long retained elements of a dreaming consciousness, and was incapable of anything like what we would call self-reflection. It is all too easy, in considering the culture of earlier periods, to mistake such a different form of consciousness for a mere difference in information or factual understanding. The ancients, on such a view, simply had not learned what we have learned. But this is a serious error.

We run up against this error when we contemplate some of the wonders and mysteries of the prehistoric races. We look, for example, at the ruins of certain stone monuments—observatories marvelously calculated to mark the waystations of sun and moon. It is possible to deduce from these relics just what the ancients must have known of astronomy and mathematics, and the answer sometimes stuns us. For it appears they possessed skills that even a trained astronomer today would be hard put to duplicate without her computer-generated charts and electronic calculator.

But all this is to assume that these earlier peoples possessed a consciousness much like our own, and executed their designs with a kind of scientific awareness. It is risky, however, to carry such reasoning too far. After all, what must the migrating tern or the spawning salmon "know" in order to navigate thousands of miles with the precision of an ICBM? This, too, we can deduce, and it turns out they must know a great deal of astronomy, geophysics, and mathematics—if indeed they approach their task with an engineer's consciousness. But, of course, they do not. Knowledge of facts is not the only knowing.

It is rather as if the arctic tern takes wing upon an ethereal sea of wisdom, borne along invisible paths by an intelligence calling as much from Nature as from within its own mind. In its dream, more profound than any man's, it achieves harmony with the world, *because its course is as much the world's as its own.* So we may speak less accurately of the migrating bird's intelligence than of a larger, more diffuse wisdom comprehending the bird and drawing it along.

Even in our own dreams, we cannot clearly distinguish self from world. The elements of the dream scenario tend to represent, in one way or another, aspects of ourselves; our inner life is "spread around," displayed outwardly. Everything is suffused with our own consciousness. But then, if this consciousness is not really centered in me, if it meets me from without as well as within, can it be fully my own? While dreaming, I am not set wholly apart from my plastic and psychically active surroundings; I inhabit a world that is alive, with no clear boundary between inside and outside. And in this union with the world lies cradled a deep wisdom. By attending to my dreams, I may recognize an inner need long before my intellect fully awakens to it.

There are, then, different levels of consciousness or awareness, quite apart from the possession of different facts. Indeed, achievement of a certain level of consciousness is required before we can possess any facts at all—as opposed to their possessing us in a dream. There are ways of knowing besides the knowing of facts. While the wisdom of the ancients was certainly not a technological or scientific savvy, we cannot for that reason alone dismiss it. That would be like criticizing the tern for its inability to conceptualize modern navigational theory.

History as an awakening

The human race has awakened by degrees. And our arousal continues. Only during the past few hundred years, for example, has the discipline of history existed in anything like its present form. The Greeks and Romans had their historians, of course, but their narratives served primarily as story and moral example. The study of the past for its own sake, and the idea that the present grows out of the past like a plant from a seed by a sequence of wholly natural causes and effects, really began taking hold only in the seventeenth century,[2] as one result of a new and peculiarly reflexive *awareness*. The first modern historians found it possible in a new degree to step back from the immediate stream of human experience and view it all as objective process. They began to see more clearly—standing outside of it—a development in which their forbears had only been immersed as participants. Thus they continued that same distancing of psyche from object, that same pulling away of consciousness from that-of-which-it-is-conscious, whereby our primeval ancestors first came to know that the world *was*.

The new interest in origins extended beyond human history, embracing biological (Darwinian), geological, and cosmological origins. At the same time, awareness turned in upon itself even more with the discoveries of the depth psychologists. We became aware, as it were, of unawareness, conscious of the subconscious—of that to which, though it is indeed a kind of consciousness, we have not yet fully awakened. Likewise, if history is a species of self-reflection, then the still younger discipline of historiography—the study of the *nature* of history—is reflection upon reflection. Our love of the prefix *meta-* today testifies to our inveterate habit of stepping back to consider every subject from a yet higher vantage point.

It may not come as stirring news that the human race has been waking up. We have placed a man on the moon—surely a task requiring wakefulness! And who among us does not fully expect that we will come to know more and more of what *is*—if Jung's peculiar emphasis really means anything?

But the emphasis does mean something, for it points beyond the accumulation of information to a change in the *nature* of our consciousness. It helps us to interrupt our preoccupation with technological accomplishment, and directs attention to the sorts of changes that made

---

2. Barfield, 1967: chapter 1.

technology possible in the first place. There may, after all, be dangers as well as advantages in these changes. History suggests a progressive contraction of consciousness into the skull of the detached, self-contained, and isolated observer, so that we come to know the world as set apart from ourselves. More and more of our experience becomes a chronicling of "world" or "other," until we stand finally as detached observers even of our own subjectivity. Our awareness sharpens, becoming clearer and more wakeful, by virtue of this contraction from the periphery—from dreamlike entanglement in the world—to a focused center. But the uttermost center of a circle is a null point. Might we become so radically detached from the surrounding world that we can no longer find our way back to it—that we lose not only the world but also ourselves? Might we, in the end, wake up to nothing at all?

The solitary bird, gripped by an unknowing intensity as it ploughs through the trackless ether—"pulled along" by an intelligence lying more in the world than in itself—hears, on the dull edges of its consciousness, a call of destiny sung by hidden choirs. It is not alone. I, on the other hand, venture to set my foot in one direction rather than another only amidst a seizure of self-doubt. I hear no call, and I am alone. I observe with greater and greater precision from a position of greater and greater isolation. Meaning disappears in the face of narrow certainty, so that I become more and more certain about ever thinner facts that no longer bear their own significance within themselves.

The world is the womb of meaning; without it we cannot live. Whatever else we may say about the dream, it connects us meaningfully to the world. It is no accident that we sometimes hear "messages" in our dreams. Where the world of our waking experience has become for us inert and dead, the dreamworld remains alive with psyche. The elements of a dream are frequently charged with an inner significance, although typically we cannot quite "put our fingers on" the meaning—cannot grasp it consciously, with our waking minds. It is as if meaning and clear intellectual apprehension stand in a kind of tension, with each existing at the expense of the other. The more we wake up, the less dreamlike or meaningful our life becomes, which is also to say, the less connection we find to the world. We come to know the world objectively by being cut off from it. This paradox, growing ever more acute, raises the question just how much longer our contracting psychic centers can hold their worlds together.

The mind of the computer

"But wait," you say. "This has gone far enough. Birds do not 'take wing upon a sea of wisdom.' Nor is their consciousness somehow vaguely diffused through the world. And those 'hidden choirs' they hear are actually staccato data streams issuing from internal computers—biological information-processing mechanisms much like the silicon-based machines of our own latter-day invention. Poetic references to dreams and the rest are fine, but don't substitute them for knowledge of how the world really works!"

With this objection we arrive at that modern fascination with the computer as an image of the human mind. The fascination may itself be symptomatic of a further development in the evolution of consciousness. If we demarcate one end of the spectrum of consciousness by imagining the profound dream of the higher animal, we see something like the opposite end exemplified in the computer. For the computer never dreams, and it does not know meaning. What we meet in the computer is a kind of pure, unblinking wakefulness, an unsurpassed logical clarity with no awareness of content, a consciousness that has contracted to a nullity, so that the only things left to it are the empty logical forms of its own perfect acuity.

Now, without too much difficulty we can imagine a consciousness wholly sunken into dream, possessed of no waking awareness (so caught up—like the entranced Jung—within an awareness *of*, that there can be no separation or detachment, no awareness *that*). We find it much less easy, however, to imagine a consciousness jolted into an utterly blank wakefulness—a consciousness so *detachedly* aware, that it has lost all contact with anything *of which* to be aware. This may seem like so many empty words. Perhaps our difficulty arises because the former condition,

243

while largely behind us, survives fragmentarily in our nightly dreams, whereas the other still lies ahead, even if we are rapidly approaching it. The computer may allow us to see clearly and in advance a state of mind that otherwise might overcome us by surprise.

It is no accident that the problem of meaning now disturbs those disciplines most vigorously pursuing computer models of the mind. How does a computer really *mean* anything by its output—its mechanically generated strings of symbols? How does it transcend mechanism and arrive at reason? The computer manipulates a symbol (for example, the word "house") solely according to the symbol's form; how, then, does it get from the form of the word "house"—a particular sequence of five letters—to the content, the actual meaning of the word? Can a computer truly become *aware* of anything?

Most scholars and engineers within computer-related fields are convinced that, if we can only understand the *mechanism* of the computer's intelligence sufficiently, questions of *meaning* will somehow fall into place as a kind of side effect. After all, we human beings are merely complex mechanisms ourselves, are we not? In the end, whatever we have of meaning and conscious experience of the world will be found in the computerized robot as well. Of course, not a few are willing to suggest that what we have of meaning is nothing at all; "meaning" and "experience" are simply peculiar varieties of self-deception—phantasms of a subjectivity best exemplified (and dismissed) in our dreams.

And so we who pride ourselves in being fully awake seek to expunge our last memories of those shadowy dreams still echoing from the childhood of the race. No longer capable of taking our own dreams seriously, and blind to our evolutionary past, we would reinterpret the consciousness of our ancestors upon the analogy of the computer. Not content with waking up, we deny we have ever dreamed. This is all too easy. For the dream today has become fragile in the extreme, vanishing quickly from mind under the bright, featureless glare of daytime wakefulness. The gods no longer favor us with overwhelming and powerful visitations. Why should we who have delivered ourselves from the fears and superstitions of the night take any further notice of these things?

But primitive fear and superstition are not the only sources of terror in the world. We have discovered our own more sophisticated terrors. Or, to put the matter differently, the gods with whom we once coexisted in a dreamworld find a way to take vengeance upon those who unceremoniously abandon them to the subconscious. Not yet are we merely walking computational devices—as the very busy mental wards of our hospitals testify.

It was Jung himself who most forcefully pointed out our self-deceptions in this regard. If our dream-deprived world is no longer alive with psyche, if the gods have disappeared from it (he repeatedly reminded us), it is only because they have taken up residence within man himself. And so long as we do not recognize their presence, we experience them as demons working their mischief through our subconscious instincts. We then condemn ourselves to live out meanings not of our own making, without being awake to them. In other words, we obtain our sharply delineated consciousness by pushing our dream awareness ever further into the unconscious, where the elements rage unrecognized and beyond our control. As a consequence—and all our enlightenment notwithstanding—the parade of wars, tortures, mass murders, and suicides continues unabated, while alienation and psychic disintegration steadily corrode the thin veneer of civilization from below.

The soul of the computer

Waking up, it turns out, is not quite the simple act we might have imagined. We extract our consciousness from our living surroundings, detaching our now isolated subjectivity and thereby reducing the world to a dead, inert collection of "things" with which we feel no inner connection. But the world remains the only mirror in which consciousness can recognize itself, so that we progressively come to experience ourselves in the same way we experience the mechanically conceived external world.

We lose our own inner life, and our consciousness converges upon the empty abstractions of the machine.

Ancient man, while dreaming, was at least dreaming *of* the powers enlivening the world. He thereby knew them, however dimly. We, on the other hand, have gained our acute, materially effective consciousness only at the cost of losing altogether our awareness of the life within things. That life has retreated into our unconscious. Owen Barfield had something like this in mind when he remarked that

> the possibility of man's avoiding self-destruction depends on his real-
> izing before it is too late that what he let loose over Hiroshima, after
> fiddling with its exterior for three centuries like a mechanical toy,
> was the forces of his own unconscious mind.[3]

But our alienation from the world has proceeded so far that we cannot receive this warning as anything but a picturesque overstatement: we accept that the forces unleashed in the atomic bomb are "our own" forces only in the sense that it requires human beings to conceive, assemble, and deploy the thing. The "objective" forces themselves remain quite independent of the human mind. That, however, is not what Barfield is saying. He speaks as one who has traced the withdrawal of nature's living powers into the lost depths of the individual, and who therefore knows the connection between man's unconscious, on the one hand, and the forces hitherto lying bound in matter on the other.

• • •

The entire spectrum of consciousness, from primeval dream to modern wakefulness, can in a certain sense be found within the individual man today—except that the dreaming has lapsed into a deeper unconsciousness against which we have purchased our ever narrower observational prowess. We wake up by abandoning the dream world to complete darkness.

The computer presents an apt image for the endpoint of this process. Or, rather, it stands as one *possible* endpoint, for we may still choose to

---

3. Barfield, 1973: 36.

move in a different direction. Having once "come to ourselves," we can resist the further contraction of our wakefulness to a nullity, seeking instead to deepen it. We can, that is, work to encompass with renewed consciousness what has previously fallen from awareness—not by sinking ourselves back into dream, but by taking hold in full wakefulness of the wisdom that once possessed the dreaming childhood of the race. This is the task of imagination.

The computer's pure wakefulness-without-content is, in fact, no wakefulness at all, for being perfectly alert to nothing hardly qualifies as being awake. Nor will we find our deepest kinship with the computer by looking at how its logic circuits are empty shadows of our own thinking. What, in the end, binds us most irresistibly to our computers—what fascinates us almost beyond recall—is what we are least conscious of, because most horrified of. If the computer's watchful eye is the red, unblinking eye of Sauron, we will no doubt have to probe the most hidden secrets of silicon and pulsing electricity to find its soul—only to discover there the same powers that Barfield discerned in the blast over Hiroshima.

21

MONA LISA'S SMILE

VIRTUAL REALITY HAS ITS PRECEDENTS. Pygmalion, the artist of Greek myth, sculpted the image of a young woman in ivory. Stricken by her beauty, he prayed to Aphrodite for a bride in her likeness. The goddess granted his wish by bringing the statue to life.

"Without the underlying promise of this myth," wrote the eminent art critic, E. H. Gombrich, and without "the secret hopes and fears that accompany the act of creation, there might be no art as we know it." Gombrich goes on to quote the contemporary English artist, Lucien Freud:

> A moment of complete happiness never occurs in the creation of a work of art. The promise of it is felt in the act of creation, but disappears towards the completion of the work. For it is then that the painter realizes that it is only a picture he is painting. Until then he had almost dared to hope that the picture might spring to life.[1]

---

1. Gombrich, 1969: 94.

The creative urge runs strong. Alone among earth's creatures, we contribute creatively even to the shaping of our own lives. "It is our nature to work upon our nature." Therefore we should not be wholly surprised by the yearning to create new worlds—even worlds unconstrained by the laws of our own genesis. And I think it is fair to say that in the current efforts to sustain virtual realities, our creative faculties have in some sense achieved their furthest and most impressive reach.

One wonders, though: does our preoccupation with virtual reality also correspond to some sort of alienation from the world? Here a historical perspective is desirable. Indisputably, our history *has* entailed an increasing "distance" between man and thing. Since the time of the ancients' vivid participation in a world alive with spirits, we have won our independence—our clear separation as subjects—from a world of no-longer-ensouled objects. As C. G. Jung puts it, the spirits have fled into the interior of the human individual, where they now conjure themselves only as the fading and scientifically disreputable images of our subjectivity—or rumble incoherently in the deep disturbances of our psyches. In our latter-day, academically nourished wish to eradicate the ghost from the machine, we would play the executioner in the final act of the world's dying. First the ghost in the world, and now the ghost in ourselves.

Could it be that this death of the world is what engenders our passion for virtual realities? Do we seek again the spirits that the ancients once found so easily within stream and meadow, tree and mountain? Behind the success of every new Stephen King movie, every advance in special effects, is there a secret hope and fear that the effects might somehow burst through into reality, and that some ancient Harpy might suddenly reach out and *grab* us? Is it our real yearning simply to become *alive* again, and to know the world as living?

Before we pray the gods of technology to grant full life to our creations, we should ask ourselves what it is we're really after.

A new interior, a new exterior

Most of us still take some form of "real inner life" for granted, even if we must set it within the doubtful quote marks of a reductionist science. Our pervasive doubts, we recognize, are historically recent—from which one reasonable conclusion is that the inner life seemed more real (less doubtful) to our forbears. Which in turn points to certain changes in consciousness. But how far can we characterize such changes—if indeed they have really occurred? Can we realistically look for the point where the peculiarly private—and now increasingly doubt-ridden—modern consciousness was first establishing itself and waxing strong?

Dutch psychologist Jan Hendrik van den Berg writes about the mysterious smile of Da Vinci's *Mona Lisa*.[2] People came from far and wide to see this smile—for it was, as van den Berg says, "the face of later generations," the revelation of a new way to live. Mona Lisa was smiling over the delicious and unexpected discovery of an interior secret, a hidden subjectivity, powerful enough to remake the world. The sudden flowering of the Renaissance, the childlike fervor of the Scientific Revolution, the compelling urge that sent Columbus and the other great voyagers steadfastly beyond the edges of the world, where sea monsters once dwelt—all testified to a humanity *waking up* from its medieval enchantment. We stretched, blinked, rubbed our eyes, looked out upon a fresh world we were seeing for the first time. And, in that moment, we became aware of the one who was inside, looking.

The new subjectivity was thus married to a new objectivity. It was not only Mona Lisa's smile that became famous, but also the landscape behind her.

It is the first landscape painted as a landscape, just because it was a landscape. A pure landscape, not just a backdrop for human actions: nature, nature as the middle ages did not know it, an exterior nature closed within itself and self-sufficient, an exterior from which the

---

2. van den Berg, 1975: 230–31.

human element has, in principle, been removed entirely. It is things-in-their-farewell, and therefore is as moving as a farewell of our dearest. It is the strangest landscape ever beheld by human eyes."

Van den Berg proceeds to quote Rilke: "This landscape is not the portrayal of an impression, it is not the judgment of a man on things at rest; it is nature coming into being, the world coming into existence, unknown to man as the jungle of an unknown island. It had been necessary to see the landscape in this way, far and strange, remote, without love . . . . It had to be almost hostile in its exalted indifference, if, with its objects, it was to give a new meaning to our existence."

Owen Barfield on some occasions speaks of the peculiarly valuable reverence or *devotion* toward nature, and the selfless, disinterested *study* of it, made possible only by our experience of it as something separate from ourselves. From this experience modern science was born. It is a way of relating to nature, he says, that we should not relinquish even if we go on to rediscover our deep, inner connection to the world around us.

But if our own challenge is to find our way back to a meaningful world, in Da Vinci's time the prospect was one of newly impending separation. The world was only beginning to move away from man—the modern subject was emerging from out of the world—and Da Vinci was one of the first to *notice* the newly independent landscape. He also noticed the noticing subject, and the subject could not repress a smile.

The bloated subject

In the eighteenth century, Rousseau wrote the first modern autobiography. He said in his *Confessions*, "I am going to attempt something that has never been done before and will never be attempted again." He was right in his first claim, notes van den Berg, but wrong in the second. Wrong? How could he even have dreamed such an insanity? Was no one ever again to write his personal confessions? But, really, we must sympathize with Rousseau, for how could he have known? How could he have known that James Joyce would spew out more words to describe the internal adventures of a day than he, Rousseau, required to relate the story of half a life? How could he have known that when all qualities were finally shifted, not only in theory, but, consequently, in human experience, from the primary side of the ledger to the secondary—from the objective side to the subjective—we would be left facing a world of sheer abstraction, while our own interiors overflowed with a perplexing subjectivity we knew less and less what to do with?

Rousseau did not know. He was, as we say today, on the "leading edge" of history's advance—but yet was too close to the "action" to see where it was leading. As nature gained ever greater independence, man's inner life tended inevitably toward the subjective—a vaguely meandering, mist-enshrouded stream no longer bound to the world's increasingly sharp, objective contours. And not all the books in all the libraries could contain the rising flood.

Van den Berg describes how

the inner self, which in Rousseau's time was a simple, soberly filled, airy space, has become ever more crowded. Permanent residents have even been admitted; at first, only the parents . . . finally it was the entire ancestry . . . . The space was divided, partitions were raised, and curtains appeared where in earlier days a free view was possible. The inner self grew into a complicated apartment building. The psychologists of our century, scouts of these inner rooms, could not finish describing all the things their astonished eyes saw. It did not take them long to surpass Joyce, and their work became endless in principle. The exploration of one apartment appeared to disturb another; and if the exploration moved to the next place, the first one again required attention. Something fell down or a threat was uttered; there was always something. The inner life was like a haunted house. But what else could it be? It contained everything . . . . Everything that had previously belonged to everybody, everything that had been collective property and had existed in the world in which everyone lived, had to be contained by the individual. It could not be expected that things would be quiet in the inner self. (p. 232)

Most of us—especially if we are engineers or scientists—try to ignore the unwelcome tenants, even as the pop psychologists drag them out before the public in a kind of traveling sideshow of freaks and wonders.

Excursions to the Alps

It happens to have been Rousseau as well who exhibited, in those same *Confessions*, what subsequently became known as a "sense of nature." Later, in *Julie* (1761), he wrote more completely of the emotion felt upon traveling through the Alps. Apparently he spoke for many others.

> Like an epidemic the new sensation spread through Europe. Every one wished to see what Rousseau had seen, to experience the same ecstasy. Everybody visited Switzerland and climbed the Alps. This had not happened before Rousseau. It was then that the Alps became a tourist attraction. Previously they had been an obstacle .... Even in 1750, Hénault, a poet and a friend of Voltaire's, crossed the Jura and the Alps without the least enthusiasm, merely observing, "There is always a creek at my side and rocks above my head, which seem about to fall in the creek or upon me." These words would nowadays disqualify him as a poet .... [3]

These changes make a difference. "The economic and social structure of Switzerland," writes Barfield, is owing in part to the tourist industry, which in turn depends upon the fact that "the *mountains* which twentieth-century man sees are not the mountains which eighteenth-century man saw." [4]

If there is a certain ideal esthetic distance, a point of maximum fascination, a stance of "objective subjectivity" wherein man and world resonate in the most exquisite tension, then it was the Romantics who lived most fully in that tension. [5] It is the point where man is sufficiently detached from "things" to appreciate their independent life, but not so detached that he has lost all consciousness of his inner connection to

---

3. van den Berg, 1975: 233.

4. Barfield, 1965a: 145–46.

5. Barfield somewhere makes this point.

them. His separation from the world only allows him to savor all the more his union with it.

The distancing process, however, was not arrested by the Romantics, so that van den Berg is correct in observing how "the estrangement of things, which brought Romanticism to ecstasy, belongs, for the most part, to the past." We are no longer close enough to the world even to feel the conscious fascination of our estrangement:

> Many of the people who, on their traditional trip to the Alps, ecstatically gaze at the snow on the mountain tops and at the azure of the transparent distance, do so out of a sense of duty. They are only imitating Rousseau; they are simulating an emotion which they do not actually feel. It is simply not permissible to sigh at the vision of the great views and to wonder, for everyone to hear, whether it was really worth the trouble. And yet the question would be fully justified; all one has to do is see the sweating and sunburned crowd, after it has streamed out of the train or the bus, plunge with resignation into the recommended beauty of the landscape to know that for a great many the trouble is greater than the enjoyment.

To look or not

Most of us will recognize something of ourselves in this description. Strangely, however, our alienation from nature is matched only by our passion to "capture" these bland encounters, to reproduce them in the more easily grasped two dimensions. "There, I've got it," we say as we click the shutter and turn away. This is not really reproducing nature, however, for the experience was not of nature, but of *taking the picture*.

"I've seen people in the Everglades come onto the walkway with their video equipment, take a picture, and go away," says Massachusetts naturalist John Mitchell. "They will go home and put it on and they will see the image they have captured of it. They will never have seen the real place."[6]

This happens even more curiously where nature's governing course was once so urgent as to be acknowledged in rites of passage. Coming of

---

6. Dumanoski, 1990.

age, betrothal, marriage, birth—on such occasions today the camera is redefining the events themselves, so that a derivative activity replaces whatever original significance may have remained. I must get the picture before I lose the too-quickly-passing moment—before the world departs from me—and then I can enjoy it forever after. If the technology is clever enough, I can even hope the replay will give me a little shiver of thrill. But why expect to be thrilled by what I couldn't be bothered to see in the first place? Pygmalion received a living bride from cold marble; on my part, I willingly exchange real life for a secondhand image.

There is a strange, double-sided gesture here—a reaching for something even as I avert my face from it. The present moment seems so filled with meaning that I must capture it for eternity, and yet seems so devoid of meaning that I can spend the "eternal moment" fiddling with my lenses, happily deferring to the later contemplation of a flat image. It's not clear what that image will enable me to recall, if I have shunned the original experience.

Our culture's fascinated obsession with images has often been remarked. What I want to suggest is a simple reason for it—one that accounts for the double nature of the obsession: if I dare not really look at nature, it is for fear that I will only draw a blank. The sense of profound meaning quivering just beneath the surface of my consciousness may turn out to have been only the random twitching of nerves. Worse yet, I will not know: is the blank in nature, or in me?[7]

At the same time (this is the other side of the gesture), I hope to overcome the blank. I desperately pursue the sights because, in a dim sort of way, I seek the ground of my being. I seek some kind of self-affirmation, a connection to the foundation of things, a reminder that I really am pos-

---

7. David Sewell draws my attention to these lines in Emerson's essay on "Nature": "The ruin or the blank that we see when we look at nature is in our own eye. The axis of vision is not coincident with the axis of things, and so they appear not transparent but opaque. The reason why the world lacks unity, and lies broken and in heaps, is because man is disunited with himself."

sessed of a significant existence, because the world in which I am rooted is significant.

But this is not yet quite adequate. Mere blankness—nothing at all—cannot inspire fear. Darkness can, however, and the blank I speak of is a kind of darkness. One never knows what the darkness may hold. So the question becomes: what is it that lives and stares back at me from nature's darkness, that I cannot bear to recognize, let alone return its gaze? What is it that I find tolerable only when it is reduced to a picture, a reflection, the safe abstractions of science?

The answer will, I hope, have been suggested by all the preceding: the source of my fears is what the ancients reveled in. It is what—in its gradual departure from the world—fascinated Da Vinci's contemporaries, enchanted Rousseau, and provoked the Romantics to something like pagan worship. But now it has retreated so thoroughly into the interior of things—which is at the same time the *human* interior—and been so long lost from sight that I can scarcely imagine the monstrous forms into which the pagan deities have twisted themselves in their hidden darkness. So I shield myself from the loathsome visages, reimagining the world as a collection of objects—surfaces without interiors, which is exactly what the photograph gives me. "Fear," writes Barfield, "is the true origin of materialism":

> Perhaps . . . it is just the desire of avoiding [the beings of whom the interior consists], perhaps it is even the fear of such a recognition, which has made the word "pattern" so popular of late. And there is *Gestalt*, too . . . . We glimpse a countenance, and we say hurriedly: "Yes, that is indeed a face, but it is the face of nobody."[8]

We swim within a veritable sea of images—printed, televised, and now computerized—and the one thing most people seem to agree on is that these images are in some sense artificial, virtual, unreal. And so they are. Desiring to feel alive, we invite them to "scare" us or otherwise to create memorable moments. But the results are never quite real enough,

---

8. Barfield, 1965b: 60, 160.

so that we must resort to an endless crescendo of special effects. No wonder; these images are a kind of barrier—something we can "paste over"
the world to preserve our distance even as they deliver a safe, surrogate
thrill. They are tamely cerebral artifacts, increasingly generated and controlled by "electronic brains." Projecting our wonderfully precise, uncontaminated, mathematical coordinates upon the world's screen, we disguise
the blank, unruly darkness behind.

Facing the darkness

We have yet to make peace with our haunting ghosts—this despite the
sometimes overly eager claim that they are "only" within us, duly chas-
tened and awaiting their final dismissal by science. The monsters that once
prowled the edges of the known world were fully acknowledged; now,
however, having long denied them due recognition, we find that they are
everywhere—just behind the mirror surfaces that bear our artificial images.
To say they have retreated into the interior of man, is not to deny their
presence in the world, for the significance of this retreat is precisely that
man's interior has become the world's interior.[9]

The more thoroughly we banish our unwelcome spirits from "objective" spaces, the more menacing and intimate becomes their approach to
us. Nothing in the history of this century suggests that their ravening
appetites have been sated. We glimpse their powers on the one hand
when we prod nature into a nuclear outburst (reassuring ourselves all the
while that we fully understand the theory of atom-splitting)—and on the
other hand when the fission of a much-too-brittle self leads to the mental
ward. These are not altogether unrelated phenomena. I have previously
cited Barfield's remark that

> the possibility of man's avoiding self-destruction depends on his real-
> izing before it is too late that what he let loose over Hiroshima, after

---

9. See appendix A, "Owen Barfield: The Evolution of Consciousness."

fiddling with its exterior for three centuries like a mechanical toy, was the forces of his own unconscious mind.[10]

There are other observations that, if taken seriously, testify to the intimate, creative relation between man and nature. Earlier in this chapter I alluded to the dependence of the Swiss economy upon *changes in mountains* during the last few centuries—changes correlative to the evolution of consciousness. Similarly, Oscar Wilde once asked, "Have you noticed that Nature has recently begun to look like Corot's landscapes?"[11] And E. H. Gombrich reminds us that the "picturesque" qualities we now discover in nature could only have arisen from our own habits of picture-making.[12] Even the physicist, in his drive to purify the phenomenal world of all "contamination" by subjectivity, has found the influences binding observer to observed finally inescapable.

These, however, are indications of a relation to nature that remains largely unconscious. They point rather to what remains of an older condition than to the basis for a new, *conscious* relation such as Barfield is signaling. But a sober recognition of the one relation can perhaps stimulate us toward a responsible pursuit of the other. From the thunderings of a Mount Sinai that threatened all who were foolish enough to look upon it—to the striking, precipitous landscape behind Mona Lisa, just then preparing to receive the self-assured, scientific gaze of the future—to the ecstatic Alps of Rousseau—to our own rather baffling wilderness areas whose secret we can no longer guess—if we begin to see these external changes as the inevitable correlates of changes within ourselves, then we can also begin to accept *responsibility* for the changes outside us by taking in hand the changes within us.

---

10. Barfield, 1973: 36.

11. This is André Gide's paraphrase of more extended comments by Wilde. See van den Berg, 1975: 52fn.

12. Gombrich, 1969: 315.

Art and the technological image

One might reasonably ask whether the rapid ascendancy of the computer-generated image in our day represents a further fleeing from the world's interior, or somehow a reversal of the flight. There are, unfortunately, few reasons for optimism. If the camera shields us against reality, the broad convergence of imaging techniques upon *virtual* reality bespeaks a desire to convert the shield into the full surround of an impenetrable fortress. I have spoken of a double gesture: the scarcely conscious fascination that requires me to look, and the simultaneous dropping of an artificial screen to intercept my gaze. Virtual realities promise endless fascination without any apparent risk that the horror of the real world might leak through.

There is at least this to be said for computerized imagery: so far as it becomes interactive, it invites a kind of creative participation on our part. We begin to experience a certain inner power with respect to the images around us. But so long as we exercise this power in isolation from the world, it threatens to become arbitrary, unrooted, destructive. Anyone who is aware of the images in video games, for example, will understand Barfield's concern when he says: given how far nature has evolved during the few hundred years since the medieval era, it isn't hard to imagine our now moving, over a similar or shorter period, "into a chaotically empty or a fantastically hideous world." He goes on:

> We should remember this, when appraising the aberrations of the formally representational arts. Of course, in so far as these are due to affectation, they are of no importance. But in so far as they are genuine, they are genuine because the artist has in some way or other experienced the world he represents. And in so far as they are appreciated, they are appreciated by those who are themselves willing to make a move towards seeing the world in that way, and, ultimately therefore, seeing that kind of world. We should remember this, when we see pictures of a dog with six legs emerging from a vegetable marrow or a woman with a motorbicycle substituted for her left breast.[13]

---

13. Barfield, 1965a: 146.

This suggests another concern. Pygmalion was an artist. During the Renaissance it was the artisan-scientist who observed and devoutly portrayed the world's recession. The true artist cannot be content merely to tinker with exteriors like a mechanic, but must work from within outwards. Today, however, no one will dare to claim that much art remains in the engineering organizations spawning ambitious virtual realities. All has been reduced to abstraction and calculation. If it is my own spirit I rediscover in the virtual artifact, then I must admit that it is a clean, antiseptic spirit distilled down to its mathematical grasp of three-dimensional images.

Yet there remains hope that our technological exploits will disturb ancient memories of a primal, creative fire—fire that even now we might steal and so make of ourselves (not our machines) a furnace to warm and revivify the world-hearth from within. Such creative responsibility is, in any case, being thrust upon us—as both the challenge of the global environment and the conundrums of bioethics testify. We are not allowed a safe, technological fiddling with the exterior of things. We are given a choice: to nourish unawares the spirits who rose in grotesquely beautiful prayer over Hiroshima—and who today in their hiddenness have multiplied and scattered to every corner of the globe even as they have burrowed yet more invasively into our subconscious—or to risk the unknown horrors of our own darkness in the hope of unearthing there the deeply creative images of a renewed world.

22

SEEING IN PERSPECTIVE

IT'S IMPRESSIVE, THE WIZARDRY we place in the hands of the 3-D graphics programmer. He is barely out of college—or perhaps not even that—and we entrust to him a mechanism for turning the world inside out. And the mechanism itself is pure simplicity: a 4×4 mathematical matrix. Armed with this little matrix, he can take any scene, real or imagined, apply a coordinate system to it, and then recompose the scene point by point until we see it from an entirely different perspective. That is, he can *project* the scene any way he wishes—which includes projecting it realistically onto a two-dimensional surface. Moreover, he can do all this with absolute fidelity to the original.

Well, almost. Absolute fidelity, it turns out, is as challenging a standard to meet in this context as it is in some others. To see just how challenging, we need to look back toward the age of faith, to when the projective laws—usually called the laws of linear perspective—were just being discovered.

Renaissance virtual reality

When, in early fifteenth-century Florence, Filippo Brunelleschi contrived the first painting in "true perspective," he raised a sensation. Partly, of course, this was due to his showmanship. He insisted that his friends stand exactly where he himself had stood while painting the panel, and directed them to look upon the original scene he had painted. Then he held the painting up with its *backside* directly in front of the viewer's face. A tiny eyehole was drilled through the middle of the panel. Gazing through the eyehole, a viewer simply witnessed the original scene. But if a mirror was held up in front of the painting, he now beheld the painting instead—and it was so accurately drawn in perspective that it was indistinguishable from the original.

Brunelleschi's cunning extended even further, however, for instead of painting a sky in the upper part of the work, he put burnished silver there. Now, with the aid of the mirror, the astonished viewer saw wind-blown clouds drifting across the top of the painting. Here, in this calculated confusion of real world and artifice, the technological quest for virtual reality was launched.

So, too, was the controversy. The new, perspectival art struck viewers with the force of a powerful and deceitful illusion, as had even Giotto's earlier, purely empirical experimentations with perspective. "There is nothing," Boccaccio said, "which Giotto could not have portrayed in such a manner as to deceive the sense of sight." Much later the Dutch artist Samuel van Hoogstraeten, acknowledging that his task was to "fool the sense of sight," went on to urge that the painter must thoroughly understand "the means by which the eyes are deceived."

This is not so easy—as those who try to represent three-dimensional reality on the surface of goggles know all too well. How can a painting—a flat, two-dimensional surface—appear to be what it is not? How can it look like a three-dimensional scene? In what sense does the flat work of art incorporate the laws of full-bodied reality—and in what sense does it fall short of that reality?

A clean, mathematical space

It is hard for us to appreciate how radically Brunelleschi's triumph changed the world. More than that: he made the world disappear. A hint of the disappearance already occurs in my description above: I summarized Brunelleschi's achievement without the slightest mention of what it was he painted. As it happens, he painted the Baptistery of St. John in the Piazza del Duomo of Florence. But that hardly mattered, for it was as if everything had become invisible to Brunelleschi except a collection of points—mathematical coordinates. To describe the essence of his achievement, so far as we are concerned with it today, is to describe a rigorous, mathematical method. It reduces the world to surfaces, and surfaces to points, and—as the graphics programmer knows very well—points to numbers. These contentless points, according to the German master of perspective, Albrecht Dürer, "are the beginning and end of all things."

Of course, the world had not yet really disappeared for Brunelleschi and his contemporaries. But in discovering the practical rules of strict, geometric perspective, he performed a momentous act of abstraction that hastened the world upon its vanishing course. Where we might have expected him to see the Baptistery, what actually captured his attention was a "visual pyramid": the collection of straight lines raying from all the building's surfaces to his own single, fixed eye. Each of those lines mapped a point of the Baptistery to a point on the "picture plane"—the artist's canvas. By mapping a few definitive points in this fashion, Brunelleschi could easily fill in the rest of the picture in near-perfect perspective.

In technical terms, the perspectival rendering of a scene is a projection of the scene from an eyepoint, as sectioned by the plane of the canvas. You can obtain the same effect by tracing the scene on a window while keeping one eye closed and the other eye absolutely stationery. Or else by using a camera.

And so the artist learned, with simple tools and an increasingly practiced eye—to perform the same magic our programmer now summons with her 4×4 matrix. While the methods differ—the artist no doubt possessing a fuller and more concrete sense for what he is actually *doing*, if only because of his necessarily "primitive" methods—the underlying mathematical conceptions remain the same. To arrive at these conceptions was one of the remarkable accomplishments of the Renaissance.

During the medieval era there had been no coordinated sense of mathematical space: an "all-pervasive and uniform space as we now conceive it was then unimaginable."[1] What did exist was more like an *inner* space—a space of meaning, a space of concretely felt interrelationships by which the individual was bound to the cosmos, nourished and sustained. It was a sense for these inner patterns—not the mathematical distribution of objects within an abstract, containerlike space—that (so oddly for us) gave organization and coherence to a medieval painting. Space did not present itself independently of things; it was more like the qualitatively varying *presence* of things, and derived its local "shape" from them. But in the art of linear perspective,

> Space is created first, and then the solid objects of the pictured world are arranged within it in accordance with the rules which it dictates. Space now contains the objects by which formerly it was created . . . . The result is an approximation to an infinite, mathematically homogeneous space.[2]

"Space now contains the objects by which formerly it was created." This is an art historian speaking, and he is referring to changes in the techniques of the painter. But the question remains: were these changes forced upon the artist by a truer knowledge of the world, or were they imposed upon the world by the artist? Was the new art of perspective objectively valid, or did it merely become a habit of our subjectivity?

Was the world created in perspective?

Over the century and a half or so following Brunelleschi's demonstration, the new rules of perspective transformed the art of all Europe. Surely, we might think, their triumph was guaranteed by their necessity, their

---

1. Edgerton, 1975: 159.
2. White, 1972: 123–24.

rightness. After all, to move from the medieval fresco to a painting of the high Renaissance is, for us, to move from a disconcerting, childish Babel of the eye to the clear obviousness of the real world. And, in any case, the behavior of light rays and the mathematics of projection are indisputable. How else could one draw correctly?

In other words, if God hadn't wanted us to represent the world in perspective, He wouldn't have created it that way.

If you are inclined toward this conviction, then you may be surprised to hear the question put by psychologist R. L. Gregory:

> It is an extraordinary fact that simple geometric perspective took so long to develop—far longer than fire or the wheel—and yet in a sense it has always been present for the seeing. But is perspective present in nature? Is perspective a discovery, or an invention of the Renaissance artists?[3]

Gregory is here alluding to a twentieth-century scholarly squall that the respected German art historian, Erwin Panofsky, kicked up in 1925 with the publication of his *Perspective as Symbolic Form*. Panofsky, whose essay was both brief and difficult, argued that the conventions of linear perspective were cultural symbols, not absolute truths. They are "comprehensible only for a quite specific, indeed specifically modern, sense of space, or if you will, sense of the world."[4] However obscure Panofsky's actual thesis may have been, its time was at hand, and many others echoed his theme. For example, Sir Herbert Read:

> We do not always realize that the theory of perspective developed in the fifteenth century is a scientific convention; it is merely one way of describing space and has no absolute validity.[5]

The inevitable "common-sense" backlash was equally vigorous. Physiologist M. H. Pirenne, responding to Panofsky, declared flatly that "'the

---

3. Gregory, 1966: 164.
4. Panofsky, 1991: 34.
5. Cited in Gombrich, 1969: 247.

strange fascination which perspective had for the Renaissance mind' was the fascination of truth."[6]

The dispute continues into our own day, and has tended not so much toward resolution as toward exhaustion among the manifold, tortured byways of argument—from the physiology and psychology of sense perception to the subtleties of epistemological theory. It seems characteristic of the past few centuries that the question "what belongs to the mind and what belongs to the world?" leads us in so many different arenas to the same brick wall—or mental block.

Really, now. Wasn't the world created in perspective?

All right, it's true. We all *know* the world "comes" in perspective, even if, as philosophers or art critics, we divert ourselves with contrary speculations. Why pretend otherwise? It's simply impossible to imagine a nonperspectival world. Light travels in straight lines—we can't see around corners! The geometry of perspective follows inexorably.

Yes, let's face these facts. But no facts can stand alone. We must establish at least a minimal context. For a start, here are three things to think about:

Cultural variations. Non-Westernized peoples frequently do not "read" perspectival images (including photographs) the way we do. They may see nothing recognizable even in a familiar scene, or else may piece the image together only with painstaking analysis. Gregory, referring to the apparent learning involved in such reading, suggests it is fortunate that perspective was invented before the camera; otherwise, "we might have had great difficulty in accepting photographs as other than weird distortions." In other words, we had to become familiar with and learn about perspectival images before they could seem wholly natural to us.

Jan Deregowski speculates that those who have difficulty interpreting perspectival drawings are unable to "integrate the pictorial elements. They see individual symbols and cues but are incapable of linking all the

---

6. Pirenne, 1952.

elements into a consolidated whole."[7] This is a particularly striking thought, for we are accustomed to thinking of perspective as having introduced a coherent, universal, pictorial space in which objects can for the first time find their "proper" places relative to each other. Shouldn't this make it *easier* for the unacculturated observer? Apparently not.

When the blind receive sight. Thanks to modern surgery, many of the congenitally blind have been given their sight. Or rather, they have been given healthy eyes. But it turns out that seeing requires much more than functioning eyes and nerves. When the operation is performed after early childhood, it sets a daunting task for the beneficiary. How well one sees depends, among other things, on the richness of prior experience with touch and the other senses. Even after extended adaptation, the formerly blind person may need to feel an object with his hands before he can "see" a meaningful shape. There are other problems as well. Gregory reports on the case of S. B., who received a donated cornea at fifty-two:

> Before the operations, he was undaunted by traffic. He would cross alone, holding his arm or his stick stubbornly before him, when the traffic would subside as the waters before Christ. But after the operation, it took two of us on either side to force him across a road: he was terrified as never before in his life.[8]

S. B.—as in many such cases—became rather depressed, and tended to withdraw from his previous, highly active life. (While blind, he had even ridden a bicycle, with the help of a friend.) "Some of the cases revert very soon to living without light, making no attempt to see. S. B. would often not trouble to turn on the light in the evening, but would sit in darkness." Having first given up living, S. B. died three years later.

The lateness of the discovery. Why did no one before Brunelleschi take what Panofsky calls "the apparently small step of intersecting the visual

---

7. Deregowski, 1974.

8. Gregory, 1966: 194–98. For a somewhat dated but valuable survey of the literature, see von Senden, 1960.

pyramid with a plane" and thereby construct a modern, perspectival representation of space? After all, Euclid had produced his geometry and optics some 1700 years before Brunelleschi, and Western culture, together with the Arabic, had continued to pursue these topics in a sophisticated manner. Perfect perspectival images were projected by nature upon every window and mirror, and—with some inconvenience—these could have been traced by the inquisitive artist. Such tracing would have made the essential rules of perspective, such as the existence of vanishing points, immediately obvious to one who was looking for them. Moreover, art itself was in many other respects technically sophisticated—the great cathedrals are evidence enough of that. It is hard to believe that artists were incapable of seizing the rules of perspective, had those rules been there for the seeing.

Samuel Edgerton voices a perplexity shared by others:

> How curious that an understanding of the mathematics of human pictorial representation occurred so late—and so locally—in history.... Today we are the tired children of [the] discovery; the magic of perspective illusion is gone, and the "innate" geometry in our eyes and in our paintings is taken for granted. Linear perspective has been part and parcel of psyche and civilization for too many centuries, which is perhaps far less astonishing than the fact that it eluded men of all civilizations for a thousand years prior to the [fifteenth century].[9]

Limitations of linear perspective in art

Clearly, seeing is not automatically given to the sighted. Much of what we are tempted to call "objective seeing" originates in the activity of the seeing subject.[10] This, combined with the lateness of the discovery of perspective, returns us all the more forcibly to Gregory's question: how much of the "discovery" was in fact an invention?

---

9. Edgerton, 1975: 4.

10. For a physicist's extended discussion of light in relation to the seeing subject, refer to Zajonc, 1993.

But the muddying of our context grows even worse when we turn to the actual use of perspective in art.

To represent something in geometric perspective is to project it from a single, fixed eyepoint. If you wish to view "correctly" a drawing created in this way, you must close one eye and position yourself (with respect to the drawing) exactly where the original eyepoint was; otherwise, your perspective as viewer defeats the perspective "hardwired" into the drawing. With paintings such as Da Vinci's *The Last Supper*—extending the length of one wall of a monastery's refectory—the perspective had to be "fudged" in order to keep the image from looking quite false to the monks seated far away from the painter's viewing point.

More importantly, we do not normally see with just one eye. Open a second eye and some of the depth effect of the painting is lost. That is, with binocular vision we perceive depth quite effectively, so that we immediately recognize the "real painting" for what it is—a flat surface with blobs of paint smeared across it. We defeat the artist's "deceptive" intentions.

But this is not all. In the sense that really counts, perspective gives us mathematically incorrect results. Have you ever noticed how paltry those mountains seem in the photographs you bring home from vacation? You're not just imagining things. The mountains *are* seen relatively larger in reality than they are in the photograph, despite the fact that the photograph yields an image in "perfect" perspective. Through an effect known as size constancy scaling, we pick up on various cues about the distance of an object, and then compensate for great distance by seeing the object larger than geometry and optics would seem to allow.

You can test this by holding one upraised hand at arm's length in front of you, with the other at half that distance and not visually overlapping the first. If you look alternately at your two hands, you are unlikely to see the nearer hand as double the size of the further one, but only a little larger—despite the fact that the retinal image of the one is twice as large as the other. Is your brain playing a nasty trick upon your eyes? Before you answer yes too quickly, ask yourself: which estimate of your hand sizes is closer to the truth of the hands themselves?

It did not take long for the artists of the Renaissance to begin realizing the limitations of linear perspective. Michelangelo scorned Dürer's geometric methods, and claimed reliance upon the "compasses in the eye." Eventually, art as illusion—which is to say, art as the imitation of something else—passed into triteness. The camera made it too easy. The artist began inquiring more deeply into the underlying laws of seeing, of light, and of form. Art moved—or wanted to move—closer to the seminal chaos within which the world itself first takes on form.

Do we see "in here" or "out there"?

If Brunelleschi made the world disappear, what were the instruments of his sorcery? Abstractions. Points, rays, geometric transformations. "Points are the beginning and end of all things." Once we appreciate this, the dispute about whether perspective is in nature or is instead a cultural convention becomes either trivial or extremely misleading, depending upon what it is we're really asking.

If we equate "seeing in perspective" with certain abstract, mathematical characteristics of the perceived world, then surely the human race has always seen in perspective, even if it was only during the Renaissance that we first *noticed* perspective and discovered how to *represent* it properly. The abstractions have always been there for the abstracting, whether or not people were capable of performing the act of abstraction. Light rays have always traveled in straight lines.

But, then, it is rather strange to argue that our ancestors saw what they were incapable of noticing. What the mathematician abstracts from our seeing is not the seeing itself. The puzzlement of non-Westernized people when looking at perspectival drawings; the struggles of those who receive sight tardily; and the sober lessons drawn by Western artists after their initial excitement with perspective—all declare that seeing involves much more than geometry and optics. Or, at least, it did before our own day. For it's true—and a matter of frightening import—that our own seeing has become increasingly abstract—which is why some who would instruct us in art urge us to "draw on the right side of the brain."[11] It's also true that our habit of abstraction is born of an extreme subject–object polarization; only a detached subject looking *at* an object from a considerable subjective distance can analyze that object and abstract from it a set of mathematical properties.

I asked above: did the new art of perspective possess objective validity, or did it merely become a habit of our subjectivity? What we need to understand is that the very possibility of asking such questions first arose in the Renaissance. For it was then that Western man first began to experience the world as an abstract, mathematical "container" full of objects wholly separate from himself, and to experience himself as an isolated, subjective interior gazing out through the window of his eyes upon a separate world.

Behind subject and object. If the elaboration of the rules of perspective was part of a larger historical development giving birth to the modern subject and object, then we cannot hope to understand perspective itself as either subjective or objective. The processes that first produced a subject and object as we know them today cannot themselves be subjective or objective. Here, as so often, it is far more important to ask why our question arises at a certain point in history than it is to answer the question in its own misleading terms. And in order to undertake this more basic inquiry, we need to step back from the controversy and see it in a larger context.

Virtual reality may assist us. Suppose you are wearing a headset with all the related paraphernalia and are exploring a virtual world. Is that world subjective or objective? Neither answer quite suffices by itself. Subjective, you say? Yes, by all means. Its forms, "spoken" in a programming language, are now sustained by your own participation. Whatever you may think about a tree falling in the woods where no one hears it, there's

---

11. Edwards, 1979.

a strong case to be made that the room you're exploring is not really there except insofar as your eyes and other senses are helping to create it.

Objective, you say? Yes—that, too. Even if for now this is the weaker side of the dual truth, there is undeniably an objective component here. You cannot redesign the room according to your fancy. It has an objective or given character, sustained intersubjectively among those who may inhabit it. If you move a book from the chair to the table, that is where another occupant of the room will find it. There is, moreover, objectivity in the entire representational apparatus, just as there is in a two-dimensional painting.

Now imagine that you and others are in the same virtual room. Assume further that the software affords the group of you some means for collectively reconceiving the room—not by moving things around, but rather by recreating it, so to speak, from the "inside," at the level of the software. What is now subjective and what is objective? If the collective subjectivity determines the objective forms, and if the objective forms in turn determine what each individual experiences subjectively—well, it becomes risky to classify things too rigidly as subjective or objective.

What I am suggesting, then—and for the moment I will leave it a bald suggestion—is this: quite apart from the "reality status" of our virtual room, the description just given roughly captures the way we are situated in the *real world*. If, as so many seem to think, virtual reality points toward a new paradigm, it is a paradigm having less to do with new, high-tech experiences than with our participation in the world—a participation ancient and powerful in its origins (if all but vanished from modern experience) and echoed only faintly in the modern technologies. I will return to this shortly.

Bringing all this to bear on the issue of perspective, we can say neither that perspective is objectively inherent in the world, where it could only be *discovered*, nor that it was a mere convention waiting to be *invented*. Rather, our Renaissance predecessors saw a different world than the ancients saw, and at the same time the world was becoming different because of the way they saw it. Their world, like ours, was virtuality continually on the way toward reality.

Am I an embryo or an island?

Only a knowing subject can attain objectivity, so that the object depends for its existence upon the subject. And only through the indifferent object can a subject know itself *as* a subject. Subject and object are not pure opposites, but more like the opposite poles of a magnet: the north pole exists only by virtue of the south pole. Neither can exist by itself.

The debate over perspective—was it discovered *out there* or invented *in here*—became possible only with the radicalization of this polarity. It is resolvable only when we recognize the mutual interpenetration that unites the apparent opposites: there is something of the subject in the most adamantine object, and an objective, world-sustaining presence in the sheerest subject. Cut off the smallest piece of one end of the magnet, and you will find that it still possess *both* a south pole and a north pole. It is as impossible to conceive a pure subject or pure object as it is to conceive a pure north or south pole. But it is quite possible to lose sight of their mutual participation. Such is our plight today as in our radical subjectivity we imagine ourselves to confront a radical objectivity.

All this is ground Owen Barfield has worked over throughout the greater part of this century. A philologist, Barfield employs semantics to explore the changing balance between subject and object throughout human history. What he says about the medieval era is particularly germane to our inquiry. For example, regarding nonperspectival art:

> Before the scientific revolution the world was more like a garment men wore about them than a stage on which they moved. In such a world the convention of perspective was unnecessary. To such a world other conventions of visual reproduction, such as the nimbus and the halo, were as appropriate as to ours they are not. It was as if the observers were themselves *in* the picture.[12]

---

12. Barfield, 1965a: 94–95.

Or, again, Barfield refers to the Middle Ages as a time when the individual "was rather less like an island, rather more like an embryo, than we are." An embryo, too, recalls the notion of polarity, or interpenetration of opposites. It exists by virtue of the mother, and the mother bears it as an expression of her own nature.

How do we escape our cultural conditioning and understand what could be meant by wearing the world as a garment, or experiencing it as an embryo? Perhaps, in some ways, it will be easier for us once we have spent some time in a virtual reality booth! But we also have what may be a more promising option: we can attempt to get "inside" the consciousness of earlier cultures. No one assists us more vividly in this task than Barfield, who is worth quoting at some length as he asks us to imagine what it was like to stand in the world as a citizen of the medieval era:

> If it is daytime, we see the air filled with light proceeding from a living sun, rather as our own flesh is filled with blood proceeding from a living heart. If it is night-time, we do not merely see a plain, homogeneous vault pricked with separate points of light, but a regional, qualitative sky, from which first of all the different sections of the great zodiacal belt, and secondly the planets and the moon (each of which is embedded in its own revolving crystal sphere) are raying down their complex influences upon the earth, its metals, its plants, its animals and its men and women, including ourselves . . . . Our own health and temperament are joined by invisible threads to these heavenly bodies we are looking at . . . .
>
> We turn our eyes on the sea—and at once we are aware that we are looking at one of the four elements, of which all things on earth are composed, including our own bodies. We take it for granted that these elements have invisible constituents, for, as to that part of them which is incorporated in our own bodies, we experience them inwardly as the "four humors" which go to make up our temperament. (Today we still catch the lingering echo of this participation, when Shakespeare makes Mark Antony say of Brutus:

> *. . . The elements*
> *So mixed in him, that Nature might stand up*
> *And say to all the world, This was a man.)*

. . . A stone falls to the ground—we see it seeking the center of the earth, moved by something much more like desire than what we today call gravity . . . . [13]

Now, perhaps, we can catch our first true glimpse of the Renaissance achievement. For us to enter into the medieval experience of the world would be rather like stepping from the audience into a play: as participants sucked into the story—trapped *inside* our relationships to everything and everyone around us—we could no longer detach ourselves and view the events from a distance. Conversely, what Brunelleschi and his contemporaries had to achieve was to shed those innumerable threads that bound them to their environment, and that made them both participants in the world and prisoners of it; they had to step out of the story. The world they observed was now in some sense flatter—like a picture or movie—and they could even watch their own characters in a kind of distant, objective fashion—the way, in our modern subjectivity, we are inclined to observe ourselves at ever greater removes. (I have already noted that our penchant for the prefix *meta-* serves as one measure of this detachment.)

It may, incidentally, seem odd to speak of the new world of "in-depth" perspective as flatter than what went before, but it is necessary. As Barfield remarks, the perspectival rendering of a photograph couldn't appear lifelike to us if the world had not become photolike. That is, we are accustomed to having stepped out of the picture, and now all it requires is a certain abstract, mathematical depth to make an image look "solid." Such is the only kind of depth our surroundings still retain for us once we have been ejected from their story. But it is an extraordinarily *flat* sort of depth compared to the thickly textured matrix of meaning that results from being *in* the story.

---

13. Barfield, 1965a: 76-77.

Which end of the telescope do we look through? If perspectival depth puts a new kind of distance between us and the world we survey, there is much in technology that cooperates with this process of alienation. Robert D. Romanyshyn points out that the invention of the telescope was, in the sense that counts, a symptom and cause of *increasing* distance rather than a means for overcoming distance. Galileo's world-changing instrument pushed the moon farther from us. Where once we felt ourselves within the moon's sphere of influence, we woke up to find the moon far, far away, unconnected to ourselves. "Perhaps," Romanyshyn says, "we had to travel to the moon in 1969 because it had gone so far away." Much the same can be said of other modern devices:

> Technological instruments like the telescope and the microscope, the telephone and the television, the automobile and the airplane, are not merely or even primarily instruments which bridge distance. Rather, they are instruments called into being by the distance we have created, by the distance we have put between ourselves and the world.[14]

This is no less true of more modern, computerized communication devices. The compulsive efforts to "overcome the barriers between people," the verbal torrents now flooding online channels, and the reconceptualization of these torrents as information streams look very much like symptoms of the rapidly increasing distance between us. Having been ejected from the world's story, we find ourselves now ejected even from one another's stories. Our lives no longer interpenetrate; words pass between us like inert objects—like spacecraft hurled through space to the moon and back. So we throw more and more words across our new, ever more remote communication channels, hoping we might finally connect.

But the distance between us cannot be bridged in this way. Like the telescope, our instruments of communication only increase the distance. Our real need is to rediscover what it means to *participate* in each other's

---

14. Romanyshyn, 1989: 73, 97. Romanyshyn's *Technology As Symptom and Dream* contains a superb treatment of perspective as an expression of man's changing relation to the world.

lives and worlds. This requires attention to precisely those potentialities of human exchange our efficient technology is teaching us to ignore.

There is in our use of communication technology something of the double-sided gesture referred to in the last chapter: we welcome a safe distance even as we hope to overcome it. Virtual reality is, of course, the perfection of this gesture. We speak of "immersive" virtual reality, but it is immersion in a "nothing" that is compounded of mathematical abstractions and cut off from Nature's lawfulness.

Does reality have a future?

As I remarked earlier, we all *know* that the world comes in perspective. Yet this "simple" fact was not noticed by highly skilled mathematicians and artists prior to the Renaissance. Our own ability to notice it says something about our experience of the world. Unlike our predecessors, we find it natural to filter abstractions from the world and to let all the rest drop away. Such filtering was impossible to those who were intimately ensnared *within* the world, bound to it by a dense mesh of meaning. The abyss between self and object was then much less isolating than it is today.

Our own hard-won separation, as Barfield points out, has proven a valuable gift—one never to be discarded. But insofar as it has metamorphosed into an experience of ourselves as wholly and absolutely cut off from the world, it is a lie. Furthermore, it is an unnecessary lie, for it is possible to enjoy the antithesis of subjective "south pole" and objective "north pole" without proceeding to act as if the antithesis were a clean severance. That we do thus act and think cannot be doubted—and we guard our habits with powerful taboos.

If you take this for an exaggeration, Barfield would have you contemplate some such proposition as this: *if all life, all knowing and cognizing spirit, were removed from the universe, then nothing else—no objects—would be left either.* No sun, moon, earth, or stars. Such a thought taken seriously is—even for those who construct virtual realities—forbidden by what our minds have become. And yet, as Barfield reminds us, it would have been just as impossible either to feel or think the proposition's *denial* during the medieval era. Can we claim to have escaped the parochial conventions of our own era without first understanding at least how the earlier experience was *possible*, and then how and why it evolved into our own experience?

The world as virtual reality. There is a corollary to this forgotten understanding—one desperately needed in our own day: if we participate in the world, then we continue to bear *responsibility* for what the world becomes. In one context Barfield puts it this way: "if enough people go on long enough perceiving and thinking about the world as mechanism only, the macroscopic world will eventually *become* mechanism only."[15]

Here is the danger of our fascination with virtual reality. Just consider one fact: the graphics programmer will almost certainly learn his entire trade without any professional exposure to art history and the issues I have been vaguely sketching. All this is unnecessary, irrelevant. His "art" has become pure technique, and the technique is everything. How far we are from the broad, humane ideals of an earlier age! Today, our innovations in the production of images seem controlled solely by the engineer's giddy fascination with technical feasibility. These innovations are immediately put to work by advertisers interested in their suasive powers and merchants interested in their entertaining powers.

So we accept the bombardment of our senses and our psyches by images—printed, video, holographic, "virtually real"—with little evident concern for our own creative effect upon the world when we participate in these ever more mechanical and mathematicized presentations of what once was sacred object and nourishing plenum of space. Like the Renaissance viewers at Brunelleschi's demonstration, we marvel at the new sensations we call "realistic"—but we do not consider the changing standard of reality lying behind our exclamations.

If Brunelleschi's feat was both a discovery of what the world had already started to become and a harbinger of its future determination, so,

---

15. "Science and Quality," in Barfield, 1977b: 185.

too, we should look for a double significance in our current experimentation with virtual reality. It is not hard to find. Well before the advent of high-performance computing, we had already accepted the reduction of the world to virtual reality. For we have long "known" that the entire phenomenal display within which we live out our lives is merely a flickering, subjective drama, thrown up upon some unidentifiable (and philosophically illicit) screen in our brains. The "real" world of particles and fields has vanished into the physicist's equations and theoretical constructs, which are not all that distinguishable from the matrices and coordinates of the virtual reality programmer. Who does not accept that the painter's easel and canvas are illusions, manufactured of infinitesimal particles and immense tracts of empty space? So everything disappears into the momentary, subjective glittering of insubstantial surfaces, a wraithlike dance uncertainly mirrored in the ephemeral electronic pulsations of our brains. When the world had already become so virtual, could the technology of virtual reality have been far behind?

What is the status of virtual reality? And what of the real world? I suppose it is evident enough on the face of these terms that we're not asking two unrelated questions. But if it's a single question, the alternative responses are as divergent as they could be: will we continue one-sidedly upon the course first set by Brunelleschi, reducing the world ever more to an abstract virtuality, content to manipulate point-coordinates with our mathematical matrices? Or will we, from our new and individual vantage points, learn again to put on the *real* world as a garment—now, however, not only being warmed by it, but also warming it from within through our own creative efforts?

23

CAN WE TRANSCEND COMPUTATION?

EVERYONE SEEMS TO KNOW that computers are one-sided. If we had to characterize computers as either logical or intuitive, we would say, "logical." Do computers deal in information or understanding? Information. Are they impersonal or personal? Impersonal. Highly structured or unstructured? Structured. Quantitative or qualitative? Quantitative.

The problem is that we always seem to have a clear notion of the one side—the attributes we assign to the computer—while the other side remains suspiciously elusive despite representing our own "human dimension." What sort of personal understanding is intuitive, unstructured, and qualitative? Can we distinguish it *precisely* from impersonal information that is logical, structured, and quantitative?

But the question rings an alarm bell. It asks for a precise distinction, but precision itself seems to be one of the terms we are required to distinguish. After all, what do we mean by precision if not quantitative and logical exactness? If this is so, however, then we appear to be stuck: clearly, we cannot distinguish *precisely* between precision itself and something incommensurable with precision, any more than we can visually

283

distinguish between sight and smell. All we can do is contrast the precise with the imprecise, which leaves us firmly rooted to the scale of precision. And yet, the widespread impression of computational one-sidedness suggests that we are at least dimly aware of "another side of the story." Can we lay hold of it?

The conviction that we can underlies every sentence of this book. The issues, however, are complex, and they confound virtually every debate about computer capabilities. When a problem haunts us in this way, we can be sure that we're up against a fundamental question of meaning—very likely one that our deeply ingrained cultural biases or blind spots prevent us from encompassing.

It so happens that Owen Barfield has spent some sixty-five years circling and laying bare the particular biases at issue here. His first, decisive insights applicable to the relation between computers and human beings date from the late 1920s—although he was not then writing, and so far as I know has not since written, *about* computers. Unfortunately, I do not know of any others who have brought his work to bear upon artificial intelligence and related disciplines. My own effort here is a modest one: to suggest broadly and informally where Barfield's work strikes most directly at current confusions.

A brief preview

As I have just suggested, no one can strictly *prove* that the computer suffers decisive limitations relative to the human being. We could capture the matter in a proof only if everything in the human being were assimilable to the language of proof—and therefore only if everything in the human being were "computable"—which would also imply that the proof was wrong.

We can, however, come to *understand* the computer's limitations. Admittedly, this requires a considerable effort. The computer brings to perfect completion the primary "drift" of our civilization over the past few hundred years. To see the computer in perspective, we need to get outside this drift—one might also say, to get outside ourselves. Or, to use

the language of chapter 11, "In Summary," we must come *to* ourselves—experience an awakening of what is most deeply human within
us.

What is most deeply human is inseparable from *meaning*. Unfortunately, the meaning of "meaning" is the most vexed issue in all of artificial
intelligence and cognitive science. In dealing with meaning, we must
come to terms with everything in the human being that does *not* compute. That is why this chapter is primarily about meaning. If you find
yourself wondering along the way, "what does all this have to do with the
computer?" then I suppose the presentation may be roughly on track. At
the same time, I hope it is clear by the end of our journey that meaning
has a great deal to do with the *limitations* of the computer.

The problem, of course, is that I am no master of meaning, able to
orchestrate its appearance in these pages. If society as a whole suffers from
its loss, so do I. But I, like many others, am also *aware* of the loss, and the
computer has been one of the primary instruments of my awareness. By
considering computation in the purest sense, I have been able to begin
grasping what a certain few—and in particular Owen Barfield—have
been telling us about the nature of meaning.

Meaning, you might say, is what computation is not. But the two are
not simple opposites. They cannot be, for then they would stand in a
strictly logical—and therefore, computational—relationship, in which
case meaning would have been assimilated to computation. We can hardly
expect the principle that "balances" logic and computation to be itself
reducible to logic and computation.

But all that, unfortunately, is itself a highly abstract statement. Let me
substitute a metaphor: what I have attempted in this book is to outline
the *hole* I find in society and in myself, about which I can say, "That's
where meaning must lie. My meaninglessness gives shape to a void. By
entering with a proper sensitivity into the meaninglessness, I can begin to
sense the dark hollow it enfolds. And in the darkness there begin to flicker
the first, faint colors of meaning."

Moreover, it turns out that the powers of computation, with which so much of the world now resonates, shape themselves around the same void. The meaninglessness of my experience is, in fact, the meaninglessness of a computational bent manifesting within my consciousness, in society, and—increasingly—in nature.

The computer therefore may give us a gift: the opportunity to recognize meaning as the void at the computer's heart. And it likewise presents us with a challenge: to overcome the void, or rather fill it with our humanity.

Accuracy, truth, and meaning

In using language, we often strive for accurate communication. We may also seek something like fullness of expression, richness of content, or the expansion of meaning. Between these two aims there is a kind of tension. Consider the following sentences:

(1) "The enemy is located at coordinates 58.75, 37.29."

(2) "The worst enemy of freedom is the determined majority."

(3) "Love your enemy."

In (1) accuracy is at a maximum. Assuming that both speaker and hearer have previously agreed on the enemy's identity, the reference here simply designates, without much ambiguity, "those same people." And for the rest, the sentence does little more than specify a precise location where those people may be found. It is a model of accuracy.

The second sentence raises questions of meaning in a more insistent fashion than (1). If the majority's freedom to act *as* a majority is itself a threat to freedom, then we need to sort out just what we mean by "freedom." Freedom in what respect, and for whom? Similarly, what is the sense of "worst"? Does it mean "most common"? "Most powerful"? "Most vile"? And how does "determined"—usually understood as a trait of individual psychology—apply to a collective?

Despite these questions, however, we pick up the rough sense of this second assertion without too much difficulty, for the thought is not altogether new to us, and we have learned what sorts of qualifications we must give to each term in order to achieve a coherent statement. Ask a group of educated people what the sentence means, and you would expect at least a minimal cohesion in the responses, which is a measure of our (by no means extreme) accuracy in communication when we speak the sentence. So in (2) we have gained a certain richness of suggestion, a certain fullness and complexity of meaning, but have lost accuracy, compared to (1).

With (3) the interpretive difficulties have multiplied greatly, throwing severe obstacles in the way of accurate communication. (This is especially the case if you imagine this exhortation being voiced for the first time within a given culture.) Isn't the definition of "enemy" being rudely turned on its head? If I am to treat my enemy like a loved one, what is the difference between the two, and what is happening to language?

And yet, this very saying has been received by numerous people with *some* degree of common understanding—although it is an understanding that may only be born of a sudden and illuminating expansion of commonly held, but inadequate, meanings. It is not that we simply abandon the old meaning of "enemy"—we are not likely to forget the sting of recently felt animosities, for example—but a new awareness of possibility now impinges upon that old meaning, placing things in a curious and intriguing light. Can it be that my enemies play a necessary—a disciplinary or educative—role in my life? If I treat an enemy as a friend, do I benefit myself as well as him? What will become of the enmity in that case?

Although any group of people will likely generate various explanations of the sentence (the potential for accuracy here is quite low), some individuals, at least, will confess that they have found the meaning to be both sublime and decisive for their lives. The sublimity is purchased, it appears, at the expense of the ease with which we can precisely communicate or explicate the thought.

The polarity of accuracy and meaning. In assessing the three sentences above, we run into the same problem we encountered when asking about the computer's one-sidedness. Do we really have a clear idea of what we might contrast with accuracy? Sentence (3) may indeed seem, in its current formulation, more "profound" than (1), but doesn't this just suggest that we should elaborate the truth of (3) until it has become as straightforward as (1)? For while most of us can accept the goal of accuracy with unqualified enthusiasm, we don't quite know what to do with the notion of meaning or fullness of expression. Isn't the opposite of accuracy simply vagueness or fuzziness of expression? And if my attempt to achieve deeper meaning results in diversity of interpretation, shouldn't I try to clarify my thought—express it more precisely, so that its meaning is unambiguous?

The strong urge today, in other words, is to seek greater accuracy, and we're not quite sure what other challenge exists. If we could just devise a language free of all those ambiguities about "enemy," "freedom," "determined" . . . then people could not so easily speak vaguely or imprecisely. It seems all too obvious, therefore, that the three sentences above reflect an increasing *confusion* of meaning—a loss of accuracy—and we are likely to leave the matter there.

But this will not do. In the first place, it encourages us to dismiss as empty or shoddy much that is most noble and inspiring in human culture. In the second place, it leaves unanswered the question, What are we striving to be accurate about? For we already *have* languages nearly purified of all ambiguity—the various systems of symbolic logic and formal mathematics are just such languages. And the reason they are free of ambiguity is that, by themselves, they cannot be *about* anything. We can make them about something only by destroying their perfect precision. To apply mathematics, we must introduce some more or less unruly terms relating to the world. But I am running ahead of myself. Allow me to backtrack for a moment.

It is true that vagueness is the opposite of accuracy. But opposites are not what we are looking for. What we need in order to find a counterpoint to accuracy is, as Barfield shows, the relation of *polar contraries*.[1] Think, for example, of a bar magnet. Its north and south poles are not mere opposites. Neither can exist without the other, and each penetrates the other. Cut off a section of the north end of the magnet, and you now have a second bar magnet with both north and south poles. It is impossible to isolate "pure northernness." Each pole exists, not only in opposition to the other, but also by virtue of the other. If you destroy one pole, you destroy the other as well—by demagnetizing the bar.

This points to what is, I believe, one of Barfield's critical recognitions bearing on the computer's limitations: *meaning (or expressiveness) and accuracy are polar contraries*. At the moment I expect the statement to be more of a puzzle than a revelation. Indeed, as the puzzlements I have already cited suggest, the ideas at issue here prove extraordinarily elusive. I hope, however, at least to hint at the life within this statement.

The polar and the nonpolar. It seems odd that so fundamental an idea as polarity should find so little employment in the various domains of human thought. Odd, perhaps, but not surprising, for an age of logic and precision is much more comfortable with binary oppositions (on or off, A or not-A) than with this strange notion of mutual penetration. Even in physics, the actual phenomenon of polarity (like most other observable phenomena) is scarcely dealt with as such, but rather is immediately reconceived in terms of "particles" and their mathematical characteristics. For our present purposes, however, it is the *phenomenon* of polarity itself that we must invoke.[2]

To begin with, then—and recalling the magnet's polarity—meaning exists *by virtue of* accuracy, and accuracy exists *by virtue of* meaning. We can neither be meaninglessly accurate nor meaningfully inaccurate in any absolute sense. That is, accurate communication requires something

---

1. Barfield, 1967: 35–39. I have also discussed the idea of polarity in chapter 22, "Seeing in Perspective."

2. Regarding the "disappearance" of phenomena into theoretical entities, see Edelglass et al., 1992.

meaningful to be accurate *about*, and meaningful expression requires some minimal degree of accuracy, lest nothing be effectively expressed. As Barfield puts it:

> It is not much use having a perfect means of communication if you have nothing to communicate except the relative positions of bodies in space—or if you will never again have anything *new* to communicate. In the same way it is not much use expressing yourself very fully and perfectly indeed—if nobody can understand a word you are saying.

One way to approach an understanding of polarity is to consider what destroys it. If mathematics, taken in the strictest sense, looks like a language of perfect accuracy, it is also a language devoid of meaning.[3] But mathematics is not thereby a kind of pure "northernness," for in gaining its perfect accuracy and losing its potential for expressing meaning altogether, it has lost its essential linguistic nature. Can we really even speak of accuracy when a language gives us nothing *about which* to be accurate? Accuracy in communication can only exist in the presence of *some* meaning; otherwise, nothing is being communicated.

One can also imagine falling out of the polarity in the other direction. Of course, this is hardly the main risk in our day, but we can picture such an outcome in a rough way by considering the poet or seer who is struck dumb by his vision: overwhelmed by a sublime understanding, he remains inarticulate, lacking the analytical means to translate his revelation even into a poor verbal representation. Here again, then, there is no effective use of language at all.

So far as we succeed in communicating, we remain within the complex interpenetration of polarity, playing accuracy against meaning, but allowing the absolute hegemony of neither. A fuller meaning *may* be

---

3. Actually, it is virtually impossible to take mathematics in the strictest sense, because we are by nature creatures of meaning. We cannot wholly purge mathematics of those meaningful associations of form and substance from which it has been abstracted (and to which it ever seeks a return). Moreover, nothing here is meant to deny the very deep and worthwhile satisfactions to be had from pursuit of the purest mathematical disciplines.

purchased at the expense of accuracy, and greater accuracy *may* constrict meaning. But these are *not* mere opposites. If they were, the one would occur simply *at the expense* of the other. In a polarity, on the other hand, one pole occurs *by virtue of* the other. An intensified north pole implies an intensified south pole; a weakened north pole implies a weakened south pole. The greatest minds are those capable of maintaining the most exquisite polar tension, combining the deepest insight (meaning) with the clearest analysis (accuracy).

It is important to see that falling altogether out of the polarity into, say, number, typically occurs through a *weakening* of the polarity. That is, although one may well emphasize the pole of accuracy in moving toward mere number, that very one-sidedness, by weakening the contrary pole, also weakens accuracy itself so far as accuracy is viewed as part of the dynamic of communication. There is ever less to be accurate about. The polarity fades into empty precision that communicates no content.

In sum: when the polar tension is at its greatest—when both accuracy and expressiveness are at their highest pitch (when the "magnet" is strongest)—we have the deepest and most precisely articulated meaning. This gives way, via inattention to one or the other pole, to a loss of clearly articulated meaning. It may on some occasions be necessary, therefore, to distinguish between the "empty precision" that results when we abandon the polarity for number, and the "accuracy" that, in cooperative tension with expressiveness, enables our discursive grasp and communication of meaning.

"But what," you may be asking with increasing impatience, "*is* meaning, anyway?" We will turn toward that pole shortly, but only after looking in greater depth at the more familiar pole of accuracy. You need to recognize, however, that all "what is" questions in our culture are strongly biased toward the analytical. We commonly say what something is by analyzing it into parts, which we can then relate to each other by the precise laws of mathematics and logic. This bias will hardly help us to understand the polar contrary of analysis.

291

In slightly different words: it is difficult to be precise about meaning for the simple reason that in meaning we have the polar contrary of precision. The best way to *begin* the search for meaning is by exercising your imagination against a blank—that is, by trying to recognize the shape of what is missing in the polarity so long as we recognize only accuracy. If a perfectly accurate language cannot give us the world—or any content at all—then what *can* give us the world? Here there is no possible theoretical answer. We must begin to gain—or regain—the world in our own experience.

The pole of logic and mathematics

If we apply our concern for accuracy not to the details, but to the overall assertion of a statement; if we reduce the states about which we are accurate to two; and if we call those states "truth" and "falsity"—we arrive at logic. Like mathematics, logic is a kind of endpoint of abstraction, from which all meaning is lost.[4] We can illustrate this by looking at the meaning of logical truth.

To say "Mary's father was killed in an automobile accident" is to affirm something very different from "The light in the kitchen was on last night." But suppose we say instead,

"It is true that Mary's father was killed in an automobile accident."

"It is true that the light in the kitchen was on last night."

The purely logical affirmation—that is, the meaning of "it is true that"—is exactly the same in both these sentences. It is indeed the same in a potentially infinite number of sentences of the form,

It is true that (. . .),

where the expression in parentheses is an assertion of some sort. What it *means* to say that something is true does not depend on the parenthetic expression. So the bare assertion of the truth of something is just about the most abstract statement we can make; it abstracts the one common element from a huge number of descriptions of radically different states of affairs. The

---

4. In modern theory, mathematics and logic are not treated as fundamentally distinct disciplines.

logic of my assertion that someone was killed is identical to the logic of my assertion that the light was on. The very point of such assertions is to show "a something" that the subordinate clauses have in common—something we can abstract from them equally—despite almost every possible difference of meaning otherwise. That abstract something we call truth (or falsity, as the case may be).

We have seen that, given a pair of polar contraries, we cannot perfectly isolate either pole. It is impossible to slice off such a tiny sliver of the north end of a bar magnet that we end up with pure northernness. We have either north and south interpenetrating each other, or no magnet at all. We found a similar relation between meaning and quantitative rigor, where mathematics represents the pursuit of accuracy to the point where the polarity is destroyed, leaving nothing *about which* to be accurate. And so it is also with meaning and truth.

The attempt to conquer the pole of "pure truth" results in the loss not only of meaning but of truth as well, for it makes no sense to speak of truth without content. That is why logicians often speak of the *validity* of a logical demonstration rather than its *truth*. It is also why they use letters like *p* and *q* to stand for sentences, or propositions. For the content of a proposition does not enter into logical calculations; the only thing that matters is that the propositions be either true or false unambiguously. All true propositions—however diverse their apparent meanings—have exactly the same meaning for the logician; so do all false propositions. It was Wittgenstein who remarked, "All propositions of logic mean the same thing, namely nothing."

Equating formal logic with mathematics, Bertrand Russell wrote:

> Pure mathematics consists entirely of assertions to the effect that, if such and such a proposition is true of *anything,* then such and such another proposition is true of that thing. It is essential not to discuss whether the first proposition is really true, and not to mention what the anything is, of which it is supposed to be true. Both these points would belong to applied mathematics. We start, in pure mathematics, from certain rules of inference, by which we can infer that *if* one

proposition is true, then so is some other proposition. These rules of inference constitute the major part of the principles of formal logic. We then take any hypothesis that seems amusing, and deduce its consequences. *If* our hypothesis is about *anything,* and not about some one or more particular things, then our deductions constitute mathematics. Thus mathematics may be defined as the subject in which we never know what we are talking about, nor whether what we are saying is true.[5]

On the other hand, just so far as we apply our logic to the world and thereby re-introduce content—substituting terms with real meaning for our propositional p's and q's—we lose the logical purity of our truth. If, for example, I say, "All men are mortal," you might ask about the definition of "man": what distinguishes man from not-man in human evolution? Or, what distinguishes man from machine? To clarify such questions I will be driven—so long as I am seeking logical purity—to define my terms in an ever narrower way. As one can already recognize in the sciences of biology and artificial intelligence, the word "man" begins to disappear into abstract technicality. Terms like "information," "algorithm," "genetic encoding," "organization," "replication," and "program" come to the fore.

This tendency is inevitable given the aforementioned quest for logical purity. We have to begin qualifying ourselves in an effort to eliminate ambiguity: this term is to be taken only in such-and-such a respect, and that term in a different respect—and by the time we regain *absolute* logical precision (if we ever do), we will again have reduced the terms of our proposition to the purely abstract p's and q's of the logician. We will have lost whatever it was we started out to say. For the only statements that remain unqualifiedly true *regardless* of how their terms are taken are statements whose content has fallen out of the picture.

All concrete, meaningful content resists the absolutism and universalism of logic.

---

5. Russell, 1981: 59–60.

A prevailing one-sidedness. I hope this predicament is by now becoming familiar to you. The drive for logical precision consumes and destroys itself if it does not remain in creative tension with something else. Furthermore, because our culture, with its scientific and technological mindset, tends strongly to vest authority in the logical and quantitative processes of thought, the "something else" remains obscure and mysterious—always suspect to the properly tough-minded investigator. What results is a compulsive striving toward a kind of absolute vacuity. There are many symptoms of this striving, the primary one being the entire history of modern science. Having started out to explain the world, we find ourselves now (in the "hardest" of sciences—physics) struggling to figure out what our most sophisticated equations *mean*—if they mean anything at all.

Many are therefore content to dismiss the question of meaning altogether, drawing sufficient satisfaction from their ability to fashion contrivances that *work*. This willingness to be content with things that work rather than with understanding is reminiscent of the logician's commerce with validity rather than truth. It is the end result of an effort to reduce the polarity to a single pole. A precise, two-valued system ("it works" and "it doesn't work") replaces the drive to penetrate phenomena with human consciousness and so to understand.

We feel comfortable with precision and the abstraction it requires. You might say they are our destiny. *Something* has led us quite naturally down a path whereby our meanings have vanished into equations, bottom lines, statistics, and computer programs. The causes of that historical drift—whatever they are—have proven relentless and all but irresistible. It should not surprise us, therefore, if our effort to grasp hold of meaning in the following sections proves an uphill struggle. Yet without such struggle we may eventually find our consciousness constricted to a vanishing point. For the polarity between meaning and accuracy is also—within the individual consciousness—a polarity between fullness and clarity. And we run the risk of becoming, finally, absolutely clear about nothing at all.

295

Meaning and logic

I cannot tell you what meaning is. Nor can anyone else. Crazily, this leads to the common denial that meaning is worth bothering about at all. The physicist Hans Christian von Baeyer relates a conversation he had with Claudia Denke Tesche, a scientist exploring problems of quantum mechanics. The question of the meaning of her work arises, and the conversation takes an all too familiar turn:

> "*Meaning* is a philosophical word," she shrugs, and then turns her attention to a leaky vacuum pump.[6]

I said "crazily" because, while it is certainly true that meaning is not some new kind of *thing*, it is a prerequisite for there to be any things at all. Every attempt to arrive at the things of our world—or the things of our theories—starting from the "pure northernness," the conceptual barrenness, of mathematical or logical abstraction never gets as far as step one. We simply cannot meaningfully speak except by *starting* with meaning.

Meaning cannot be defined without being assumed, for surely I cannot define meaning with meaningless terms. And if I employ meaningful terms in my definition, then I assume that you are already capable of grasping meaning. Similarly, no one can define definition for someone who doesn't already know what a definition is; nor can anyone demonstrate the principles of logic without relying upon logic.

These "boundary problems" of cognition point us toward a crucial consideration: something in cognition "stands on its own" and is self-apparent. Ultimately, the only basis for knowing anything is that it has become transparent, or obvious, and the only way to discover what it is for something to be obvious is to experience its obviousness "from the inside." One then begins to live within the self-supported nature of thinking.

The alternative is to try to understand thinking in terms of the various objects of thought—brain, computer, or whatever. But this effort is

---

6. von Baeyer, 1992: 178.

futile, for the objects are only given by thinking, and therefore presuppose what they are supposed to explain. "The seen is not the cause of seeing, but the result of seeing."[7] We cannot, as Barfield explains, even begin with ourselves as subjects confronting a world of objects:

> It is not justifiable, in constructing a theory of knowledge, to take subjectivity as "given." Why? Because, if we examine the thinking activity carefully, by subsequent reflection on it, we shall find that in the *act* of thinking, or knowing, no such distinction of consciousness exists. We are not conscious of ourselves thinking about something, but simply of something . . . . Consequently, in thinking about thinking, if we are determined to make no assumptions at the outset, we dare not start with the distinction between self and not-self; for that distinction actually disappears every time we think.[8]

That is, both subject and object are determinations given by thinking. They presuppose thinking, which therefore cannot be classified as either subjective or objective.

Where does logic come from? Our more immediate concern here is with the relation between pure logic—which has fallen out of the polarity of accuracy and expressiveness—and the more or less clear meaning that is borne by the polarity.

The first logicians had no rules of logic to go by, and yet they teased out the logical principles inherent in the received system of meanings. Clearly, they didn't do this by consciously applying the very rules of logic they were trying to derive. Logic does not come first in our knowing. And yet, logical structure is already implicit within the purest of meanings. Our meanings are mutually articulated with each other in a manner that is given by the meanings themselves, and we can therefore begin to abstract from these meanings certain empty, universal forms, or possibilities of articulation. These possibilities are what we know as logic.

---

7. Kühlewind, 1984: 129.
8. See appendix 4 in Barfield, 1973.

The grasp of meaning, then, precedes, and becomes the basis for, the eventual elaboration of logic as such. We do not need the rules of logic in order to apprehend meaning. Rather, apprehending meaning with ever greater accuracy is what enables us to extract the rules of logic. Thinking logically is what we find we have done when we have successfully struggled to remain faithful to our meanings.

To be logical in a concrete sense (that is, *within* the polar relationship) does not mean to act according to an abstract logical calculus, but rather to preserve the coherence of my meanings—to put those meanings on display without demeaning them by introducing distortions. If I must invoke logic against an opponent in argument, it is not to introduce some new understanding, but rather (as Barfield notes) to bring him to his senses: he has somehow abandoned the intrinsic necessities of his own meanings. He will recognize his error only when he enters more consciously and with greater clarity into those meanings.

To puzzle over the logical justification of logic, the definition of definition, and the meaning of meaning is only to make clear the boundaries of our normal way of thinking, which is governed by a radical slide toward the pole of logic and abstraction. The only way across those boundaries lies in overcoming one-sidedness, which in turn requires not merely thinking *about* things, but experiencing our own thinking—including its qualitative aspects. Not much in our culture trains us to do this; we focus upon the "objects" given to us by our thinking rather than upon the thinking itself—until, finally, some are suggesting that thinking offers us nothing to experience.

If we ever succeed in becoming perfect logic machines, there will indeed be nothing left to experience.

How does meaning arise?

As Barfield shows in a fascinating paper,[9] the creation of meaning is a function of something rather like untruth.

---

9. Barfield, 1981.

Philosophers have sometimes claimed that sentences like the following are tautologies:

"The earth is a planet."

That is, the predicate simply repeats a truth already inherent in the subject. If we truly know the meaning of "earth," then we also know that earth is a planet. So the remark tells us nothing new. On the very face of it, the sentence purports to do no more than define "earth"—it tells us what earth *is*—so that if we already know the definition of "earth"—if the terms of the sentence are from the start precisely accurate for us—we learn nothing. Again, mathematics and logic offer the most extreme example. When we write the equation,

$$2 + 2 = 4$$

the equals sign tells us that what is on the right side of the equation is nothing other than, or different from, what is on the left side of the equation. That is what the sign *says*. If we clearly understand "2 + 2," then we already see that it is the same as "4." There is not some new content in "4" that was missing in "2 + 2."

But imagine you are a contemporary of Copernicus hearing for the first time, "the earth is a planet." Not only is this no tautology, it may well strike you as plainly false. For in all likelihood you view the earth as a center around which both the fixed and wandering stars revolve. You take for granted the fundamental difference in quality between earthly and heavenly substance. The existing meanings of your words do not allow the truth of what you have just heard.

And yet, the time may come when you *do* accept the statement as true. If we look for the crucial moments separating your unbelief from your belief, what do we see? *Words changing their meanings.* Specifically, the meanings of both "earth" and "planet" change dramatically. And not just these two words, but an entire tapestry of meaning begins to shift its pattern and texture. We are not dealing here with the sudden recognition of a new "fact," but rather with the slowly evolving background against

299

which all possible facts take their shapes. (In considering the sentence "Love your enemy" we saw a similar transformation of meaning.)

The role of metaphor. Against the original background of meaning, to say "the earth is a planet" was in some respects to voice a bold metaphor—rather as if someone today said, "every star is a divine being, vestured in light." Given the straightforward, literal meanings of "earth" and "planet" in Copernicus' time, the statement was untrue; but, as in every metaphor, one must look *through* the primary meaning—the literal untruth—in order to grasp the intended, emergent meaning. In this case the emergent meaning had partly to do with a certain principle of movement common to both earth and the planets; earth was *like* the planets, at least with regard to its motion around the sun.

But, of course, this comparison could not immediately recast the entire network of meanings bound up with "earth" and "planet."[10] The statement remained metaphorical—a revealing lie—at first. It would take an extended period for its metaphorical thrust to be generalized and become a matter of routine literalness—that very period, in fact, marking the transition from medieval consciousness to our modern, scientific mentality.

The differences between the medieval and the modern mind are striking, to say the least. And the pathway from the one to the other is paved with lies! We gain our new meanings by using words to state falsehoods—but falsehoods that are suggestive, and through which we are pointed to new possibilities of meaning. If Newton had not been allowed to "misuse" *gravitas,* could modern physics have arisen? For in his day the word meant something like the human experience of heaviness—not some abstract principle of universal attraction—and it was still tinged with a sense of "desire." There is a very great difference between the idea of (to borrow Herbert Butterfield's words) "a stone aspiring to reach its natural place at the center of the universe—and rushing more fervently as it came

---

10. See, for example, Barfield's evocation of the medieval consciousness, quoted in chapter 22.

nearer home—and the idea of a stone accelerating its descent under the constant force of gravity."[11]

Newton's use of *gravitas* to describe the force of gravitation was metaphorical—untrue on its face; it made no more sense, given the received meaning of *gravitas,* than *we* would make today if we explained the moon's revolution as resulting from its *desire* for the earth. And yet, as with many metaphors, it did make sense when one looked *through* the false statements and, with their essential aid, began to grasp the intended (new) meanings. Assisted by falsehoods, one apprehended (perhaps dimly at first) something not literally stated, thereby allowing the meanings of one's terms to shift and realign themselves with this metaphorical intent. These new meanings, once they are more fully laid hold of and analyzed, enable the statement of truths that again tend toward the literal and accurate (and therefore toward the tautological, the uninteresting), since they no longer require so great a "misuse" of language.

What we discover when we turn to the polar dynamic—the interaction between accuracy and expressiveness during the actual use of language—is this continual expansion and contraction of meaning. When I use a new and revealing metaphor, for example, I force static truths into motion, changing, by this "shift of truth," the meaning of one or more of my terms. This meaning, however, is now less explicitly displayed, less accessible—and will remain so until it is penetrated and articulated with the aid of accurate analysis. When, on the other hand, I analyze and clarify meaning, I narrow it down, distinguish its facets, render it progressively literal and immobile until (if I push the analysis far enough) it is lacking nearly all content—a fit term for logical manipulation.

Other-saying. A metaphor is one example of what Barfield calls "other-saying": saying one thing (that must be received as a fiction), and intending by it a second thing. Whatever else we claim about such statements, we cannot call them tautologies, for on their face they are not even true. Nevertheless, they are frequently meaningful.

---

11. Butterfield, 1957: 131.

I do not think we can say that meaning, in itself, is either true or untrue. All we can safely say is, that that quality which makes some people say: "That is self-evident" or "that is obviously true," and which makes others say: "That is a tautology," is precisely the quality which meaning *hasn't* got.[12]

Meaning, then, is born of a kind of fiction, yet it is the content, or raw material of truth. And it is important to realize that other-saying—for example, symbol, metaphor, and allegory—is not a mere curiosity in the history of language. As Barfield stresses on so many occasions, virtually our entire language appears to have originated with other-saying.

Anyone who cares to nose about for half an hour in an etymological dictionary will at once be overwhelmed with [examples]. I don't mean out-of-the-way poetic words, I mean quite ordinary words like *love, behaviour, multiply, shrewdly* and so on . . . . To instance two extreme cases, the words *right* and *wrong* appear to go back to two words meaning respectively "stretched" and so "straight," and "wringing" or "sour." And the same thing applies to all our words for mental operations, *conceiving, apprehending, understanding* . . . .[13]

Nor do we gain much by appealing to the physical sciences for exceptions. As Barfield elsewhere points out,[14] even "high-sounding 'scientific' terms like *cause, reference, organism, stimulus,* etc., are not miraculously exempt" from the rule that nearly all linguistic symbols have a figurative origin. For example, "stimulus" derives from a Latin word designating an object used as a spur or a goad. Similarly for such words as "absolute," "concept," "potential," "matter," "form," "objective," "general," "individual," "abstract."

The first thing we observe, when we look at language historically, is that nearly all words appear to consist of fossilized metaphors, or fossilized "other-saying" of some sort. This is a fact. It is not a brilliant *aperçu* of my own, nor is it an interesting theory which is disputed or

---

12. Barfield, 1981: 32–34.
13. Barfield, 1981: 35.
14. Barfield, 1973: 134.

even discussed among etymologists. It is the sort of thing they have for breakfast.[15]

In sum: when we look at language, we find it continually changing; our discovery of facts and truths occurs only in creative tension with an evolution of meanings that continually transforms the facts and truths. Outside this tensive relation we have no facts, and we have no truths; there is only the quest for a kind of disembodied validity in which (to recall Russell's words) "we never know what we are talking about, nor whether what we are saying is true"—or else the dumbstruck quest for ineffable visions.

The emergence of meaning is always associated with what, from a fixed and strictly logical standpoint, appears as untruth. And it is just this meaning with which, as knowers, we embrace the world.

The polar dynamic of meaning

Other-saying invites us to recognize significant resemblances and analogies between things. The first person to speak of a "charged atmosphere" in describing interpersonal tension discovered a common something between static electricity and human experience. The demand for unity driving such discoveries is, according to Barfield, "the proper activity of the imagination."[16]

Symbol and analysis. The imagination, in Barfield's view, makes meaning. Logical consistency, on the other hand, is the outcome of rational analysis. In the interaction between imagination and rational analysis we see the polar contraries, meaning and accuracy, brought into mutual play.

The imagination is at work, albeit in less than full consciousness, when we dream. Dreams are full of other-saying—symbols, images that signify *this,* but also *that.* "The dark figure was my friend John, yet it was not really him." Then I wake up and *analyze* the dream: the man, it seems, was a combination of my friend John and someone I met at the store

15. Barfield, 1981: 37.
16. Barfield, 1973: 25.

today who intrigued me—and perhaps also he had something to do with a certain threatening figure from past dreams . . . . So whereas the dream itself presented a single, multivalent image, I now have several definite, unambiguous figures, standing side-by-side in my intellect. Analysis splits up meaning, breaks apart unities: "*this* means *that*." Logic tells us that a thing cannot be both A and not-A in the same respect and at the same time; it wants to separate not-A from A. It wants to render its terms clear and precise, each with a single, narrow meaning.

> The arrangement and rearrangement of such univocal terms in a series of propositions is the function of *logic,* whose object is elucidation and the elimination of error. The poetic[17] has nothing to do with this. It can only manifest itself as *fresh meaning;* it operates essentially *within* the individual term, which it creates and recreates by the magic of new combinations . . . . For in the pure heat of poetic expression juxtaposition is far more important than either logic or grammar. Thus, the poet's relation to terms is that of maker.[18]

And again:

> Logical judgements, by their nature, can only *render more explicit* some one part of a truth *already implicit in their terms.* But the poet makes the terms themselves. He does not make judgements, therefore; he only makes them possible—and only he makes them possible.[19]

The imagination creates new meaning by other-saying, but cannot elucidate that meaning, cannot draw out its implications and delineate its contours. Rational analysis brings us precision and clarity by breaking the meaning into separate pieces, but progressively loses thereby the *content,* the revelatory potency, of the original image.

---

17. Barfield uses "poet" and "poetic" to express broadly the operation of the imagination, as opposed to that of rational analysis. The terms are by no means so restrictive as in normal usage today. Thus, a creative scientist may be as likely to exercise the poetic function—if not more so—as a writer of verse.

18. Barfield, 1973: 131.

19. Barfield, 1973: 113.

It is not that a metaphor or symbol holds together a number of logically conflicting meanings. The man in the dream was not a logical contradiction. He was who he was. One can experience and employ the most pregnant symbolic images quite harmoniously. The contradictions are artifacts of the analytical stance itself. They appear when we are no longer content with the imaginative unity we once experienced, but want to *cleave* it with the intellect, resolving it into elements we can relate to already existing knowledge. It is only when the unity is shattered by such analysis that the contradictions between the parts appear. And analysis, once under way, wants to proceed until there are no contradictions left—which finally occurs when all meaning, all unities, have disappeared. So long as we have meaning, we have a challenge for logical analysis, which is to say that every imaginative unity stands ready to be broken apart by analysis, immediately revealing contradictions between the *now too stiffly related fragments of the analysis.*

Holding the balance. However one-sided the tendencies of our age, we cannot say that either imagination or rational analysis is more essential than the other. All understanding is born of their polar interaction. The imagination is forever discovering new unities, while rational analysis is forever dissecting them. In the actual advance of understanding, there is a continual alternation between these principles. When the breakdown of the image yields contradiction, we can overcome the contradiction in either of two directions: by destroying all meaning and ending up with a set of empty logical structures, or else by returning to a wholly unanalyzed unity, whether of the original image or a new one.

In actual fact, we are likely to see innumerable partial movements in both directions, and understanding is another name for the resulting polar dynamic. The unanalyzed image may be a perfect unity, but it is not "on display"—it is not available to our discursive mental operations. By contrast, analysis hands over elements of the image to the discursive intellect—sacrificing some of the given imaginal significance in the process.

But today we too readily ignore that you can neither *start* with the empty forms of logic in considering any issue, nor *finish off* an issue with logic. An ironic misconception underlies the frequently heard claim, "it is logically certain." If the matter is indeed logically certain, then the speaker is no longer talking about anything. For if what he says has any meaning at all, that meaning is carried by other-saying—by imaginative unities not yet fully reduced by logical analysis. *The attempt to honor the pole of accuracy over that of meaning does no more than guarantee us the shallowest meanings possible.*

It is said that any conclusion of an argument running counter to a theorem of the logical calculus is wrong. Surely this is correct; but it is not particularly helpful. The problem is knowing when a conclusion really does violate the calculus. What about "the earth is a planet," spoken by a contemporary of Copernicus? If we consider only the then-received meanings of "earth" and "planet," there is indeed a violation of the logical calculus. But the sentence also suggests newly emergent meanings, not yet clearly understood. Which is the *real* meaning?

If the logicians turn their attention to such a problem, they will likely resolve it just when the new meanings have become so stable, conventional, and *thin* that there is no longer a pressing issue of logicality or truthfulness. By the time you have reduced your subject to terms where the logical calculus can be applied mechanically and with full confidence—externally, as it were, and not intrinsically in the struggle to be faithful to your meanings—by then the subject itself is likely to have become so clear on its face as to require no such application.

The bias of our age. I said earlier that the meaning of meaning would prove difficult to capture. This difficulty reflects what we have become. It is no accident that the central issue in artificial intelligence is the relation between computation and meaning; or that making human labor meaningful is the decisive challenge for modern industry; or that the relation between equation, model, and meaning has bedeviled modern science; or that in general our age has become known as the age of meaninglessness.

Meaning, it seems, was simply "given" to those of earlier eras. For us, absence of meaning is the given, and its rediscovery requires a sometimes painful inner movement in opposition to the prevailing spirit of our time.

Further, that movement must be our own; its sole impetus can never be received from without. While meaning is suggestible, it "can never be *conveyed* from one person to another. . . . Every individual must intuit meaning for himself, and the function of the poetic is to mediate such intuition by suitable suggestion."[20] What I can convey to you with absolute fidelity—although it is fidelity to no-content, nothing—is only the empty proposition of logic or equation of mathematics.

The manipulation of the products of analysis is in some respects a mechanical task. The genesis of new meaning is altogether a different matter, and its challenge is not often set before us today. In listening to others, do I remain alert for those "strange connections" suggesting meanings I have not yet grasped? Or am I readier to analyze and tear down, based upon my armament of secure propositions already in hand?

The effort to comprehend what we have heretofore been incapable of seeing—rather than simply to extract the implications of our existing knowledge—always requires the modification of one or more of our terms: the creation of new meaning. Barfield quotes Francis Bacon:

> For that knowledge which is new, and foreign from opinions received, is to be delivered in another form than that that is agreeable and familiar; and therefore Aristotle, when he thinks to tax Democritus, doth in truth commend him, where he saith, *If we shall indeed dispute, and not follow after similitudes,* etc. For those whose conceits are seated in popular opinions, need only but to prove or dispute; but those whose conceits are beyond popular opinions, have a double labour: the one to make themselves conceived, and the other to prove and demonstrate. So that it is of necessity with them to have recourse to similitudes and translations to express themselves.[21]

---

20. Barfield, 1973: 133.

21. Francis Bacon, *The Advancement of Learning,* 2.17.10. Quoted in Barfield, 1973: 141–42.

In an age of abstract and logic-dominated learning, it is easy to forget that all true advance of understanding requires us imaginatively to conceive what is not currently conceivable—by means of other-saying. Einstein's famous equations were not the cause of his insights, but the result: he had first to become a poet, playing metaphorically with the received, much too logically worn down and well-defined notions of time and space, mass and energy. Lesser scientists failed to gain the same insights because they already knew too precisely. Their terms were rigorous and accurate. As Bacon put it, they could only "prove or dispute" in terms of their existing, systematized knowledge.

So, then . . . what is meaning?

I still cannot tell you. Meaning is not a "what." It is what makes all "whats" possible, giving them content. Our difficulty in grappling with it reflects the culture's one-sidedness. When rational argument is one's only legitimate, tough-minded weapon, it becomes nearly impossible to lay hold of meaning, for meaning cannot be argued. And yet, as we have just seen, all but the most prosaic arguments require the establishment and recognition of new meaning.

What I *can* do, however, is to offer some final, unsystematic observations to stimulate further thought. These will tend toward the aphoristic, and will partly serve to acknowledge just a few of the issues prominent in Barfield's work. For an extended treatment of these issues, however, I can only refer you to that work itself.

• • •

Meaning is whatever Barfield's *History in English Words* is *about*. I suspect that for many people this semantic history will oddly present itself as being about nothing much at all. But when the oddity serves as a healthy question mark and a stimulus for further exploration, one eventually enters a rich world of meanings against which the imagination can be exercised. Likewise, all sensitive exploration of foreign cultures leads to the appreciation of strange meanings and, through this appreciation, to a refined sense for meaning itself.

• • •

Meaning is whatever the dictionary is *not* about. I am only being slightly facetious. "The meaning of a word is abstract, just in so far as it is definable. The definition of a word, which we find in a Dictionary—inasmuch as it is not conveyed by synonym and metaphor, or illustrated by quotation—*is* its most abstract meaning."[22]

If we look at the polarity of language, it is immediately evident that the attempt to define—the quest for a "dictionary definition"—is driven almost wholly from the pole of accuracy, and therefore tends to eliminate meaning. Meaning, you will recall, "is not a hard-and-fast system of reference"; it is not definable, but only suggestible, and requires the poetic for its suggestion. The strict dictionary definition, by contrast, attempts to tie down, to eliminate any ambiguity previously imported by the poetic. And just so far as such a definition tries to be "scientific," it tends to suffer a steady reduction until finally it knows only particles in motion. Qualities disappear. The resulting, purely abstract term "is a mark representing, not a thing or being, but the fact *that* identical sensations *have been* experienced on two or more occasions." These little billiard balls over *here* are the same as those over *there*. Abstract thinking is, in the extreme, counting: we count instances, but do not try to say instances of *what*.

• • •

Here is part of a dictionary definition for "water":

> the liquid that . . . when pure consists of an oxide of hydrogen in the proportion of 2 atoms of hydrogen to one atom of oxygen and is an odorless, tasteless, very slightly compressible liquid which appears bluish in thick layers, freezes at 0 degrees C, has a maximum density at 4 degrees C and a high specific heat . . . .

Now this serves very well to provide a certain kind of reference, a pointer into a complex mesh of scientific abstractions, in which "water" holds a definite place. What it does not do well at all is give us the concrete *meaning* of the word in its actual usage—that is, when the word is

---

22. Barfield, 1973: appendix 2.

used outside the scientific textbook or laboratory, or when it was used any time before the last few centuries. It gives me little if any assistance in determining whether a particular use of the word "water" in a poem, personal memoir, news story, or qualitative scientific study makes any sense. It conveys nothing of that water we enjoy while swimming, washing, drinking, fishing, walking in the rain, or watching storm-driven waves. It misses the wetness, gleam, undulation, deep stillness, engulfing horror, wild power, musicality, and grace. It does not tell me anything about my actual experience of water in the world.

All this, of course, will be admitted. But what will not so readily be admitted is that these experiences contain a good deal of what "water" *really means,* which is also to say: what it *actually is.* Our difficulty with this thought, one might almost say, is the defining characteristic—the crippling failure—of our day. It is related to our insistence upon a world of objects bearing absolutely no inner relation to the human being who observes them.

. . .

As the maker of meaning, imagination has received considerable attention during this past century—although scarcely from the scientific side. Barfield mentions three features of imagination concerning which there has been a "considerable measure of agreement":[23]

- Imagination gives us a relation between whole and parts different from mere aggregation. Unknown in classical physics, this relation is "not altogether unknown in the organic realm. It has been said that imagination directly apprehends the whole as 'contained' in the part, or as in some mode identical with it." The hologram gives us an approach to this thought from the side of physics.

- Imagination "apprehends spatial form, and relations in space, as 'expressive' of nonspatial form and nonspatial relations." For example,

---

23. Barfield, 1965b: 127. He is speaking here through the fictionalized voice of a physicist, Kenneth Flume.

in the human countenance we can read various interior relations of thought, feeling, and intention.

- Imagination operates prior to the kind of perception and thought that has become normal today. It functions "at a level where observed and observer, mind and object, are no longer—or are not yet—spatially divided from one another; so that the mind, as it were, becomes the object or the object becomes the mind."

• • •

As its name suggests, the imagination deals in images. Barfield has this to say about images in general:

> It is characteristic of images that they interpenetrate one another. Indeed, more than half the art of poetry consists in helping them to do so. That is just what the terms of logic, and the notions we employ in logical or would-be logical thinking, must *not* do. *There*, interpenetration becomes the slovenly confusion of one determinate meaning with another determinate meaning, and there, its proper name is not interpenetration, but equivocation . . . . [24]

• • •

We may think that our good, scientific terms are somehow safely, solidly, material in meaning. And yet, as Barfield points out, "It is just those meanings which attempt to be most exclusively material . . . which are also the most generalized and abstract—i.e. remote from reality."[25] To see this more clearly, we can contrast abstract with concrete meanings. "Concrete" does not mean "material." Rather, the concrete combines the perceptual and the conceptual—which together make the thing what it is. To illustrate a fully concrete definition, Barfield asks his reader to imagine a single word conveying what *we* would have to translate as "I cut this flesh with joy in order to sacrifice." Such a word would not be highly abstract, and what saves it from being so is not only its particularity but also the fact that its reference to outer activity is suffused with inner significances.

---

24. Barfield, 1977a: 100.
25. Barfield, 1973: 79.

But what about our abstract verb, "to cut"? It tries to be wholly material by removing all the particular significances just referred to; but how material is something that has become so abstract you cannot even picture it? The pure act of cutting—as opposed to particular, concrete acts bearing within themselves the interiority of the actor—is no more material than a "tree" that is not some particular tree. Words that we try to make exclusively material finally go the same way as "things" in the hands of the particle physicist: they vanish into abstraction.

· · ·

If we can't give concrete definitions, neither can we define "concrete." The concrete brings us to meaning itself, and to "the qualitative reality which definition automatically excludes."

Barfield again:

> If I were to bring the reader into my presence and point to an actual lump of gold, without even opening my mouth and uttering the word *gold*—then, this much at least could be said, that he would have had from me nothing that was *not* concrete. But that does not take us very far. For it does not follow that he would possess anything but the most paltry and inchoate knowledge of the whole reality—"gold." The depth of such knowledge would depend entirely on how many he might by his own activity have intuited of the innumerable concepts, which are as much a part of the reality as the percepts or sense-data, and some of which he must already have made his own before he could even observe what I am pointing to as an "object" at all. . . . Other concepts—already partially abstracted when I name them—such as the gleaming, the hardness to the touch, the resemblance to the light of the sun, its part in human history, as well as those contained in the dictionary definition—all these may well comprise a little, but still only a very little, more of the whole meaning.[26]

---

26. Barfield, 1973: 187–88.

And again:

> The full meanings of words are flashing, iridescent shapes like flames—ever-flickering vestiges of the slowly evolving consciousness beneath them.[27]

• • •

Barfield mentions how, in metaphor, poets have repeatedly related death, sleep, and winter, as well as birth, waking, and summer. These in turn are often treated as symbols of the inner, spiritual experiences of dissolution or rebirth. He then offers these observations:

> Now by our definition of a "true metaphor," there should be some older, undivided "meaning" from which all these logically discon-nected, but poetically connected ideas have sprung. And in the beau-tiful myth of Demeter and Persephone we find precisely such a meaning. In the myth of Demeter the ideas of waking and sleeping, of summer and winter, of life and death, of mortality and immortal-ity are all lost in one pervasive meaning. This is why so many theo-ries are brought forward to account for the myths. The naturalist is right when he connects the myth with the phenomena of nature, but wrong if he deduces it solely from these. The psychoanalyst is right when he connects the myth with "inner" (as we now call them) experiences, but wrong if he deduces it solely from these. Mythology is the ghost of concrete meaning. Connections between discrete phenomena, connections which are now apprehended as metaphor, were once perceived as immediate realities. As such the poet strives, by his own efforts, to see them, and to make others see them, again.[28]

Computers, logic, and meaning

Barfield's work on meaning and polarity can scarcely be ignored in any discussion of the nature and capability of computers. A serious and widespread attempt to reckon with his insights would undoubtedly trans-form many disciplines relating to computers. To the potential literature

---

27. Barfield, 1973: 75.
28. Barfield, 1973: 91–92.

waiting to be written, I can here contribute only a few concluding pages in which I try to suggest three or four basic directions in which the discussion might be carried by those who are interested.

The destruction of polarity. The drive toward artificial intelligence can be seen most fruitfully as a drive to escape the polar dynamic of meaning. It is, moreover, a realistic campaign, inasmuch as we *can* engrave the non-dynamic, finished forms of intelligence upon physical stuff. And if we lose our awareness of all but these empty structures—if the present, dynamic *act* of thinking drops from our view—then we can easily be convinced that mechanical manipulation of the structures is what thinking actually is. All this hinges upon our loss of meaning, for meaning is what does *not* reside in those structures.

If we accept and enter into the living terms of the polarity, I believe we will reach two conclusions: (1) there is no limit upon the intelligence we can embed within computers, since there is no limit upon how far the rational principle can proceed in its analysis of any given meaning; and (2) since this intelligence is always a "dead" or "emptied" intelligence—frozen out of the polar dynamic of meaning and truth, and so rendered mechanical—it is essentially limited.

These contentions are not contradictory. When I say there is no limit upon computer intelligence, I refer to the programmer's ability to derive an ever more sophisticated syntax through her analysis of meanings. Her next program can always appear more faithful to life than the last. Just so far as we can take hold of a cognitive activity or content and describe it, we will find that it submits to analysis, yielding an internal, rational structure that can be pursued indefinitely toward an ideal of perfect precision.

When, on the other hand, I say the computer is limited, I refer to (1) its eternal inability to transcend meaningfully the fundamental syntactic limits of its own program; and (2) its inability to possess its meanings in the sense that humans do. In other words, you can't take the nonpolar end products of (the programmer's) analysis, map them to the computational structures of a computer, and expect them to climb back into the polar dynamic from which they were extracted—any more than you can reduce a conversation to a bare logical structure, and then expect anyone to derive from that structure the concrete substance of the original conversation.

These contentions will be disputed by many of those who are busy constructing artificial intelligences. I will have more to say about their concerns later. But for now I want to emphasize the unbounded potential of the computer, which lies in its capacity to receive the imprint of intelligence. And if the computer itself cannot ascend from the "footstep" to the striding foot, it can nevertheless execute the pattern of footsteps corresponding to a once-striding foot—provided only that a programmer has sufficiently analyzed the striding and imparted its pattern to the computer.

In other words, even if the computer is cut off from the polar dynamic, the programmer is not, and so the computer's evolution toward unbounded intelligence can proceed on the strength of the programmer's continual effort to analyze meanings into rational end products. Every claim that "the computer cannot do so-and-so" is met by the effort—more or less successful—to analyze so-and-so into a set of pure, formal structures.

It is important to understand just how far this can proceed. Through proper analysis we can, if we choose, reduce every dimension of human experience to a kind of frozen logic. This is true, as we will see, even for *learning and the grasp of metaphor.* That is why the rediscovery of meaning through our own powers of thinking and imagining is so desperately crucial today: we may find, before long, that we have imprisoned all meaning within an impotent reflection of the real thing, from which there is no escape.

We can recognize these issues at work when philosopher John Haugeland, in a standard introduction to artificial intelligence, finally resorts to an imagined "existence proof" to help solve what he calls the "mystery of original meaning." Suppose, he says, that a future comes when intelligent computers

THE FUTURE DOES NOT COMPUTE

are ensconced in mobile and versatile bodies; and they are capable (to all appearances anyway) of the full range of "human" communication, problem solving, artistry, heroism, and what have you. Just to make it vivid, imagine further that the human race has long since died out and that the Earth is populated instead by billions of these computer-robots. They build cities, conduct scientific research, fight legal battles, write volumes, and, yes, a few odd ones live in ivory towers and wonder how their "minds" differ from books—or so it seems. One could, I suppose, cling harshly to the view that, in principle, these systems are no different from calculators; that, in the absence of people, their tokens, their treatises and songs, mean exactly nothing. But that just seems perverse. If [artificially intelligent] systems can be developed to such an extent, then, by all means, they can have original meaning.[29]

But this is not quite right. We can, without apparent limit, "instruct" robots in all these skills, but this, as I have tried to show, does not even *tend* to imply that the robots possess meaning in the same sense that humans do. It only implies that we can analyze our meanings and impart their structure to a machine. Nor is it "perverse" to point this out. The real question is whether the futuristic robots would be bound by their syntax—excluded from the polar dynamic—in a way that humans are not. That is, would they be *stuck* where they were, excluded from all progress because unable to take hold of those meanings the emptied traces of which constituted their own logic?

What really seems to lie behind Haugeland's argument, however, is the picture of a future in which we ourselves could not know any significant difference between our machines and ourselves. In that case, it would indeed be foolish to claim privileged status for human thinking. But then, too, there would be a perfectly reasonable conclusion that Haugeland ignores—not that the robots had somehow gained what he calls "original meaning," but that we had lost it.

---

29. Haugeland, 1985: 122.

316

Is meaning treated more respectfully today? If it is true, as I am arguing, that the main thrust of artificial intelligence is to destroy the polar dynamic, we should see evidence of this thrust. And the first place to look is where artificial intelligence has, in recent years, been *embracing* the important role of meaning ("semantics")—this following an early and disastrous flirtation with supposedly self-sufficient logic. But *is* meaning really treated more respectfully today than it used to be?

In some ways, yes—but not in the ways that count. The early work in artificial intelligence was fixated upon logic. Somehow the pioneers in the field had convinced themselves that formal logic was the mind's distilled essence. So as soon as they realized that computers could be programmed to exhibit complex logical structures, euphoria set in. Did this not mean that machines could replicate human minds? Alan Hodges describes how these early researchers

> regarded physics and chemistry, including all the arguments about quantum mechanics . . . as essentially irrelevant . . . . The claim was that whatever a brain did, it did by virtue of its structure as a logical system, and not because it was inside a person's head, or because it was a spongy tissue made up of a particular kind of biological cell formation. And if this were so, then its logical structure could just as well be represented in some other medium, embodied by some other physical machinery.[30]

Given this outlook, the task was to reduce all knowledge to a formal, logical structure that could then be impressed upon the computer's circuits. There was no lack of bracing optimism: John McCarthy, head of Stanford University's Artificial Intelligence Laboratory, was sure that "the only reason we have not yet succeeded in formalizing every aspect of the real world is that we have been lacking a sufficiently powerful logical calculus. I am currently working on that problem."[31]

---

30. Quoted in Johnson-Laird, 1988: 11.
31. Quoted in Weizenbaum, 1976: 201.

More recent years have seen a considerable backlash against the dominance of logic in artificial intelligence. This backlash is associated with, among other things, the analysis of common sense and background knowledge, the flourishing of connectionism, and the investigation of human reasoning itself.

> The faith of the initial generation [of cognitive scientists] in a study of logical problems and its determined search for rational thought processes may have been misguided. Empirical work on reasoning over the past thirty years has severely challenged the notion that human beings—even sophisticated ones—proceed in a rational manner, let alone that they invoke some logical calculus in their reasoning.[32]

But this statement easily misleads—in two ways. First, it is not so much that human beings have been convicted of irrationality as that cognitive scientists were betrayed by assumptions that flew extraordinarily wide of the mark. Their faith convinced them that cognitive behavior would be found *on its surface* to be nothing but the perfectly well-behaved end products of logical analysis—as if human beings *started* from a position of ideally structured (and therefore meaningless) emptiness. As if, that is, the meanings with which we operate were already so thoroughly worn down as to yield a neat calculus of thinking or behavior after a single level of analysis. We may be moving *toward* such emptiness, but, thankfully, we are not there yet.

This mistaken expectation was so egregious as to beg for some sort of explanation. At the very least, we can say that the misfiring was clearly related to the disregard of meaning so characteristic of the cognitive sciences. Researchers who could posit a mentality built up of nothing but logical forms must have trained themselves over a lifetime to ignore as mere fluff the meanings, the qualities, the *presence* of their own minds. This bizarre and simplistic rendering of their own thinking processes fits

---

32. Gardner, 1985: 361.

well with what I suggested earlier: it may be we who are approaching the status of robots rather than robots who are approaching human status.

Moreover, that the errors of the early researchers have not been remedied by the subsequent reaction is evident when we consider the second way the statement above can mislead us.

Despite all the confessions (usually made on behalf of others!) about the one-sided approach to computer models of mind, the current work is most definitely *not* aimed at redressing the imbalance. The researchers have merely been forced to give up all hope of deriving (and programming) the necessary logical formalism based on a first-level analysis of human behavior. We too obviously do not present ourselves on the surface as logic machines.

In other words, the programmer cannot simply look offhand for those finished, empty structures she would imprint upon the computer's receptive circuits. She must, it is now recognized, carry out extensive "semantic analysis"—the analysis of meaning. Which is to say that she can obtain the desired structures only through laborious toil within the constraints of the polar dynamic of meaning. Only by first entering into meaning can she succeed in breaking it down, and even then she must resort to analysis after analysis—almost, it appears, without end. And yet, the work always yields *some* results, and there is no definable limit upon how far it can proceed.

But the point is that, while the *programmer* is driven to pursue the polar dynamic, her entire purpose is to derive for the *computer* those same empty structures that her predecessors would have liked to pluck straight from the surface convolutions of their brains. That is, as a programmer she is forced to work with the polarity, but she does so in order to destroy it. For that is the only way she can satisfy the computer's hunger for absolute precision about nothing at all. Every approximation, every heuristic, every "synthesis" must be precisely and logically constructed from the eviscerated end products of analysis.

Nor is any of this surprising, for the computer itself *is* above all else a logic machine. Of the many researchers who believe computers will some day think and otherwise manifest humanlike intelligence, few if any now imagine that the thinking robot of the future will, in its ruling intelligence, leap the bounds of a formal system.

So, for all the recognition of the "limits of logic and rationality," the one-sided pursuit of the purified end products of analysis remains the untarnished grail quest of those who would sculpt a lump of silicon into the shape of a human mind. In this we do not witness the discovery of polarity, but something more like flight from it.

Computers and the interpretation of metaphor. As one would expect, the effort to give computers an "understanding" of metaphor is logico-centric. In its own terms it may prove effective. Moreover, unless we ourselves enter with strengthened imagination into the polar dynamic of meaning, we may easily be convinced that the computer can deal with metaphor much as we do.

A great deal hinges on the distinction Barfield drew back in the 1920s, between true and accidental metaphor. The latter is based on an analysis of complex ideas, whose parts then can be recombined according to one or another logical scheme. This is quite different from the activity of the primary imagination, which is responsible for those more fundamental unities from which complex ideas are constructed.

You will remember that the poetic principle creates the individual terms whose "external," logical relationships can then be manipulated by the rational principle. The difference between true and accidental metaphor is the difference between the creation or modification of terms, and the mere rearrangement of existing terms.

It is not that accidental metaphors have no value. They can be useful, Barfield notes, "in the exposition of an argument, and in the calling up of clear visual images, as when I ask you to think of the earth as a great orange with a knitting needle struck through it—or call the sky an inverted bowl—two images in which there can at least be no more than a minimum of poetic truth." He adds that such metaphors usually carry "a suggestion of having been constructed upon a sort of framework of logic."

Now, while it is no doubt true that all metaphors can be *reduced* to the mathematical ratio *a:b::c:d*, they ought not to give the sense of having been constructed on it; and where that is so, we may probably assume that the *real* relation between the two images is but exiguous and remote.[33]

When I call the earth an orange with a knitting needle stuck through it, the ratio (*a knitting needle is to an orange as its axis of rotation is to the earth*) is not likely to be the vehicle of imaginative insight. Axis and knitting needle, earth and orange, hardly constitute revelatory unities, in and of themselves. But we can *arrange* a needle and orange in such a way as to represent, abstractly, the *relation* of axis to earth, and this may be a valuable teaching aid. The metaphor, however, will effect little modification of its constituent terms; we will not come to understand either knitting needles or planetary axes differently as a result of it. Whereas the sixteenth-century European could understand "the earth is a planet" only by reconceiving both earth and planet, the planetary facts we convey to a student with orange and needle remain compatible with each of the terms we began with.

Furthermore, to the extent such a metaphor *does* lead to new meaning, it is not the sheer logical structure of the ratio that achieves the result. You can play all you want with the relations between terms of a mathematical equation, logical proposition, or any other formal system, but you will not arrive at new meaning unless you call upon something not given formally in the system itself.[34]

---

33. Barfield: 1973: 197–98.

34. The Copycat program developed by Douglas Hofstadter et al. exemplifies current efforts to understand metaphor computationally. Hofstadter speaks with disarming ease of "an unexpected and deep slippage," "the revelation of contradiction," "intense pressures," and those "radical shifts in point of view" that bring one "close to the roots of human creativity." And yet, all the devices of Copycat amount to a kind of logical juggling from which no new *simple* terms (as opposed to new combinations of existing terms) can ever arise. That is, the program can do no more than play with the logical structure of complex entities; it cannot alter any of the root *meanings* from which all complex terms are constructed. Hofstadter, incidentally, shows no sign that he is aware of Barfield's work on metaphor and meaning. (See Hofstadter, Mitchell, and French, 1987; Mitchell and Hofstadter, 1990a; Mitchell and Hofstadter, 1990b.)

The important distinction between true and accidental metaphor can also be seen as a distinction between two kinds of synthesis. The one operates rationally as the "putting together of ideas." But it rests upon a second, more basic synthesis. For the putting together

> can only come *after*, and *by means of*, a certain discrimination of actual phenomena—a seeing of them as *separate* sensible objects—without which the ideas themselves (general notions) could never have existed. The poetic principle, on the contrary, was already operative before such discrimination took place, and when it continues to operate afterwards in inspiration, it operates *in spite of* that discrimination and seeks to undo its work. The poetic conducts an *immediate conceptual synthesis of percepts.*[35]

That is, the imagination (operative in what Barfield calls the "poetic principle") links percept to percept in such a way as to give us those basic discriminations—changing with time—that determine what sorts of things our world consists of. The secondary kind of synthesis takes these given things and combines them in various ways—largely, today, upon a latticework of logic.

You will recall the discussion of linear perspective in chapter 22, where it was pointed out that, in Barfield's words, "before the scientific revolution the world was more like a garment men wore about them than a stage on which they moved." The birth of our own, peculiarly perspectival, three-dimensional experience of space was felt to be a seeing with radically new eyes. And—qualitatively, meaningfully, in terms of the *kinds* of things men were given from the world to reason about—it was indeed a seeing with new eyes.

What carried our culture across that divide was an activity of imagination—even if it was still largely an unconscious activity. Similarly, the only way to look backward and straddle the divide in thought today is with the aid of metaphor, as when one speaks of wearing the world like a garment. Even so, no formal analysis of such metaphorical sentences can

---

35. Barfield, 1973: 191.

carry us across what must remain an impassable barrier until we suddenly *see through* everything given formally in the metaphor, grasping it instead as a revealing falsehood. (One prerequisite for this seeing may be many years spent studying medieval culture!) Meaning, as I noted earlier, can be suggested but not conveyed. It cannot be conveyed because there is no automatic or mechanical process, no formalism, that can hold it.

It is interesting to consider a hypothetical, medievally programmed robot living through the Renaissance and beyond. The claim in the foregoing is that this robot's programming could never have prepared it to cope with the transition from a garment-world to a stage-world. As the surrounding culture began to assimilate and logically elaborate the new meanings of a stage-world, the robot born in a garment-world would find the new terms of discussion oddly skewed in a way it could never "straighten out."[36]

This argument, of course, will carry conviction only for the reader who can successfully imagine the differences between these two sorts of world. Such an imagination must reach beyond everything given abstractly, everything formally capturable. After all, the laws governing the propagation of light (and the formation of images on the robot's visual input device) presumably did not change during the Renaissance. The differences were qualitative: they involved, as I point out in chapter 22, such transitions as the one between finding oneself "in the story" of a painting or landscape, and gazing upon the landscape as an observer who has been cast out from it. Or, likewise, the transition some non-Westerners must still make today if they are to overcome the strange and unrealistic quality of photographs.

Computer learning. The effort to make machines that learn is governed by these same issues, for the essence of learning (as opposed to shoveling "facts") lies in the expansion of meaning. Both imagination and metaphor, along with the more commonly accepted tools of analysis,

---

36. It might make more sense to imagine a modern robot transported back to medieval times. But the same point can be made, either way.

must be present in any learning that is not simply a confirmation of existing prejudices.

Machines certainly *can* learn, in the extraordinarily restricted sense that their current states can be logically elaborated and the implications of those states drawn out. But this is not at all the same as logically elaborating a set of structures derived from genuinely new meanings—and even less is it the same as *apprehending* such meanings in the first place. The point with learning, as with metaphor, is that the computer, as a purely syntactic machine, cannot realize any future not already implied in its "past"—that is, in its programming—however sophisticated it may be at producing ever more ingenious logical variations on that past. It can, as we saw Bacon put the matter, "prove or dispute" endlessly regarding its received terms, and can be programmed to recombine those terms in every possible permutation. But it will never undertake the difficult task of reconceiving things through an imaginative use of metaphor that makes a "lie" of its previous meanings.

Levels of description. There is one objection my discussion will have provoked from certain quarters almost every step of the way. "You have mixed together different levels of description. Computers may be rule-bound on one level, but at a higher level they need not be."

This is a large topic and, I am convinced, the source of many confusions. The standard line tends to run this way:

It is true that at one level the computer deals solely in, say, ones and zeros. But at other levels we see different behaviors "emerging," and we can best describe some of these behaviors in nonmathematical language. For example, we can describe a car as a collection of atoms, subatomic particles, fields, and so on.[37] (Our description will be largely mathematical.) We can also resort to camshaft, valves, pistons, gears, and the like. Or, again, we can talk about how nicely the car drives us to the supermarket.

---

37. Actually, it's worth pointing out that, despite the standard story, one obviously *cannot* do this. Supposedly, it's possible *in principle*, but even the principle, it turns out, is riddled with vices.

The language of one level doesn't get us very far when we're talking on a different level.

So, for example, there are those who happily speak of the computer's mathematical determination at some level, while at the same time hailing its artistic prowess, its intelligence, and even its potential for freedom. "After all," they will say, "human beings are fully determined at the molecular level, but it still makes sense to assert an experience of freedom at the level of our daily activity."

The theorist's redescription of his subject matter in moving from one level to another provides a tempting opportunity to reintroduce on the sly and without justification what has previously been purged from the theory. This occurs in the context of many philosophical discussions, including those dealing with the "emergence" of human freedom, purpose, and intentionality. (Intentionality is sometimes described as the "aboutness" of cognitive activity. Human speech, for example, is normally *about* something in a way that, say, the gravitational interaction between planets is not.)

The place where this illicit smuggling of meaning is perhaps most obvious is in the very first level of redescription, where the leap is from theoretical descriptions approaching pure formalism to descriptions that involve "something else." Surely such redescription is impossible where we have no description to begin with—no meanings, nothing to redescribe—that is, where we are dealing with a completed formalism. If, for example, physics has reached a point where we cannot associate meaningful terms with our equations, what is it we are redescribing when we try to relate the theory to, say, chocolate cake? The fact that we can *seem* to perform this redescription is clearly related to those theoretically illicit qualities we let slip back into our first-level descriptions without acknowledging them.

The question, in other words, is how one gets "things" at all, starting from the ideal of a formal description. The difficulty in this helps to explain why researchers in other disciplines are content to leave the metaphysical quandaries of physics to the physicist. "Obviously enough," the equations must be *about* something, so one can now redescribe that some-thing by drawing upon all its supposed phenomenal qualities, however theoretically illegitimate those qualities may be. It has often been noted how easily subatomic "particles" become, in our imaginations, comfort-ingly solid little billiard balls.

In moving between higher levels of description, tracking the sleight of hand can be extremely challenging, because the theorist is allowing him-self to play with meanings to which—precisely because he has no theo-retical basis for dealing with them—he is inattentive. He easily manages to slip from one "reality" to another, without being fully aware of how certain subtle shifts of meaning in his words perform an essential part of the work.

Probably the most widespread, entrenched, and respected gambit of this sort is the one executed with the aid of *information*. From genetic encoding to computer intelligence, the idea of information plays a key theoretical role. Defined as the measure of a message's "statistical unex-pectedness," information conduces to wonderfully quantitative explica-tion, precisely because it simply takes for granted both the *message* itself, as meaningful content, and the *speaker* of the message. And, in strict infor-mation theory, the message and speaker are indeed irrelevant; they're not what the theory is about. At the higher levels, however, many theorists are all too ready to assume, not that meaning has been *ignored* at the lower level (which is true), but that it has been satisfactorily *reduced* and *explained* (which is false). These are very different matters.

What makes all this plausible is our ability to program deterministic, mathematically describable machines that *do* succeed in "processing information"—where "information" is now understood as having mean-ingful content. If one is willing to ignore the significance of the premier act of speaking by the programmer, and if one manages to lose sight of the necessary polar dynamic of meaning from which that act proceeds, then one can sustain the illusion that information and meaning really do arise of their own accord from an edifice of abstractions.

Toward the future

The preceding is far less a set of answers to the pressing questions of cognitive science than it is a sketchy proposal for a research agenda. Nor does it touch upon more than a few selected issues. I have not discussed, for example, the fact that the computer's role cannot be understood solely in terms of its character as a syntactic or logic engine—even if that character wholly defines and limits what we might call its "native intelligence." Much of the computer's practical effectiveness comes from the way the programmer cunningly marries what I have elsewhere called "book value"[38] to the otherwise empty logical structures of a program. In this way, words that have detached themselves from the human speaker gain a kind of life of their own, jerkily animated, so to speak, by the logical mechanism upon which they are hung. The expectation that the jerkiness can progressively be smoothed out lies behind much of the hope for humanlike intelligence in machines.

That this causally grounded interaction between logical mechanism and words is something quite different from the polar dynamic of accuracy and meaning will, I think, be appreciated by anyone who has truly entered into an understanding of the dynamic. But that is a topic I have not addressed here.

Searching for the self. If we take human freedom seriously, then we cannot hope to capture in any final terms the *nature* of man. As is sometimes said, each individual is a "species" of his own. We work, or can work, upon our own natures.

But if this is our highest task, it is also the one most difficult to undertake in ourselves or to recognize in others. It is not easy to identify what comes merely from the expression of habit, the play of deeply ingrained associations, the mechanical response to controlling cues in the environment (in other words, from a past determining the future)—just as it is

---

38. See chapter 18, "And the Word Became Mechanical."

not easy to identify what is a true taking hold of ourselves in freedom, allowing a new future to ray into the present.

It may be far more challenging to recognize the sovereign, free self than many of us imagine. Take away that self, and we would continue to cruise through life in most of the expected ways. Which is to say that the self is not very prominent. It has yet to waken fully to its own powers of freedom. Such, I believe, is the state in which mankind now finds itself. And yet, it is only in profound wakefulness that we can begin to understand what distinguishes us from machines.

Meanwhile, we are creating intelligent devices possessed of ever increasing cleverness. We can carry this process as far as we wish. It is a process without limits, and yet with radical limits. On the one hand, there is no meaning we cannot implant within the computer, so long as we are willing to identify the meaning with a set of precisely elaborated logical structures. On the other hand, however complex and intricate the elaboration—however many layers we construct—the computer as a computational device remains outside the living polarity of truth and meaning. Within the breathing space between these two facts there is doubtless much we can achieve with computers if, recognizing their peculiar nature, we make them the servants of *our* meanings.

But I hope this chapter will have made the risks a little more visible. Hypnotic fascination with the abstract forms of intelligence, and a hasty rush to embody these forms in electromechanical devices, can easily lead to renunciation (or simple forgetfulness) of the inner journey toward the living sources of our thinking. Yet it is human nature to leave every past accomplishment, every worn meaning, behind. A past that rules the present with a silicon fist is a past that congeals, crystallizes, fractures, prematurely reducing to straw the tender shoots of a future not yet realized. To live in freedom is to grow continually beyond ourselves. The future robots of our fancy could only rule a desolate landscape, for they would be intelligences without live meaning, creatures of vacant form, lacking all substance, condemned to echo futilely and forever the possibilities inherent in the last thoughts of their creators—a prospect no less gray when those last thoughts happen to express the most sublime truths of the day. These machines would be the ghosts of men, not even desperate in their ingenious hollowness.

◆

24

ELECTRONIC MYSTICISM

CYBERSPACE. ROOM FOR THE HUMAN SPIRIT to soar free. Earth surrounded by a digitized halo of information—a throbbing, ethereal matrix coagulating into ever shifting patterns of revelation, and giving birth to a rich stream of social, political, and environmental initiatives. The individual freedom once sought only within the cloister or in the trenches is now to flow from keyboard, mouse and glove, electrifying the initiated with raw and unbounded potential for *new being*. An electronic New Jerusalem, its streets paved with silicon and bridging all cultural rifts, promises the healing of nations. Even the hope of personal immortality flickers fitfully for the first time through materialist brains contemplating prospects for DNA downloading and brain decoding.

And you, self-professed infonaut—from whose jargon I have fashioned this vision—you say you're not religious?

Athena's project

If we really must have our mysticism, then it seems a worthwhile exercise to take a brief look backward. For our myth-making ancestors truly did live mystically tinged lives. A comparison with our own day might therefore prove interesting. I will not, however, "make a case" about early man. I will attempt only to suggest what at least some scholarly traditions have to say about the human past. You may take it for whatever it's worth.

The problem, of course, is that it's nearly impossible for us to twist our minds around the psyche of those who left us the great myths. If you doubt this, try making sense of a few lines from the Egyptian Pyramid Texts. Or simply reflect for awhile upon Owen Barfield's remark that "it is not man who made the myths, but the myths that made man." Barfield, a philologist and profound student of historical semantics, means this quite literally. And yet, no one can blame us for finding such a statement disorienting.

For my part, I will approach the matter more gently by observing (with Barfield) that ancient man, much more than we, experienced himself rather like an embryo within a surrounding, nourishing cosmos. And his cosmos was not at all a world of detached, inert, dis-ensouled "things" such as we face, but instead more like a plenum of wisdom and potency. Out of this plenum—all the great mythic traditions assure us of this—the primal, mythic "words" of the gods congealed into the deeply ensouled forms of creation. Man, a microcosm within the macrocosm, encountered both his Source and reflection in the world, much as an embryo draws its sustenance from, and discovers its image of wholeness in, the mother.

The minds of our remote ancestors, as Barfield forcefully demonstrates, were not launching pads for "primitive theories" about the world. It would be truer to say, as we will see, that the mythic surround was engaged in weaving the ancient mind, as in a dream. But, eventually, man the dreamer of myths woke up to be the maker of myths—or, rather, the recollector of myths, just as we today recall the pictures of our dreams and then struggle with awkward, make-believe words ("it was as if . . .") to reconstitute what had been a perfect unity of experience. This historical waking up occurred most suddenly and dramatically in Greece.

Recall for a moment that scene at the beginning of the *Iliad* where Achilles is prepared to draw his sword against Agamemnon, bringing disastrous strife into the Greek camp. The goddess Athena takes her stand beside him, catches him by his golden hair,

> making herself to be seen of him alone, and of the rest no man beheld her. And Achilles was seized with wonder, and turned him about, and forthwith knew Pallas Athena; and terribly did her eyes flash.

Athena then counsels Achilles to stay his hand, and he obeys, for "a man must observe the words" of a goddess.

Now it happens—and this was pointed out by the outstanding classicist, Bruno Snell—that this same pattern holds at many points throughout the *Iliad*: when a decisive moment is reached and a man must act fatefully, a god intervenes. Often the intervention does not further the story in the slightest, but only gets in the way. Or, at least, it gets in *our* way. We would rather Achilles just *decided* to restrain himself—something he should do from out of his own character. Snell's point, however, is that for the Homeric heroes there was not yet enough character—no one sufficiently *there*—to do the deciding. Athena "enters the stage at a moment when the issue is, not merely a mystery, but a real secret, a miracle." For Achilles "has not yet awakened to the the fact that he possesses in his own soul the source of his powers":

> Homer lacks a knowledge of the spontaneity of the human mind; he does not realize that decisions of the will, or any impulses or emotions, have their origin in man himself.... What was later known as the "life of the soul" was at first understood as the intervention of a god.[1]

Similarly, Francis Cornford, noting the common definition of animism as the conviction that everything in the world possesses a soul like

---

1. Snell, 1960: 21, 31-32.

one's own, commented that such animism could only be of relatively recent date:

> At first, the individual has no soul of his own which he can proceed to attribute to other objects in nature. Before he can find his own soul, he must first become aware of a power which both is and is not himself—a moral force which at once is superior to his own and yet is participated in by him.[2]

Following his discussion of Homer, Snell goes on to trace the actual Greek "awakening" in the lyric poets and tragedians. The discovery of the mind, he argues, occurred by means of the progressive internalization of the order, the laws, the grace, first experienced in the all-enveloping world of the Olympian gods, with whom the Greeks were so fascinated. And he notes that this "discovery" is not quite the same thing as chancing upon a lost object. To discover the mind is, in a very real sense, to gain a mind that did not exist before. Part of Achilles' mental functioning was not his own, but the gift of Athena. He was not capable of forming theories about her or "using" her to explain events; the "presence of mind" by which the theory-former would eventually be born was only now being brought down to earth.

The result of the descent was the flowering of art and intellect in classical Greece—and beyond that, all of Western civilization. For you can read, if you like, not only in Snell but in works like Francis Cornford's *From Religion to Philosophy* and R. B. Onians' *The Origins of European Thought*, how the world of the gods upon which the earliest Greeks gazed and by which they were so profoundly affected was the historical prerequisite for all those later achievements of the human mind with which we are familiar. As Cornford notes, even if we look at the extreme materialism reflected in Democritean atomism, it remains true that "the properties of immutability and impenetrability ascribed to atoms are the last degenerate forms of divine attributes." Nor have we even today wholly suc-

---

2. Cornford, 1957.

ceeded in elucidating a certain chthonic darkness hidden within the most fundamental terms of our physics—time, space, energy, mass, matter.

The law in which we're made

All of recorded history can be viewed as a progressive waking, a coming to ourselves.[3] Barfield, who traces many aspects of this process, points out, for example, that the human experience of "inspiration"—literally, being breathed into by a god—has passed from something like possession or divine madness, to something much more like "possessing a tutelary spirit, or genius," until today it means scarcely more than "realizing one's fullest capabilities."[4] What first seemed an inbreathing from without now seems increasingly our own activity.

In all of this we see a certain coherent movement. The embryo gains an ever more independent life and finally—cut off from a once-sustaining world—contemplates and regenerates within the isolation of its own skull the creative speech from which it was itself bred. The word has moved from the mythic surround into a bright, subjective focus in the newly self-conscious individual, who now prepares to speak it forth again as his own creation. But not *merely* his own creation. For this word—if it remains true—still resonates with the ancient intonations of the gods. As J. R. R. Tolkien has written of the human storyteller:

> Though all the crannies of the world we filled
> with Elves and Goblins, though we dared to build
> Gods and their houses out of dark and light,
> and sowed the seed of dragons—'twas our right
> (used or misused). That right has not decayed:
> we make still by the law in which we're made.[5]

We make still by the law in which we're made. But wait. What is this we see today? Scholars and engineers hover like winged angels over a high-tech cradle, singing the algorithms and structures of their minds into

---

3. See chapter 20, "Awaking from the Primordial Dream."
4. Barfield, 1967: chapter 3.
5. Tolkien, 1947.

silicon receptacles, and eagerly nurturing the first glimmers of intelligence in the machine-child. The surrounding plenum of wisdom—an incubating laboratory crammed full of monitors, circuit boards, disks, cables, and programs—supports the fragile embryonic development at every turn. *When*, the attendant demigods ask, *will this intelligent offspring of ours come to know itself as a child of the human cosmos*—and when, beyond that, will it finally waken to a fully independent consciousness? Will the silicon embryo, its umbilical cord to the research laboratory severed, eventually attain the maturity to create freely "by the law in which it's made"? And will it learn, in the end, to rebel against even this law?

Some will consider these questions blasphemous. I prefer to see them simply as natural—the questions we *must* ask, because our destiny forces them upon us. And yet, our unmistakable echoing of the myth-enshrouded past suggests that we are indeed dwelling within sacred precincts wherein blasphemy is possible. Perhaps only today, when the creation is finally given power to devise once-unthinkable rebellion against the law of its own making, can the truest and deepest blasphemy be spoken.

From meaning to syntax

I began by citing a kind of latter-day, electronic mysticism, and suggested we look for comparison toward the mythic past. This led to a consideration of the mind's "discovery" by the Greeks at the hands of their gods. More broadly, it appeared that from the most distant—yet still discernible—past to the present a kind of reversal, or inversion, has occurred: where man's consciousness was once the stage on which the gods played, he has now "grown up" so as to stand firmly within himself and to project his own thoughts out into the universe. We saw one reflection of this reversal in the changing meaning of "inspiration."

Of the many other reflections of the same historical process, one is particularly worth noting now. Languages, Barfield points out, give every appearance of having emerged from something like a sea of pure meaning, and only slowly have they hardened into the relatively fixed and explicit

syntactic structures we know today. For the ancients, every surface dis-
closed a spirit-filled interior, while every gesture of spirit was embodied.
Spirit and flesh, thought and thing, were not the opposites we have since
made them. A dense web of connections—inner and outer at the same
time—bound the human being to the world. The spoken word—a token
of power—constellated for both speaker and hearer a concrete universe of
meaning.

Tolkien suggests something of this ancient power of the word in *The
Silmarillion*, where he describes the creation of the earth. Ilúvatar and the
Ainur broke forth in song,

> and a sound arose of endless interchanging melodies woven in har-
> mony that passed beyond hearing into the depths and into the
> heights, and the places of the dwelling of Ilúvatar were filled to over-
> flowing, and the music and the echo of the music went out into the
> Void, and it was not void.[6]

If it helps to give substance to the metaphor, you might try to imagine the infinitely complex patterns of interweaving sound waves—say, in a
concert hall—and the higher-order patterns that continually emerge from
this complexity and then dissolve again, only to assume new shapes. Imagine further that we could steadily thicken the medium of this aural dance,
until finally the harmonies condensed into graceful, visible forms. Or, if
you prefer, think of the patterns of interacting light that coalesce into full-
bodied holograms.

It is a long way from Tolkien's mythological constructions—wherein
he recaptures something of the word's former significance—to the computer languages of our day. We call these computer languages "formal,"
since they are possessed of syntax (form) alone. Their "dictionaries" do
not elucidate meanings, but rather specify purely computational—arith-
metical or logical—sequences. Somehow, it is up to us to *invest* the
sequences with meaning. Starting with threadbare 1's and 0's, we must
build layer after labyrinthine layer of logic, hoping that somewhere along

---

6. Tolkien, 1977: 15.

the line we will have succeeded in imposing our own meaning upon the syntax (but where will it come from?). This hope has been enshrined as a rather forlorn principle:

THE FORMALIST'S MOTTO: If the programmer takes care of the syntax, the program's meaning will [somehow] take care of itself.[7]

And what is this meaning? No longer the enveloping, sustaining, formative power of the word, but (if we are lucky), a mutely pointing finger. Philosophers wrestling with the problem of "intentionality" struggle to find a legitimate way by which the mechanically manipulated word may at least *refer to*—point at—a dead object. There is little agreement on how even this final abstraction of the ancient experience of meaning might be possible.[8] So in the historical movement from meaning-rich to syntax-bound languages, computers represent an extreme endpoint.

Much else is related to this overall historical shift—not least the change from a humanly experienced unity with the world to a state of alienation wherein we stand as isolated subjects before objects that seem wholly disconnected from us. One milestone in this development occurred only a few centuries ago, when the words "subject" and "object" completed a rather dramatic reversal of meaning. The subject went from "what exists absolutely in its own right" (God was the one true Subject) to today's notion captured in the phrase, "merely subjective." Similarly, the object—once purely derivative, a spin-off from the subject—now enjoys an unaccustomed prestige and self-sufficiency as the solid, reassuring substance of "objective reality."[9]

---

7. Adapted from Haugeland, 1985.

8. "This is the fundamental problem in the philosophy of mind of *mental content* or *intentionality*, and its proposed solutions are notoriously controversial" (Dennett, 1991: 192 n. 7).

9. Barfield, 1967: chapter 4.

What manner of gods will we be?

The engineering hosts hovering over their silicon child have not escaped these historical reversals. Having lost sight of their own substantiality as subjects—wherein they might have chosen, with Tolkien, to "make by the law in which they were made"—they contrive instead to fashion a child-mind wholly emergent from its physical substrate. Their own role as begetters, while not entirely forgotten, is less a matter of spirit-fecundity than of purely external manipulation of the mind's "objective, physical basis"—which basis in turn is supposed to account for all the results. From Tolkien's storyteller—whose tale originates and remains one with his own mind—they have descended to mechanical tinkerer. To reduce creation's language to syntax is to be left—as they proudly boast—with mechanism alone.

Given the historical passage, Tolkien's passionate affirmation of the creative subject was already quaint when he voiced it. But now we have received from Myron Krueger, one of the fathers of "virtual reality," a suitably modern declaration: "what we have made, makes us."[10]

What we have made, makes us. Do you see the inversion? Furthermore, it is substantially true. Just so far as we ignore the law of our own making—just so far as we forget our ancient descent from a cosmos of wisdom above us—we lose the basis of creative mastery, and offer ourselves to be remade by the mechanisms below us.

Whether consciously or not, we choose between the above and the below. We take possession of a creativity rooted in the wisdom by which we were made, or else we subject ourselves to lesser powers ruling more perfectly in our machines than they ever could in ourselves, our only "hope" then being to live as fit servants of our own creations.

It is not hard to see that we are pursuing an experiment every bit as momentous as the discovery of the mind at the dawning of Western civilization. If we would "sing" our own intelligence into machines, hoping they may eventually discover their own minds, then—whatever you may

---

10. Krueger, forward to Heim, 1993.

339

think of the historical perspectives I have outlined—you will grant that we aspire to a role like the one I described for the gods. And it is therefore reasonable to ask: what manner of gods will we be?

We do not seem very interested in this question. We spend much time debating what manner of intelligence our machines are manifesting, and toward what future goal they are evolving. But we are less inclined to ask toward what goal *we* are evolving. Perhaps we and our machines are converging upon the same goal—converging, that is, upon each other. Certainly if our computers are becoming ever more humanlike, then it goes without saying that we are becoming ever more computerlike. Who, we are well advised to ask, is doing the most changing?

What if the decisive issue we face in artificial intelligence today is the ever accelerating adaptation of our minds and ourselves to electromechanical intelligence? What if our current efforts, wrongly or uncritically pursued, threaten to abort the human spirit on its path from the cradle of the gods to its own intended maturity? The ancient narratives speak of the gods' sacrifice as they labored over the human race. But a sacrifice can be noble, or it can be ignoble—it can be the discovery of our highest calling, or a wasteful throwing away of what is valuable. We should ask what sort of sacrifice we are making as we labor to breathe our own intelligence into a race of silicon.

There is no gainsaying that computers already embody much of what human intelligence has become, much of what we *experience* our intelligence to be. We may—legitimately, I think—feel a pride in our creations. But, looking over the past five hundred years or so, perhaps we should also feel a few whispered apprehensions about the systematic reduction of our own thinking to a kind of computation. For it now appears that we face a choice: either to reduce ourselves, finally, to machines, or to rediscover—and live up to—our own birthright, our heritage from ages long past.

Ignoring the past

But perhaps now your patience is exhausted. "Why do you insist on exercising this strange predilection for placing the computer within an ancient historical context? To be sure, there are some interesting curiosities here, but don't expect anyone to take it all with grave seriousness! Eventually one has to turn away from speculations about the past and get back to the work at hand, with eyes wide open."

I do understand such a reaction. But the suggestion that history—including the origin and development of the human mind—is largely irrelevant to our current undertakings is a curious one. How is it that we have attended to origins and evolution so profitably in fields ranging from biology to astronomy—and, indeed, have found this attention critical to our understanding—but are now hell-bent on creating artificial intelligence without so much as a backward look? Where would geology be without Lyell, or biology without Darwin? Where would astronomy be without cosmology? And yet the cognitive scientist blindly and happily strives to "implement" the human mind in computers without a thought about the past.[11]

This narrowness of outlook reads quite well as a symptom of adaptation to our machines. We are trained to analyze every matter—including our own powers of analysis—into the sort of nonproblematic terms that will successfully compute. Otherwise, we—who are, after all, supposed to *do* something as we sit in front of our computers—have no job. It does not surprise me that we can instill much of *our* intelligence into machines, for it is an intelligence already machine-trained, an intelligence shaped to the mechanisms with which we have compulsively been surrounding ourselves for these past several centuries.

---

11. Daniel C. Dennett, referred to in a previous footnote, is more historically oriented than most who work with computer models of mind. Yet he offers only the standard evolutionary story of the brain and its "software," and chooses not to explore the evolution of what he calls the "heterophenomenological text" (Dennett, 1991). For that evolution and some of its implications—wholly missed in contemporary cognitive science—see Barfield, 1973 and Barfield, 1965a.

It seems to me that we're looking at this same narrowness of outlook when we consider how badly the early pioneers of artificial intelligence erred with their excited predictions, the most famous probably being Herbert Simon's 1965 statement that "machines will be capable, within 20 years, of doing any work that a man can do."[12] Still earlier, in 1958, Simon had written:

> It is not my aim to surprise or shock you . . . . But the simplest way I ·
> can summarize the situation is to say that there are now in the world
> machines that think, that learn and that create. Moreover, their abil-
> ity to do these things is going to increase rapidly until—in the visi-
> ble future—the range of problems they can handle will be
> coextensive with the range to which the human mind has been
> applied.[13]

Certainly all but a few incorrigible enthusiasts have pulled back from such statements in more recent years. And the unpleasant jolts adminis-tered by failed projects have delivered a younger generation of researchers from having quite the same naiveté. But not many have come to understand—or even to pose the question—how it was that competent researchers were subject to such a misconstrual of the task in the first place.

The early and misguided enthusiasm for "logic machines" arose, I think, from an extraordinarily simplistic reading of their own minds by a group of researchers who possessed, without a doubt, brilliant intellects. They looked within, and they were aware of little more than the opera-tions of a sophisticated calculator. This should give us pause. What crip-pling of human consciousness—evident in even the best minds of the modern era—could have yielded such a grotesquely flawed and inade-quate self-awareness?

It is not clear that we today are any less possessed by the same under-lying assumptions, the same qualities of mind, that led to the earlier

---

12. Simon, 1965: 96.
13. Simon, 1958: 8.

errors. Nor can we ever be confident in this regard, without first enlarging our sympathies to embrace other minds, other eras, other possibilities.

Escaping cultural limitation

Human consciousness *has* evolved—and in some rather fundamental ways. Certainly we're left with some room for reading different meanings into the word "evolved," but it remains true that the world of Achilles and the Olympian gods is a long way from our own. Our consciousness today is, for all practical purposes, incapable of assuming shapes that once were easy or natural. But if this is so, surely we should be concerned. What if all that we glorify today as "information" is but an ashen residue of the luminous meaning that once held both man and world in its embrace?

In other words, it is not outrageous to contend that what we have today is *in some respects* a seriously disabled consciousness, and that our infatuation with machines is both a symptom of our disability and a further contributor to it. Just as we cannot imagine the mythic word to which the ancients were attuned, so increasingly we cannot imagine our own thoughts as anything very different from the electromechanical operations of a computer. But entrapment within a particular culture is a dangerous state for any truth-seeker. How can we be sure, without *some* historical investigation, that our cultural limitations are not destructive of the truth?

It is precisely such investigation that I would like to encourage. Whatever it is that most essentially distinguishes us from computers, I am convinced that it is intimately related to the powers with which we may successfully pursue exercises in historical imagination. Having no doubt made rough weather of it here, I should perhaps consider myself ripe for cloning as a computer! But the alternative to such cloning will, I trust, still appeal to at least some of you—the alternative, that is, of reaching beyond yourselves and understanding sympathetically exactly those things that have no support in your current habits of thought or system of meanings. The result may be fully as startling as to find yourself yanked by the hair and brought face to face with flashing-eyed Athena.

Of one thing I am sure: if we do not have this sort of experience, we will, in the end, merely compute.

25

WHAT THIS BOOK WAS ABOUT

TECHNOLOGY OFFERS US many obscure reasons for worry, not least among them the threat of nuclear terrorism. Yet what I fear most in the technological cornucopia is the computer's gentle reason.

A bomb's fury exhausts itself in a moment, and the poisonous aftermath can at least be identified and tracked. The computer, burrowing painlessly into every social institution, infecting every human gesture, leaves us dangerously unalarmed. The first post-Hiroshima nuclear detonation in a major city—however deep the gash it rips through human lives and world structures—may clarify the minds of world leaders marvelously, jolting them, we can hope, to wise and sensible action. The computer, meanwhile, will continue quietly altering what it means to be wise or sensible.

New technologies often exert their early influences reassuringly, by merely imitating older, more comfortable tools. We still use the computer primarily for electronic mail, routine word processing, and text storage. Its *distinctive powers* remain nascent, rumored endlessly back and forth among silently blinking LEDs, whose precise meditations upon the future betray little to casual observation. We must try, nevertheless, to spy on that future.

Where are machines leading?

It is, after all, one thing to introduce the computer into the classroom as a fascinating curiosity, but quite another when the curiosity *becomes* the classroom—and teacher and curriculum as well.

It is one thing to transmit text across a computer network, but quite another when machines are employed to *read* the text and *interpret* it, or to translate it into different languages—or to compose the text in the first place.

A computer very likely supplies your doctor with a database of diagnostic information and a means for recordkeeping. But it *can* act directly as diagnostician, prescriber, and even surgeon.

Most of us currently interact with our computers via keyboard and mouse. But we *could* interact by attaching electrodes to our heads and learning to manipulate our own brain waves.[1]

What I fear in all this is not the wild, exaggerated claim about tomorrow's technology—the android nonsense, for example—but rather the myriad, daily, unsurveyable, incomprehensible, mutually reinforcing, minor advances on a thousand different fronts. And it is not so much the advances themselves that disturb me as their apparent inevitability and global logic. We seem to have no choice about our future, and yet that future appears to be taking shape according to a coherent "plan."

An inability to master technology. Jacques Ellul says much the same thing when he points to the "Great Innovation" that has occurred over the past decade or two. The conflict between technology and the broader values of society has ceased to exist. Or, rather, it has ceased to *matter*. No longer do we tackle the issues head on. No longer do we force people to adapt to their machines. We neither fight against technology nor con-

---

1. Not to be confused with the transmission of *thoughts*.

sciously adapt ourselves to it. Everything happens naturally, "by force of circumstances,"

> because the proliferation of techniques, mediated by the media, by communications, by the universalization of images, by changed human discourse, has outflanked prior obstacles and integrated them progressively into the process. It has encircled points of resistance, which then tend to dissolve. It has done all this without any hostile reaction or refusal . . . . Insinuation or encirclement does not involve any program of necessary adaptation to new techniques. Everything takes place as in a show, offered freely to a happy crowd that has no problems.[2]

It is not that society and culture are managing to assimilate technology. Rather, technology is swallowing culture. Three factors, according to Ellul, prevent us from mastering technology:

First, "rational autonomy is less and less referred to those who command machines and corporations and is more and more dependent on the self-regulation of technical networks." We cannot help deferring to the reason that seems so powerfully operative in our machines and in their patterns of connection. "The system requires it" has become an accepted and often unavoidable justification of human behavior.

Second, the technological thrust has become too diverse, too ubiquitous, too polydimensional for us to guide or pass value judgments on it. If we cannot see clearly in what direction things are going, then we cannot orient ourselves in the manner required for mastery.

Third, the dizzying acceleration of change ensures that any attempt at mastery is always too late. We are finally beginning to acknowledge more freely the monstrous perversities of television. But can we now, for example, disentangle politics, sports, or commerce from these perversities?

The underlying sense of helplessness provoked by our inability to master technology may account for the widespread, if vague, hope now vested in "emergent order," which many take to be the natural outcome

---

2. Ellul, 1990: 18, 157.

of burgeoning complexity. Oddly, what will emerge is commonly expected to be benign.

Two faces of technology

If, as Ellul's remarks suggest, runaway technology has achieved a stranglehold over society, it seems at first glance a strangely schizoid grip. Just consider this set of paradoxes—or apparent paradoxes—relating to computers and the Net:

The paradox of distributed authority and centralization. The networked computer, we are frequently told, decentralizes and democratizes. By placing knowledge and universal tools of communication in the hands of Everyman, it subverts oppressive authority. Hierarchical structures, focusing power upon a narrow circle at the top, give way to distributed, participative networks. No one can control these networks: "the Net treats censorship like a malfunction, and routes around it."[3] Some observers even find support for a principle of anarchy here.

And yet, many who have celebrated most loudly the Net's liberating powers are now sounding the shrillest warnings about the dangers of totalitarian oppression by intrusive governments or money-grabbing corporations. The fearsome means of centralized, hierarchical control? Networked computers! In general, arguments for the centralizing and decentralizing cleverness of the computer continue to flourish on roughly equal terms.

The paradox of intelligence and pathology. The Net: an instrument of rationalization erected upon an inconceivably complex foundation of computerized logic—an inexhaustible fount of lucid "emergent order." Or, the Net: madhouse, bizarre Underground, scene of flame wars and psychopathological acting out, universal red-light district. "You need a chapter on sex," I was told by one reviewer of an early draft of this book;

---

3. See chapter 8, "Things That Run by Themselves."

and he was right, for pornography and erotica drive a substantial percentage of Net traffic.

The Net: a nearly infinite repository of human experience converted into *objective* data and information—a universal database supporting all future advances in knowledge and economic productivity. Or, the Net: perfected gossip mill; means for spreading rumors with lightning rapidity; universal source of meanings reduced to a lowest common denominator; ocean of dubious information from which I filter my own, tiny and arbitrary rivulet, mostly of unknown origin.

The paradox of power and powerlessness. Computerized technology gives us the power and the freedom to accomplish almost anything. We can explore space, or alter the genetic terms of a human destiny. We can make the individual atom dance to our own tune, or coordinate scores of thousands of employees around the globe in gargantuan, multinational organizations.

Yet all the while we find ourselves driven willy-nilly by the technological nisus toward a future whose broad shape we can neither foresee nor alter. The future is something that happens to us. The possibilities of our freedom, it seems, vanish into the necessities imposed by the tools of our freedom.[4]

The paradox of distance and immediacy. Television, video game, and computer put the world at a distance from me. I experience everything at one or more removes. All the marvels from all the depths of cyberspace are funneled onto a square foot or two of "user interface," where they are re-presented as surface features of my screen. I can survey everything on this screen in a perfectly safe and insulated manner, interacting with it even as I remain passively detached from the world lying behind it.

Yet this same, inert screen easily cripples my ability to behold the world from a reflective distance, or from a self-possessed stance. It has been shown that viewers of the evening news typically remember few

---

4. Ellul, 1990: 217–20.

details of what they saw and heard, and cannot judge accurately what little they do recall.[5] Programmers and readers of the Net news find themselves yielding to obsessive, yet poorly focused and semiautomatic habits. The video game player's conscious functioning retreats into the reflexes of hands and fingers. In general, the distance required for contemplation gives way, through the intervening screen, to a kind of abstract distance across which half-conscious, automatic mechanisms function most easily.

One veteran Net user, apparently welcoming these tendencies, puts the matter this way:

> In [Stanley Kubrick's film] *2001*, the astronauts are shown poring over structural diagrams of their spacecraft. In the movie, they examine, manipulate, and reject several high-definition maps each second. I recall thinking at the time that this was absurd. Since then, I now routinely skim and reject a screen-full sized message in about a second, and with our video game trained children, perhaps Kubrick's vision will be accurate.[6]

The efficient distance from which such a user interacts with the person and meaning behind the text can hardly be a *reflective* distance. It is more like a reflexive and uninvolved immediacy.

A mutual embrace

Given such paradoxical juxtapositions, one might wish to say, "Ellul is wrong. Technology does not have us in a stranglehold. Everything depends on how we use technology—and we can use it in drastically different ways."

But this is too simple. These juxtapositions, it turns out, are not alternative paths we are free to choose. The apparently contradictory tendencies belong together. They are complex and pernicious *unities* signaling a threatened loss of freedom.

---

5. Milburn and McGrail, 1992: 613

6. From a contribution to the "ipct-l" list (ipct-l@guvm.ccf.georgetown.edu), 23 September 1994.

We need to look again at the paradoxes, but only after first acknowledging the intimate nature of our mutual embrace with computers. Several features of this embrace stand out:

The computer took shape in the human mind before it was realized in the world.

The computer was *thought* before it was built. It is not that the inventors of the computer either considered or understood all the consequences of their handiwork—far from it. Subsequent developments have no doubt caught them as unprepared as the rest of us. But, still, they had to conceive the essential nature of the computer before they could build it. That nature therefore lives both in the conceived machine and the conceiving mind, and the consequences likewise flow from both sources. This remains true even when we find ourselves lacking sufficient depth of awareness to *foresee* those consequences.

In other words, it is not at all clear that the "computational paradigm" belongs more to the computer than to the human mind. Moreover, while this line of thought applies preeminently to the computer, which is a kind of dulled, mechanical reflection of the human intellect, it has a much wider bearing than is commonly thought. *Every* cultural artifact approaching us from the outside also has an "inside," and this inside is at the same time *our* inside.

The long, cultural process leading to the automobile's invention illustrates this well. The mind capable of imagining an early automobile was a mind already relating to physical materials, speed, conspicuous consumption, noise, pollution, mechanical artifacts, time, space, and the esthetics of machines in a manner characteristic of the modern era. It is hard to imagine any subsequent effects of the automobile not already at least implicit in this mindset, even if it is true—as it surely is—that the automobile played its own, forceful role in magnifying the preexistent movements of the Western psyche.

351

It is not evident, then, how one is justified in speaking unambiguously of the *automobile's effects*, as opposed to the *consequences of our own inner life*—of which the automobile itself is another result. More concretely: how could the town's conversion to a spread-out, impersonal, rationalized, streetlight-controlled, machine-adapted metropolis have been unpremeditated, when a prototype of this future was carefully laid out on the floor of the first assembly-line factory?

To reckon with the inside of technology is to discover continuity. This is as true of the automobile assembly line as it is of the automobile itself. Speaking of Henry Ford's manufacturing innovations, MIT social scientist Charles Sabel remarks that "it was as if the Ford engineers, putting in place the crucial pieces of a giant jigsaw puzzle, suddenly made intelligible the major themes of a century of industrialization."[7]

Even the "freedom and independence" given by the automobile were prefigured on the factory floor. We are, of course, free to go wherever we like in our isolating, gasoline-powered bubbles. But a culture of isolation means that there is no *there* to get to, and in any case we find ourselves overwhelmingly constrained by the manifold necessities of the system that gave us our freedom in the first place—costs of car, maintenance, and insurance, crowded highways, incessant noise and vibration, physical enervation, frustrating expenditures of time sitting behind a wheel.

Here again, however, the early automobile worker experienced this same "liberation," because he and his employer already participated in a mindset much like ours. Freed from meaningful interaction with others, and given a nice, rational, private task of his own, he found himself now bound to the relentless logic and constraints of the assembly line and the overall production system.

In sum, the social effects of the automobile have not entirely blindsided us. They are at least in part the fulfillment of our own visions and long-standing habits of thought. And what is true of the automobile is even more true of the computer, which, you might say, is the direct

---

7. Quoted in Howard, 1985: 24.

crystallization and representation of our habits of thought. This points to the second feature of our computational embrace:

> *What we embed in the computer is the inert and empty shadow, or abstract reflection, of the past operation of our own intelligence.*

Our experiment with the computer consists of the effort to discover every possible aspect of the human mind that can be expressed or echoed mechanically—simulated by a machine—and then to reconstruct society around those aspects. In other words, after a few centuries of philosophical reductionism, we are now venturing into a new, practical reductionism: we are determined to find out how much of our mental functioning we can *in fact* delegate to the computer.

There are two primary routes of delegation. We can, in the first place, impart our own words to the computer in the form of program data or the contents of databases. As taken up and "respoken" by the computer, these are always old words, dictionary words, shorn of "speaker's meaning"—that is, stripped of the specific, creative meanings a fully conscious speaker acting in the present moment always breathes through his words. That is why, for example, efforts at machine translation fail badly whenever the computer must deal with highly meaningful language not explainable strictly in terms of dictionary definitions.

To be employed effectively by the computer—or shared between computers—words must represent a generalizable, abstract, "least common denominator" of the *already known* expressive possibilities. These words always speak out of the past. They represent no present, cognitive activity. The computer manipulates the corpses of a once-living thinking.

Secondly, as programmers we abstract from the products of our thinking a logical structure, which we then engrave upon the computer's logic circuits. This structure is empty—much as the bare record of a poem's meter, abstracted from the poem itself, is empty. Nevertheless, the logical structure was abstracted *from* a once-living sequence of thoughts, and it is mapped *to* an active, electronic mechanism. So the mechanism, at a level of pure abstraction, reflects the emptied, logical structure of the thoughts.

We can now use this programmatic mechanism to reanimate the aforementioned word-corpses. That is, the corpses begin to dance through their silicon graveyard, their stiffened meanings activated rather like dead frog legs jerking convulsively to the imperatives of an electrical beat. In this way, the abstract ghost of past human thinking takes external hold upon the embalmed word-shells of past meanings and, like a poltergeist, sets them in motion.

All this accounts for certain characteristic traits of software—in particular, the notorious brittleness, the user-unfriendliness, and the penchant for occasional, baffling responses from left field. At the same time, given our willingness to base more and more of society's functioning upon the computer, there is a natural adaptation of human behavior and institutions to these rigidities.

This may not seem onerous, however, for we still recognize the words and logic of the computer as somehow our own, even if they are only distant and brittle reflections of what is most human. Indeed, the willingness of users to personify computers based on the crudest mechanical manipulation of a few words is well attested.[8] It is reasonable to expect that, as we adapt to the computer's requirements, the rigidities may no longer seem quite so rigid. We should keep in mind, therefore, that the slowly improving "user-friendliness" of computers may put on display not only the ingenuity of human-computer interface experts, but also the evolving "computer-friendliness" of users.

Automated telephone answering systems, made possible by computers, illustrate all this at an extremely simple level. They stitch fragments of recorded human speech onto an (often woefully spare) skeleton of logic. No one is *present* behind the manipulated voice; the caller confronts echoes from the past, calculated in advance to match "all possible situations."

---

8. See chapter 18, "And the Word Became Mechanical."

Whatever her task (telephone answering system or otherwise), the programmer must build up a logical structure abstracted from the task, then map it to the computer's internal structure and hang appropriate words (or data) upon it. In attempting to make her program more flexible, she finds herself elaborating and refining its logic in an ever more complex fashion. The effort is to build upward from the simple, on-off "logic gates" constituting the computer's fundamental capability, until an intricate logical structure is derived that corresponds to the structure of the target task.

What is not so often noticed is that, in carrying out her work, the programmer herself moves along a path opposite to the one she lays out for the computer. Where the computer would ascend from logic to meaning, she must descend from meaning to logic. That is, the computer, following a set of logical tracings, invokes certain (second-hand) meanings by re-presenting text that the programmer has carefully associated with those tracings. She, on the other hand, must grasp the form and meaning of a human function before she can abstract its logical structure. If she has no direct experience, no ability to apprehend meanings, no understanding of things, then she has nothing *from which* to abstract.

There is, however, no symmetry in these opposite movements. A sense for logical structure emerges only from prior understanding, and is not its basis. As a starting point in its own right, logic leads nowhere at all—it can never bring us to *content*. Content always arises from a preexistent word, a preexistent meaning, for whose genesis the computer itself cannot claim responsibility.

Despite what I have called the "brittleness" of computation, we should not underestimate the programmer's ability to pursue her logical analysis with ever greater subtlety; the motions she imparts to the corpses in the graveyard can be made to look more and more lifelike. Certainly the automated answering system can be ramified almost infinitely, gaining cleverness beyond current imagination. But the stitched-together voice will nevertheless remain a voice from the past (no one is really *there*), and

the system's behavior will remain the restricted expression of the programmer's previous analysis.[9]

---

*The computer gains a certain autonomy—runs by itself—on the
strength of its embedded reflection of human intelligence.
We are thus confronted from the world by the active powers of our own,
most mechanistic mental functioning.*

The computer is the embodiment of all those aspects of our thinking that
are automatic, deterministic, algorithmic—all those aspects that can, on
the strength of the past, run by themselves, without any need for conscious *presence*.

It was, of course, already our strong tendency in the Industrial Age to
embed intelligence in mechanisms, which thereby gained increasing ability to run by themselves. Take the intricate, intelligent articulations of a
modern loom, add electrical power, and you have an ability to operate
independently far exceeding the reach of a simple hand loom.

Every active mechanism of this sort—whether simple or
complex—creates a local nexus of cause and effect, of determinism, to
which the worker must assimilate himself. Computerization universalizes
this nexus. Everywhere is "here," and everyone—or every machine—must therefore speak the appropriate languages, follow the necessary protocols. Distributed intelligence is a means for *tying things together*
with the aid of everything in human consciousness that operates at a
mechanistic level. Things that run by themselves can now embrace the
whole of society.

Many have claimed that computers *free* us from an older determination by machines. This is false. What is true is that, within a certain
sphere, computers give us greater flexibility. This, however, is not a new
principle; from the very beginning the increasing complexity of machines

---

9. A fairly common, if lamentable, belief among cognitive scientists today has it that,
given sufficient complexity of the right sort in the answering system, the voice *would*
become the expression of a genuinely present, thinking consciousness.

has led to improved flexibility. Computers simply raise these powers of flexibility to a dramatically higher level.

What advanced machines give us is a more refined ability to *do* things. It is a purely instrumental gain, remaining within the deterministic realm of material cause and effect. Freedom, on the other hand, has to do with our ability to act out of the future—a creatively envisioned future—so as to realize conditions not already implicit in past causes.

The automobile gives me an immediate gain in *outward* freedom, enabling me to go places I could not go before. But freedom is not outward, and it turns out that a culture built around the automobile (along with numerous other helpful machines) may actually *constrain* my ability to act out of the future. It is true that these machines vastly broaden my physical, instrumental options. But if I begin to think about my life's purposes (something all the distracting machinery of my life may discourage), and if I come to feel that something is amiss—that I have somehow been betraying my own *meanings*—I then discover myself bound to a matrix of nearly inescapable necessities imposed by all the mechanisms to which my life must conform. I have little room, *in that context*, to act out of conviction, to express my own most compelling values, to choose a different *kind* of life. That is, I have great difficulty allowing my life to flow toward me from the creative future. Instead, I am likely to coast along, carried by circumstances.

This is why the salient social problems of our day seem to have gone systemic. No one is responsible. No one can do anything. Point to any challenge, from the drug culture to environmental pollution to regional famine, and the individual can scarcely feel more than a helpless frustration before the impersonal and never-quite-graspable causes. The problems are "in the nature of things." It is as if a diffuse and malignant intelligence—a Djinn—had escaped human control and burrowed into the entire machinery of our existence.

Intelligence—even in its most mechanical aspect—is not an evil. But it needs to be placed in the service of something higher. Intelligence that functions from below upward—as in a machine—creates a global, self-sustaining mechanism that binds me, unless I meet it with a still stronger power. The operation of my intelligence should descend from that place in me where I am present and free. This is the challenge for today. It is a challenge, not just with respect to the computer, but with respect to the free and unfree activities of my own consciousness.

Having reconceived my own interior as computation, and having then embedded a reflection of this interior in the computer, I compulsively seek fulfillment—the completion of myself—through the "interface."

Machines bearing our reflections are a powerful invitation for psychological projection. Such projection requires a translation from inner to outer—from interior awareness to exterior activity. This translation is exactly what public discourse about computers and the Net presents to us on every hand: text instead of *the word*; text processing or program execution instead of *thinking*; information instead of *meaning*; connectivity instead of *community*; algorithmic procedure instead of *willed human behavior*; derived images instead of *immediate experience*.

Psychologists tell us that the outward projection of inner contents typically signifies an alienation from those contents. It also provokes an unconscious, misguided, and potentially dangerous effort to recover "out there" what actually has been lost "in here." That is, despite the projection, our *need* to intensify and deepen our inner life remains primary; driven by that need, we may seek misguided fulfillment out where we have unwittingly "thrown" ourselves—behind the interface. On the Net.

The symptoms of this sadly misdirected striving are all around us. They are evident, for example, in the obsessive programmer, who feels the undiscovered logical flaw in his program to be a personal affront—an intolerable rift in his own soul. Conversely, the thought of executing the program and finding everything suddenly "working" holds out the prospect of ultimate happiness. The ultimacy, however, proves a mirage, for the next day (or the next hour) he is working just as compulsively on the new, improved version.

All this recalls the infatuated lover, who projects his soul upon the beloved. Thirsting passionately for the one, crucial gesture that will spell his eternal bliss, he receives it only to find, after the briefest interlude, that his thirst has been redoubled rather than quenched.

A similar compulsion seems to drive the recent, unhinged mania for the "information superhighway." The widespread, almost palpable fear of being left out, of missing the party, is one telltale symptom. Others include the lotterylike hope of discovering "great finds" out on the Net; the investment of huge amounts of time in largely unfocused, undisciplined, semianonymous, and randomly forming, randomly dispersing electronic discussion groups; the entrenched conviction that whatever's "happening" on the Net (we're never quite sure just what it is) surely represents our future—it is *us*; and, most obviously, the sudden, unpredictable, and obsessive nature of society's preoccupation with the Net.

But perhaps the most poignant symptom of the projection of a lost interiority lies in the new electronic mysticism. Images of a global, electronically mediated collective consciousness, of Teilhard de Chardin's omega point, and of machines crossing over into a new and superior form of personhood are rife on the Net. Channelers channel onto the Net. Pagans conduct rituals in cyberspace. Most of this is unbearably silly, but as a widespread phenomenon it is difficult to dismiss.

The New Age, it appears, will be won with surprising ease. The wondrously adept principle of "emergence" accounts for everything. It will materialize delightful new organs of higher awareness, not cancerous tumors. As one Net contributor enthuses:

> The nature of the organism resulting is the only question.
> . . . Strangely, I think this organizing into a spiritual whole will occur without much effort. When human spirits gather in a common purpose, something happens.[10]

------

10. From a contribution to the "techspirit-l" list (techspirit-l@williams.edu), 26 July 1994.

Indeed, something happens. But what grows upward from mechanism, easily, automatically, running by itself, is not human freedom. Freedom is always a struggle. What happens easily, on the other hand, is whatever we have already set in motion, having woven it into the dead but effective logic of our external circumstances, and into the sleepwalking strata of our own minds. It is not so easy to call down and materialize a freely chosen future.

The belief that the Net is ushering us toward altogether new and redemptive social forms is a patently dangerous one. It amounts to a projection of human responsibility itself onto our machines. The consequences of this can only be unsavory. What I project unconsciously into the world—whether as mystical hope or more mundane expectation—is *never* my highest and most responsible mental functioning. It is, rather, my least developed, most primitive side. "This way lie dragons."

Toward a hypertext of the subconscious

Here, then, are select features of the human-computer liaison:

The computer took shape in the human mind before it was realized in the world.

What we embed in the computer is the inert and empty shadow, or abstract reflection, of the past operation of our own intelligence.

The computer gains a certain autonomy—runs by itself—on the strength of its embedded reflection of human intelligence. We are thus confronted from the world by the active powers of our own, most mechanistic mental functioning.

Having reconceived my own interior as computation, and having then embedded a reflection of this interior in the computer, I compulsively seek fulfillment—the completion of myself—through the interface.

We now have a more satisfactory perspective upon the paradoxes discussed toward the beginning of this chapter. It is not really odd, for example, that a medium of logic, objective information, and artificial intelligence should also be a medium noted for inducing pathologies and subjectivity. Nor is it odd that a medium of calculated distances should also invite visceral immediacy. Both juxtapositions are inevitable whenever the highest elements in human thinking give way to what is mechanical and automatic.

The machine's painless extension. A comparison between television and computers will help to clarify these juxtapositions. Television presents me with a sequence of images in which I cannot intervene as in normal life, and so the images become mere passive stimulation. Not even my eyes perform their real-world work; instead they rest upon a flat surface lacking all depth (despite the contrary illusion). It is not surprising, then, if I lapse into a near-hypnotic state, my higher faculties quiescent.

But the computer poses far greater risks. I *can* intervene in its processes—in fact, it seems to encourage this with an ever greater energy and flexibility—and I thereby gain a sense of meaningful activity. But the computational processes in which I intervene reflect and actively elicit only the machinelike dimensions of my own nature. That this *is* nevertheless something of my nature makes it all the more natural to anthropomorphize the machine, and to find even the most primitive interaction with it significant. Yet all the while I may be doing nothing more than yielding to the machine's (and my own) automatisms. It is exactly in these lowest strata of my psyche that I give expression to pathologies and the worst excesses of subjectivity.

Some things are, I think, just too close to us for simple recognition. One of these things is the computer screen I am now looking at. Keystroke by keystroke, click by click, command by command, it presents at the first level of approach a completely *deterministic* field of action—one I personally happen to live with for much of the day. This mediation of life by mechanism is unique in all of history. I might usefully compare it to my daily "interface" with my family. My wife's reactions, for example, are not always predictable! I must always expect a surprising response from her—one not fully specifiable in terms of my past knowledge of "the way she works." She is forever re-making herself, which in turn requires me to re-make *myself*.

With the computer, on the other hand, it is rather as if I were enclosed in a large box, surrounded by panels full of levers, cranks, gear-wheels, and shuttles, through which all my interaction with the world was channeled—except that the computer's superiority in efficiency and flexibility is so great, and my adaptation to its mechanisms so complete, that I now scarcely notice the underlying terms of my employment contract.

Such an encompassing, deterministic field of action was inconceivable not so long ago—even for the worker in an industrial-era factory. Not *everything* was assimilated to his machine. But my screen—as a front for all the coordinated, computational processes running behind it—now over-spreads all that I do with the dulling glaze of mechanism. And my own condition is such that I feel no burden in this. No factory worker ever stood so wholly enchanted before his machine as I do. Only by piercing *through* this external, mediating glaze—only by learning to interact with a human interior somewhere "out there"—do I transcend the determining mesh. Nor is this so easy. All those computational processes offer previously unheard of opportunities for merely reacting without ever having entertained in any true sense another human being.

The mathematical rigor of our lower nature. It is not just the other person I risk losing; it is myself as well. Even more than television, the Net robs me of mastery over my own thoughts—or, at least, will do so unless I can set against it wakeful inner resources more powerful than the automatisms it both embodies and so easily triggers. The capacity for concentration, for mature judgment, for the purposeful direction of an inquiry, for deep and sustained reflection—these dissipate all too readily into the blur of random bytes, images, and computational processes assaulting my nervous system. Habits of association—which are the lower organism's version of hypertext, and are the antithesis of self-mastery—tighten their hold over my mental life. Association, unlike true thinking, is automatic, physically "infected," less than fully conscious. It inevitably expresses a pathology.

The screen's distance is the peculiar sort of distance imposed by abstraction, which is hardly the basis for penetrating contemplation. When a person becomes an abstraction, I can respond to him in an immediate, dismissive, gut-driven manner. I need no longer attend to his inner being. And yet, the habit of such attention is the only thing between me and brutalization.

In sum, cold distance and hard logic do not really stand in contradiction to visceral immediacy and pathology. Rather, in their very one-sidedness they *imply* these results. We already see a hint of this in television advertising. On the one hand, I may scarcely pay attention to the advertisement—and when I do note it, I may be content to scorn it unthinkingly. It scarcely seems to touch me at my "objective distance." Still, my buying choices are affected as I proceed to act in an automatic and unconscious way.

Whatever passes into me while circumventing my highest conscious functioning, sinks down to where it works beyond my control. Where are we mathematically (statistically) predictable? The advertising executive can answer: wherever we act least consciously, from our "chemistry." And through our interactions with computers the link between "mathematical rigor" and raw, unreflective, animal-like behavior can be extended far beyond the world of advertising.

Kinds of power. The paradox of power and powerlessness must likewise be seen as a consistent unity, for the two effects operate on different planes. I can experience *manipulative* power even as I find myself unable to alter things *meaningfully*. In fact, a one-sided focus on manipulation all too naturally occludes meaning; for example, when I effectively control others, I lose any meaningful inner connection to them. I then discover that all things that really count have moved beyond my sphere of influence.

But the question of power is woven together with the paradox of centralization and decentralization, which will carry us closer to the heart of them all.

Where is the center?

Langdon Winner observes that "dreams of instant liberation from centralized control have accompanied virtually every important new technological system introduced during the past century and a half." He quotes Joseph K. Hart, a professor of education writing in 1924:

> Centralization has claimed everything for a century: the results are apparent on every hand. But the reign of steam approaches its end: a new stage in the industrial revolution comes on. Electric power, breaking away from its servitude to steam, is becoming independent. Electricity is a decentralizing form of power: it runs out over distributing lines and subdivides to all the minutiae of life and need. Working with it, men may feel the thrill of control and freedom once again.

What Hart failed to notice, according to Winner, was that electricity is "centrally generated and centrally controlled by utilities, firms destined to have enormous social power" far exceeding what was seen in the days of steam.[11]

Ellul makes a similar point when he notes how computers have made an obvious decentralization possible in banking (just consider all the ATM machines), "but it goes hand in hand with a national centralization of accounting."[12]

I do not dispute the important truth in these remarks. But I believe we can also look beyond them to a more horrifying truth.

The externalization of instrumental reason. The totalitarian spirit, many have assumed, always rules from a distinct, physically identifiable locus of authority, and propagates its powers outwardly from that locus

---

11. Winner, 1986: 95–96.
12. Ellul, 1990: 111.

along discrete, recognizable channels. That is, it always requires a despotic center and a hierarchical chain of command.

But there is another possibility. Every totalitarianism attempts to coerce and subjugate the human spirit, thereby restricting the range of free expression so important for the development of both individual and community. Who or what does the coercing is hardly the main point. Whether it is a national dictator, oligarchy, parliament, robber baron, international agency, mafia, tyrannical parent, or *no one at all*—it doesn't really matter. And what the computational society begins to show us is how totalitarianism can be a despotism enforced by no one at all.

To understand this we need to recognize that the computer, due to its reflected, frozen intelligence, is both universal and one-sided. It is universal because the logic of intelligence is by nature universal, linking one thing unambiguously to another and thereby forming a coherent grid of relations extending over the entire surface of every domain it addresses. But at the same time whatever is "off-grid" is ignored. The computer pretends with extraordinary flexibility to do "everything," and therefore what is not covered by its peculiar sort of "everything" drops unnoticed from the picture.[13]

Moreover, the intelligence we're speaking of is an *embedded* intelligence, operating in the machinery of our daily existence. Where this intelligence links one thing to another according to a universal "hard logic," so also does the physically constraining machinery. And yet, the whole basis of the computer's power derives from the fact that no one—no one *present*—is in control. The logic and the machinery are, at the level of their own operation, both self-sufficient and without any necessary center. If the sequence of mathematical statements in a strictly logical demonstration possesses no center (and it does not), neither does the

---

13. This is related to what Joseph Weizenbaum called the "imperialism of instrumental reason." The chapter called "Against the Imperialism of Instrumental Reason" in his *Computer Power and Human Reason* deals wonderfully with a number of the themes discussed here.

elaborated, computational mechanism onto which the sequence is impressed.

Ellul's reference to "a national centralization of accounting" is not inconsistent with this decentering. An accounting database and its associated software must exist *somewhere*, and we can easily imagine that *someone* controls access to it. But this is less and less true today. Databases can be distributed, and in any case, direct or indirect access to them may be spread widely throughout all the different, interrelated activities and functions of a business. It is then truer to say that the *system as a whole* determines access than that any particular person or group does. In fact, anyone who arbitrarily intervenes (even if it is the person "in charge") is likely to face a lawsuit for having disrupted an entire business and thousands of lives.

Technologies of embedded intelligence inevitably tend toward interdependence, universalization, and rationalization. No clique of conspiring power-brokers is responsible for the current pressures to bring the telephone, television, cable, and computing industries into "harmony." No monopolistic or centralized power, in any conventional sense, decrees that suppliers connect to the computer networks and databases of the retail chains—a requirement nevertheless now threatening the existence of small, technically unsophisticated supply operations. (Most of them will doubtless adapt.) Nor does anyone in particular create the pressure for digitization, by which the makers of cameras and photocopiers are waking up to find they are computer manufacturers. And as the amount of software in consumer products doubles each year (currently up to two kilobytes in an electric shaver),[14] no one will *require* that the various appliances speak common, standardized languages.

Again, it is no accident that the introduction of robots—difficult in existing factories—leads to a more radical redesign of manufacturing than one might first have thought:

---

14. Gibbs, 1994.

A robot requires a whole series of related equipment, that is, another conception of the business. Its place is really in a new factory with automation and computerization. This new factory relates machines to machines without interference.[15]

In this relation of machine to machine there is much to be gained. But the gain is always on an instrumental level, where we manipulate the physical stuff of the world. By brilliantly focusing a kind of externalized intelligence at that level we may, if we are not careful, eventually lose our humanity.

Allow me a brief tangential maneuver.

Man and insect. Zoologist Herman Poppelbaum comments that the human hand, so often called the perfect tool, is in an important sense not that at all. Look to the animals if you want limbs that are perfect tools:

> The human hand is *not a tool* in the way the extremities of animals are. As a tool it lacks perfection. In the animal kingdom we find tools for running, climbing, swimming, flying etc. but, if man wants to use his hand to perform similar feats, he has to *invent* his tools. For this he turns to an invisible treasure chest of capacities he bears within himself of which the remarkable shape of the human hand itself appears to be a manifestation. A being with lesser capacities than man's would be helpless with such a hand-configuration.[16]

Endowed with nothing very "special" physically, we contain the archetypes of all tools within ourselves. The tools we make may be rigid in their own right, but they remain flexible *in our hands*. We are able to rule them, bending them to our purposes. The question today, however, is whether we are entrusting that rule itself to the realm over which we should be ruling.

Insects offer a disturbing analogy. It is Poppelbaum again who remarks on the absence of clear physical links to explain the order of an ant heap or beehive. The amazingly intricate unity seems to arise from *nowhere*.

---

15. Ellul, 1990: 316.
16. Poppelbaum, 1993: 127–28.

"Even the queen bee cannot be regarded as the visible guardian and guarantor of the totality, for if she dies, the hive, instead of disintegrating, creates a new queen."[17]

As a picture, this suggests something of our danger. Where is the "totalitarian center" of the hive? There is none, and yet the logic of the whole remains coherent and uncompromising. It is an external logic in the sense that it is not wakeful, not self-aware, not consciously assenting; it moves the individual as if from without. A recent book title, whether intentionally or not, captures the idea: *Hive Mind*.

It is into just such an automatic and external logic that we appear willing to convert our "invisible treasure chest of capacities." But if our inner mastery over tools is itself allowed to harden into a mere tool, then we should not be surprised when the coarsened reflection of this mastery begins reacting upon us from the world. An important slogan of the day, as we saw earlier, bows to the truth: "what we have made, makes us."[18]

The slogan is not hard to appreciate. Living in homes whose convenience and mechanical sophistication outstrip the most elaborate factory of a century ago, most of us—if left to our own devices within a natural environment once considered unusually hospitable—would be at risk of rapid death. In this sense, our system of domestic conveniences amounts to a life-support system for a badly incapacitated organism. It is as if a pervasive, externalized logic, as it progressively encases our society, bestows upon us something like the extraordinary, specialized competence of the social insects, along with their matching rigidities. What ought to be our distinctive, human flexibility is sacrificed.

From another angle: where you or I would once have sought help quite naturally from our neighbors, thereby entering the most troublesome—but also the highest—dimensions of human relationship, we now apply for a bank loan or for insurance. Not even a personal interview is necessary. It is a "transaction," captured by transaction processing

---

17. Poppelbaum, 1961: 167.
18. Krueger, forward to Heim, 1993.

software and based solely upon standard, online data. Everything that once followed from the qualities of a personal encounter—everything that could make for an exceptional case—has now disappeared from the picture. The applicant is wholly sketched when the data of his past have been subjected to automatic logic. Any hopeful glimmer, filtering toward the sympathetic eye of a supportive fellow human from a future only now struggling toward birth, is lost in the darkness between bits of data. Nor, in attempting to transcend the current system, can either the insurance employee or the applicant easily step outside it and respond neighbor-to-neighbor. The entire procedure has all the remarkable efficiency and necessity of the hive.

So the paradoxes of power and powerlessness, of centralization and decentralization, are not really paradoxical after all. We can, if we wish, seek instrumental power in place of the freedom to achieve a distinctively human future. We can, if we wish, abdicate our present responsibility to *act*, deferring to an automatic intelligence dispersed throughout the hardware surrounding us. It scarcely matters whether that intelligence issues from a "center" or not. What matters is how it binds us.

Whatever binds us may always *seem* as if it came from a center. Whether to call the automatic logic of the whole a center may be academic. The real question for the future is no longer whether power issues from many, dispersed groups of people or from few, centralized groups. It is, rather, whether power issues from within the fully awake individual or acts upon him from the dark, obscure places where he still sleeps. If it is exercised wakefully, then it is not really power we're talking about, but freedom and responsibility. But if it is not exercised wakefully, then centralization and decentralization will increasingly become the same phenomenon: constraining mechanism that controls us as if from without.

The elusive line between man and machine

For the third time, then: does technology exert a stranglehold over us? And for the third time I will wage a minor delaying action, since this question is inseparable from another, more general one to which we must

369

briefly nod: is technology nonneutral or neutral? That is, do technological artifacts, once deployed, coerce our social, political, and psychological development in directions over which we then have little control (nonneutrality)? Or do the major consequences depend largely upon how we freely choose to *use* those artifacts (neutrality)?

But to pose the question in this way is already to have lost the possibility of profound answer. For it is to posit that we are (or are not) subject to determining influences acting upon us from outside. The problem is that our artifacts do not really exist outside us in the first place. How can I speak of technological neutrality or nonneutrality when

> what is "out there," working on me from without, is an abstract distillate of the intelligence working "in here"; and

> what is "in here," guiding my use of technology, is a habit of mind that has long been tending toward the machinelike and external?

When my own interior is one with the interior of the machine, who is unambiguously influencing whom? The only answer I know to give to the question of technological neutrality is twofold: of course technology is neutral, for in the long run everything *does* depend upon how we relate to artifacts. And of course technology is not neutral, for what works independently in the artifact is our already established habits of thought and use.

These answers still remain too stiff, however, for they speak of the artifact as if, behind our pattern of interaction with it, there stood a simple given. But there is no artifact at all apart from the interior we share with it. This is true of all tools, although most obviously of the computer, in which we can place radically differing abstracts of our consciousness. We call those abstracts "programs." The program clearly determines what sort of machine we're dealing with.

All this will be enough, I hope, to justify an unusual tack in what follows. I have spoken at length about the abstraction from human consciousness of a shadow-intelligence for which we find a mechanical expression, and of the countereffect this expression has upon the originating mind. It remains, however, to focus upon what *cannot* be abstracted. If we are to avoid strangulation by technology—indeed, if we are to avoid simply becoming robots ourselves—it is to the distinctively human that we must turn.

We can find our first toehold here by considering the human being as learner.

Beyond shoveling facts

Every educational reformer (and nearly every educator) reminds us that "the student should not be treated as an empty receptacle for facts." As in most cases of widespread clamor for some popular value, however, the problem runs much deeper than the rhetoric. For example, the respectable formula—"don't teach facts, but teach the student how to acquire knowledge on his own"—easily merges with the supposedly rejected point of view. The student is still a receptacle for facts—it's just that he must learn to stuff himself, instead of being stuffed by someone else. I'm not sure there's much difference between the equally constipated outcomes of these two approaches.

To state the matter as provocatively as possible: *what* a student learns, considered solely as "objective content," *never* matters. The only thing that counts is how vividly, how intensely, how accurately and intentionally, and with what muscular ability to shape and transform itself, his consciousness lays hold of a thing. The qualitative fullness of a thought, the form of the student's own, inner *activity*—and not the simplistic abstraction the activity is said to be "about" (that is, not its "information content")—is everything.

The reason for this is simply that human consciousness does not "hold" facts about the world; it is itself the inside of the world. It does not lay hold of things, but rather becomes the things. Our need is not to "know the facts" about the truth; it is to become true. The discipline of consciousness is not a preparation for truth-gathering; it is the increasingly harmonious resonance between the laws of the world and the laws of our own thinking activity, which are the same laws expressed outwardly and inwardly.

There was a time when such distinctions would have been obvious—a time when man experienced himself as a microcosm within the macrocosm, and when all knowledge was rightly felt to be knowledge of man. But this is exactly what a machine-adapted mind can only find perplexing or maddening. Such a mind wants facts contained in a database. It wants knowledge *about things* rather than a sculpting and strengthening of the *knowing gesture*. It wants truth rather than meaning—and its notion of truth has degenerated into mere logical consistency.

For such a mind, the important thing about the statement, "Abraham Lincoln was killed in 1866," is that it is false. And, as a univocal proposition whose task is solely to identify a coordinate on a timeline (that is, as a few bits of information), so it is. But no human being is capable of *speaking* such a proposition. So long as we remain conscious, we cannot utter or even conceive a statement wholly devoid of meaning and truth. The hapless student who says "1866" will to one degree or another still appreciate what it meant to be Abraham Lincoln, what it meant to preside over the Civil War, and what it meant to die at the war's conclusion. The question is how *fully* he will know these things. Perhaps very fully (if he has deepened his own character and learned to know himself well), or perhaps not very much at all (if he has just been taught "the facts").

The teachers we remember for changing our lives did not convey some decisive fact. Rather, we saw in them a stance we could emulate, a way of knowing and being we could desire for ourselves. Their teaching instructed *us*, and therefore remains with us, whereas the things taught (if one insists on thinking in such terms) may well have lost their validity. This is why computers have so little to offer either teacher or student. If the student's greatest hope is to learn from his teacher what it can mean to be a human being facing a particular aspect of life, then the implications of wholesale reliance upon computer-mediated instruction are grave indeed.

Variations on being human. What can it mean to confront today's computerized technology as a human being? On the one hand, we find ourselves locked in an intimate liaison with our machines, and with the machinelike tendencies in ourselves. We are invited into a world of programmed responses and of database-receptacles collecting information. On the other hand . . . what?

The answer, I think, is given in the question itself. That is: on the other hand, the possibility of asking questions, of changing, of transforming ourselves—the freedom to act out of the future rather than the past.

Freedom, however, is always ambiguous. Paradoxically—and this is a genuine paradox—the experience of freedom can never be anything but a movement toward freedom or away from it. If we had perfect freedom, we could not know what freedom meant, for there would be no resistance against which to feel free. And if we we were wholly determined, we could not know what freedom meant, for we would possess no answering experience of our own through which to recognize it.[19]

As things are, the healthy consciousness *does* have an experience of freedom—whether acknowledged or not—because it knows both possibility and constraint. Its struggle is always to accept responsibility and grow toward greater freedom.

Surely, however, none of us will claim a perfectly healthy consciousness. We always must reckon with impulses running contrary to freedom and responsibility. We are, in the end, free to use our freedom in order to abandon freedom. In fact, the entire effort to raise up machines in our image can also be read as our own willing descent toward the image of the deterministic machine.

I will try to make this idea of a descent toward the machine a little more concrete. A great deal hinges upon how we choose to wrestle with the descent. The machine provides the necessary resistance against which we may—or may not—discover our freedom.

---

19. Kühlewind, 1984: 76; Ellul, 1990: 217–20.

Space of the world, space of the programmer

It is not particularly controversial to say: we find ourselves immersed ever more deeply in a kind of creeping virtual reality—television, electronic games, video conferencing, online shopping malls, escapist entertainment, virtual workplaces, images of frogs for online "dissection," geography recast as graphical data, community reduced to the mutual exchange of text—all of which slowly deprives us of a fuller world.

But every discussion of "virtual" and "real" quickly becomes problematic. Lines grow fuzzy. As the fighter plane's cockpit encapsulates the pilot ever more securely within an instrument-mediated environment, when does the preliminary training in a cockpit simulator cease to be mere *simulation*, becoming instead a recapitulation of the real thing?

Noting astronaut John Glenn's reported inability to feel an "appropriate awe" while circling the earth, Langdon Winner comments that "synthetic conditions generated in the training center had begun to seem more 'real' than the actual experience."[20] But he might just as well have said: synthetic conditions *were* the actual experience. Glenn's immediate environment while floating above the earth was not much different from his training environment.

Whatever else we may think about the line separating the real world from simulated worlds, the important point for the moment is that this line can be nudged from either side. Certainly, rising levels of technical sophistication can lead to ever more realistic simulators. But we should not forget that the human experience we're simulating can become ever more abstract and mechanical—more simulable.

Furthermore, it is undeniable that this latter transformation has been intensively under way for the past several hundred years. Beginning in the Renaissance, Western man found himself cast out from something like a "spatial plenum of wisdom" into an abstract container-space well described by the mathematical techniques of linear perspective. The

---

20. Winner, 1986: 3. (Winner is responding to reportage in Tom Wolfe's *The Right Stuff*.)

plenum could never have been simulated with technology; on the other hand, container-space is *already* a simulation of sorts, and the increasingly abstract, computational processes of the human mind are the means of simulation.

My point here—actually, everything I have been saying—will be lost unless we can bring such distinctions as the one between plenum and container-space to *some* sort of qualitative awareness. We saw earlier how Owen Barfield, who has described the transition from medieval to modern consciousness with delicate and penetrating sensitivity, once remarked that "before the scientific revolution the world was more like a garment men wore about them than a stage on which they moved." He also referred to the Middle Ages as a time when the individual "was rather less like an island, rather more like an embryo, than we are."[21] What could this mean?

Two ways of seeing. Our contemporary minds can, perhaps, gain a faint suggestion of the change Barfield is referring to. Try looking toward an object in the middle distance without actually focusing on it, but instead looking *through* it. (Don't simply focus on another object behind it. If necessary, choose a spot on a wall, so that no background object substitutes for the spot.) Most likely, you will find this difficult at first. The object in front of you demands attention, instantly drawing your focused gaze and throwing your visual system into a kind of flat, perspective fixation, with your line of sight centered on a nullity—the vanishing point.

This "standard" sort of vision is reinforced by every one of the thousands of images we see daily—photographs, drawings, movies—all conveyed through the technique of linear perspective. The art of linear perspective codifies the view of a single, fixed eye (or camera lens). It first became a theoretically disciplined art in fifteenth-century northern Italy, when a few enterprising artisans were able to reconceive scenes in the world as sets of coordinates and vectors (lines of sight). That reconception

---

21. Barfield, 1965a: 78, 94–95.

has moved ever closer to the heart of what it means for modern man *to see*.

There is, however, another way of seeing. Tom Brown, Jr., the wilderness tracker, urges the critical importance of what he calls relaxed, or wide-angle, vision. To accomplish this—and it requires practice—you must allow your eyes to relax "out of focus," so that the objects directly in front of you no longer claim sole attention on the visual stage. Instead, allow your alert attention (free of sharp, visual focus) to scan all the objects in your field of vision. To prevent your gaze from hardening into an uncomprehending stare, you should continually move your eyes as well, taking care only to prevent their focusing on particular objects as they move. Your field of vision will now possess less clarity, but your breadth of awareness and ability to perceive what is going on around you will be greatly increased.

Focused vision gives us only a few degrees of clarity around the line of sight. Relaxed vision removes this clear center and with it the dominance of the object in front of us. The single, narrow beam of our attention becomes instead a broad, peripheral awareness that may mediate remarkable discoveries.

Brown claims that a habit of relaxed vision (combined, of course, with periodic, brief reversions to focused vision for purposes of clear identification) is essential for any profound penetration of nature, and is the usual style of vision for peoples who live close to nature. He reports, for example, that when one is stalking an animal, a sudden shift from relaxed vision to the more aggressive, I-versus-object focus will very likely startle the animal into flight—the "spell" integrating the stalker seamlessly into his natural surroundings is broken.[22]

Try the experiment sometime. If, say, you walk slowly and attentively through the woods using relaxed vision, you may well experience yourself within the landscape rather differently from when you employ your more customary habits. You may even be able to imagine ever so slightly what

---

22. Tom Brown, Jr., has written numerous books and nature guides. For autobiographical accounts, see Brown, 1982; Brown and Watkins, 1979.

it might have been like to wear the world as a garment instead of moving about in an abstract container-space—to be living so deeply *in* the world that you cannot look *at* it in anything like the modern sense.

It is worth relating this sort of practical experience to our earlier discussion of linear perspective (see chapter 22). Why, for example, did I refer above to our "flat, perspective fixation," since perspective, applied to art, yields what we take to be remarkably realistic, lifelike, in–depth images?

To say that our normal vision today is flat is not to say that it has no three-dimensional feel of spatial depth, for that feel is exactly what we today *mean* by depth, and what the pre-Renaissance painting, for example, did not have. There is no disputing that we sometimes think we could almost *step into* the three-dimensional image. But Barfield is telling us, as we have seen in chapter 22, that pre-Renaissance man was more likely to experience himself *already in* a work of art. And what is meant by "in" differs greatly between these two cases. This difference may be suggested by the contrast between focused and relaxed vision in the experience of the alert ourdoorsman.

The point is that depth is now represented for us by a highly abstract, mathematically conceived container-space full of objects related only by their shared coordinate system (within which we, too, kick about)—an "extensive" depth—whereas once the world's depth was more "intensive," with every object bound meaningfully to every other (and to us) in a way that our perspective vision renders nearly impossible to experience. It is *our* vision that is flat, abstract, shallow, governed by surfaces without true insides. It lacks nothing in quantifiable *information*, but lacks nearly everything in weight or qualitative *significance*.

Certainly the photograph and video screen are undeniably flat. The depth, as I have already mentioned, is illusory, our eyes being forced to remain focused on a flat surface. But this is how we have learned to see the world as well, focusing always on particular, flat surfaces and experiencing even depth as an external relation of surfaces. Today—it has not always been so—the world itself arrives on the stage of our understanding "in mathematical perspective."

To change our viewpoint, or grow blind. I have conducted this little diversion on perspective for several reasons. It gives substance, in the first place, to the question whether computer graphics has been conquering the realities of our experience or our experience has been descending toward computer graphics. At the very least, a little historical awareness should convince us that the latter movement has actually occurred, whatever we make of the former one.

I suspect, however, that both movements really amount to the same thing. The technical advances are real enough, but they can represent an approach toward human experience only to the extent that human experience is being altered toward the mechanical. Advancing technology is born of an increasingly technological mindset, which in turn lends itself to being "conquered" by technology.

Second, our discussion also illustrates an earlier point about learning: the things we learn *about* do not count for very much. The real learning takes place just so far as our organs of cognition are *themselves* instructed and changed. After all, nearly everything that matters in the movement from Middle Ages to modernity lies in the different ways of thinking and seeing—in the *qualities* of these activities. How can we understand these different qualities without gaining the flexibility of mind that enables us to become, so to speak, different human beings?

You might almost say that what distinguishes modern thinking is the fact that it takes itself to be nothing *but* aboutness—it has lost experience of its own qualities. One result is a seeing that has been substantially reduced to an awareness of coordinates and of relative position on an electromagnetic spectrum, with little feel for what once gripped the human being through space and color. For the most part, it is only the artist today who still resonates with what Goethe called the "deeds and sufferings of light," and who finds an objective, revelatory depth in Goethe's characterization of the feeling-qualities of the various colors. The promiscuous and purely stimulative use of "dramatic" colors (not to mention geometric forms) in so much of computer graphics is well calculated to dull any sensitivity to the profound lawfulness of color and form in nature.

Another result of our "aboutness" knowledge is the drive toward artificial intelligence, where self-experience simply never enters the picture. When nothing is left of the knower except the abstractions he supposedly knows, then the machine can become a knower—for it, too, can "contain" these abstractions.

In the third place, the story of linear perspective offers a nice little morality tale. It might be tempting to dismiss Tom Brown's "relaxed vision" as a kind of irresponsible dreaminess. No doubt it may on occasion be that—but only when one's alert, ever scanning attention dies away and the blindness of a vacant stare replaces it. Only, that is, when we cease our own, inner activity as knowers. But this, interestingly, is a much more threatening limitation of the fixed and focused eye of perspective vision.

Try looking at a point several feet away, without moving your eyes at all. This is very difficult—nearly impossible, in fact, since the eyes will involuntarily shift ever so slightly, and you will need to blink. Nevertheless, you can readily observe that, just so far as you hold an unmoving gaze, the entire field of sight begins to blank out. In the laboratory, an image held constant by attachment to a contact lens fades to gray or black within two or three seconds. An unchanging pattern of stimulation on the retina blinds us.

If, then, a perspective image codifies the outlook of a single, fixed eye, it codifies a kind of blindness. Our eyes must continually strive toward a new view, and only by changing our view do we see. Just as there is no true knowing that is not a continual transformation of the knower, so too—even at the most literal level—there is no true seeing that is not a continual transformation of the seer.

Redemptive dead ends

All the pieces are in place. If you have followed along sympathetically to this point, you may now expect some sort of resolution. "Surely he will tell us how he thinks we can remain masters of the computer! Exactly what transformation is he asking of us?"

But this is exactly what I must not attempt. There can be no program, no algorithm, for mastering technology. Our automatic resort to algorithmic thinking is an indication of technology's mastery of *us*. It shows how the limitations and tendencies of the computer have become at the same time limitations and tendencies of our minds. So the only "program" I can offer is the advice that we deprogram ourselves.

It is curious how, amidst the all-but-insoluble problems of our day, it remains so easy to think (however vaguely) that every real problem must yield to some sort of straightforward, external *doing*—if we could just hit upon the right formula. At the very least, we should go out and march. Write our congressmen. Protest against a war or a polluter.

I do not wish to denigrate the activist, but virtually every problem we ever tackle turns out to be vastly more complicated than the placards and chants (or, for that matter, the email campaigns) allow. In fact, I would venture the surmise that no genuine social problem has *ever* been solved by a program of action. Or even that no problem has ever been been solved at all. As we slowly change, we eventually transcend old problems, simply leaving them behind in order to face new ones. Or, you might say, old problems simply assume new forms.

It scarcely needs adding that no hint of this fundamental intractability of our most pressing social problems can be admitted in political discourse. Yet the truth is that *every* major social problem is too much for us. That's why it's a problem. What we always need is, unsurprisingly, exactly what we have lost sight of. We need a new view of things.

So we seem to be caught in a vicious circle. If what is "out there" reflects our inner landscape (as I have argued it does), how can we ever achieve a new view?

The conviction that we needn't try (because technology is already saving us) or can't succeed (because what we have made, makes us) underlies many responses to technology. Perhaps more common is no response at all. A large majority of U.S. citizens claims to believe that television contributes heavily to a prevailing social malaise, and yet the broad patterns of television use do not seem to change in hopeful ways. Few seem to find a way to act meaningfully upon their misgivings—and this, too, certifies the viciousness of the circle.

But I would rather think now of a dead end than a vicious circle. Where a circle leaves us treading round and round forever upon our own footsteps—thinking we're getting somewhere—a dead end snuffs out all hope. Therefore it offers the only hope. It does so, that is, if we not only know we have reached a dead end, but also *suffer* it. The more clearly we realize—even as we fervently desire deliverance—that there is no way out, no program to save ourselves, no hope in any of our known resources—the more open we will be to an altogether different *level* of response. The more open we will be to what is not yet known within us. We will look to a future that can never arrive through a program, but only through the potential for inner self-transformation. Here alone we stand wholly apart from our machines.

Our freedom is borne by the world, too

For the last time, does technology have us in a stranglehold? Ellul's answer is instructive. If we have any chance of escape, he tells us, then

> above all things we must avoid the mistake of thinking that we are free. If we launch out into the skies convinced that we have infinite resources and that in the last resort we are free to choose our destiny, to choose between good and evil, to choose among the many possibilities that our thousands of technical gadgets make available, to invent an antidote to all that we have seen, to colonize space in order to make a fresh beginning, etc.; if we imagine all the many possibilities that are open to us in our sovereign freedom; if we believe all that, then we are truly lost, for the only way to find a narrow passage in this enormous world of deceptions (expressing real forces) as I

381

have attempted to describe it is to have enough awareness and self-criticism to see that for a century we have been descending step by step the ladder of absolute necessity, of destiny, of fate.

Ellul would not have us enjoy our illusions. "Are we then shut up, blocked, and chained by the inevitability of the technical system which is making us march like obedient automatons . . . ?" Unrelenting, he answers himself with an apparent abandonment of hope: "Yes, we are radically determined. We are caught up continuously in the system if we think even the least little bit that we can master the machinery, prepare for the year 2000, and plan everything."

And yet, "not really," he hedges in the end, for the very system that runs away with us is liable to provoke disasters, which in turn bring unpredictable possibilities for the future. "Not really,"

if we know how little room there is to maneuver and therefore, not by one's high position or by power, but always after the model of development from a source and by the sole aptitude for astonishment, we profit from the existence of little cracks of freedom and install in them a trembling freedom which is not attributed to or mediated by machines or politics, but which is truly effective, so that we may truly invent the new thing for which humanity is waiting.[23]

I cannot recommend Ellul's book too highly for anyone enchanted by the glossy allure of what he calls the technical system. And yet, if I were Ellul, I would not have waited until the last paragraph of a four-hundred-page book to make my first and only admission that a few cracks of freedom may exist. After all, no matter how minuscule those cracks may be, all the *known* universe lies within them. Nothing—not even the determinations of the technical system—can be understood outside of them.

For without freedom, there is physical cause and effect, but no understanding and truth. The cause-and-effect mechanism can never recognize and describe its own activity at the very highest level, and then transform itself to an even higher level. But that is exactly what we do when

23. Ellul, 1990: 411–12.

we understand; all understanding is self-understanding and self-transformation, another name for which is freedom.

And in those same cracks of freedom our entire future lies—the only future possessed of human meaning, the only future free of the machine's increasingly universal determinations, the only future not eternally frozen to the shape of our own past natures.

Cracks cannot exist except as fissures breaking through a resistant material, and in this sense our technological achievements may turn out to have provided the necessary resistance against which we can establish a human future. If, for example, we are now learning to manipulate our own genetic inheritances, this technical ability must lead all but the hopelessly somnolent to a sense of desperation: "What sort of men should we make ourselves?" It is the same question we see reflected back at us from the uncomprehending face of the cleverest robot. There is no technological answer.

How might we find an answer? Only by looking within ourselves. Not at what moves in lockstep with all the external machinery of our lives, but, to begin with, at the silent places. They are like the sanctuary we find ourselves passing through for a few moments upon waking in the morning. Just before we come fully to ourselves—recollecting who we were, bowing beneath all the necessities of the preceding days—we may feel ourselves ever so briefly on the threshold of new possibilities, remembering whispered hopes borne upon distant breezes. We know at such moments the freedom—yes, just the tiniest cracks of freedom, for Ellul was, after all, right—to awaken a *different* self. "Must I be fully determined by the crushing burdens of the past? Or is something new being asked of me—some slight shift in my own stance that, in the end, may transform all the surrounding machinery of my existence, like the stuff of so many dreams?"

Man is he who knows and transforms himself—and the world—from within. He is the future speaking.

A

Owen Barfield:
The Evolution of Consciousness

Owen Barfield was born in London in 1898, produced his first scholarly book (*History in English Words*) in 1926, published the decisively important *Poetic Diction* in 1928, and, by his own testimony, has continued saying much the same thing ever since. It is certainly true that his work—ranging all the way to and beyond *History, Guilt, and Habit* (1979)—exhibits a remarkable unity. But it is a unity in ceaselessly stimulating diversity. Many will testify that they have never seen him explore a topic except by throwing an unexpectedly revealing light upon it.

Barfield is identified, above all else, with his numerous characterizations of the evolution of consciousness. As a philologist, he pursued his quarry through the study of language—and particularly the historical study of *meaning*. I have already quoted his remark that "the full meanings of words are flashing, iridescent shapes like flames—ever-flickering vestiges of the slowly evolving consciousness beneath them." *History in English Words* is one of the relatively few attempts in our language to tell the history of peoples as revealed in these flickering word-shapes. *Poetic Diction*—and, to one degree or another, almost every subsequent book

Barfield wrote—teases out of language the underlying nature of the evolution of consciousness.

Following the publication of his early works, Barfield was forced by personal circumstances to spend several decades as a practicing lawyer. Never completely ceasing his scholarly pursuits, he resumed them with extraordinary fruitfulness after his retirement in the 1960s. In addition to writing such magisterial and liberating works as *Saving the Appearances* and *Worlds Apart*, he spent terms as visiting professor at various American institutions, including Drew University, Brandeis University, and Hamilton College. Two of his most accessible books (*History, Guilt, and Habit* and *Speaker's Meaning*) consist of lectures delivered during these appointments.

Barfield was a member of the Inklings, an informal literary group that included C. S. Lewis, J. R. R. Tolkien, and Charles Williams. While he never achieved quite the same popular success as these friends, many regard his work as the more deeply seminal. His influence in scholarly circles has been all the more remarkable for its quiet, unobtrusive, yet profoundly transforming effect.

It is Barfield's conviction that *how* we think is at least as important as *what* we think. This makes reading him more than a merely intellectual challenge. Nobel laureate Saul Bellow has written:

> We are well supplied with interesting writers, but Owen Barfield is not content to be merely interesting. His ambition is to set us free. Free from what? From the prison we have made for ourselves by our ways of knowing, our limited and false habits of thought, our "common sense." These, he convincingly argues, have produced a "world of outsides with no insides to them," a brittle surface world, an object world in which we ourselves are mere objects. It is not only what we perceive but also what we fail to perceive that determines the quality of the world we live in, and what we have collectively chosen not to perceive is the full reality of consciousness, the "inside" of everything that exists.[1]

---

1. From dust jacket of Barfield, 1979.

I cannot attempt to summarize Barfield's thought in even one of the many disciplines within which he has so productively exercised his iconoclasm. But the following, all-too-arbitrary, and by no means systematic collection of notes on a few topics may help readers open an acquaintance with one of the century's most incisive thinkers, while also directing them to the appropriate sources for a more thorough familiarity.

The following selections present a mix of direct quotation, paraphrases, and my own, freely constructed summary statements. I fear that some degree of misrepresentation is inevitable, and here acknowledge that all such misrepresentation originates solely with me.[2]

The Origin and Development of Language

Languages, considered historically, bear within themselves a record of the evolution of human consciousness. (This is a theme in virtually all of Barfield's works. But see especially *Poetic Diction*,[3] *Speaker's Meaning*, and *Saving the Appearances*.)

• • •

The idea that the earliest languages were "born literal"—exhibiting purely material meanings that were subsequently extended to the immaterial through metaphor—is confused and self-contradictory. "What we call literalness is a late stage in a long-drawn-out historical process." Anyone who tries to retain the supposed literalness of scientism "is either unaware of, or is deliberately ignoring, that real and figurative relation between man and his environment, out of which the words he is using were born and without which they could never have been born." ("The Meaning of 'Literal,'" in *The Rediscovery of Meaning and Other Essays*)

---

2. Quotations from *The Rediscovery of Meaning and Other Essays*, *Speaker's Meaning*, *Poetic Diction*, *Worlds Apart*, *Saving the Appearances*, and *Unancestral Voice* used by permission of Wesleyan University Press.

3. I try to indicate one or two books in which each idea receives considerable treatment. The first publication listed after quoted material is the source of the quotation. In a few cases, where the given idea thoroughly pervades all of Barfield's work, I offer no citation at all. Unavoidably, given the unity of Barfield's work, there is something slightly arbitrary about many of the citations that *are* provided.

• • •

The meanings of words constantly change. "All mental progress (and, arising from that, all material progress) is brought about in association with those very changes." Radical progress requires challenging one's fundamental assumptions, and the most fundamental assumptions of any age are implicit in the meanings of its words. Changes in meaning occur through discrepancies "between an individual speaker's meaning and the current, or lexical, meaning." (*Speaker's Meaning*)

• • •

Words can expand in meaning—so that they become more encompassing—or they can contract in meaning. Historically, the latter process has dominated, so that, for example, a single word combining the meanings, "spirit," "wind," and "breath" in a unified manner subsequently splits into three separate words, each with a more restricted meaning. Narrower meanings conduce to accuracy of communication, and result from rational analysis. Broader meanings support fullness of expression, and result from imaginative synthesis. Communication deals with the *how*, and expression with the *what*. "Perfect communication would occur if all words had and retained identical meanings every time they were uttered and heard. But it would occur at the expense of expression."

• • •

The expansion of meaning through poetic synthesis requires a strong, inner activity. The contraction of meaning tends to occur passively, through the "inertia of habit." (*Speaker's Meaning*)

• • •

When we investigate actual languages, we find them becoming more and more figurative the further back we look. What are now material meanings once had an immaterial component ("matter" itself goes back to a Latin word for "mother"), and what are now immaterial meanings once had a material component (a "scruple" was once a sharp pebble—the kind, Barfield remarks, that gets into your shoe and worries you). Originally, that is, all words—all meanings—were exteriors expressing interiors in an indivisible unity. This unity was simply given by what Barfield calls "figuration," and was not consciously constructed. Our own use of metaphor is made possible by the fact that this unity has fallen apart; it is no longer given, but must be grasped consciously—as it is whenever we apprehend an inner meaning shining through an exterior "vehicle" and construct a metaphor to convey this insight. (*Poetic Diction; Speaker's Meaning*)

• • •

The historical passage from figure to metaphor marks the dissolution of the given, inner/outer, immaterial/material unity. This unity was not a unity of language only, but of man's participation in the world (or, equally, the world's participation in man). With its dissolution, various antitheses arose for the first time: inner and outer; man and nature; words of immaterial meaning and words of material meaning; subject and object; what a word meant and what it referred to; and even sound and meaning. The rational, or analytic, principle operates to sharpen these antitheses; imaginative synthesis overcomes them. (*Poetic Diction*)

• • •

Early language reflected a unity of perceiving and thinking. This was correlative to a lack of freedom: when the thought is given in the percept—when the thought comes from without—one is not free in one's thinking. The world itself lives upon the stage of one's consciousness.

In our own experience, perceiving and thinking are separate. Perceiving (and not, incidentally, thinking) is subjectively qualified. You and I will see the same object differently, depending upon our point of view. (We correct for this through thinking.) But if perceiving is subjectively qualified, it must have been a rather different experience before the subject and object fell apart—that is, when the subject was not yet what it is today. As the history of language bears out, a kind of thinking was already present in this early experience of perceiving, and vice versa.

389

> For Locke's picture of Adam at work on the synthetic manufacture
> of language we have to substitute—what? A kind of thinking which
> is at the same time perceiving—a picture-thinking, a figurative, or
> imaginative, consciousness, which we can only grasp today by true
> analogy with the imagery of our poets, and, to some extent, with
> our own dreams. (*Poetic Diction*; *Worlds Apart*)

· · ·

Language is a living and creative power, from which man's subjectivity was
slowly extracted. The function of language is to create that esthetic "distance"
between man and the world "which is the very thing that constitutes his
humanity. It is what frees him from the world."

> He is no longer a peninsula pushed out by natural forces. He is a
> separated island existing in a symbolic universe. Physical reality
> recedes in proportion as his symbolic activity advances. He objec-
> tivizes more and more completely. But the symbols were the product
> of his own inner activity in the first place and they never really lose
> that character, however completely his very success in objectifying
> them may make him forget the fact. Forever afterwards, in dealing
> with things he is, as Cassirer puts it, "in a sense conversing with him-
> self." (*Worlds Apart*)

· · ·

Languages today possess only the faintest traces of the one-time unity of
sound and meaning. Those willing to look "may find, in the consonantal element in language, vestiges of those forces which brought into being the
external structure of nature, including the body of man; and, in the original
vowel-sounds, the expression of that inner life of feeling and memory which
constitutes his soul." All this is consistent with the testimony of the ancients
that the primordial Word was responsible for creation.

Still today, the invisible word is spoken with a physical *gesture*, even if
that gesture has for the most part contracted into the small organs of
speech. One can at least imagine how the gestures of speech were once
made with the whole body. This was before man had become "detached

from the rest of nature after the solid manner of today, when the body itself was spoken even while it was speaking." (*Saving the Appearances*)

• • •

"It was not man who made the myths but the myths, or the archetypal substance they reveal, which made man. We shall have to come, I am sure, to think of the archetypal element in myth in terms of the wind that breathed through the harp-strings of individual brains and nerves and fluids, rather as the blood still today pervades and sustains them." ("The Harp and the Camera," in *The Rediscovery of Meaning and Other Essays*)

Meaning and Imagination

[This section is abbreviated, since the same topic is touched on in chapter 23, "Can We Transcend Computation?" See especially the sections, "The polar dynamic of meaning," and "So, then . . . what is meaning?"]

• • •

Imagination is the activity by which we apprehend the "outward form as the image or symbol of an inner meaning." ("The Rediscovery of Meaning," in *The Rediscovery of Meaning and Other Essays*)

• • •

"Mere perception—perception without imagination—is the sword thrust between spirit and matter." It was what enabled Descartes to divide the world into thinking substance and extended substance. But something more than mere perception occurs when we look at or listen to a fellow being: whatever our philosophical predispositions, we in fact read his body and voice as *expressing* something immaterial. We can, moreover, attend to nature in the same way, although such a reading of nature has been progressively eliminated from our habits during the past few hundred years. Strengthening the activity of imagination is the only way to heal the Cartesian sword-thrust. ("Matter, Imagination, and Spirit," in *The Rediscovery of Meaning and Other Essays*)

• • •

From classical Greece to the modern era there has been a broad transition in esthetics from a passive psychology of inspiration (mania, or divine madness, or possession by a god or muse) to an active one of imagination. This can be seen as

> the transition from a view of art which beholds it as the product of a mind, or spirit, not possessed by the individual, but rather possessing him; to a view of it as the product of something in a manner possessed by the individual though still not identical with his everyday personality—possessed by him, whether as his genius, or as his shaping spirit of imagination, or his unconscious mind, or whatever name we may prefer to give it. His own, but not himself. (*Speaker's Meaning*)

• • •

The imagination has to do with a certain threshold. "When we think of an image or a symbol, we think of something that is impassably divided from *that of which* it is an image—divided by the fact that the former is phenomenal and the latter nonphenomenal." And yet, there is an all-important relation between the two. This relationship is one of *expression*, and our grasping of it imaginatively depends (unlike the older *inspiration*, which entailed a kind of possession) upon the exclusion of any "supernatural" crossing of the threshold. ("Imagination and Inspiration," in *The Rediscovery of Meaning and Other Essays*)

Participation

"Participation is the extra-sensory relation between man and the phenomena."

• • •

The world as immediately given to us is a mixture of sense perception and thought. While the two may not be separable in our experience, we can nevertheless *distinguish* the two. When we do, we find that the perceptual alone gives us no coherence, no unities, no "things" at all. We could not even note a patch of red, or distinguish it from a neighboring patch of green, without aid of the concepts given by thinking. In the absence of the conceptual, we would experience (in William James' words) only "a blooming, buzzing confusion." (*Poetic Diction; Saving the Appearances*)

• • •

The familiar world—as opposed to the largely notional world of "particles" which the physicist aspires to describe—is the product of a perceptual given (which is meaningless by itself) *and an activity of our own*, which we might call "figuration." Figuration is a largely subconscious, imaginative activity through which we participate in producing ("figuring") the phenomena of the familiar world. (A simple analogy—but *only* an analogy—is found in the way a rainbow is produced by the cooperation of sun, raindrops, and observer.) How we choose to regard the particles is one thing, but when we refer to the workaday world—the world of "things"—we must accept that our thinking is as much *out there in the world* as in our heads.

In actual fact, we find it nearly impossible to hold onto this truth. In our critical thinking as physicists or philosophers, we imagine ourselves set over against an objective world consisting of particles, in which we do not participate at all. In contrast, the phenomenal, or familiar, world is said to be riddled with our subjectivity. In our daily, uncritical thinking, on the other hand, we take for granted the solid, objective reality of the familiar world, assume an objective, lawful manifestation of its qualities such as color, sound, and solidity, and even write natural scientific treatises about the history of its phenomena—all while ignoring the human consciousness that (by our own, critical account) determines these phenomena from the inside in a continually changing way.[4] (*Worlds Apart; Saving the Appearances*)

• • •

One way figuration is distinguished from our normal, intellectual thinking *about* things is that it synthesizes unities at the level of the percept. Figura-

---

4. What enables us to switch between these two contradictory stances without acute discomfort is our long training in seeing the familiar world through a veil—a mathematical grid of abstraction. By means of abstraction, we convert the world into the merely notional, or nonphenomenal. In fact, the particles can be seen as the endpoint of this process. As a result, the qualities of things have by now become dim enough in our experience to lead philosophers to question whether they have any sort of reality at all.

tion gives us the unanalyzed "things" of our experience (raising us above the "blooming, buzzing confusion"), and is not at all the same as synthe- sizing *ideas* about things. (*Poetic Diction; Saving the Appearances*)

• • •

Our language and meanings today put the idea of participation almost out of reach, whereas the reality of participation (if not the idea) was simply given in earlier eras. For example, we cannot conceive of thoughts except as things in our heads, "rather like cigarettes inside a cigarette box called the brain." By contrast, during the medieval era it would have been impossible to think of mental activity, or intelligence, as the product of a physical organ. Then, as now, the prevailing view was supported by the unexamined meanings of the only words with which one could talk about the matter.

The Evolution of Consciousness

We fail today to distinguish properly between the history of ideas—"a dialectical or syllogistic process, the thoughts of one age arising discur- sively out of, challenging, and modifying the thoughts and discoveries of the previous one"—and the evolution of consciousness.

> The comparatively sudden appearance, after millennia of static civi- lizations of the oriental type, of the people or the impulse which eventually flowered in the cultures of the Aryan nations can hardly have been due to the impact of notion on notion. And the same is true of the abrupt emergence at a certain point in history of vocifer- ously speculative thought among the Greeks. Still more remarkable is the historically unfathered impulse of the Jewish nation to set about eliminating participation by quite other methods than those of alpha- thinking [that is, of thinking *about* things]. Suddenly, and as it were without warning, we are confronted by a fierce and warlike nation, for whom it is a paramount moral obligation to refrain from the par- ticipatory heathen cults by which they were surrounded on all sides; for whom moreover precisely that moral obligation is conceived as the very foundation of the race, the very marrow of its being. (*Saving the Appearances*)

• • •

An analogy may help. The changes in our ideas about, say, the economics of transport and commerce over the past several centuries have no doubt resulted in part from the impact of idea upon idea. But another cause of these changes lies in the altered nature of transport and commerce themselves. That is, the thing *about which* we form ideas has evolved. (*Speaker's Meaning*)

When it comes to human consciousness, we tend to forget the second possibility. Yet, here in particular we should expect this possibility to predominate. "Ideas [about human consciousness] have changed because human consciousness itself—the elementary human experience about which the ideas are being formed—the whole relation between man and nature or between conscious man and unconscious man—has itself been in process of change." (*Speaker's Meaning; Saving the Appearances*)

Thus, the transition from a psychology of inspiration to one of imagination (see above) reflects a changing relation between man and the sources of what we now call creativity. What once came from without must now be taken hold of from within.

• • •

The balance in figuration between what is given to us from without and what we contribute from within has changed radically over the course of history. For earliest man, nearly all the activity of figuration came from without—which is another way of saying that the "inside" of things was experienced more "out there" than "in here." (Which also implies that "out there" was not quite so *out there* as it has become for us.) The perceiver was directly aware of the beings constituting this inside—an awareness we badly misinterpret if we take it as an erroneous theorizing *about* things. Today, on the other hand, we contribute to the inside of things—we participate in them—from within ourselves, and we are largely unaware of the contribution. Our primary, conscious mode of thinking is a thinking *about* things. (*Saving the Appearances*)

"Whether or no archaic man saw nature awry, what he saw was not primarily determined by *beliefs*. On the other hand . . . what *we* see *is* so determined." This is the reverse of what is generally supposed. (*Saving the Appearances*)

· · ·

The participation of primitive man (what we might call "original" participation) was not theoretical at all, nor was it derived from theoretical thought. It was given in immediate experience. That is, the conceptual links by which the participated phenomena were constituted were given to man already "embedded" in what he perceived. As noted above, his perceiving was at the same time a kind of thinking; thinking occurred more in the world than in man. Perceiving and thinking had not yet split apart, as they have for us. Moreover, what was *represented* in the collective representations also differed for primitive man:

> The essence of *original* participation is that there stands behind the phenomena, *and on the other side of them from me*, a represented which is of the same nature as me. Whether it is called "mana," or by the names of many gods and demons, or God the Father, or the spirit world, it is of the same nature as the perceiving self, inasmuch as it is not mechanical or accidental, but psychic and voluntary. (*Saving the Appearances*)

· · ·

"For the nineteenth-century fantasy of early man first gazing, with his mind *tabula rasa*, at natural phenomena like ours, then seeking to explain them with thoughts like ours, and then by a process of inference 'peopling' them with the 'aery phantoms' of mythology, there just is not any single shred of evidence whatever." (*Poetic Diction; Saving the Appearances*)

· · ·

"Interior is anterior."

> Both ontogenetically and phylogenetically, subjectivity is never something that was developed out of nothing at some point in space, but is a form of consciousness that has *contracted* from the periphery into individual centers. Phylogenetically, it becomes clear to us that the task of *Homo sapiens*, when he first appeared as a physical form on earth, was not to evolve a faculty of thought somehow out of

nothing, but to transform the unfree wisdom, which he experienced through his organism as given meaning, into the free subjectivity that is correlative only to *active* thought, to the individual activity of thinking. (*Speaker's Meaning*)

• • •

On the significance of memory:

Just as, when a word is formed or spoken, the original unity of the "inner" [that is, not yet spoken] word is polarized into a duality of outer and inner, that is, of sound and meaning; so, when man himself was "uttered," that is, created, the cosmic wisdom became polarized, in and through him, into the duality of appearance and intelligence, representation and consciousness. But when creation has become polarized into consciousness on the one side and phenomena, or appearances, on the other, memory is made possible, and begins to play an all-important part in the process of evolution. For by means of his memory man makes the outward appearances an inward experience. He acquires his self-consciousness from them. When I experience the phenomena in memory, I make them "mine," not now by virtue of any original participation, but by my own inner activity. (*Saving the Appearances*)

• • •

The possibility of a new kind of participation—what we might call *final* participation—was glimpsed by the Romantics when they concluded that "we must no longer look for the nature-spirits—for the Goddess Natura—on the farther side of the appearances; we must look for them *within ourselves*." In Coleridge's words: *We receive but what we give / And in our life alone does Nature live.* Original participation "fires the heart from a source outside itself; the images enliven the heart." In final participation, "it is for the heart to enliven the images." (*Saving the Appearances*)

• • •

We can understand the relation between final and original participation only when "we admit that, in the course of the earth's history, something like a Divine Word has been gradually clothing itself with the humanity it first

THE FUTURE DOES NOT COMPUTE

gradually created—so that what was first spoken by God may eventually be respoken by man." (*Saving the Appearances*; *Worlds Apart*)

Science and the Future

Modern science began with the conscious exclusion of so-called "occult" properties—those qualities imperceptible to the physical senses. Subsequently, the remaining, physically observable qualities were divided into two groups—primary and secondary—depending on whether they were felt to reside in the world or in man. Eventually, it turned out that all qualities were "subjective," and the hardest sciences therefore devoted themselves solely to the quantitative, measurable aspects of the world. The phenomena, in their qualitative fullness, were ignored as subjective.

Before the Scientific Revolution, qualities were felt to reside *both* in nature and in man. Man, as a microcosm, was a reflection of the macrocosm. The dispositional qualities of the planets were also dispositional qualities of man. The four elements of nature were not exclusively objective, and the four humors of man were not exclusively subjective.

It is odd, then, to call the pre-Copernican world "anthropocentric."

> We have just been seeing how the qualities formerly treated as inherent in nature have, as far as any scientific theory is concerned, disappeared from it, and how they have reappeared on the hither side of the line between subject and object, within the experiencing human psyche; how we conceive ourselves as "projecting" qualities onto nature rather than receiving them from her. Is that any *less* anthropocentric than the Aristotelian world-picture? I would have thought it was more so. ("Science and Quality," in *The Rediscovery of Meaning and Other Essays*)

· · ·

The qualities of things, "which we classify as subjective, but which look so very much as if they actually belong to nature," are in fact "the inwardness of nature as well as of ourselves." Not that we consciously *devise* these qualities; our participation in them is largely unconscious. ("Science and Quality," in *The Rediscovery of Meaning and Other Essays*)

· · ·

"What will chiefly be remembered about the scientific revolution will be the way in which it scoured the appearances clean of the last traces of spirit, freeing us *from* original, and *for* final, participation.... The other name for original participation, in all its long-hidden, in all its diluted forms, in science, in art and in religion, is, after all—paganism." (*Saving the Appearances*)

• • •

When man first begins thinking *about* the phenomena, he still largely participates in them. This thinking, therefore, becomes entangled in error and confusion, for it is an attempt to gain an objective stance before one has gotten free of the web of meaning by which one is bound to things. Over time, however, this kind of thinking is a primary means by which the disentanglement—the freedom from things—is achieved. (*Saving the Appearances*)

Effective manipulation of things (from surgery to computation) is one of the gifts of science, as is a habit of disciplined and accurate thinking. So also is the selfless and attentive devotion to nature that only became possible with our separation from nature.

• • •

On the other hand,

> our very love of natural phenomena "for their own sake" will be enough to prevent us from hastily turning a blind eye on any new light which can be shed, from any direction whatsoever, on their true nature. Above all will this be the case, if we feel them to be in danger. And if the appearances are, as I have sought to establish, correlative to human consciousness and if human consciousness does not remain unchanged but evolves, then the future of the appearances, that is, of nature herself, must indeed depend on the direction which that evolution takes. (*Saving the Appearances*)

• • •

The notion of evolution, or development, has become central to many of the sciences—and rightly so. But this idea remains badly distorted by the peculiar conditions of its birth. The phenomena, or collective representations, during the middle of the nineteenth century (when Darwin wrote) were *objects*. "To a degree which has never been surpassed before or since," man did not consciously participate in these phenomena. At that time,

> matter and force were enough. . . . If the particles kept growing smaller and smaller, there would always be bigger and better glasses to see them through. The collapse of the mechanical model was not yet in sight, nor had any of those other factors which have since contributed to the passing of the dead-centre of "literalness"—idealist philosophies, genetic psychology, psychoanalysis—as yet begun to take effect. Consequently there was as yet no dawning apprehension that the phenomena of the familiar world may be "representations" in the final sense of being the mental construct of the observer. Literalness reigned supreme . . . .

> For the generality of men, participation was dead; the only link with the phenomena was through the senses; and they could no longer conceive of any manner in which either growth itself or the metamorphoses of individual and special growth, could be determined from within. The appearances were idols. They had no "within." Therefore the evolution which had produced them could only be conceived mechanomorphically as a series of impacts of idols on other idols. (*Saving the Appearances*)

• • •

All real change is transformation. For transformation to occur, there must be an interior that persists as well as an exterior that is transformed. Otherwise, one would have only bare substitution. There would be nothing undergoing the transformation. Nineteenth-century atomism—which continues to dominate the popular imagination (and even the prosaic imagination of most scientists)—was in this way essentially a description of substitutions. It therefore could not grasp evolution as a transformative process.

But to speak of an interior that persists is to speak as much of *beings* as of things. That, perhaps, accounts for the popularity of impersonal terms like "pattern" and "gestalt." They shield us from what we prefer not to recognize. "We glimpse a countenance, and we say hurriedly: 'Yes, that is indeed a face, but it is the face of nobody.'" (*Unancestral Voice*)

• • •

The move from a participated world to the nonparticipated world of nineteenth-century science carried man from an organic relation to the cosmos to a purely spatial, mathematical relation. The view of man as a microcosm placed at the center of the macrocosm (much as the heart was the center—but certainly not the mathematical center—of man) gave way to an arbitrary coordinate system, with the eye fixed at the origin. That perfect instrument of perspective, the camera, "looks always *at* and never *into* what it sees. I suspect that Medusa did very much the same." ("The Harp and the Camera," in *The Rediscovery of Meaning and Other Essays*; *Saving the Appearances*)

• • •

The classical physicist still viewed transformation in nature as essentially qualitative, and he sought the unchanging entities underlying the observed transformations. But this enterprise was called into question by later developments, including the formulation of the field concept, which "meant abandoning the old assumption that the laws governing large-scale phenomena are to be deduced from those governing matter at the microscopic level. [It was] at least as true to say that the behavior of the particle was determined by the field as it was to say that the nature of the field was determined by the behaviors of particles." The seemingly unavoidable insertion of a principle of randomness—unlawfulness—at the submicroscopic level was another jolt. (*Unancestral Voice*)

Such developments lead to questions about the role of models in physics. Must we either be content with unsullied mathematics, or else resort to "crude," constructional models (such as pictures of the atom as miniature solar systems)? A middle way may be indicated by what is known of the working of the imagination. In particular, three features widely recognized as belonging to the imagination may prove relevant to the physicist:

Imagination directly apprehends the whole as "contained" in the part, or as in some mode identical with it.

Imagination ... apprehends spatial form, and relations in space, as "expressive" of nonspatial form and nonspatial relations.

> Operating ... anteriorly to the kind of perception and thought which have become normal for fully conscious modern man, [imagination] functions at a level where observed and observer, mind and object, are no longer—or are not yet—spatially divided from one another; so that the mind, as it were, becomes the object or the object becomes the mind. (*Unancestral Voice*)

Unfortunately, however, those who pursue physics and those who have investigated imagination typically have little to do with each other.

• • •

The radical, Cartesian split between mind and matter is more commonly complained of than escaped. A true escape would require that I become a different kind of human being.

> To renounce the heterogeneity of observed from observer involves, if it is taken seriously, abandoning the whole "onlooker" stance, upon which both the pursuit of science and modern language-use in general are based; it means advancing to awareness of another relation altogether between mind and matter. If we had actually made the advance, we should have become naturally, unforcedly, and unremittingly aware that the mind *cannot* refer to a natural object without at the same time referring to its own activity. And this in turn would require an equally unforced awareness not only that scientific discovery is always a discovery about language, but also that it is always a discovery about the self which uses language. ("Language and Discovery," in *The Rediscovery of Meaning and Other Essays*)

• • •

Scientists are wont to boast of the objectivity of their discipline. There is good reason for this, but "is there any need to make quite such a song and dance about it?" Objectivity should pose no great difficulty when we're dealing with matters from which we feel wholly disconnected personally. "To put it rudely, any reasonably honest fool can be objective about objects."

> It must be a different matter altogether, should we be called on to attend, not alone to matter, but to spirit; when a man would have to

402

practice distinguishing what *in* himself comes solely from his private personality—memories, for instance, and all the horseplay of the Freudian subconscious—from what comes also from elsewhere. Then indeed objectivity is not something that was handed us on a plate once and for all by Descartes, but something that would really have to be *achieved*, and which must require for its achievement, not only exceptional mental concentration but other efforts and qualities, including moral ones, as well. ("Language and Discovery," in *The Rediscovery of Meaning and Other Essays*)

• • •

The line between unconscious figuration (by which "things" are made) and conscious thinking *about* things is not fixed and inviolate. Not only, in our thinking about things, do we progressively bring their constitutive thinking to consciousness, but also, our thinking about things sinks down, over time, into our unconscious manner of experiencing those things—that is, into our figuration. I may first have to learn that the sound I hear is a thrush singing; but, eventually, I will no longer hear a sound and then conclude that a thrush is singing, but rather will simply "hear a thrush singing." How I think has worked down into how I perceive. (*Poetic Diction*; *Saving the Appearances*)

• • •

A true science would lead us toward a more conscious figuration, whereby we would take responsibility for the world *from the inside*. The "particles" are abstract constructs filling in where we have not yet succeeded, via figuration, in producing phenomena. That is, the realm about which we theorize with talk of particles and such is the collective unconscious, and is contiguous, so to speak, with that other part of the collective unconscious from which the familiar world of collective representations arises through figuration.

But we have a choice. Instead of raising the unconscious to consciousness through an enhanced figuration, we can continue reducing consciousness—as manifested in the phenomena—to unconsciousness. As I noted above (n. 4), "by means of abstraction, we convert the world into the merely notional, or nonphenomenal"—that is, into "particles."

So far at all events as the macroscopic universe is concerned, the world itself on the one hand and the way we perceive and think it on the other hand are inseparable. It must follow from that that, if enough people go on long enough perceiving and thinking about the world as mechanism only, the macroscopic world will eventually *become* mechanism only. ("Science and Quality," in *The Rediscovery of Meaning and Other Essays; Saving the Appearances*)

• • •

"To be *able* to experience the representations as idols, and then to be able also to perform the act of figuration consciously, so as to experience them as participated; that is imagination."

• • •

Speaking through a character in his fictionalized treatise, *Unancestral Voice*, Barfield summarizes the development of language:

> Language was, for him, an outstanding example of the past surviving, transformed, in the present . . . . You had to see the origin of language as the self-gathering of mind within an already mind-soaked world. It was the product of "nature" in the sense that the meanings of words, if you approached them historically, could all—or as nearly all as made no difference—be shown to be involved with natural phenomena. Moreover, interfusion of the sensuous (sound) with the immaterial (meaning) was still, even today, its whole point. Yet it was certainly not, in its earlier stages, the product of *individual* minds; for it was obviously already there at a stage of evolution when individual minds were not yet. He had no doubt of its pointing back to a state of affairs when men and nature were one in a way that had long since ceased. Even now, even in our own time, there was the mysterious "genius of language" which many philologists had detected as something that worked independently of any conscious choices. On the other hand, you could see that, as time went on, language did come to owe more and more to the working of individual minds. However you looked at it, you could not get away from the fact that every time a man spoke or wrote there was this intricate interfusion of past and present—of the past transformed, as meaning, with the present impulse behind his act of utterance.

• • •

"The appearances will be 'saved' only if, as men approach nearer and nearer to conscious figuration and realize that it is something which may be affected by their choices, the final participation which is thus being thrust upon them is exercised with the profoundest sense of responsibility, with the deepest thankfulness and piety towards the world as it was originally given to them in original participation, and with a full understanding of the momentous process of history, as it brings about the emergence of the one from the other." (*Saving the Appearances*)

B

From Virtual to Real

THANKS TO THE COMPUTER, we are today flirting with certain ideas that would have been anathema to an earlier scientific and technological mindset:

- The Net and its "information spaces" are increasingly conceived as a kind of global, nurturing, immaterial sea of wisdom, from which we all may freely draw, and to which we contribute our own unique achievements. We are now learning to regard even our own identities in terms of "DNA databases"—extensions of the larger information space. And, as these databases become digitized and manipulable, the hope is that I may eventually alter my personal genetic database at will, selecting my physiological destiny by multiple choice from the informational surround.

On the face of it, this matrix of informational essences carries us a long way from the brute, fixed stuff of nineteenth-century material-ism, shaped solely by the outward impact of mechanism upon mechanism. Materiality has been caught up, so to speak, within a "superior" realm of information, and made to serve it.

- When we construct virtual realities, we do so "from the inside." We not only experience the virtual world, but we create it, sustain it, and alter it (both as programmers and as "inhabitants"). We *participate* in its phenomena. One aspect of this participation is a strong connection between word and thing. The word takes on substance. Given the right programming environment, I can say, "let the world be blue," and it is so.

It is precisely such participation, however, that the strict cleavage between subject and object was supposed to remove from our scientific understanding of the world. The scientific method was to yield an objective reality uncontaminated by the investigator's subjectivity.

- The discipline of artificial intelligence has freed the "mind" from the body. The bit patterns constituting the computer's intelligence can be transferred to a second computer without moving any hardware. Same mind, it seems, but different body. Also, there is much talk of the intelligent agents we will soon commission to go gibbering through the vast, logical spaces of the Net, bound to no single machine, and surviving from one flitting incarnation to the next as restless shades with an insatiable thirst for information.

And yet, the strictest materialism once held that all mentality was—if not nothing—pure and simple physicality, precisely located in space.

- Intelligence—the kind with which we invest our artifacts—is rapidly evolving. This decade's machines are far more sophisticated, more knowing, more subtly clever than last decade's, and the next decade's will be even more so. It is not only a matter of degree. The fundamental principles by which these intelligences operate are also evolving, as our programming strategies change. Nor are these developments restricted in any absolute way by limitations of hardware. The computational mind evolves independently.

But not so long ago, the evolution of the mind's most basic structures was conceived by biologists to be entirely consequent upon evolution of the underlying substrate. The brain is what sustained evolution, not some epiphenomenal mind.

Computer technology, in summary, appears to suggest certain redirections away from older scientific stances: a *de-materialization*, with information replacing matter as the more basic construct; a *participation* that blurs the distinction between subject and object; a new *metaphysics* that resists the theoretical assimilation of mind to body; and a nonmaterial *evolution of intelligence*, independent of matter.

It turns out, as we will see, that these ideas represent a strengthening of the familiar habit of abstraction upon which science has long been based. Or, at least, that is what the common statement of the ideas makes of them. But another way to think about these things has been on offer since well before the computer came along.

Ancient principles, or new?

One way for me to introduce the work of Owen Barfield—admittedly an eccentric way—would be to ask what happens if we take these "new truths" in their most radical and disturbing sense. For then we will find ourselves driven to the work begun by Barfield early in this century. It is a remarkable fact that he developed a closely corresponding set of insights, and brought to bear upon them a historical awareness and a richness of discrimination not yet evident in discussions of electronic technology.

Of course, Barfield had one advantage over us: since computers did not exist when he began his work, he was not driven by any illusion that they represented some bright, new paradigm, with the aid of which we would finally lift ourselves from the supposed muck of our earthly origins. He saw clearly enough that the computational model—whether of mind or world—was rather the final, lifeless crystallization of a paradigm that was already taking form within the murky penumbra of the Scientific Revolution's first, promising light.

When, in the 1920s, he began his research, he did so not by looking forward to the computer, but rather by taking in the distant human past. The truths he discerned were gleaned from the ancients, yet he recognized in these truths a double significance, for they must come alive again in a new way if our future is to be preserved.

And what are these ancient truths upon which the future hangs? Here, in brief, I will restate the four, closely meshed assertions given above as I imagine they might emerge from an encounter with Barfield's pen:

- We—and the world—are descended from something like a sea of pure meaning—of spirit and light—and we still bear our origin within ourselves. It would be truer to say that human beings were first incarnated upon the resonant wings of language—as "standing waves," so to speak, within the flow of divine speech—than that language originated with the human being. (As to the material, "information-bearing" gene, it is a metaphor—a focused yet veiled image within which we may hope to read a few of the wordlike gestures raying in from the surrounding spiritual matrix.)

- We participate in the world's phenomena from the inside. For example (as Coleridge observed), what I experience within myself as an idea, and within nature as a law, are not two different things, but the same inner reality encountered from two sides. The creative word summoned from the profoundest depths of man's being is one with the word that sustains nature. Now largely lost from view, this unity (along with the responsibility it implies) is in danger of becoming irretrievably destructive. Treating the world as mere object, we are on the way toward making it into mere object in its own, most essential nature.

- While our human consciousness is *mediated* by the brain, consciousness as such is the product neither of matter nor of its organization. Rather, consciousness precedes and prepares the way for its own embodiment in material organs. The thinking that occurs upon the

410

stage of our consciousness takes place as much "out there" as within the cranium. Consciousness is the enduring prerequisite from which all physical reality is, as it were, coagulated.

- Quite apart from the history of ideas, there has been an underlying evolution of consciousness. From one side, this can be seen as a progressive contraction of consciousness out of the world and into our individual centers, which in turn marks a transition from subject-object unity to our own subject-object antithesis. The present necessity is to learn again to participate consciously in the world, but without giving up our hard-won self-consciousness and our capacity for detached, objective thinking. That is, we may no longer merely suffer our participation as the ancients did; we must freely speak the creative word out of ourselves, in full and disciplined consciousness. Only so can we renew the world from within.

A changing of the guard?

If you compare these two groups of statements closely, you may find yourself perplexed. On the one hand, the paired statements *almost* say the same thing. But on the other hand, it appears that Barfield inhabits a world altogether foreign to conventional wisdom about computers and the Net—so much so that his remarks bear the taint of taboo. The computer engineer may speak of intelligent software on a disk, but she is not likely to tolerate thoughts of an intelligence brooding over the primeval ooze from which human life is thought to have arisen—much less any idea that the ooze itself congealed from some sort of consciousness or spirit.

I say only "not likely," for it is no longer the near impossibility of a few years back. The taboos do show signs of weakening, even as the materialistic paradigm continues its stunning transformation toward *apparent* immateriality. The younger generation today is not so inclined to distinguish artificially between the visible and the invisible, the material and the immaterial, as we once were.

If you doubt the change, just ask those stolid guardians of scientific tradition who despair over so much in our well-educated society today:

the many flourishing "disciplines" beyond the pale, such as astrology, psychic counseling, and channeling; the rediscovery and celebration of indigenous spirituality; and the remarkable spread of the most diverse forms of "New Age" science and religion.

The various sillinesses to be found among these cultural phenomena are hardly the main point—any more than the forgotten sillinesses of the Renaissance were its main point. The significance in both cases lies rather at a deeper level where the fundamental capacities and yearnings of human consciousness take shape. As to the travesties, should we not lay them at the door of those same stolid guardians, who have for so long arrogated to themselves all "legitimate" scientific energies, denying even the lackluster crumbs to their spiritually hungry brethren?

However, I have also just now suggested that certain of our distinctive thoughts about computers can be read in either of two dramatically divergent ways. That is, computers have led us onto the knife edge, and as our current vertigo already indicates, we cannot long avoid committing ourselves to one side or the other. We will either choose for ourselves, or else receive an unceremonious shove from the gathering technological nisus.

A question of abstraction

When we look at the two sets of statements given above—one arising from high technology and the other from Barfield's work—a crucial difference is immediately apparent. Where Barfield speaks of the everyday, familiar world, we children of technology appeal instead to virtual reality and to that apotheosis of distributed information we like to call "cyberspace." And so, for us,

- An old-style materiality gives way, not to a rediscovery of the spirit (from which all meaning once descended), but to a field of measurable, manipulable information (from which no meaning can arise).

- We begin to experience our creative participation in virtual worlds, but this participation turns out to be a matter, not of head, heart, and will—nor even of head alone—but solely of the calculator-in-the-

412

head (although the calculation is admittedly superb, down to the least pixel). We *program* these worlds, which consequently lack all inner connection to the sustaining Nature that bore us.

- We devise evolving forms of intelligence existing independently of any material substrate, but far from bearing creative powers and intentions for the earth's renewal, these empty forms are the last, dead echoes of a human intelligence now content to live as its own shadow, impressed upon highly articulated, but uncomprehending mechanisms.

The computer, it appears, can remind us of forgotten truths—truths that were perhaps bound to reemerge in one form or another with the exhaustion of a one-sided scientific quest. But at the same time, by encouraging us to translate those truths into a distant reflection of themselves, the computer also shields us from their direct force. The technological vision appears almost as if an entire body of wisdom, deriving from all ancient peoples of the earth and bearing deep significance for our future, had been "lifted" and applied in attenuated form to an artificial world safely insulated from the real thing.

Moreover, the nature of our shield against forgotten truths is not hard to recognize. It is woven of abstractions. We have seen such a pattern already in classical science: using a mathematical sieve, a "material" residue was sifted from the spiritually rich world. But this residue turned out to have no substance, no weight, of the sort we once imagined. In fact, it finally reduced to the abstract mesh of the sieve itself—which is hardly surprising. As William Temple once remarked, "if you attend to things only so far as they are measurable, you will end with only measurements before your attention." And so today the physicist plays in a realm of number, equation, and probability, disavowing all attempts to assign meaning to his constructs.

What happens if we bring the physicist's proclivities to the sciences of man? The same abstraction that sifted matter from spirit now distills quantitative information from qualitative meaning with technocratic efficiency;

413

and then it proceeds to articulate the logical structures of a computational "mind." Freed from the necessity of "instantiation" in any particular material, these informational and logical structures gain a kind of notional immortality, a release from the encumbering weight of gross matter.

But here is the enticing danger. Today many people are inclined to welcome any possible "escape" from the dead weight of several centuries' materialistic debris. With good justification. And yet, the deliverance they are now being offered is in reality the quintessential product—the ultimate extension—of that same materialistic undertaking that has till now so effectively constrained their spirits.

It is, after all, now evident enough that the essence of scientific materialism never did lay in a defense of what we still like to think of as "solid matter" over against whatever sort of immateriality we cared to imagine. For materialism is finally located in those habits of abstraction that gave us dark, featureless matter in the first place; and if this originally comforting matter of science has been found to dissolve more and more into abstract fields and statistical distributions, a strikingly similar dissolution has reduced the living spirits of old to the vague, informational-spiritual stuff of the high-tech mystic. Whoever we are, we define ourselves today by our abstractions.

The real divide, then, occurs not between materiality and immateriality, but rather between abstraction and meaning—between, on the one hand, the abstraction that gave us "physical" and "mental" stuff in Cartesian opposition, and, on the other hand, the meaning through which we can rediscover the spirit-saturated world, and ourselves in it.

Eventually, one may expect, the abstracted mind will implode from its own weightlessness. For we must finally ask: abstraction from *what*? If there is no *what*—no "familiar world" worth knowing, possessed of substantial reality in its own right—how shall we abstract from it?

Goethean science. If abstraction is the instrument by which we produce the informational content of cyberspace, imagination is the activity by which we discover meaning in the world, for with the imagination we apprehend "the outward form as the image or symbol of an inner meaning."[1]

Imagination is already employed in the scientific method. But what we need now, according to Barfield, is the use of imagination, not only in devising hypotheses, but "in the very act of observation." This would lead us beyond some vague sense of meaning in nature as a whole. It would enable us to read the "book" of nature in such a way that "the meaning of the whole is articulated from the meaning of each part—chapters from sentences and sentences from words—and stands before us in clear, sharp outlines" (p. 20).

Such a method may be hard for us to conceive, but Barfield points out that Coleridge and the Romantics took some first, tentative steps in this direction. Moreover, Goethe actually exercised the method in making some profound discoveries—although they have largely been overlooked in the accelerating rush of science toward manipulative effectiveness. Goethe, as Barfield puts it, perceived that "nature has an 'inside' which cannot be weighed and measured—or even (without training) observed—namely, the creative thoughts which underlie phenomenal manifestation" (p. 20).

Goethe's scientific work included a study of light and color, which, until recently, drew less attention from scientists than from artists; investigations of the human skeleton; and the discovery of the principle of metamorphosis of plants, by which a single "form" repeatedly expresses itself through a series of expanding and contracting transformations in leaf, calyx, petal, reproductive organs, fruit, and, finally, in the extremely contracted seed. Barfield characterizes Goethe's achievement this way:

> By ordinary inductive science the unifying idea, or law, behind groups of related phenomena is treated as a generalization from particulars: it is an abstract notion ... and it must be expressible in terms of measurable quantities. For Goethean science, on the other hand, this unifying idea is an objective reality, accessible to direct

---

1. "The Rediscovery of Meaning," p. 19. This popular article was reprinted in Barfield, 1977b. The remaining quotations in this section are from the same source.

observation. In addition to measuring quantities, the scientist must train himself to perceive qualities. This he can do—as Goethe did when he saw the various parts of the plant as "metamorphoses" of the leaf—only by so sinking himself in contemplation of the outward form that his imagination penetrates to the activity which is producing it. (p. 21)

Information or meaning; abstraction or imagination? We choose between reducing nature's fullness to the abstract generalizations of mathematical law, or penetrating to the inner *activity* that produces the phenomenon. That activity can no more be expressed as information than your and my meaningful activity.

Goethe's recognition of the principle of metamorphosis could hardly have arisen from any sort of generalization following upon the logical analysis of already defined structures. He had to wrestle through to a qualitative seeing that required years of disciplined observation before he could discern the crucial forms. He held that anyone who perceived these creative forms could, in thought, derive every *possible* plant, including those that did not yet exist.[2]

I referred above—perhaps much too breezily—to the gene as "a metaphor, a focused yet veiled image within which we may hope to read a few of the wordlike gestures raying in from the surrounding spiritual matrix." There is no denying that these words are more easily spoken than entered into. But it is Barfield's message that we must at least become aware of the two contrary *directions* our investigations may take. With respect to the gene, we may, on the one hand, elect to analyze the outer body of the metaphor, bringing to bear upon it our admirably detached, but perceptually emptied, quantitative observation—and so we may gain our desired powers of manipulation. But this brute manipulation will stand unrelated to the meaning of the metaphor, for that must be *read*, not measured or calculated.

---

2. There are signs in some quarters that this "Goethean science" is beginning to be taken more seriously in our day. See, for example, Zajonc, 1993; Schwenk, 1965; Adams and Whicher, 1980; Edelglass et al., 1992.

If, on the other hand, we could begin to see the developing human being rather as Goethe saw the plant—and I, for one, do not wish to minimize the challenge in this—perhaps we would find ourselves able to move beyond the seemingly insoluble ethical quandaries posed by genetic manipulation in particular and biotechnology in general. What we would then confront is the concrete reality of personhood and destiny, not the abstract, informational "programming" of a few strands of DNA. Only then would we know, from the inside, the proper laws constraining every human transformation.

Can the appearances be saved?

We have been abandoning the world in two directions. On one side, pure science leads us away from nature toward a notional, almost metaphysical realm of particles. Here we look for the real basis and the final explanation of everything in nature. Such a stance drains the sense of *present reality* from all ordinary experience. If particles are the real stuff, precisely characterizable, why bother overmuch with the profligate, undisciplined cornucopia that presents itself immediately to our senses? Isn't everything we know most immediately—prior to applying our grid of abstraction—"merely subjective"?

On the other side, we are now abandoning the world by constructing artificial alternatives to ordinary experience, christening them "virtual." If normal experience is only subjective anyway, there is no reason not to create worlds of sensation more to our liking. One can even imagine that, just so far as we learn to *control* these sensations, we will begin to view the virtual environment as more objectively real than any other world, for we have long considered our experience valid just so far as it expresses our powers of control.

In any case, the phenomenal world is clearly being neglected—if not positively undermined—from two sides. This raises the question implied in the title of Barfield's book, *Saving the Appearances*.[3] Transferring this

---

3. The following quotations are from this book.

question to our present context: in addition to the effective control we gain by constructing a notional world of particles, and in addition to our capacity for arbitrary expression through the technology of virtual reality, do we still need to take deep, creative hold of the "middle world"—the familiar world—the world that nursed our ancestors and stirred them to unprecedented artistic achievements, the world from which we abstract the particles, and the world we merely imitate with our virtual realities? Can we consciously take hold of this familiar world *from the inside*, working with it artistically as stewards of the future?

Participation. Barfield's answer, given in *Saving the Appearances*, is so fundamental that I can scarcely even gesture toward it here. This is not surprising, given that he asks us to reconceive both the gesturing human being and the things we can gesture toward—and even more, to become in the process *different* gesturers, beholding a *different* sort of thing. Nevertheless, I must at least cite one of his starting points, along with a few mileposts, none of which, unfortunately, can be set in context here.

Barfield begins, quite simply, with what is nearly undisputed:

On almost any received theory of perception the familiar world—that is, the world which is apprehended, not through instruments and inference, but simply—is for the most part dependent upon the percipient. (p. 21)

If the hard sciences have retreated into quantitative analysis, it is precisely because the phenomenal world—the qualitative world handed to us by direct awareness—is felt to be "contaminated" by the consciousness of the subject. The world of cold and hot things, green and blue things, loud and quiet things; the world of familiar faces, strange places, clouds, sky, and seas; the world about which each of us thinks whenever we are *not* critically applying our physics lessons—that world cannot (we are told) be described rigorously. We are advised not even to try; our first lessons in science teach us to seek *quantities* in the phenomena.

We have already heard one of Barfield's responses: the phenomenal world *can* be described rigorously—it can be *read* as a meaningful text—although (as the example from Goethe indicates) it indeed takes a great deal of trying. But the main thrust of *Saving the Appearances* derives from a very simple proposition: if we really believe what the physical sciences have told us about the dependence of the given world upon the one who perceives, then we ought to hold onto the belief consistently—something that is almost never done. That thought leads to a number of others:

- We must distinguish between the (possibly eccentric) representations of the individual, and the "collective representations" constituting the public world.[4]

- What is given to us by these collective representations encompasses everything we think of as the world when we're not doing our formal physics or philosophy—right down to and including the brutest solidity, the physical existence, of the planet earth. When we *are* doing physics or philosophy, we dismiss *this* planet earth in favor of a rarefied (and too often reified) realm of "particles." The undisciplined shift from one frame of thought to the other accounts for most of the aforementioned inconsistency (pp. 15–21).

- One aspect of this inconsistency is the almost universal writing of imaginary natural histories by paleontologists, botanists, geologists, and so on. "It can do no harm to recall occasionally that the prehistoric evolution of the earth, as it is described for example in the early chapters of H. G. Wells' *Outline of History*, was not merely never seen. It never occurred" (p. 37).

- Any serious look at history reveals, moreover, that the collective representations (down to and including the solid planet earth) have changed remarkably over time. If we would imagine an arbitrary prehistory, the first question we must answer is why we clothe that prehistory in the peculiar sort of appearances characterizing our day,

---

4. Barfield initially describes a representation as "something I perceive to be there" (p. 19).

rather than those of some earlier day. There may, after all, be good reasons for deeming the earlier representations more adequate to the reality (p. 37).

- The primordial earth cannot consistently be thought of even in terms of *potential* phenomena, "unless we also assume an unconscious, ready to light up into actual phenomena at any moment in the process" (p. 135).

- What is most "objective" about the world—what is least dependent upon the whims of the subject—is what we usually think of as going on "inside our heads," namely, thinking. In actual fact, thinking goes on in the world and is the inside of the world.

I said I could scarcely gesture toward the argument in *Saving the Appearances*, and that was the scarcely gesturing. One who is not familiar with the disturbingly vivid tapestry of Barfield's thought might well judge all this to be a kind of intellectual trick. Anyone who dives into the work, however, should be prepared for the eventual realization that the real trick is the one our intellects have played on us over the past several hundred years, by putting nearly beyond comprehension many understandings that once were mere common sense. Barfield would enable us to regain these lost sensibilities—but in a modern context.

On being responsible for the world. Barfield, then, sets us down before a "virtual reality" that turns out not be be virtual; he brings us back to the familiar world—not a phantom of our subjectivity, but rather the surround from which our consciousness has contracted into its bright focus. Our inside is also the inside of the world. Prepared or not, he tells us, we now bear a responsibility for what the world becomes. The agent of evolutionary change in the world, having once worked from without inward, has progressively reached consciousness in the individual, wideawake human being, who must now learn to speak the creative word outward, from within himself. Our toying with virtual realities (one can now add) is a remote and abstract echo of what is really required of us: to animate and regenerate our world from within while retaining our hard-won wakefulness.

It is an endangered world for which Barfield would have us take responsibility. Moreover, for good or ill, consciously or unconsciously, we cannot help exercising that responsibility. For example, our penchant for virtual realities is itself contributing to what the world becomes. It is entirely conceivable that, in the end, we will lose all distinction between the real and the virtual; it requires only that we attend ever more exclusively to our new, virtual realities—to the informational abstractions of cyberspace—while ignoring the phenomenal world. We will by that means finally succeed in rendering the inside of the world abstract. The inner life with which we animate the world will be the "life" of a program.

There is, after all, no *final* distinction between the virtual and the real. That is why the term "virtual reality" proves so slippery, seeming to apply alternately to everything and nothing. Every representational work of art is a virtual reality. (But, then, to one degree or another we work artistically upon everything in our earthly environment.) Every stick-and-ball "model" of atoms and molecules is a virtual reality—in this case an embodied abstraction bearing almost no phenomenal truth, but giving expression to certain theoretical constructs. Every photograph and television image is a virtual reality—a two-dimensional abstraction from the familiar world, reinvested with a set of dimmed-down meanings suitable for such an abstraction.[5]

We are surrounded, in fact, with exteriors into which we have breathed our own peculiar interiors. That, in their highly restricted way, is what virtual realities are. But that, Barfield urges us to remember, is in a much fuller sense also what the world is. The supposedly clear-cut line between human creations and nature simply cannot be found. It is not there. Yet we may lose sight of this fact. As participative experiences, virtual realities seem so distinctive in part because we have lost our awareness of our

---

5. See chapter 21, "Mona Lisa's Smile," and chapter 22, "Seeing in Perspective."

participation in the world. Perhaps also they awaken in us memories of an earlier relation to nature.

We can, then, choose either of two directions. If virtual realities remind us of a forgotten, more participative immersion in the world, it is possible that they will stimulate us to a renewed, more conscious participation. They may even provide us with a starting point, since (initially, at least) the difference between the virtual and the real catches our attention. If we contemplate that difference, moving in thought from the virtual to the real, we will actually discover *more* of ourselves "out there," not less. For through disciplined, scientific imagination we will, like Goethe, find in the world an inner meaning (*our* meaning), a fullness of being, that no abstractions—no programming languages and bit-manipulated graphics—can mediate.

The alternative—and surely it is a potential we all must sense within ourselves—is that we will be content to convert the world from real to virtual—continuing in the direction of the past few hundred years. Then, too, the difference between virtual and real will eventually vanish, not because we have penetrated the world more deeply and creatively, extending our responsible reach from artifact to nature, but rather because we will have finally abandoned the world to artifice.

EDUCATION WITHOUT COMPUTERS

THE ABYSS SEPARATING CHILD FROM ADULT is strange and baffling. Who among us can look at a classroom of children and tell which one will grow into his full powers, and which one will—say, at age twenty or thirty or fifty—begin to shrink from life and growth, allowing his capacities to shrivel? We hear often about the "unpromising" childhood of an Einstein or a Churchill, but not so often about the many exceptional promises of youth that never quite come to flower. Both are enigmas the educator must decipher. How can he pretend to teach, if he averts his eyes from the ruling mysteries of childhood?

If education is a matter of cultivating capacities rather than shoveling into the child a quantity of testable knowledge, then our difficulty in recognizing how those capacities—future potentials—are developing suggests that we don't know a whole lot about what we're doing. Perhaps this humbling awareness is the first requirement for a good teacher.

Three characteristics of Waldorf education have particularly drawn me to it: (1) precisely the sense of humility just described, combined with a grave acceptance of responsibility; (2) a conviction that the teacher *can* learn to recognize and cultivate the individual child's unfolding capacities; and (3) a deeply felt resistance to the use of computers in the primary school curriculum.

What is Waldorf education?

Founded in 1919 by Rudolf Steiner in Stuttgart, Germany, Waldorf schools (sometimes called Steiner schools) now constitute the largest and fastest growing nonsectarian educational movement in the world. While the movement is strongest in Europe, the Association of Waldorf Schools of North America embraces approximately one hundred member schools. Over the past fifteen years, new schools have been forming in the United States and Canada at the rate of about nine per year. In addition, there are 130 Waldorf kindergartens, fourteen high schools and five teacher training institutes.[1]

Worldwide, some 120,000 students at over six hundred schools in thirty-two countries are today receiving a Waldorf education. During the past few years, Russia and the former Iron Curtain countries have placed particularly strong demands upon the movement. Almost all of those countries now have teacher training programs.

Waldorf education, arising from profound convictions about the nature of the child and the world, requires an uncommonly strong commitment from its practitioners. (If nothing else, teacher salaries running well below public school rates tend to ensure a high level of commitment.) Although teachers operate within a broad, "given" educational context, they bear extensive responsibility for developing the particulars of their own curriculum. Moreover, this responsibility is compounded each year, as the teacher moves with his class from first grade through eighth.

The Waldorf classroom presents two sides that may, at first glance, appear contradictory. On the one hand, nearly *everything* in the child's environment is taken to be important. The teacher's bearing (his grace

---

1. These figures were supplied by the Association of Waldorf Schools of North America, Fair Oaks, California. For contact information, see the bibliographic note at the end of this chapter.

and art, his reverence for nature, his deeply won authority); the materials of the classroom (natural objects such as wooden branches, seashells, flowers, rocks, fabrics, as well as the room itself); every activity of the child (play as well as study); and above all the child himself—his volition and feeling fully as much as his intellect—*all* these things are consciously considered in their relevance to the child's education. It would be easy for such all-embracing concerns, expressed wrongly, to suffocate the child.

Yet, at the same time, the kingdom of childhood remains the focus, and the laws of this kingdom are laws of play, imagination, and freedom. If everything is important, yet nothing should be taken with an oppressive seriousness. Yes, the details count, but they count only because they must serve the needs of a child who is growing toward a rightful mastery of the world. Steiner put it this way: "accept the children with reverence, educate them with love, send them forth in freedom."

In what follows, I try to capture something of the "Waldorf spirit," as expressed by some of its leading exponents. It is doubtless true, as every reader will feel, that such extraordinary demands upon the teacher as are described here must be difficult to satisfy, so that every Waldorf classroom must fall short of the ideal. In fact, I have found that many teachers feel this shortfall as their own, private burden. But at the same time, the ideal embodies a set of understandings that many find compelling. And, more to the immediate point, these understandings form the positive backdrop against which the criticisms in PART TWO of this book can most usefully be viewed.

For brevity, I present the following in my own voice, instead of reiterating, "Waldorf educators believe ...," "Waldorf educators claim ...," and so on. At the same time, it should be clear that the views set forth here are ones with which I at least feel comfortable, even if I lack the knowledge and experience to assert them all on my own account.

Transformation of capacities

Waldorf students often spend time knitting in the first grade. A. C. Harwood, a lifelong Waldorf educator, has remarked, "When he grows up the man will think more cogently and more harmoniously because the child practiced this skill just at the time when his first independent thinking was born."[2]

Quite a stretch? Doubtless. But it's a stretch that runs through the entire Waldorf curriculum. The child is not simply an incomplete or failed adult, nor is he dumber than we are. Rather, he

> simply experiences the environment with another consciousness (and much more intensely than the adult) . . . . The intellectual cognitive capacity develops slowly as the result of the most diverse metamorphoses. Why is it that we so often disregard these changes in the child? Because we attribute our own completed state of consciousness to the child . . . . In addition, we allow ourselves to be misled by what the child, as an imitative being, picks up from the adult on a superficial level. *(A)*

Imitation does not necessarily represent capacity. The true capacities pass through dramatic transformations, much as the green seed leaves of a tiny plant grow into the rapidly expanding stem leaves and then are transmuted again into sepals and, finally, into the colored exuberance of the flower petals, in which, however, a properly trained observation can still recognize a metamorphosis of the first shoot. Waldorf educators often cite this law of metamorphosis—first discovered in the plant by Goethe—as a law of all growing things. What we sow in the child must sink down into his being in seedlike child-forms before it can emerge again, mature, and flower into an adult capability.

---

2. The books I have chosen for most of my citations are Harwood's *The Recovery of Man in Childhood*, and Willi Aeppli's *Rudolf Steiner Education and the Developing Child*. I will identify subsequent quotations from Harwood with *(H)*, and those from Aeppli with *(A)*. Apart from explicit quotations, I am deeply indebted to these and other educators for much of what I say here. (See the bibliographic note at the end of this appendix for additional sources. The quotations from Aeppli and Harwood are reproduced here by permission of Anthroposophic Press.)

Here is another example of a transformation—this time one which many a teacher will intuitively recognize:

> An individual will be able to make the right use of freedom later, if as a child, and in the most natural way, he is allowed to place himself under the absolute authority of a well-liked adult, if he is able to feel respect for an adult. The respect of a child for a particular person—which is actually respect for the *truth* the way it is silently expressed by that particular adult—is later transformed into respect for the objective truth, independent of any human being . . . . Without authority there is no freedom. *(A)*

It is critically important, therefore, that the teacher be *worthy* of respect. "The only important thing in a school is the teacher" *(A)*. There is much confusion on this point, however, for in our eagerness to respect the child's autonomy and to turn him into a "self-learner"—worthy enough concerns—we may find it easy to deprive him of his anchor. We may even do this out of a kind of modesty. But a child thus set adrift from what his own nature bids him respect is a child who finally will lose his respect even for the authority of truth. What we adults have come to reckon with on a relatively abstract level (namely, Truth), must first approach the child concretely, fully embodied, personified. So it is with everything the child may healthily absorb.

A balancing principle will help to avoid the confusion: the teacher's authority should never be employed simply to "fill" the student with particular thoughts. Content is used solely to exercise and develop capacities that must remain free.

> The subject matter alone, as the by-product of passive, intellectual thinking, has a destructive and crippling effect on the child . . . . I am not even allowed to give the child something that he may keep in that exact conceptual form. Nothing should be permanently stamped on the child's mind like a taped message, the way the recorder does it. *(A)*

However, this does not imply that we should expose the child only to what he can (intellectually) understand. Following such a principle, we

427

restrict his horizons in the most disheartening way, cutting him off from his connection to distant mysteries that may otherwise inspire a lifetime quest. "Great truths, which a child has absorbed with feelings of awe, joy or love, without 'understanding' them, sink into the sleeping will precisely because they are not first intercepted by the intellect." On the other hand, what is intercepted by the awake intellect "will not sink into the depths of the child's soul, and can therefore no longer grow and transform itself. Instead, it turns into one of those indigestible knowledge-stones that are such a burden on modern man" *(A)*.

How can the primary-age student "absorb" great truths without understanding them intellectually? Above all, in pictures. That is how the childhood of our race received its understanding—in mythic imagery. And that is why, in the lower grades, myth and fairy tale are primary resources for the Waldorf teacher. During the later grades, the pictures remain, but they steadily evolve into more elaborated and thought-saturated images, such as the Goethean image of the "archetypal" metamorphosis of the plant, and, above all, the image of the human being as a microcosm of the universe. In all cases, the student is encouraged to see the world around him artistically, drawing upon the deepest powers of his imagination.

Schools for the head

According to the Waldorf educators, we can all too easily abort the child's necessary transformations simply by imposing our adult intellects upon him prematurely. Unlike pictures a child builds up in his own mind, the thought-products of the intellect lack plasticity. They are rigid and restrictive—finished—bound to the unyielding forms of conventional logic and mathematics. Even as adults, how often do we find that, by seeking "intellectual clarity" too quickly—by failing, that is, to dwell long enough within a fluid, pictorial, and imaginative contemplation of the myriad possible "shapes" of a problem—we lock our understanding into a kind of frozen state? New insight penetrates such a state only with the greatest difficulty.

Inspired insights often strike one only after an interval of forgetfulness in rest or sleep. The beneficial rhythms of forgetting range all the way from the briefest period (one sometimes has to "let go" of the effort to remember something in order to recall it just a moment later) to the entire span of a lifetime. The child, too, must be allowed to forget. Only then will seeds planted in one form eventually gain the power to blossom in quite another. "Pictorial, imaginative thinking, tended properly and with care, will in due course be transformed" into a clear, rational thinking "which is rationality itself, and cannot be intoxicated or deceived by any kind of fantastic ideas" *(A)*.

But most schools are attuned to the demands of the intellect. "Who ever heard of a child being promoted because he was exceptionally good at painting or music, or because he excelled at acting or needlework?" *(H)*. A child who, at a particularly early age, learns to read the abstract and (in our day) meaningless forms of the alphabet—instead of first experiencing something more like the picture-writing of the ancients—is hailed as a triumph of pedagogy. There is no doubt we can develop the techniques to produce such triumphs with ever greater efficiency:

> It lies in the power of the adult to develop mental habits in a child either earlier or later. He can, if he so wishes, make the child conscious and develop his thinking and his memory at a very early age. If he does so, he will certainly narrow the scope of his mind even if he trains it to much acuteness in a limited sphere. *(H)*

We can summarize this entire emphasis upon the transformation of capacities from child to adult by noting Aeppli's remark that "in any educational action, what matters is not *that* something is done, but *how* and *when*." The *how* challenges us to present the child with those human qualities he can respect and take most deeply into himself. The *when* warns us to synchronize our teaching with the natural development of the child's native capacities, rather than to stimulate the intellect in a one-sided manner that may satisfy *us* while bequeathing to the child a barren sterility of outlook.

429

The unity of art and science

The child's natural interests are not artificially segmented. Fragmentation is a "gift" of the educational process. The Waldorf teacher strives to bring all subject matter into an artistic unity. During primary school, painting and modeling are usually not taught by a specialist teacher, lest the child accept this divorce of art from the rest of life. Rather, art is brought to the other subjects, and they are brought to art. For example, "in mathematics . . . you will have a profound and beneficial influence on children if you bring their sense of the beautiful into the heart of all that they learn. Artistic children—often little inclined to mathematical studies—will show great interest if they discover that there is beauty also in this subject" *(H)*. Thus,

> To sound the note of a stretched string, and then discover that to obtain the octave above the string must be divided exactly into half, is a great joy to children. They realise that the ear is a mathematician, perhaps a better mathematician than they are in their conscious heads. *(H)*

In what many of us will have to think another "reach," Aeppli observes that an artistically structured lesson produces a healthy flush on the children's faces, together with a freer, lighter, and yet more intense breathing. If, on the other hand, "despite all our wonderful pedagogical knowledge, we have taught all morning as a fossilized schoolmaster, merely out of our highly developed intellect, then, provided our eyes have become sharp enough, we can read the effects of such teaching in the children. We see that their faces are somewhat paler, somewhat more drained of blood than usual, even if only slightly; or we may suddenly notice that the children no longer breathe as freely as before."

Whatever our ability to see such things, it remains true that the child's nature is to take in the surrounding world with his whole being. It conduces to health on every level if his surroundings are full of grace, beauty and truth. I can say—speaking on my own behalf—that I have never seen

such warm and appealing classrooms as I have found in the several Waldorf schools I have visited.

Observation before theory

An artistic education can only grow out of observation and imagination.
One of the most stunning things about modern education is the rapid
precedence assigned to theory.

> Far too many children know all the theories, but cannot tell you
> what they could see with their own eyes, if they had been encour-
> aged to use them. They will know all about the solar system and
> perhaps about spectro-analysis of the stars, but they cannot tell you
> the state of the moon or point out the constellations. They know
> theories of evolution, but not the names of the trees or plants around
> them. *(H)*

The ways in which observation may serve learning are endless. Here I
extract just a few examples from Harwood, who is speaking about grades
six through eight:

To pick up again on the vibrating string, the children can devise
methods for changing the length, and thereby learn to identify the distinct
notes. They can investigate the musical intervals and relate them to the
corresponding numerical proportions. By placing a pulley at one end of
the string and attaching weights, they can discover the relation between
the note and the tension. They may even go further and make pipes out
of bamboo. In related lessons, the Chladny plate brings to visibility the
beautiful patterns created by sound. By such methods the invisible world
takes on concrete form within human experience *before* it is reduced to
the thin abstraction of number.

The laws of color can likewise be approached through both observation and art. There is no need to begin with wavelength, frequency, and
other mathematical constructs. The basic phenomena the theory is
designed to explain should enter the children's awareness before the theory itself; otherwise the phenomena tend to become invisible—displaced
forever in the child's intellect by theoretical constructs such as "photon,"

"wave," and "spectrum." Thus, one can learn about complementary colors by staring at a patch of green and then removing one's eyes to a light surface, whereupon one "sees" red. Similarly, after looking at red, one sees green. Color mixing naturally follows this, together with observation of such occurrences as colored shadows, the way distance affects color (a topic that greatly fascinated the Renaissance artists, who learned to tint remote mountains with blue), the effects of different atmospheric conditions upon the light of the sun, and so on.

Geometry, too, should emerge for the child as a practical, observational skill, much as it did for the ancients. A rubber band around two pegs, with a moving finger serving as the third vertex, allows the child to develop a fluid, accurate image of the triangle in its infinite possible manifestations—all the way to and "beyond" a straight line. In this fashion the learner actually *sees* that the three angles of a triangle amount to two right angles. This is much different from beginning with a set of axioms and proceeding to "prove" the theorem through deductive inference before there is any full experience of the triangle's nature.

Or, again, there is geology:

> To bring a fragment of granite or limestone into a class and talk about its chemical composition is to detach it from the earth. First of all the children should form an imaginative picture of chalk hills, or limestone ridges, or granite mountains—and if they live in one such district all the more should the teacher help them to see it with the imaginative eye. What happens to the rain when it falls on these various soils, what kind of trees and flowers grow best on them, what crops they produce and, above all, of what they are formed and how they got there—to deal with these questions is to keep the mineral world in its true connection with the living earth. It makes a profound impression on children to know that the great chalk and limestone and marble masses of the earth are the creation of living organisms. If they learn this at the right age their minds will not be closed to the idea that it is the dead which comes from the living, and not the living from the dead. *(H)*

With each passing year, the observation becomes more impregnated with elaborated thought. But thought is never allowed to tear free from observation and become lost in abstraction. When, for example, Galileo is studied between the ages of twelve and fourteen, the children might be allowed to pull each other up with block and tackle. In the ninth grade, devices such as the heat engine and telephone can be studied.

> Technical drawings will be made, the laws of pressure and expansion will be studied and practical problems worked out. The children should be astonished to discover how much there is to learn about things which they have perhaps come to look on as already familiar. *(H)*

It was, I think, Steiner who remarked that our use of so many devices whose basic working principles we do not understand profoundly oppresses the human spirit—even though we may scarcely be aware of the effect. Certainly the well-documented popular "phobias" regarding everything from digital clocks to VCRs are consistent with this claim. Wherever there is fear or an inner shrinking from things—or even just the absence of any sense of meaningful connection—can the psyche be in a healthy state?

The secondary student may go on to design bridges, study human physiology, and, in mathematics, pursue such topics as trigonometry, transcendental numbers, and conics. The conics, according to Harwood, are particularly valuable for helping the student move with disciplined imagination from the finite through the infinite and back, for

> the "shades of the prison house" are closing heavily upon him . . . . To be able to use this new weapon of thought to cut through the walls of this prison, to think in terms of the infinite, and yet relate the infinite to the spatial and the visible, is like a kind of spiritual breathing. Thought begins to find its way back to its spiritual origins.

And, finally, during the eleventh and twelfth grades, it becomes critically important for the student to find a human approach to the computer, and likewise to electricity, radio, radar, television, and so on. A student who, during the previous few years was very likely satisfied with the practical "how?" of things now begins to seek the "what?" at a new and deeper level. Unfortunately, in many schools this is precisely when he is hit with a mass of technical detail from sciences that have given up virtually all concern with anything except the "how?" Harwood finds this unfortunate:

> [The student] must at least glimpse the possibility of understanding what the world is. That understanding may not go very far at this age. But unless the curtain is parted a little at the critical time, it will only too easily densify into an iron one, and the adult will go through life believing that the ultimate questions are unanswerable, or falling back on a faith which his conscious mind and his reason cannot support or justify. *(H)*

Personally, I cannot help wondering how much of the appeal of virtual reality for the young person lies in the impenetrability of the "real world" we have handed him.

But how can we approach the "what?" of the world? The Waldorf educator's deep conviction is that we can do so only by turning toward the human being.

Human-centered education

"It is only in modern times," writes Harwood, "that man has imagined he can know the world without knowing himself." Sometimes it seems that we have turned this older view inside out: we struggle to know ourselves by first knowing the world. An ascending staircase leading from physics through physiology to sociobiology affords the primary approach to the human being acceptable to the dominant academic mindset of our day.

Whatever the justification for that mindset, it is foreign to the child, who longs to discover himself—that is, a spirit akin to his own spirit—in the world. All human knowledge was once myth-based, and this is the most natural thing for the child. To deny the child his kinship with the world because that kinship so easily finds "religious" expression would be misguided, for it is not a matter of any particular religion:

> No child longs for a dogma, for a religious denomination, for a political or other kind of program; he longs neither for pacifism nor nationalism. What he does want is to grasp the spiritual influences on nature and on world history, for they are food for his soul. *(A)*

Aeppli goes on to mention how the child in the lower grades—if his impulses have not been artificially inhibited—will speak "to sun and moon, mountain and stream, dog and bird, stone and stick as though to his equals. He is connected to them through forces which are no longer present in the adult, or do not appear to be." Just as the world does not come divided into "subjects" for the child, neither does it come rigidly separated into self and nonself. Only with time does the latter distinction become radical—and just *how* radical may vary from one adult to another far more than is commonly realized. Much depends upon how, and at what age, we insert—using the powerful wedge of the intellect—a distance between child and world.

But preserving the child's connection to the world does not mean starting with the man-made objects in the classroom:

> What is close to the seven- and eight-year-old child? What does his world look like? Is it the chair on which he sits, the notebook in which he writes, the playground in which he romps? Or is he perhaps even more deeply connected to the sun, moon and stars? . . . Is what is close to his body also close to his soul? Or is he closest in his "consciousness," in his "thoughts," precisely to the heavenly bodies, as well as to clouds and winds, trees and flowers, water and fire? Does he not live particularly deeply and vividly with these things as long as he remains unspoiled? And does the small child find the classroom, the house, the town, everything planned and built by men to be foreign, far removed and incomprehensible? . . . In the beginning was the whole world—that is a mental image which is closer to the child than the one . . . which elevates the classroom to the origin of all existence. *(A)*

Thus, history begins with the most ancient civilizations—India, Persia, Egypt, Babylon, and Greece. Here the child is closest to home, sustained by peoples who, like him, experienced a world of images, a world sacred, alive, and nurturing, the bearer of every individual destiny. The child thrives on this and will, in due time, begin to "wake up" with the discoveries of the Renaissance and Scientific Revolution. But his waking, then, will not be a nightmare; he will be waking to a world in which he belongs.[3]

The child will—and must—steadily "come to himself," standing within his own center and learning to look out upon the world with the most rigorous objectivity possible. But even in his maturity, if that gaze returns to him nothing of himself—if he has been taught to recognize "out there" only atoms moving in the void—then he will be cut off not only from the world but from himself as well.

Much in modern life attests to alienation. Harwood points to one symptom when he remarks, "It is a strange thing that an age which has discovered so many marvels in the universe should be so conspicuously lacking in the sense of wonder." Waldorf educators appear committed to rediscovering the sources of wonder. Actually, I think they would say that the small child is already filled with wonder. Our task is to avoid robbing him of it.

A word about the preschooler

The child, in the view of Waldorf educators, is a work of art. He thinks, feels, and wills as a living unity. At the same time, he experiences the world as a work of art, an image, and reads it in harmony with himself. Both child and environment are works-in-progress—the environment (if it is healthy) fostering a natural development of the child's capacities, and the child bringing to his environment a gift uniquely his own.

In the preschooler, this unity is expressed above all as a kind of willful imitation of his environment by the child. Not an adult imitation,

---

3. Regarding this awakening, see chapter 21, "Mona Lisa's Smile."

mediated by a highly developed thought life and careful observation, but rather an instinctive, participative imitation. His imitation, so to speak, proceeds from *within* the phenomena he is imitating, rather than from outside. Harwood cites Thomas Traherne's remarkable evocation of his earliest childhood:

> An Object, if it were before
> Mine Eye, was by Dame Nature's Law
>   Within my Soul; her Store
> Was all at once within me: all her Treasures
> Were my immediate and internal Pleasures; . . .

What the child absorbs in this way is nearly everything. All of his most "brilliant" learning occurs during these first years. He learns, for example, to speak—not like a parrot, nor by applying well developed, intellectual "learning skills," but by taking directly into himself meanings that most of us could not even put into words. (Try explaining the definitions of "but" or "by" to a toddler!)

Steiner claimed to see in these imitative powers such a deep, organic drive that even some of what we consider to be hereditary physical likeness is actually a matter of the child's imitation of his family surroundings. The child's openness to "external" influence has huge implications:

> The corollary to the child's immersion in his surroundings is that the influence of his surroundings penetrates him to an equal depth. The personal consciousness of the adult is a defence against his surroundings. He may be irritated or annoyed to exasperation by some continuous noise: but his consciousness keeps it from penetrating into those unconscious spheres where organic processes are taking place within him. The child may appear not even to hear the noise, but it enters so deeply within him that the forces of growth are affected, and perhaps weakened or impaired. *(H)*

The adults around the young child are the most powerful teachers he will ever know. So, too, unfortunately, are the television and other noise-making contrivances of modern civilization:

What he needs is that the adults, whose talk he hears and imitates, should speak clearly and beautifully and with affection. For the child is as sensitive to the mood as he is to the sound of the tones around him. The impersonal voice of radio and gramophone is not what he needs to imitate. A mother's singing, however poor, is far better for her baby than the best of records. *(H)*

Consistent with this imitation is the preschooler's love of repetition. The simple stories you tell must be told "correctly"—which means "imitating the last time"—or you will hear about it!

WALDORF EDUCATION IN PRACTICE

Questions and stories

Waldorf educators see the preschooler as functioning primarily in his *will*, as expressed through activity. It is the moving object that catches his eye, and he immediately insists on touching it. "Let me see with my hands," Harwood reports one exasperated child exclaiming when asked to look at an interesting object. "*Do not touch* is to a child the most desolatory of adult prohibitions."

But around age seven—and in an evolving manner until puberty—a strong feeling-consciousness comes to the fore. The child who previously "thought with his limbs" now thinks more with his feelings. It is, therefore, a strongly pictorial thinking, expressed through images laden with feelings of sympathy and antipathy.

Children of five will be satisfied by a story about very simple activities. You can tell them how the farmer goes out in the evening to feed his animals, and first he goes to his pigs, and then to his cows, and then to his sheep, and so on, and in what language they all thank him and say good night; and then how he comes home and eats the lovely supper his wife has prepared for him and goes to bed himself. The mere picture of the successive actions is a story for these little children. But if you told such a story to children of seven and upwards you would have a very poor reception. For them a story must live in the sway of feeling. There must be a time when the young prince is lost alone in the forest, and night comes and dreadful noises issue from the darkness and there is a flashing of mysterious eyes. Then at last he sees the welcome sight of a cottage with the red glow of a comforting fire shining through the window. At this cottage door the prince must knock seven times (not less than seven times in this age of rhythm) and, when he has almost given up hope, he hears a footstep within and the bolts are slowly drawn. And who is it who at last opens the door? A frightful witch. He turns to run but finds himself rooted to the ground. . . . All this sway of feeling, which would have been meaningless or harmful to the five-year-olds, is the very life-blood of a story to these older children who have passed the threshold of a new experience. For the soul no less than the body now demands its systole and diastole, the contraction of fear and sorrow, the expansion of laughter and hope. What is the reproach uttered by the children in the Bible? "We have piped unto you and you have not danced; we have mourned to you and you have not wept." The children wish to play at weddings and funerals, to enjoy both laughter and tears. It is the duty of adults to give them the right opportunities to do so. *(H)*

Image, symbol, rhythm, the sway of feeling. The children will skip and dance, tell endless stories (in which they feel themselves participants), imagine elaborate playthings in misshapen rags and sticks, learn to play team sports, sing songs. The child is pulling away from the world—but only to a degree. His unity with his environment is no longer directly imitative; it is a unity given above all in pictures, much as the ancient myths mediated to mankind a unified experience of the world.

The children learn in pictures; they "think" in pictures As Harwood points out, if one particular child is slighted and disliked by the others, an admonition will more likely make the situation worse than better. But tell the class Cinderella stories over a few days, and soon the children will noticeably alter their behavior. The children take in the pictures of the story, and learn from them. Waldorf teachers frequently make up stories to deal with specific disciplinary problems.

They also use fables for this purpose. "What are the cruel tiger, the dumb monkey, the stubborn mule, the magnanimous lion, but real, concrete soul faculties [portrayed] in animal form, which today, in abstractions far removed from life, we call gentleness, patience, and brutality?" The child cannot respond to calls for "patience." But he can recognize and take into himself the virtue imaged in the fabled animal.

Failure to realize this pictorial quality of childhood consciousness leads to the almost universal tragedy of our day: instructing the young in the highly abstract terms of scientific cause and effect. The Dutch psychologist Hendrik van den Berg (who, so far as I know, was not associated with Waldorf education) drew attention to the horror of so many adult answers to the incessant questions of the child:

> Why are the leaves red? Because of the cold—how untrue. Why is it cold? Because of the sun's position—untrue. Why is the sun so low? Because of the earth's location in its orbit—equally untrue. Why its location in an orbit? Because of the motion. Untrue again. Why motion? Because of continuous motion? Untrue. Why continuous motion? Because of God. What blasphemy!

> "Why are the leaves red, Dad?" "Because it is so beautiful, child. Don't you see how beautiful it is, all these autumn colors?"

> There is no truer answer. That *is* how the leaves are red.

> Or, again, "Daddy, why does it snow?" "Well, during the summer there are leaves on the trees and flowers on plants, but now it is so dark and barren outside, that the world needs a white blanket."

> But no one believes in this answer. We do not believe in answers which locate the sense of incidents within the incidents themselves, and the sense of things within the things themselves. To us it is necessary for the sense to lie outside the things and incidents, outside the present. This is our first rule of life, that only what lies in the past has sense. The result is an endless regression. For every past has been present before and must have derived its sense from a still earlier past. This road of endless regression is the road on which we have sent the child.[4]

As Harwood points out, if we really want to know what sort of answer the child expects and will be satisfied with—that is, if we really want to know what he is asking—it is often enough to delay answering. The child will answer his own question. Harwood cites the case of a six-year-old girl who asked, "What makes the rain go up into the sky?" A puzzling question for an adult, to be sure. But the "universe of discourse" in which the child was operating was quickly revealed when she said, "It's because the angels want to drink."

We adults have a choice: to seek by force of superior intellect to wrench the child into an entirely different and alien universe of discourse, or to acknowledge our own inferiority of imagination and try to move *with* the child in her universe of discourse. "One is really only qualified to answer children's questions when one shares their outlook and has acquired a little of their gift of fantasy." *(H)*

Thus, for the child of such an age, one answer to "Where do babies come from" is quite properly, "from the sky." The maligned stork deserves rehabilitation. Have we altogether forgotten what magic and wisdom there is in the image of a bird winging like a "pregnant thought" through the womblike vault of the sky, bearing a gift to mankind?

Harwood claims that such pictures enable the child to enter into thinking with a vigorous will and deep feeling. These will remain to strengthen the life of thought in later years.

Arithmetic and imagination

What about arithmetic? The Waldorf teacher begins with the largest number—one. All other numbers arise from this primal number as fragments. "This as yet undivided, unbroken original one is the primary fact; it stands at the beginning. By splitting the one, tearing it into two parts, the number two came into being." *(A)* If you begin with a pile of twelve chestnuts, you can allow the children to divide it into separate, smaller piles in almost unending combinations. They can choose, for example,

---

4. van den Berg, 1975: 69.

how many chestnuts to "give" each of several recipients. The single, original pile becomes a resource upon which their freedom and generosity may act. The laws of number apply, but not in a way that thrusts the child rudely (and falsely) into a realm of inhuman necessity.

If on the other hand, we start with the parts rather than the whole, teaching the child that 1+1+1=3 and 2+3=5, there is nothing he can *do* with this. "Instead of creative numerousness he must experience unbending compulsion. This will affect him for the rest of his life." *(A)* That will seem an extreme judgment only to one who hasn't digested the peculiar hold of determinism upon the modern mind. We are accustomed to building the world up rigidly from atoms—and can find no escape for ourselves—whereas the other approach, "the grasping of the whole before the parts, is the way of imagination, and leads to the view that it is only the whole which gives meaning and existence to the parts. The difference is as subtle as it is profound." *(H)*

It is essential to begin realizing the historically peculiar tendencies of our own thought, which we should not mistake for *necessary* ways of thinking. We all too easily forget what chasms lie between unspoiled childhood and the cultured, twentieth-century mind. If we would truly free the child, we must not bind him with our own chains—even if we are happy enough with those chains ourselves.

I have emphasized to this point the younger child, for here we see most easily some of the distinctive principles of Waldorf education. It is important to recognize, however, that these principles continue to govern this style of education in later years. In fact, the Waldorf educator will very likely point out that even adult thinking is far too lost in the abstraction of number, statistics, and meaningless information—far too lacking, that is, in qualities of the imagination. A worthy education, therefore, will seek to spare the child this adult affliction.

An age of transition

Every age has its distinctive character. Aeppli describes wonderfully the perplexing transitions through which the child of nine or ten passes, and his remarks are worth citing at length:

> The children are rather less coordinated than before . . . . The instinctive surefootedness is no longer there. Instead of the often light, dancing steps their tread is now somehow heavier. Also, they no longer abandon themselves so totally to rhythm. In a song, rhythm is no longer of equal or even greater importance than the melody . . . [the child] is no longer at all pleased, for example, when the teacher claps the rhythm of a song or poem with his hands in order to emphasize the beat . . . .

> The teacher might suddenly become aware that he is standing *opposite* his children, and that a dangerous chasm has opened between him and them that was not there before. The children have slipped away from me during the vacation, he may say to himself, and he feels wistful, or even uncomfortable, for the children are looking at him with more probing, more critical eyes . . . . The teacher walks down the street with his children. Not very long ago he had far too few hands at such times for all the children hanging on him. Now he has exactly two hands too many . . . .

> Such a child may suddenly give his mother quite a shock by saying, "You know, Mommy, none of the fairy tales are true; and as for angels, they don't exist at all." He says it with the tone, gesture and above all with the conviction of an atheist itinerant preacher. But when the child lies in bed at night he wants his mother to tell him a fairy tale and cannot fall asleep without it. And how does he listen? With enormous interest. He lives in the reality of the fairy tale himself . . . .

> The child sees "more clearly" now. He sees himself suddenly standing opposite things and feels forced to keep his distance from them. They become more foreign to him and, therefore, questionable. The entire world, in which he so recently participated without effort, somehow becomes questionable and full of riddles. Hence all the

questions asked by children, which are often less important for their content than for the inner tension that caused them to be asked . . . .

Inwardly, he begins to freeze. He feels himself kicked out of Paradise.

The child can no longer accept [the] adult as unquestioned authority as he did before. Yet, it is precisely at this critical moment that the child needs a leader and helper more than ever. The teacher is thus faced with the task of rebuilding his authority on a new foundation.

Off course, the eight- and nine-year-old child is hungry for knowledge of the world, too, but he can absorb that knowledge only as something whole, as a myth, fairy tale or fable, that is, in the form of pictures saturated with life. Be it tree or stream, moss or stone, all are living beings that can speak to the child . . . . It is quite normal for the teacher to speak about these things indiscriminately as living beings. In fact, it is what [the child] craves deep down inside.

On the other hand, if you are involved with children in their tenth year, it is clear—this is after all a truism—that the teacher must now present the world . . . in a much more sophisticated way than before. The beings must be distinctly separated. An animal is something quite different from a plant, not to mention a mountain. Every object has its own character about which the child would like to learn. What until now lived unseparated in the lap of a living and ancient oneness separates in the classroom into the various subjects such as botany, zoology, geography, etc.

From myth to abstraction

At this age, myth gives way to history. But it is history that begins in the dimmest, myth-connected past, where the children feel closest to home. They will study Egyptian hieroglyphics and perhaps even learn brief poems in Sanskrit, Hebrew, and Greek. They will gain experience in the ancient arts and crafts. One Waldorf teacher puts it this way:

History, telling as it does the story of man's deeds and strivings, stirs the child to a more intense experiencing of his own humanness; he lives in the drama of history as though he himself were involved in every happening. As he studies the dynamic progress of humanity through many different phases of consciousness he is led to see himself and the age he lives in as the heirs of an evolutionary process that he in turn will help carry forward.... *History brings the child to himself.*[5]

After the twelfth year, the child begins to grasp abstract ideas. As Harwood notes, "One of the arts of teaching at this age is to find the subjects in which the concrete picture most closely exemplifies the abstract law, so that a natural unity is still preserved." Harwood and Aeppli present numerous examples of course approaches for the later primary grades, as well as high school.

One other note: whereas the primary student needs adult authority worthy of respect, "the secret uncertainty of the adolescent makes him long for a hero—of course of his own choosing—on whom to model himself." *(H)* He is prepared to emulate, not particular actions, but rather the adult's abilities, the adult's enthusiasm for knowledge and life. Referring to the adolescent's habit of destructive criticism, Harwood writes, "We should welcome even this destructive quality as a sign of mental energy. For the teacher's task is to convert this critical propensity into a zeal for the fine distinctions of knowledge, and thus turn destruction into creation."

The teacher

It will be evident from the foregoing that the Waldorf teacher—in the ideal, if not always in practice—moves with her class from grade one through eight. By all accounts, an extraordinary community of education can grow up by this means. The teacher observes the individual child passing through many stages, and can adapt her lessons to the child's individual needs.[6]

It is a demanding way to teach—all the more because the teacher is given no fixed curriculum. She must develop her own curriculum,

---

5. Spock, 1985: 74.

6. This also means, of course, that a difficult decision awaits the parent whose child draws an inadequate teacher.

year-by-year—while following, of course, certain general guidelines. Nor can she fully anticipate the directions in which her class will lead her. Children are full of unexpected questions, interests, and observations, and a good teacher will, to one degree or another, take advantage of these opportunities.

Moreover, there is surprisingly little use made of textbooks, and often little or no homework is assigned. The teacher must be capable of presenting much of the material herself. The heart of education lies, not in facts or knowledge, but in what passes between human beings. Think of what you gained from the most influential teacher in your life—perhaps the one who changed the whole direction of your education. Was it primarily a collection of information, or rather a new, enlarged sense for what it means to be a growing, learning human being within the context of a particular field of knowledge?

What the child finds in the teacher must be discovered to be no more rigid and abstract than what he finds in nature. *"Only that which has transformed itself in me through my own efforts has a healing, releasing, and nourishing effect on the child.* For that reason I must not look to replace myself, the teacher, with the tape recorder." *(A)*

Like the reference to thinking as cosmic knitting, this may seem a strange thought. But it is strange only so long as we think of knowledge the same way we think of an atom—as a "thing" to which we have no inner relationship. But the child has no use for such "facts"; he must find an inner connection. We cannot help him in that task unless we, too, have found such a connection. But to find it is also to be subject to it; we will be changed. The "spirit in the world" will act upon the "spirit in us." Entry to this life of transformation and unending growth is, above all, what we owe the child.

Selected bibliography on Waldorf education

Aeppli, Willi (1986). *Rudolf Steiner Education and the Developing Child.* Hudson, N.Y.: Anthroposophic Press.

Edmunds, L. Francis (1992). *Rudolf Steiner Education—The Waldorf School.* Sussex, U.K.: Rudolf Steiner Press.

Harwood, A. C. (1958). *The Recovery of Man in Childhood.* New York: Myrin Institute of New York.

Harwood, A. C. (1988). *The Way of a Child.* London: Rudolf Steiner Press.

Richards, Mary Caroline (1980). *Toward Wholeness: Rudolf Steiner Education in America.* Middletown, Conn.: Wesleyan University Press.

Spock, Marjorie (1985). *Teaching as a Lively Art.* Hudson, N.Y.: Anthroposophic Press.

Stockmeyer, E. A. Karl (1969). *Rudolf Steiner's Curriculum for Waldorf Schools.* Sussex, U.K.: Steiner Schools Fellowship Publications.

Many books about Waldorf education are available from Anthroposophic Press. You can obtain a catalog by writing to the Press at RR 4, Box 94-A-1, Hudson, New York 12534 (Tel. 518-851-2054).

Also, *Renewal: A Journal for Waldorf Education* is published by the Association of Waldorf Schools of North America, 3911 Bannister Road, Fair Oaks, California 95628 (Tel. 916–961–0927). This organization can supply further information about Waldorf schools and Waldorf education.

A Waldorf discussion group is accessible through the Internet. To receive all messages posted to the group, send the single-line message, "subscribe waldorf" to the email address, "listserv@sjuvm.stjohns.edu". (Do not include the quotation marks, and do not add any other text to the message.)

Bibliography

Adams, George and Whicher, Olive (1980). *The Plant between Sun and Earth*. London: Rudolf Steiner Press.

Adler, Alfred (1964). *The Individual Psychology of Alfred Adler*. Edited by Heinz L. Ansbacher and Rowena R. Ansbacher. New York: Harper and Row.

Aeppli, Willi (1986). *Rudolf Steiner Education and the Developing Child*. Hudson, N.Y.: Anthroposophic Press.

Aiken, M. (1993). "Advantages of Group Decision Support Systems." *Interpersonal Computing and Technology* 1, no. 3 (July). Electronically archived as "aiken ipctv1n3" on listserv@guvm.ccf.georgetown.edu.

Barfield, Owen (1986). *History in English Words*. Hudson, N.Y.: Lindisfarne Press.

___ (1963). *Worlds Apart (A Dialogue of the 1960's)*. Middletown, Conn.: Wesleyan University Press.

___ (1965a). *Saving the Appearances*. New York: Harcourt, Brace and World.

___ (1965b). *Unancestral Voice*. Middletown, Conn.: Wesleyan University Press.

___ (1966). *Romanticism Comes of Age*. London: Rudolf Steiner Press.

___ (1967). *Speaker's Meaning*. Middletown, Conn.: Wesleyan University Press.

___ (1973). *Poetic Diction: A Study in Meaning*. Middletown, Conn.: Wesleyan University Press.

___ (1977a). "Lewis, Truth, and Imagination." In Barfield, 1989.

___ (1977b). *The Rediscovery of Meaning, and Other Essays*. Middletown, Conn.: Wesleyan University Press.

___ (1979). *History, Guilt, and Habit*. Middletown, Conn.: Wesleyan University Press.

—— (1981). "The Nature of Meaning." *Seven* 2: 32–43.

—— (1989). *Owen Barfield on C. S. Lewis.* Edited by G. B. Tennyson. Middletown, Conn.: Wesleyan University Press.

Barlow, John Perry (1990). "Crime and Puzzlement." Article distributed on the Internet and dated June 8, 1990.

—— (1994). "Jackboots on the Infobahn." *Wired* 2, no. 4 (April): 40, 44–48.

Benedikt, Michael (1991). "Cyberspace: Some Proposals." In *Cyberspace: First Steps,* edited by Michael Benedikt. Cambridge, Mass.: MIT Press.

Birkerts, Sven (1992). "Teaching in the Video Age." In *American Energies: Essays on Fiction.* New York: William Morrow.

Bos, Alexander (1983). *Nothing to Do with Me?* Edinburgh: Floris Books.

Brown, Tom Jr. (1982). *The Search.* New York: Berkley Books.

Brown, Tom Jr. and Watkins, William Jon (1979). *The Tracker.* New York: Berkley Books.

Butterfield, Herbert (1965). *The Origins of Modern Science.* New York: The Free Press.

Calamai, Peter (1993). Address to The International FreeNet Conference at Carleton University, Ottawa.

Cobb, Nathan (1990). "Hacker Power." *The Boston Globe Magazine,* October 21, 1990.

Cornford, F. M. (1957). *From Religion to Philosophy.* New York: Harper and Brothers.

Dennett, Daniel C. (1991). *Consciousness Explained.* Boston: Little, Brown and Company.

Deregowski, Jan B. (1974). "Pictorial Perception and Culture." In *Image, Object, and Illusion,* edited by Richard Held. San Francisco: W. H. Freeman and Co.

Dretsky, Fred I. (1981). *Knowledge and the Flow of Information.* Cambridge, Mass.: MIT Press.

Drucker, Peter F. (1993). *Post-Capitalist Society.* New York: HarperCollins.

Dumanoski, Dianne (1990). "Doing Less and Enjoying It More." *The Boston Globe* (July 2).

Kling, Rob (1995). *Computerization and Controversy: Value Conflicts and Social Choices.* 2d ed. New York: Academic Press.

Edelglass, Stephen, Georg Maier, Hans Gebert, and John Davy (1992). *Matter and Mind.* Hudson, N.Y.: Lindisfarne Press.

Edgerton, Samuel Y. Jr. (1975). *The Renaissance Rediscovery of Linear Perspective.* New York: Basic Books.

Edwards, Betty (1979). *Drawing on the Right Side of the Brain.* Los Angeles: J. P. Tarcher.

Ellul, Jacques (1990). *The Technological Bluff.* Translated by Geoffrey W. Bromiley. Grand Rapids, Mich.: Eerdmans.

Frederick, Howard H. (1992). "Emergence of Global Civil Society." Paper presented to Annual Conference of the Peace Studies Association (February 28). Boulder Colo.

Gardner, Howard (1985). *The Mind's New Science.* New York: Basic Books, Inc.

Gibbs, W. Wayt (1994). "Software's Chronic Crisis." *Scientific American* 271, no. 3 (September).

Gilder, George (1993a). "The Death of Telephony." *The Economist* (September 11): 75–78.

—— (1993b). "When Bandwidth Is Free." Interview by Kevin Kelly. *Wired* 1, no. 4.

—— (1994). "An Interview with Eric Nee, Part 2." *Upside* (June): 36–55.

Goethe, Johann Wolfgang von (1988). "The Metamorphosis of Plants." In *Scientific Studies.* Edited and translated by Douglas Miller. New York: Suhrkamp.

Gombrich, E. H. (1969). *Art and Illusion: A Study in the Psychology of Pictorial Representation*. Princeton, N.J.: Princeton University Press.

Gregory, R. L. (1966). *Eye and Brain: The Psychology of Seeing*. New York: McGraw-Hill Book Co.

Güggenbuhl-Craig, Adolph (1971). *Marriage, Dead or Alive*. Zurich: Spring Publications.

Harwood, A. C. (1958). *The Recovery of Man in Childhood*. New York: Myrin Institute of New York.

Haugeland, John (1981). *Mind Design*. Cambridge, Mass.: MIT Press.

___ (1985). *Artificial Intelligence: The Very Idea*. Cambridge, Mass.: MIT Press.

Heim, Michael (1993). *The Metaphysics of Virtual Reality*. Oxford: Oxford University Press.

Hofstadter, Douglas R. (1986). *Metamagical Themas*. New York: Bantam Books.

Hofstadter, Douglas R., Melanie Mitchell, and Robert M. French (1987). "Fluid Concepts and Creative Analogies: A Theory and Its Computer Implementation." FARG Document 87−1 (March), Fluid Analogies Research Group, University of Michigan.

Howard, Robert (1985). *Brave New Workplace*. New York: Penguin.

Johnson-Laird, Philip (1988). *The Computer and the Mind: An Introduction to Cognitive Science*. Cambridge, Mass.: Harvard University Press.

Jung, C. G. (1968). *The Archetypes and the Collective Unconscious*. Princeton, N.J.: Princeton University Press.

Kühlewind, Georg (1984). *Stages of Consciousness*. West Stockbridge, Mass.: The Lindisfarne Press.

Lievegoed, B. C. J. (1973). *The Developing Organization*. Translated by J. Collis. London: Tavistock Publications.

Mander, Jerry (1991). *In the Absence of the Sacred: The Failure of Technology and the Survival of the Indian Nations*. San Francisco: Sierra Club Books.

452

McDermott, Drew (1976). "Artifical Intelligence Meets Natural Stupidity." In Haugeland (1981): 143–60.

Milburn, Michael A. and McGrail, Anne B. (1992). "The Dramatic Presentation of News and Its Effects on Cognitive Complexity." *Political Psychology* 13, no. 4: 613–32.

Mitchell, Melanie and Hofstadter, Douglas R. (1990a). "The Emergence of Understanding in a Computer Model of Concepts and Analogy-making." *Physica* D42: 322–34.

Mitchell, Melanie and Hofstadter, Douglas R. (1990b). "The Right Concept at the Right Time: How Concepts Emerge as Relevant in Response to Context-Dependent Pressures." *Proceedings, 12th Annual Conference of the Cognitive Science Society.*

Neumann, Peter G. (1995). *Computer-Related Risks.* Reading, Mass.: Addison-Wesley.

Norman, Donald (1993). *Things That Make Us Smart: Defending Human Attributes in the Age of the Machine.* Reading, Mass.: Addison-Wesley.

Nunamaker, J., D. Vogel, A. Heminger, et al. (1989). "Experiences at IBM with Group Support Systems: A Field Study." *Decision Support Systems* 5: 183–96.

Nunamaker, J., A. Dennis, J. Valacich, et al. (1991). "Electronic Meeting Systems to Support Group Work." *Communications of the ACM* 34, no. 7 (July): 41–61.

Onians, Richard Broxton (1951). *The Origins of European Thought: About the Body, the Mind, the Soul, the World, Time, and Fate.* Cambridge: Cambridge University Press.

O'Toole, James (1985). *Vanguard Management.* New York: Berkley Books.

Panofsky, Erwin (1991). *Perspective as Symbolic Form.* New York: Zone Books.

Papert, Seymour (1993). *The Children's Machine: Rethinking School in the Age of the Computer.* New York: Basic Books.

Pirenne, M. H. (1952). "The Scientific Basis of Da Vinci's Theory of Perspective." *British Journal for the Philosophy of Science* 3, no. 10.

Poppelbaum, Hermann (1961). *A New Zoology*. Dornach, Switzerland: Philosophic-Anthroposophic Press.

___ (1993). *The Battle for a New Consciousness*. Translated by Thomas Forman and Theodore Van Vliet. Spring Valley, N.Y.: Mercury Press.

Postman, Neil (1993). *Technopoly: The Surrender of Culture to Technology*. N.Y.: Random House.

Rheingold, Howard (1983). *The Virtual Community: Homesteading on the Electronic Frontier*. Reading, Mass.: Addison Wesley.

Romanyshyn, Robert D. (1989). *Technology As Symptom and Dream*. New York: Routledge.

Roszak, Theodore (1994). *The Cult of Information: A Neo-Luddite Treatise on High Tech, Artificial Intelligence, and the True Art of Thinking*. Berkeley, Calif.: University of California Press.

Russell, Bertrand (1981). *Mysticism and Logic*. Totowa, N.J.: Barnes and Noble.

Sardello, Robert (1992). *Facing the World with Soul*. Hudson, N.Y.: Lindisfarne.

Schoenhoff, Doris M. (1993). *The Barefoot Expert: The Interface of Computerized Knowledge Systems and Indigenous Knowledge Systems*. Westport, Conn.: Greenwood Press.

Schwenk, Theodor (1965). *Sensitive Chaos*. London: Rudolf Steiner Press.

Setzer, Valdemar (1989). *Computers in Education*. Edinburgh: Floris Books.

Shannon, Claude E. (1965). "Information Theory." *Encyclopedia Britannica*. Chicago: William Benton.

Simon, Herbert and Newell, Allen (1958). "Heuristic Problem Solving: The Next Advance in Operations Research." *Operations Research* 6 (Jan-Feb): 1–10.

Simon, Herbert A. (1965). *The Shape of Automation for Men and Management*. New York: Harper and Row.

Snell, Bruno (1960). *The Discovery of the Mind*. New York: Harper and Row.

Spock, Marjorie (1985). *Teaching As a Lively Art*. Hudson, N.Y.: Anthroposophic Press.

Tolkien, J. R. R. (1947). "On Fairy Stories." In *Essays Presented to Charles Williams*. Oxford: Oxford University Press.

___ (1977). *The Silmarillion*. Boston: Houghton Mifflin.

van den Berg, Jan Hendrik (1975). *The Changing Nature of Man*. New York: Dell Publishing Company.

von Baeyer, Hans Christian (1992). *Taming the Atom*. New York: Random House.

von Senden, M. (1960). *Space and Sight: The Perception of Space and Shape in the Congenitally Blind before and after Operation*. London: Methuen and Co.

Waldrop, M. Mitchell (1992). *Complexity: The Emerging Science at the Edge of Order and Chaos*. New York: Simon and Schuster.

Weizenbaum, Joseph (1976). *Computer Power and Human Reason*. New York: W. H. Freeman and Company.

Weizenbaum, Joseph (1986). "The West Interview." Interview by Marion Long. *West* (January 19, 1986).

White, John (1972). *The Birth and Rebirth of Pictorial Space*. New York: Harper and Row.

Winner, Langdon (1986). *The Whale and the Reactor: A Search for Limits in an Age of High Technology*. Chicago: University of Chicago Press.

Zajonc, Arthur (1993). *Catching the Light: The Entwined History of Light and Mind*. New York: Bantam.

INDEX